Lecture Notes in Computer Science   14755

Founding Editors

Gerhard Goos
Juris Hartmanis

The series Lecture Notes in Computer Science (LNCS), including its subseries Lecture Notes in Artificial Intelligence (LNAI) and Lecture Notes in Bioinformatics (LNBI), has established itself as a medium for the publication of new developments in computer science and information technology research, teaching, and education.

LNCS enjoys close cooperation with the computer science R & D community, the series counts many renowned academics among its volume editors and paper authors, and collaborates with prestigious societies. Its mission is to serve this international community by providing an invaluable service, mainly focused on the publication of conference and workshop proceedings and postproceedings. LNCS commenced publication in 1973.

Efrén Mezura-Montes ·
Héctor Gabriel Acosta-Mesa ·
Jesús Ariel Carrasco-Ochoa ·
José Francisco Martínez-Trinidad ·
José Arturo Olvera-López
Editors

Pattern Recognition

16th Mexican Conference, MCPR 2024
Xalapa, Mexico, June 19–22, 2024
Proceedings

 Springer

Editors
Efrén Mezura-Montes (iD)
Universidad Veracruzana
Veracruz, Mexico

Héctor Gabriel Acosta-Mesa (iD)
Universidad Veracruzana
Veracruz, Mexico

Jesús Ariel Carrasco-Ochoa (iD)
Instituto Nacional de Astrofísica, Óptica y
Electrónica (INAOE)
Puebla, Mexico

José Francisco Martínez-Trinidad (iD)
Instituto Nacional de Astrofísica, Óptica y
Electrónica (INAOE)
Puebla, Mexico

José Arturo Olvera-López (iD)
Autonomous University of Puebla (BUAP)
Puebla, Mexico

ISSN 0302-9743   ISSN 1611-3349 (electronic)
Lecture Notes in Computer Science
ISBN 978-3-031-62835-1   ISBN 978-3-031-62836-8 (eBook)
https://doi.org/10.1007/978-3-031-62836-8

This Springer imprint is published by the registered company Springer Nature Switzerland AG
The registered company address is: Gewerbestrasse 11, 6330 Cham, Switzerland

If disposing of this product, please recycle the paper.

Preface

The Mexican Conference on Pattern Recognition 2024 (MCPR 2024) was the 16th event in the series, this time organized by the Instituto de Investigaciones en Inteligencia Artificial de la Universidad Veracruzana (IIIA-UV) and the Computer Science Department of the Instituto Nacional de Astrofísica, Óptica y Electrónica (INAOE) of Mexico. The conference was overseen by the Mexican Association for Computer Vision, Neurocomputing, and Robotics (MACVNR), a member society of the International Association for Pattern Recognition (IAPR). MCPR 2024 was held in Xalapa, Veracruz, Mexico, during June 19–22, 2024.

MCPR aims to provide a forum for exchanging scientific results, practice, and new knowledge, and to promote collaboration among research groups in pattern recognition and related areas in Mexico and worldwide.

In this edition, as in previous years, MCPR 2024 attracted Mexican researchers and worldwide participation. We received 68 manuscripts from authors in 10 countries: Brazil, Canada, Costa Rica, Cuba, France, Mexico, Netherlands, South Africa, Spain, and the USA. Each paper was strictly peer-reviewed by at least two members of the Program Committee. All members of the Program Committee are experts in many fields of pattern recognition. As a result of a single-blind peer review, 36 papers were accepted for presentation at the conference and included in these excellent conference proceedings.

We were very honored to have as invited speakers such internationally recognized researchers as:

- João Gama, Laboratory of Artificial Intelligence and Decision Support, University of Porto, Portugal.
- Bing Xue, School of Engineering and Computer Science, Victoria University of Wellington, New Zealand.
- Graciela González Farías, Centro de Investigación en Matemáticas (CIMAT-Monterrey), Mexico.

We thank everyone who devoted much time and effort to running MCPR 2024 successfully. Notably, we thank all the authors who contributed to the conference. In addition, we give special thanks to the invited speakers, who shared their keynote addresses on various pattern recognition topics during the conference. We are also very grateful for the efforts and the quality of the reviews of all Program Committee members and additional reviewers. Their work allowed us to maintain the high quality of the contributions to the conference and provided a conference program of a high standard.

Finally, but no less importantly, we thank the Instituto de Investigaciones en Inteligencia Artificial de la Universidad Veracruzana (IIIA-UV) for supporting this event.

We are sure that MCPR 2024 provided a fruitful forum for Mexican pattern recognition researchers and the broader international pattern recognition community.

June 2024

Efrén Mezura-Montes
Héctor Gabriel Acosta-Mesa
Jesús Ariel Carrasco-Ochoa
José Francisco Martínez-Trinidad
José Arturo Olvera-López

Organization

General Conference Co-chairs

Efrén Mezura-Montes   IIIA-UV, Mexico
Héctor Gabriel Acosta Mesa   IIIA-UV, Mexico
Jesús Ariel Carrasco-Ochoa   INAOE, Mexico
José Francisco Martínez-Trinidad   INAOE, Mexico
José Arturo Olvera-López   BUAP, Mexico

Local Arrangement Committee

Barrientos Martínez Rocío Erandi   IIIA-UV, Mexico
Cervantes Cuahuey Brenda Alicia   INAOE, Mexico
Quiroz Castellanos Marcela   IIIA-UV, Mexico

Program Committee

Antunes, F.	University of Coimbra, Portugal
Borges, D. L.	Universidade de Brasília, Brazil
Cabrera, S.	University of Texas at El Paso, USA
Cancela, P.	UDELAR, Uruguay
Caridade, C. M. R.	Instituto Superior de Engenharia de Coimbra, Portugal
Cimmino, L.	University of Salerno, Italy
Escalante-Balderas, H. J.	INAOE, Mexico
Facon, J.	Pontifícia Universidade Católica do Paraná, Brazil
Fumera, G.	University of Cagliari, Italy
Godoy, D.	UNICEN, Argentina
Grau, A.	Universitat Politècnica de Catalunya, Spain
Heutte, L.	Université de Rouen, France
Hurtado-Ramos, J. B.	CICATA-IPN, Mexico
Iwahori, Y.	Chubu University, Japan
Jiang, X.	University of Münster, Germany
Kampel, M.	Vienna University of Technology, Austria
Kim, S. W.	Myongji University, South Korea
Kober, V.	CICESE, Mexico

Körner, M.	Technical University of Munich, Germany
Lazo-Cortés, M. S.	ITTLA,TecNM, Mexico
Levano, M. A.	Universidad Católica de Temuco, Chile
Liu, C. L.	CASIA, China
Mandal, B.	Uppsala University, Sweden
Martínez-Carranza, J.	INAOE, Mexico
Mitrea, D.	Technical University of Cluj-Napoca, Romania
Montes-Y-Gomez, M.	INAOE, Mexico
Morales, E.	INAOE, Mexico
Nalepa, J.	Silesian University of Technology, Poland
Neves, A. J. R.	University of Aveiro, Portugal
Oliveira, J. L.	University of Aveiro, Portugal
Ouarda, W.	Digital Research Center of Sfax, Tunisia
Palagyi, K.	University of Szeged, Hungary
Pedrosa, G. V.	Universidade de Brasília, Brazil
Perez-Suay, A.	Universitat de València, Spain
Real, P.	University of Seville, Spain
Rejer, I.	West Pomeranian University of Technology, Poland
Ruiz-Shulcloper, J.	UCI, Cuba
Sanchez-Cortes, D.	Groupe Mutuel Holding SA, Switzerland
Sansone, C.	Università di Napoli, Italy
Schiaffino, S.	ISISTAN, Argentina
Silva, C.	University of Coimbra, Portugal
Sossa-Azuela, J. H.	CIC-IPN, Mexico
Sucar, L. E.	INAOE, Mexico
Tolosana, R.	Universidad Autónoma de Madrid, Spain
Tomasiello, S.	University of Tartu, Estonia
Torres-Moreno, J. M.	Avignon University, France
Valle, M. E.	Universidade Estadual de Campinas, Brazil
Wario, F.	ISTC, Italy
Yashina, V.	CC RAS, Russia

Additional Reviewers

Altamirano-Robles, L.	INAOE, Mexico
Ballister, I.	TU Wien, Austria
Carbajal-Hernández, J. J.	CIC-IPN, Mexico
Fonseca-Delgado, R.	Yachay Tech University, Ecuador
Gutierrez-Giles, I. A.	INAOE, Mexico
Heitzinger, T.	TU Wien, Austria

López-Lobato, A.	IIIA-UV, Mexico
Márquez-Grajales, A.	IIIA-UV, Mexico
Mucha, W.	TU Wien, Austria
Ortega-Mendoza, R. M.	UAEH, Mexico
Pérez-Espinosa, H.	INAOE, Mexico
Peregrina-Barreto, H.	INAOE, Mexico
Strohmayer, J.	TU Wien, Austria
Yang, P.	CASIA, China
Zapotecas-Martínez, S.	INAOE, Mexico
Zhang, Y. M.	CASIA, China

Sponsoring Institutions

Instituto de Investigaciones en Inteligencia Artificial de la Universidad Veracruzana (IIIA-UV)
Instituto Nacional de Astrofísica, Óptica y Electrónica (INAOE)
Mexican Association for Computer Vision, Neurocomputing and Robotics (MACVNR)
National Council of Humanities, Science and Technology of Mexico (CONAHCYT)

Contents

Computer Vision

Medical Applications of Pattern Recognition

Language Processing and Recognition

Deep Learning and Neural Networks

Pattern Recognition and Machine Learning Techniques

Identification of Spatial Dynamic Patterns of Behavior Using Weighted Voronoi Diagrams

Martha Lorena Avendaño-Garrido[1] ,
Carlos Alberto Hernández-Linares[1]([✉]) , Brenda Zarahí Medina-Pérez[1] ,
Varsovia Hernández[2] , Porfirio Toledo[1] , and Alejandro León[2]

[1] Facultad de Matemáticas, Universidad Veracruzana, Xalapa, Veracruz, Mexico
carlhernandez@uv.mx
[2] Centro de Investigaciones Biomédicas, Universidad Veracruzana,
Xalapa, Veracruz, Mexico

Abstract. This study proposes an innovative approach to analyze spatial patterns of behavior by integrating information in weighted Voronoi diagrams. The objective of the research is to analyze the temporal distribution of an experimental subject in different regions of a given space, with the aim of identifying significant areas of interest. The methodology employed involves dividing the experimental space, determining representative points, and assigning weights based on the cumulative time the subject spends in each region. This process results in a set of generator points along with their respective weights, thus defining the Voronoi diagram. The study also presents a detailed and advanced perspective for understanding spatial behavioral patterns in experimental contexts.

Keywords: Weighted Voronoi diagrams · Behavior Analysis · Spatial Dynamics Behavior Analysis

1 Introduction

The Spatial Dynamics Behavior Analysis (SDBA) focuses on analyzing the displacement of individuals, whether animals or humans, within the context of various behavioral phenomena such as learning, motivation, and fear, among others (see [9]). One of the inherent challenges of SDBA involves visualizing the quantitative relationships between spatial variables associated with the phenomena of interest and other relevant variables. In this context, SDBA requires an analysis and visual representation method capable of segmenting space into zones defined by organism behavior, thus enabling the analysis of Regions of Behavioral Relevance (RBR) and the representation of the emergence and evolution of RBR over different time points. In this study, we propose employing weighted Voronoi diagrams to address this challenge.

A Voronoi diagram is constituted by regions that divide the space according to a finite set of points called generators. Each region is associated with a single generator point and each point in the space is associated with at least one region (see

[3,6,13]). When, in addition to considering the location of the generator points, a weight is incorporated, we call them weighted Voronoi diagrams. In this paper, we focus specifically on the multiplicative weighting. It is important to mention that between the 1950s and 1970s, multiplicatively weighted Voronoi diagrams were widely used to solve problems in market and urban analysis (see [12]).

Voronoi diagrams have been highlighted as a versatile tool for exploring diverse aspects of behavioral spatial dynamics. They have been used in various fields such as urban mobility modeling to determine population concentration, travel speed, and direction (see [11,14]). Similarly, in sports science, they have been useful in characterizing collective behavior, identifying crucial moments in games, and analyzing spatial organization (see [5,7]). However, in these contexts, the potential of weighted Voronoi diagrams has not been fully exploited, limiting their use to movement classification or the determination of relevant regions in a single episode or session. In contrast, in this work, we use weighted Voronoi diagrams to analyze the change in dynamics over multiple sessions in order to describe the evolution of the individual behavior under a given spatiotemporal dynamics of the environment.

2 Weighted Voronoi Diagrams

We will consider a generator set $P = \{p_1, p_2, \ldots, p_n\} \in \mathbb{R}^2$, where each point p_i is assigned a weight $w_i > 0$, represented by the parameter set $W = \{w_1, w_2, \ldots, w_n\}$. It is considered that the weight w_i reflects the ability of the generator p_i to influence the space. This weight is used to define a weighted distance relative to p_i, denoted as $d_w(x, p_i)$. It is important to note that we will call this a distance, even though it is not in the strict sense of the definition of a metric space. In this context, we define the following.

Definition 1. *The weighted Voronoi polygon associated to a point $p_i \in P$ is the region defined by*

$$Vor_w(p_i) = \{x \in \mathbb{R}^2 : d_w(x, p_i) \leq d_w(x, p_j), \forall p_j \in P\}.$$

Definition 2. *A weighted Voronoi diagram of P is a partition of $\mathbb{R}^2$ into n regions, defined by the Voronoi polygons associated to set P, that is*

$$\{Vor_w(p_1), \ldots, Vor_w(p_n)\}.$$

The Voronoi diagram of P is usually denoted as

$$Vor_w(P) = \bigcup_{i=1}^{n} Vor_w(p_i).$$

Definition 3. *For $i \neq j$, the domain region of p_i over p_j is defined as*

$$Dom(p_i, p_j) = \{x \in \mathbb{R}^2 : d_w(x, p_i) \leq d_w(x, p_j)\}.$$

So, we have

$$Vor(p_i) = \bigcap_{j\neq i, j=1}^{n} Dom_w(p_i, p_j).$$

Definition 4. *The weighted bisector between p_i and p_j, with $j \neq i$, is defined as*

$$b_w(p_i, p_j) = \{x \in \mathbb{R}^2 : d_w(x, p_i) = d_w(x, p_j)\}.$$

Note that the domain regions of p_i and p_j correspond to spaces divided by their bisector, so we can express this set as

$$b_w(p_i, p_j) = Dom_w(p_i, p_j) \cap Dom_w(p_j, p_i).$$

Definition 5. *Given p_i and p_j, with $j \neq i$, its weighted Voronoi edge $e_w(p_i, p_j)$ is the intersection of its polygons if it is not empty and has more than a single point; that is,*

$$e_w(p_i, p_j) = Vor_w(p_i) \cap Vor_w(p_j).$$

We will call the union of weighted Voronoi edges a Voronoi lattice and the intersection of three or more Voronoi polygons a Voronoi vertex.

In the literature, four variants of weighted Voronoi diagrams are distinguished: multiplicatively weighted, additively weighted, compound weighted, and power weighted. The choice among them depends on how the values of W are used in the function d_w (see [3]).

In this paper, we will use multiplicatively weighted Voronoi diagrams. In particular, we will consider $w_i > 0$, for $i = 1, \ldots, n$, and we will use the weighted distance defined by

$$d_w(x, p_i) = \frac{\|x - p_i\|}{w_i},$$

where $\|x - p_i\|$ represents the Euclidean distance between x and p_i. Thus, the domain region of p_i over p_j is

$$Dom_w(p_i, p_j) = \left\{x \in \mathbb{R}^2 : \frac{\|x - p_i\|}{w_i} \leq \frac{\|x - p_j\|}{w_j}\right\}.$$

Note that when $w_i = w_j$, the domain corresponds to those points which are closer to p_i than to p_j. Actually, when $w_i = w_j$ for all $i, j \in \{1, \ldots, n\}$ the weighted Voronoi diagrams coincide with the classical Voronoi diagrams, and every Voronoi polygon is the set of points closer to p_i than to another p_j, with the euclidean metric. On the other hand, if $w_i < w_j$, the domain region of p_i over p_j can be expressed as

$$Dom_w(p_i, p_j) = \left\{x \in \mathbb{R}^2 : \|x - o\| \leq \epsilon\right\},$$

where

$$o = \frac{w_j^2}{w_j^2 - w_i^2}p_i - \frac{w_i^2}{w_j^2 - w_i^2}p_j, \qquad \epsilon = \frac{w_i w_j}{w_j^2 - w_i^2}\|p_i - p_j\|.$$

Then $Dom_w(p_i, p_j)$ is a closed ball with center at o and radius ϵ. Whereas for the case $w_i > w_j$, the domain region of p_i over p_j is

$$Dom_w(p_i, p_j) = \left\{ x \in \mathbb{R}^2 : \|x - o\| \geq \epsilon \right\},$$

which defines the complement of the open ball with center at o and radius ϵ. Thus, if $w_i \neq w_j$, the bisector between p_i and p_j can be written as

$$b_w(p_i, p_j) = \left\{ x \in \mathbb{R}^2 : \|x - o\| = \epsilon \right\}.$$

That is, in this case, the bisector is a circle.

In the literature we find the following result characterizing the geometry of the multiplicatively weighted Voronoi lattice (see [3]).

Theorem 1. *The edges of a multiplicatively weighted Voronoi region are circular arcs if and only if the weights of two adjacent regions are not equal, and are straight lines in the plane if and only if the weights of two adjacent regions are equal.*

Due to the wide range of applications of Voronoi diagrams, several algorithms have been developed for their generation, including techniques such as Domain Intersection, the Incremental Algorithm, and the Divide and Conquer approach, and others (see [2–4]).

In Fig. 1 we can see that multiplicatively weighted Voronoi regions are not necessarily convex.

Fig. 1. Multiplicatively weighted Voronoi diagrams, the numbers represent the corresponding weights.

3   Application for SDBA

Behavior Analysis constitutes a discipline that aims to understand the behavior of individuals, exploring both the behavior itself and the variables that influence it, including the spatiotemporal dynamics of the environment. Within this field, the study of organism movement, within the framework of behavioral phenomena and repertoires, addressed from perspectives such as organization, development, and change, is termed Spatial Dynamics Behavior Analysis (see [8]).

In SDBA, one of the main challenges lies in visualizing quantitative relationships between spatiotemporal variables of the environment and spatiotemporal features of behavior. Specifically, a clear representation of the organization, development, and evolution of interactions between variables, such as the time of stay in a specific zone, and treatment variables, such as the type of reinforcement schedule defined by the spatial-temporal constancy or variation in water delivery, is sought. This approach is applied to the study of specific behavioral phenomena, such as spatial differentiation in water-seeking situations in water-deprived rats.

Next, we will explore the use of weighted Voronoi diagrams in this context, starting with a detailed description of the experimental process, the type of data collected, and the data collection process.

3.1 Data Acquisition

The study was conducted by members of the Comparative Psychology Laboratory at Universidad Veracruzana within the facilities of the W. N. Schoenfeld Laboratory. The experimental subjects were 12 Wistar rats subjected to 22 h of water deprivation, with continuous access only to food.

A single-case experimental design was implemented within established behavior analysis protocols, but incorporating a high-resolution behavioral record for each rat (7200 data points per session). For data collection, a modular displacement chamber was employed, with an experimental space measuring $92 \times 92 \times 33$ cm in length, width, and height. Within this experimental space, four limited-availability water dispensers were placed, one in the middle of each wall of the chamber. The provided data indicate the subject's trajectory in coordinates (x, y) over time, recorded at a resolution of 5 frames per second.

Fifty sessions, each lasting 20 min, were conducted for these experiments. The studies involved the intersection of two environmental features (Fixed and Variable) within two environmental dimensions (Time and Space):

FT: *Fixed Time*, water delivery occurred every 30 s, with an availability window of 3 s.

VT: *Variable Time*, water delivery time varied, within an average of 30 s, with an availability window of 3 s.

FS: *Fixed Space*, water was delivered consistently at the same dispenser in all sessions, located at the coordinate $(50, 0)$.

VS: *Variable Space*, water was randomly delivered to one of the four dispensers.

Thus, four experiments were obtained: Fixed Time - Fixed Space (FT-FS); Fixed Time - Variable Space (FT-VS); Variable Time - Fixed Space (VT-FS); and Variable Time - Variable Space (VT-VS). Each experiment was conducted with three subjects for each combination.

Figure 2, illustrates an example of trajectories followed by some subjects in the first session for combinations FT-FS (Fig. 2(a)), FT-VS (Fig. 2(b)), VT-FS (Fig. 2(c)) and VT-VS (Fig. 2(d)).

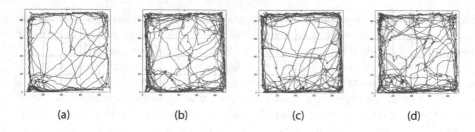

(a)   (b)   (c)   (d)

Fig. 2. Subjects' Trajectory.

3.2   Generation of Weighted Voronoi Diagrams

In order to be able to construct the weighted Voronoi diagrams with the experimental data collected, it is necessary to have a generator set up and to assign the appropriate weights to each of its points. The procedure to achieve this construction is detailed below.

First, the experimental space was divided into $n \times m$ regions of uniform size and the center of each of them was calculated, thus obtaining a set of $n \times m$ points, which we will call *initial set*. Once this division was obtained, the software **MOTUS**[1] was used to obtain the *cumulated time* by region, corresponding to the cumulative number of times the subject was in each area (see [10]). This information can be visualized as a matrix.

The following procedure was used to build the generator set and assign weights to each of its points:

1. Each point in the initial set was assigned its weight based on its cumulative time.
2. The generator set P was defined as the set of points whose assigned weights were non-zero.
3. The set W contains all the weights corresponding to the generating set P.

This procedure guarantees an accurate representation of the generator points and their respective assigned weights, providing the necessary elements for the generation of the weighted Voronoi diagrams. It can be observed that *initial set* and *cumulative time* in the region are fully determined, the first one at the moment when the parameters for the analysis are configured and the second one by data acquired from the behavioral experiment. This implies that there is no randomness in the diagram they generate. To accomplish the above, the domain intersection algorithm was implemented and executed in Python.

Figure 3 shows the data derived from the process described above, in which the experimental space, with dimensions of 92 cm ×92 cm, was partitioned into a grid of 10×10, generating an initial set of 100 points, each with its

---

[1] MOTUS, is a software that allows to generation of different graphical representations of data from the displacement of an individual, recorded as changes in (x, y) coordinates over time.

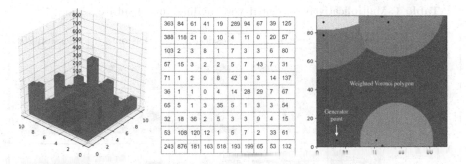

Fig. 3. Accumulated time in regions and the corresponding multiplicatively weighted Voronoi diagram. (Color figure online)

associated weight. In the multiplicatively weighted Voronoi diagram in Fig. 3, the red triangles indicate the location of the water dispensers, and the color-determined region points to the weighted Voronoi region of the generator points, represented by a black dot. The regions shown are those corresponding to the generators with the highest weights, as they are arranged in descending order. In order to streamline the visualization of the identified regions in this study, only the first five regions with the highest weights were included.

3.3 Data Analysis

To illustrate the use of Voronoi diagrams in SDBA, four subjects were selected from the twelve experimental subjects, with each subject exposed to one of the four aforementioned conditions. Tables 1 and 2, display the condition, subject, and five sessions in which the weighted Voronoi diagram of the five generators with the highest weight was generated. The Voronoi diagrams show the behavioral segmentation of the experimental space. The sessions were chosen to depict the evolution of behavioral spatial segmentation throughout the experiment-highlighting the contrast between the transition in early sessions (1 to 4) and a later session that illustrates a typical steady behavioral state. This detailed analysis of behavioral spatial evolution serves as an example of SDBA.

It is noticeable the similarity of the diagrams in session 1 between the four experiments. In all cases, the generators with more time spent were distributed between corners and dispenser zones, as Regions of Behavioral Relevance (RBR), with both circular arcs and straight-line arcs. Nevertheless, as experiments progress, different segmentations emerge between them as follows.

It is noteworthy that, for Subject 1 under the condition *Fixed Time-Fixed Space*, the generators where the subject spent the most time from session two onward are near the dispenser. These RBRs are represented in grayish blue and neon green colors, and such RBRs are also present in the last session of the experiment. Starting from session two, all RBRs are circular arcs, and the straight-line arcs disappear completely, depicting a dominance of certain regions or inequality between regions.

Table 1. Multiplicatively Weighted Voronoi diagrams of subjects 1 and 7.

On the other hand, for Subject 7 under the condition *Variable Time-Fixed Space*, although the water delivery is located in the same zone as in the condition of the first subject, the diagrams vary significantly. In this case, no single dominating region·is identified across sessions, regardless of the water delivery only being in one region. The simple variability in the time delivery induced more varied RBRs, including corners and dispenser zones. Additionally, in comparison to Subject 1, both circular and some straight-line arcs can be observed in the first four diagrams related to the transition sessions, but only circular arcs for session twenty.

In contrast, Subject 4 under the condition *Fixed Time-Variable Space*, was expected to visit each of the dispensers. From session two onward, a notable progression toward symmetric regions was observed, with straight-line arcs becoming especially prominent in session 4.

Finally, in the sessions corresponding to Subject 10 under the condition with higher variability, *Variable Time-Variable Space*, two differentiated kinds of diagrams are observed. Sessions 1–3 revealed an RBR distribution trending toward equity, characterized by prominent straight-line arcs, as expected under the Variable Space condition. However, a sudden shift occurred in session 4, where generators with more time spent were predominantly located near the bottom and left dispensers, as well as the bottom-right corner. In this scenario, RBRs were now delimited by circular arcs. Notably, in session 20, all weight generators were concentrated at the bottom of the experimental space. This transition from an equitable segmentation to a dominant segmentation, as indicated by the size of RBDs and the features of the arcs, may be attributed to heightened uncertainty in water delivery conditions resulting from the variability in both Space and Time.

Table 2. Multiplicatively Weighted Voronoi diagrams of subjects 4 and 10.

	Session 1	Session 2	Session 3	Session 4	Session 20
FT-VS Subject 4					
VT-VS Subject 10					

4 Conclusions

Multiplicatively weighted Voronoi diagrams, applied in the context of SDBA, proved to be a valuable tool for visualizing and understanding various aspects of individual behavior.

Each region in the weighted Voronoi diagram defines an RBR. The various organizations of these regions represent well-differentiated patterns of behavioral segmentation within the same experimental space. In other words, they depict distinctive spatial behavioral patterns related to the specific spatiotemporal features of the environment. Identifying these RBRs provides valuable information about behavior dynamics in relation to environmental conditions.

The weighted Voronoi diagrams evolve across experimental sessions, allowing the tracking of spatial patterns known as RBRs. The evolution of these patterns shows how behavior adapts to different conditions, offering crucial insights into a subject's behavioral adjustments over time and space.

The weighted Voronoi diagram highlights not only areas of close influence but also areas of distant influence. This aspect could help us identify not only preference patterns (i.e., RBR with approaching valence) but also those RBRs that tend to be avoided or have withdrawal valence. This feature could enrich the understanding of spatial variables and features related to a wide range of behavioral phenomena, incorporating not only preferences derived from the highest values of time spent in a given region but also aversive patterns indicated by the lowest values of time spent in a zone. It could provide a more comprehensive perspective on the dynamics of different behavioral phenomena.

The above observations highlight the utility of this tool for analyzing and visualizing spatial dynamics in behavioral studies. The ability to identify, track evolution, and distinguish spatial patterns in a perspicuous way, such as RBR, adds depth and precision to SDBA. Moreover, this capability could facilitate interpretation and informed decision-making in applied behavioral settings.

References

1. Aurenhammer, F., Edelsbrunner, H.: An optimal algorithm for constructing the weighted Voronoi diagram in the plane. Pattern Recogn. **17**(2), 251–257 (1984)
2. Aurenhammer, F., Klein, R., Lee, D.T.: Voronoi Diagrams and Delaunay triangulations. World Scientific Publishing Company (2013)
3. Boots, B., Sugihara, K., Chiu, S.N., Okabe, A.: Spatial Tessellations: Concepts and Applications of Voronoi Diagrams. Wiley, Hoboken (2009)
4. de Berg, M., Cheong, O., van Kreveld, M., Overmars, M.: Computational Geometry: Algorithms and Applications, 3rd edn. Springer, Heidelberg (2008). https://doi.org/10.1007/978-3-540-77974-2. ISBN 9783540847441
5. Eliakim, E., Morgulev, E., Lidor, R., Munk, O., Meckel, Y.: The development of metrics for measuring the level of symmetry in team formation and ball movement flow, and their association with performance. Sci. Med. Football **6**(2), 189–202 (2022). https://doi.org/10.1080/24733938.2021.1919747
6. Gallier, J., Quaintance, J.: Aspects of Convex Geometry Polyhedra, Linear Programming, Shellings, Voronoi Diagrams, Delaunay Triangulations. Department of Computer and Information Science, University of Pennsylvania, vol. 219104, pp. 31–235 (2017)
7. Gudmundsson, J., Horton, M.: Spatio-temporal analysis of team sports. ACM Comput. Surv. **50**(2), 1–34 (2018). https://doi.org/10.1145/3054132
8. León, A., et al.: Ecological location of a water source and spatial dynamics of behavior under temporally scheduled water deliveries in a modified open-field system: an integrative approach. Front. Psychol. **11**, 577903 (2020). https://doi.org/10.3389/fpsyg.2020.577903
9. León, A., et al.: Beyond single discrete responses: an integrative and multidimensional analysis of behavioral dynamics assisted by machine learning. Front. Behav. Neurosci. **15**, 681771 (2021). https://doi.org/10.3389/fnbeh.2021.681771
10. León, A., et al.: MOTUS: Software para el análisis conductual de patrones de desplazamiento. Revista Mexicana de Análisis de La Conducta **46**(1), 222–242 (2020). https://doi.org/10.5514/rmac.v46.i1.76960
11. Manca, M., Boratto, L., Morell Roman, V., Martori i Gallissà, O., Kaltenbrunner, A.: Using social media to characterize urban mobility patterns: state-of-the-art survey and case-study. Online Soc. Netw. Media **1**, 56–69 (2017). https://doi.org/10.1016/j.osnem.2017.04.002
12. Mu, L.: Polygon characterization with the multiplicatively weighted Voronoi diagram. Prof. Geogr. **56**(2), 223–239 (2004)
13. Preparata, F.P., Shamos, M.I.: Computational Geometry: An Introduction. Springer, New York (2012). https://doi.org/10.1007/978-1-4612-1098-6
14. Viloria, A., Pineda Lezama, O.B., Vargas, J.: Analysis of crowd behavior through pattern virtualization. Procedia Comput. Sci. **175**, 102–107 (2020). https://doi.org/10.1016/j.procs.2020.07.017

Pattern Recognition in Road Safety: Uncovering the Latent Causes of Accidents on Mexico's Federal Highways

Diana Zepeda-Martínez[1], Angélica Guzmán-Ponce[2],
R. María Valdovinos Rosas[1]($\boxtimes$), and David Joaquín Delgado-Hernández[1]

[1] Faculty of Engineering, Autonomous University of the State of Mexico,
Cerro de Coatepec, 50100 Toluca, State of Mexico, Mexico
{dzepedam001,rmvaldovinosr,david.delgado}@uaemex.mx
[2] Institute of New Imaging Technologies, Department of Computer Languages
and Systems, Universitat Jaume I, Av. Vicent Sos Baynat,
12071 Castelló de la Plana, Spain
aguzman@uji.es

Abstract. Land transportation in Mexico plays a crucial role in ensuring connectivity and facilitating the mobility of both people and commodity. Nevertheless, this sector confronts substantial challenges, predominantly related with road accidents. Understanding the factors that contribute to these accidents is essential to developing and implementing effective safety strategies to reduce their frequency and severity. This research uses two unsupervised methods: latent Dirichlet allocation analysis (LDA) and the K-means algorithm, to identify the underlying factors responsible for road accidents in Mexico. LDA uncovers latent thematic structures in accident reports, revealing patterns in textual descriptions, and K-means identifies groups of accidents that share common attributes. The study period is from the years 2015 and 2019. The results suggest that traffic accidents are significantly influenced by a combination of factors such as driver behavior, road conditions, weather conditions and weather patterns.

Keywords: Road Accidents · Highways · Latent Dirichlet Allocation · Latent Topics · Clustering

1 Introduction

In Mexico, in 2022 847,716 deaths were reported, 90% were due to some disease or its consequences, in the remaining 10%, traffic accidents are among the ten main causes of death.[1]. In 2020, 13,630 people died from injuries in traffic accidents,

---

[1] https://www.inegi.org.mx/contenidos/saladeprensa/boletines/2023/EDR/EDR2022-Dft.pdf.

corresponding to a mortality rate of 11 per 100,000 inhabitants[2]. About it, in 2021, an analysis of urban traffic incidents reported 340,415 accidents, where 3,849 of them had at least one death and 60,584 with injuries[3].

The analysis of traffic accidents reveals an inherent complexity in their causes and consequences. In this context, the use of machine learning (ML) and pattern recognition techniques emerges as a promising approach, with the potential to transform our understanding and response to traffic-related issues, such as the proposed by Yassin & Poooja [9], focused on accident severity in developing countries, examining factors like road conditions, lighting, weather, and casualty data (age and type). Using data from Addis Ababa's federal traffic police, including categorical and numerical data, their study implemented a hybrid method combining K-means clustering and Random Forest to identify critical variables affecting accident severity.

In Mexico, Saldana et al. [7] predict urban traffic congestion using a semi-supervised ML model. Focusing on Mexico City traffic dynamics, the study combines Support Vector Machine regression with data from Twitter, to forecast traffic events. The methodology integrates geospatial models, allowing traffic congestion to be visualized and upcoming traffic events to be predicted.

Sosa [8] applied Artificial Neural Networks (ANN) to predict car accidents in Monterrey, Mexico, analyzing variables like weather, location, time, date, type, and cause of accidents. The study used various data types across different study area sizes, including textual, categorical, time series, and images like diagrams. Using historical data from 2017, the ANN model effectively predicted accidents, though its efficiency was notably influenced by the variables, particularly the accident cause.

Daniel et al. [6] analysed the timing and occurrence of traffic accidents in Mexico City between 2014 and 2019, using data from the C5 open data portal[4]. Employing rule-based decision trees on a hexagonal grid framework, they generated rules associating points of interest with accident rates. Key findings include a high concentration of accidents in five Mexico City delegations, significant temporal patterns, and the critical role of intersections, traffic lights, and other relevant points in accident occurrences.

Hernández [4] developed a model using the information of the National Institute of Statistics and Geography on Traffic Accidents in urban and suburban areas during 2020 in Mexico[5]. The goal was to predict the severity of car accidents through data cleaning, balancing and feature selection processes. Random Forest, instance-based algorithms like KNN and ANN were implemented. The results indicate that Random Forest outperformed other models.

---

[2] https://www.gob.mx/cms/uploads/attachment/file/818181/Informe_SV_2021_HD2_compressed.pdf.

[3] https://www.inegi.org.mx/contenidos/saladeprensa/boletines/2021/accidentes/ACCIDENTES_2021.pdf.

[4] https://datos.cdmx.gob.mx/explore/dataset/incidentes-viales-c5/information/.

[5] https://www.inegi.org.mx/contenidos/saladeprensa/boletines/2021/accidentes/ACCIDENTES_2021.pdf.

From the efforts made by the scientific community, few studies focus on finding hidden patterns that allow identifying the impact that car accidents have on society in general. Derived from this, this study focuses on identifying hidden factors that precipitate the occurrence of traffic accidents on Mexican roads during the period from 2015 to 2019. For this, two unsupervised machine learning techniques were implemented: LDA and K-means algorithms.

2   Unsupervised Methods

2.1   Latent Dirichlet Allocation

The Latent Dirichlet Allocation (LDA) algorithm represents an unsupervised statistical approach employed to elucidate sets of observations that are not directly observed (latent). Let a dataset of M samples and N_d attributes, the essence of the LDA method is to model each sample as a mixture of several features (Algorithm 1). These features are represented by a multinomial distribution, which in turn is derived from a predefined Dirichlet distribution [3].

Algorithm 1. Latent Dirichlet Allocation

Require: M, N_d, α, T, ξ
Ensure: A distribution of topics and characteristics for each sample in the collection.
1: Initialize β: Matrix $T \times N$ for conditional distribution
2: **for** each sample $m = 1$ to M **do**
3:     $N_d \sim Poisson(\xi)$ ▷ Number of sample characteristics
4:     $\theta \sim Dirichlet(\alpha)$ ▷ Vector of topic mixture parameters
5:     **for** each feature $n = 1$ to N_d **do**
6:         $z_n \sim Multinomial(\theta)$ ▷ Select a topic
7:         $w_n \sim p(w_n|z_n, \beta)$ ▷ Select a word from the conditional distribution
8:     **end for**
9: **end for**

In the Algorithm 1: α sets the initial probability for the Dirichlet distribution. θ indicates how different topics are combined in a sample. z_n links the features in the samples to the underlying topics. β is a vector composed of N terms from the feature vocabulary. w is the specific features that appear in the samples.

The algorithm's outputs are: the patterns distribution or topics (β), the distribution of samples represented in the topic space (θ). To ensure the quality of the topics obtained, two metrics are used [1]: *perplexity* and *coherence*.

Perplexity. Perplexity determines how efficiently a model can handle previously unseen data [1]. In LDA, identify the optimal number of topics according to Eq. 1. Generally, there is an assumed inverse relationship between perplexity and model accuracy: lower perplexity implies higher accuracy [1]. This principle underlies the use of perplexity as a key indicator in LDA optimization, aiding in the selection of an appropriate number of topics to enhance the ability of the model to classify and understand the data.

$$Perplexity = \exp\left(\frac{\sum_{d=1}^{M} \log P(w_{dn})}{\sum_{d=1}^{M} N_d}\right) \tag{1}$$

where, N_d represents the number of features in a sample, M denotes the total number of samples in the dataset. $P(w_{dn})$ is the probability of observing a specific word w in the n-th position of the sample d, conditional on the assigned topic z_n an the distribution β for that topic.

Coherence. Coherence focuses on assessing the clarity and consistency of themes from the human view, that is to say, C_v evaluates to what degree the induced themes of an LDA model are correlated with each other, based on conditional probability (Eq. 2). The higher coherence value, greater will be the probability of obtaining greater precision from that model [1].

$$C_v = \sum_{i<j} log \frac{D(w_i, w_j) + 1}{D(w_i) + 1} \tag{2}$$

where, $D(w_i)$ is the frequency of samples containing the word w_i, and $D(w_i, w_j)$ the frequency of samples containing both words.

2.2   K-Means Algorithm

The K-means clustering algorithm is a unsupervised learning method that partitioned a dataset into K distinct non-overlapping subsets or clusters. This partitioning is achieved by assigning each data point to the cluster with the nearest mean, serving as a cluster prototype [9]. The goal of the K-means algorithm is to minimize the within-cluster sum of squares (WCSS), also referred to as inertia, represented as follow Eq. 3:

$$\sum_{i=1}^{M} \min_{\mu_j \in C} \left(||x_i - \mu_j||^2 \right) \tag{3}$$

where x_i denotes the i-th sample with N_d attributes, and μ_j is the centroid of the j-th cluster. The centroid is conceptualized as the mean position of all points in the cluster representing the centre of the cluster. The set C encompasses all clusters, where each cluster j is characterized by its centroid μ_j. The goal is to determine a division where the total sum of squared distances from each sample to the mean of its assigned cluster is minimized (Algorithm 2).

In Algorithm 2, the iterative process involves reassigning data samples among various clusters until a stable clustering configuration is achieved or when a predefined stopping criterion is met, such as a specified number of iterations [9].

Jambu's Elbow method is commonly used to find the optimal value of K [2]; this method identifies the *elbow* point in a plot of the sum of squared distances

---

Algorithm 2. K-Means

Require: M: samples, K: Number of clusters
Ensure: Cluster assignment for each instance in the dataset.
 1: Initialize *centroids*: List of K initial centroids
 2: Initialize *clusters*: List of K empty sets to store instances in each cluster
 3: Randomly assign instances to the initial centroids
 4: **repeat**
 5:    **for** each sample x in M **do**
 6:       Calculate the distance between x and each centroid at *centroids*
 7:       Assign x to the cluster of the nearest centroid
 8:    **end for**
 9:    **for** each cluster C en *clusters* **do**
10:       Calculate the new centroid as the average of the instances in C
11:    **end for**
12: **until** Convergence or maximum number of iterations achieved

---

from points to their cluster centroids against different K values. This point indicates that increasing the number of clusters does not significantly improve intra-cluster homogeneity.

3   Methodology

3.1   Information Acquisition

The data used were extracted from the official website of the Mexican Government[6]. It includes 66,008 samples from traffic accident reports between 2015 and 2019, detailing locations, road conditions, times, dates, and specifics about vehicles and victims. The data are in textual and tabular formats with numerical and categorical components. 15,038 samples were excluded due to missing data.

Each sample contains 120 attributes Also, information regarding accident victims, encompassing those injured and deceased and pedestrians, was amalgamated into a singular *victims* column. Finally, various columns about the classification of accidents and the circumstances that contributed to them were categorized. The final dataset is composed by 50,970 samples and 15 attributes.

3.2   Data Pre-processing

A cleaning phase was applied, in which less relevant attributes were excluded under the guidance of an expert in the study area, in order to preserve only relevant features. Likewise, the data were adapted to the requirements of the LDA and K-means algorithms.

For the LDA algorithm, the attributes were transformed into textual format. While for the K-means algorithm, they were kept numerical and one-hot coding was used to adjust them. This technique changes categorical variables to a binary

---

[6] https://datos.gob.mx/busca/dataset/policia-federal.

format, representing the presence or absence of a category with a numerical value. Upon completing the coding process, 195 attributes were obtained.

3.3 Uncovering Latent Patterns

The implementation of the algorithms was carried out using Python, with the main library for topic modelling, Gensim[7], and for K-means sci-kit-learn[8].

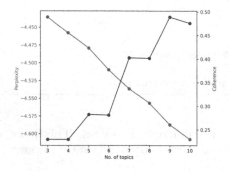 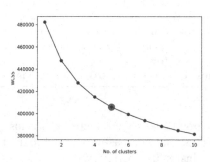

(a) Perplexity and coherence metrics for various numbers of topics.

(b) Jambu's Elbow method for optimal cluster determination.

Fig. 1. Comparative visual analysis for optimizing topic and cluster numbers using perplexity, coherence, and Jambu's Elbow method.

The effectiveness of the LDA model was evaluated using the perplexity and consistency metrics, varying from 3 to 10 topics to determine the optimal number. The lowest perplexity, indicating higher accuracy, was achieved with 10 topics, despite 9 topics showing the highest consistency. The choice of a 10-topic model was driven by the significant improvement in model predictions through minimizing perplexity (See Fig. 1a). Jambu's elbow method determined the optimal number of clusters for the K-means algorithm, identifying 5 clusters as the point with the lowest inertia decline rate (See Fig. 1b).

3.4 Assessment Metric

The silhouette coefficient (SC) was used to validate the clustering quality in this analysis (Eq. 4). From -1 to 1, it measures the similarity of a sample to its group versus others. A score near 1 indicates robust matching, -1 implies poor matching, and around 0 suggests equal distance from clusters [5]. In K-means, SC assesses the similarity of a sample to others in its group (cohesion) versus neighbouring groups (separation), calculating both within-group average

---

[7] https://radimrehurek.com/gensim/index.html.
[8] https://scikit-learn.org/stable/.

similarity $(a(i))$ and with the closest different group $(b(i))$ to measure internal coherence.

$$S(i) = \frac{b(i) - a(i)}{\max(a(i), b(i))} \tag{4}$$

For the LDA algorithm, the (SC) assess the coherence of topics extracted from a dataset, i.e. SC measures how distinctly topics are defined and how well samples map to them. A high (SC) value suggests that the samples have a solid membership to the identified topics, which indicates good topic separation and definition in the LDA model.

4   Results

4.1   Latent Topics in Accidents

In Fig. 2 reveals that in states like Nayarit, Puebla, Sinaloa, Tabasco, and Tamaulipas, morning accidents on three-lane roads are prevalent, often attributed to reckless driving and adverse weather conditions such as wind and fires. Conversely, Mexico City experiences accidents primarily from lane invasions during overtaking, frequently leading to head-on collisions and vehicle rollovers, with four to nine victims per incident (Fig. 2b). In Fig. 2c shows that in Aguascalientes, Nuevo León, Tabasco, Jalisco, and Morelos, accidents occur mainly on Sunday mornings, typically due to failures in yielding the right of way, averaging five victims. In Yucatán, Durango, and Sonora, the peak accident periods are in April and August, on Saturdays and Wednesdays, involving two victims per incident (Fig. 2d). The State of Mexico records frequent accidents on five-lane roads caused by absent road signs, unsafe loads, and fog, with an average of one victim (Fig. 2e). In Durango and San Luis Potosí (Fig. 2f), September Tuesdays see accidents mainly from driver errors, like dozing or improper parking, and vehicle malfunctions, resulting in two to six victims. Michoacán, Hidalgo, and Sinaloa report afternoon rollovers and brake failures, affecting up to six individuals. Seasonal traffic trends in October and November indicate a rise in accidents during twilight in Guanajuato, Chiapas, and Tlaxcala, possibly linked to the Day of the Dead celebrations. Lastly, July in Querétaro, Quintana Roo, Coahuila, Baja California, Campeche, and Guerrero sees the most accidents on single-lane roads due to road conditions, driver behaviour, and weather (Fig. 2j). December features night accidents on two- and four-lane roads caused by weather and driver recklessness, correlated with the Christmas and New Year festivities.

4.2   K-Means in Accidents

The K-means algorithm analysis shows that road accidents in Guanajuato, Jalisco, San Luis Potosí, Chiapas, and the State of Mexico predominantly occur during the night and early morning of Sundays in December 2015, involving 0 to 4 victims. Common causes include falling objects, driver recklessness, impacts with

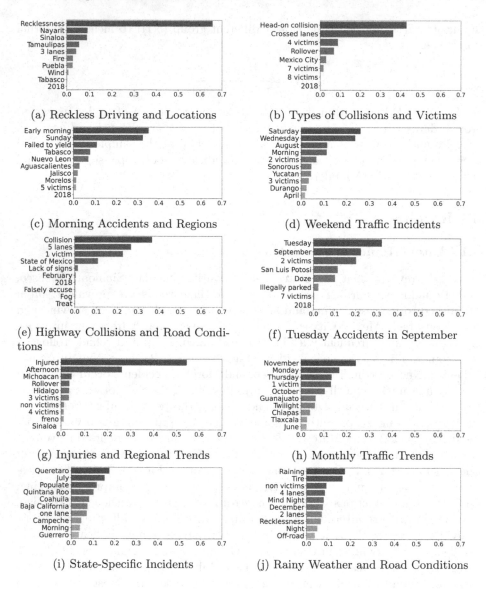

(a) Reckless Driving and Locations

(b) Types of Collisions and Victims

(c) Morning Accidents and Regions

(d) Weekend Traffic Incidents

(e) Highway Collisions and Road Conditions

(f) Tuesday Accidents in September

(g) Injuries and Regional Trends

(h) Monthly Traffic Trends

(i) State-Specific Incidents

(j) Rainy Weather and Road Conditions

Fig. 2. Topics on traffic accidents on Mexican highways from 2015 to 2019

stationary vehicles, and lane invasions, suggesting a link with weekend trips and holiday festivities during Christmas and New Year. Similarly, in December 2018, Veracruz, State of Mexico, and Jalisco experienced frequent accidents on 4-lane roads, mainly involving 1 to 2 victims from driver deviations, pedestrian collisions, and rear-end impacts, correlating with the Christmas season. In June and July 2015, incidents on four-lane highways during weekend nights resulted in 0 to 3 victims due to excessive speed and adverse weather. The trend continued in 2018 with accidents in Morelos and Guanajuato on Sunday afternoons, particularly in July and May, on two-lane roads involving excessive speed and rain. Additionally, in March and April 2015, evening accidents were frequent in Veracruz, Chiapas, and Guanajuato during weekends, causing 0 to 3 victims from driver recklessness, leading to head-on collisions on 4-lane highways.

4.3 Comparative Evaluation of Models

The results obtained are summarized in Fig. 3a. The word cloud reveals an emphasis on the terms 'victim,' 'Morning,' and 'Recklessness,' as well as several urban locations.

(a) Word cloud from the topics

(b) Word cloud from the clusters

Fig. 3. Word clouds

Additionally, the (SC) was employed to assesses the coherence and separation within the clustering, providing a quantitative evaluation of the clustering quality, determining the cohesion and separation of the structures identified by the LDA and K-means algorithms. Although K-means is inherently designed to optimize such a metric, using it with LDA allow to validate the clarity and robustness of the topics generated.K-means exhibited a substantially higher (SC) (0.5781585923153798) compared to LDA (0.0252322471173679). This finding suggests that K-means formed more cohesive and separate clusters in the dataset.

5 Conclusions

Traffic accidents in Mexico are a significant public health issue and a leading cause of mortality and injuries. This research employed LDA and K-means to analyse road accident patterns across Mexican states. LDA identified ten latent topics linked to reckless driving, collisions, and environmental influences, revealing complex accident scenarios shaped by regional traits and weather conditions. K-means categorised incidents by timing, location, and impact, highlighting prevalent trends such as night and early morning accidents during holidays, influenced by environmental conditions like rain. These methods provided a detailed understanding of the multifaceted nature of traffic accidents, emphasising the roles of driver behaviour, road conditions, and temporal factors. Recommendations include developing targeted safety campaigns and enhancing enforcement during high-risk periods. Future studies should analyse long-term trends, integrate socioeconomic and demographic data, create predictive models, and assess the efficacy of existing road safety policies.

References

1. Abdelrazek, A., Eid, Y., Gawish, E., Medhat, W., Hassan, A.: Topic modeling algorithms and applications: a survey. Inf. Syst. **112**, 102131 (2023). https://doi.org/10.1016/j.is.2022.102131
2. Amorim, B.D.S.P., Firmino, A.A., Baptista, C.D.S., Júnior, G.B., Paiva, A.C.D., Júnior, F.E.D.A.: A machine learning approach for classifying road accident hotspots. ISPRS Int. J. Geo-Inf. **12**(6), 227 (2023). https://doi.org/10.3390/ijgi12060227
3. Blei, D.M., Ng, A.Y., Jordan, M.I.: Latent dirichlet allocation. J. Mach. Learn. Res. **3**(Jan), 993–1022 (2003)
4. Hernández, J.J.O.: Aplicación y valoración de algoritmos de Machine Learning para la predicción de gravedad en accidentes automovilísticos. Ph.D. thesis, Benemérita Universidad Autónoma de Puebla (2023)
5. Lenssen, L., Schubert, E.: Medoid silhouette clustering with automatic cluster number selection. Inf. Syst. **120**, 102290 (2024). https://doi.org/10.1016/j.is.2023.102290
6. Otero, D.E.R.: Descubrimiento y representación de patrones de accidentes de tránsito en la Ciudad de México usando técnicas geoestadísticas y aprendizaje máquina. Ph.D. thesis, INFOTEC Centro de Investigación e Innovación en Tecnologías de la Información y Comunicación (2021)
7. Saldana-Perez, M., Torres-Ruiz, M., Moreno-Ibarra, M.: Geospatial modeling of road traffic using a semi-supervised regression algorithm. IEEE Access **7**, 177376–177386 (2019). https://doi.org/10.1109/ACCESS.2019.2942586
8. Sosa, E.E.C.: Análisis y predicción de accidentes automovilísticos mediante la aplicación de la red neuronal artificial de máxima sensibilidad y un prototipo de sistema web para la visualización de la información. Ph.D. thesis, Universidad Autónoma de Nuevo León (2019)
9. Yassin, S.S.: Pooja: road accident prediction and model interpretation using a hybrid k-means and random forest algorithm approach. SN Appl. Sci. **2**(9), 1576 (2020). https://doi.org/10.1007/s42452-020-3125-1

A Regression Tree as Acquisition Function for Low-Dimensional Optimisation

Erick G. G. de Paz[1]([⊠]) (iD), Humberto Vaquera Huerta[1] (iD),
Francisco Javier Albores Velasco[2] (iD), John R. Bauer Mengelberg[1] (iD),
and Juan Manuel Romero Padilla[1] (iD)

[1] Colegio de Postgraduados, 56230 Texcoco, México, Mexico
{giles.erick,hvaquera,jbauer,romero.manuel}@colpos.mx
[2] Universidad Autónoma de Tlaxcala, 90341 Apizaco, Tlaxcala, Mexico
franciscojavier.albores.v@uatx.mx

Abstract. DIRECT-type optimisation algorithms recursively explore
the domain of an objective function by means of a hierarchical partition.
In this context, a regression tree can be estimated with the exploration
data and be used to quickly reach the optimum. This regression tree
allows to apply Bayesian optimisation techniques instead of the poorly
adaptive rules applied within the original DIRECT algorithm. Although
based on a probabilistic framework, this approach can perform a deterministic search, a remarkable attribute of DIRECT-type algorithms. This
method based on a machine learning algorithm and Bayesian inference
is compared with several R libraries for optimisation, including the original DIRECT algorithm and three representative evolutionary algorithms.
For a collection of well-known benchmark functions, the proposal is statistically more reliable and robust than DIRECT with respect of dimensionality, but not enough to beat the evolutionary alternatives.

Keywords: Regression Tree · DIRECT algorithm · Bayesian
Optimisation

1 Introduction

The DIRECT optimisation algorithm is a deterministic black-box method based
on a branch and bound strategy, which produces a hierarchical partition of the
search domain into hyperrectangles. Although effective only on low dimensions
(2–6 variables), this algorithm is still in use to solve real-world problems in
several areas [8]. Since it was published a couple of decades ago, one of the key
strengths is that the algorithm is deterministic, so there is no need to perform
multiple runs, and experimental results are easily to replicate [9].

In few words, the original DIRECT algorithm iterates three deterministic
steps: 1) Select and divide the most promising subset (initially the entire domain)
into several hyperrectangular subsets, 2) Evaluate the centroid of each new subset in the objective function, and 3) Determine which subsets are considered as

promising to contain the optimum. The iteration stops when a limit of function evaluations or a desired accuracy is reach. There exists a wide variety of versions of DIRECT. The idea of changing the geometry of partition has been widely explored with partitions based on: bisections [16], polytopes [12] (Voronoi diagram), etc. Another recurrent idea is the local application of derivative-based algorithms: Newton's method [15], Interval Analysis [10], and others [17].

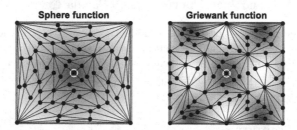

Fig. 1. Simplex-based regression trees fitted to two well-known benchmark functions

In the field of machine learning, methods such as CART or ID4.5 [13] create partitions of the data space to assign labels or mean answers. This paper proposes that the search for the optimum be guided by a regression tree, in which each function evaluation is used to approximate the objective function. Thus, relevant aspects of the search are decided by means of the local statistics estimated for each subset of the partition. Instead of performing a quasi-exhaustive search like DIRECT, the regression tree allows to infer which are the most promising subsets to contain the optimum. And, instead of invariably evaluating the centroid of each subset, the regression tree is used as an acquisition function to infer which should be the next point to evaluate in a subset. In addition to those techniques of statistical inference, the geometry of the partition is based on simplexes in order to define more adaptive subsets bounds. Further, the geometry of simplexes will prove to be quite convenient for defining a probabilistic model. As illustrative examples, Fig. 1 shows two simplex-trees fitted to well-known benchmark functions.

Section 2 formally introduces an *ad-hoc* probabilistic model and an algorithm for inferring (fitting) a regression-tree focused on optimising. Section 3 details the design of two Monte Carlo experiments for comparing our proposal with DIRECT and three evolutionary algorithms. In Sect. 4, numerical results are discussed to finally draw conclusions in Sect. 5.

2 Mathematical Framework

2.1 A Brownian Process over a *d*-Simplex

In stochastic process theory, a Brownian bridge is a probabilistic model that assigns a probability measure for each possible connecting path between two points in a continuous space. Under the assumption that the initial and final points have to be visited, the variance (uncertainty) of different possible paths around these points is close to zero. In contrast, the maximum variance is in the midst of the path due to the multiple possible routes to take. Formally,

Definition 1. *[5] Given a real function $f : \mathbb{R}^d \to \mathbb{R}$, a pair of points $\{\bar{a}_i, \bar{a}_j\} \in \mathbb{R}^d$ and their corresponding function evaluations $\{y_i = f(\bar{a}_1), y_j = f(\bar{a}_2)\}$; the* **Brownian bridge** *$F_{i,j}(w)$ is a continuous stochastic process with continuous index $0 < w < 1$, defined as:*

$$F_{i,j}(w) \sim Normal(\mu_{i,j}(w) = wy_i + (1 - w)y_j, \tag{1}$$
$$\sigma^2_{i,j}(w) = \sigma^2_0 \|\bar{a}_i - \bar{a}_j\| w(1 - w))$$

In Bayesian Optimisation, Brownian bridges are frequently used to model the behaviour of a function in any point where the actual function evaluation is unknown [4]. These probabilistic models estimate the function and also measure the uncertainty of the estimation, so they provide sufficient information to define a credible interval, i.e. upper and lower bounds for the actual function. In order to perform an *optimistic exploration* in a minimisation problem, the minimum of the lower bound is located and evaluated in the objective function as a promising solution [3]. The iteration of this strategy minimises the uncertainty around promising solutions. The minimum inside a credible interval is given by:

Lemma 1. *Let $F_{i,j}(w)$ be a Brownian bridge, with known parameter σ^2_0,* **the minimum credible realisation** *$f^*_{i,j}$ inside a credible interval with probability $1 - \alpha$ corresponds to the index $w^*_{i,j}$. Where*

1. $w^*_{i,j} = min(\frac{1}{2} + \frac{1}{2}c, \frac{1}{2} - \frac{1}{2}c)$
2. $c = (y_i - y_j)/\sqrt{(y_i - y_j)^2 + \sigma^2_0 q^2_\alpha \|\bar{a}_i - \bar{a}_j\|^2}$
3. $f^*_{i,j} = \mu_{i,j}(w^*_{i,j}) + q_\alpha \sqrt{\sigma_{i,j}(w^*_{i,j})}$
4. $\Pr(Y < q_\alpha) = \alpha$ with $Y \sim Normal(0, 1)$

Proof Hint. *Solve $\frac{d}{dw}[\mu_{i,j}(w) + q_\alpha \sqrt{\sigma_{i,j}(w)}] = 0$ for w.*

Definition 1 enounces a very simple model which is only defined for lines over the domain space $\mathbb{R}^d$. However, this model is quite useful to split a simplex set. According to [18], to efficiently compute a simplex-tree, it is necessary to bisect the simplex in an edge. Formally,

Definition 2. *[18] Let $A \subset \mathbb{R}^d$ be a simplex bounded by $d + 1$ extreme points $\{\bar{a}_1 \ldots, \bar{a}_{d+1}\}$, i.e. $A = \{\sum_{i=1}^{d+1} \bar{a}_i w_i | \sum_{i=1}^{d+1} w_i = 1; w_i \geq 0\}$. Assume, without loss of generality, the pair of points $\bar{a}_1, \bar{a}_2$ and any real $0 < w < 1$, then the subsets $A_1, A_2 \subset A$ constitutes a* **bisection of the simplex** *A. Where,*

1. $\bar{a}^* = w\bar{a}_1 + (1 - w)\bar{a}_2$
2. A_1 *is a simplex bounded by the extreme points $\bar{a}_1, \bar{a}^*, \ldots, \bar{a}_{d+1}$*
3. A_2 *is a simplex bounded by the extreme points $\bar{a}^*, \bar{a}_2, \ldots, \bar{a}_{d+1}$*

In the context of a minimisation problem subject to a simplex A, consider that the first point to be evaluated in the objective function must: 1) be a promising solution, and 2) be able to define a bisection (to recursively explore smaller simplexes). Therefore, the search for the most promising solution is subject to the edges of the simplex A. The following corollary is a direct consequence of Lemma 1 and Definition 2,

Corollary 1. *Given a real function $f : \mathbb{R}^d \to \mathbb{R}$, $d+1$ points $\{\bar{a}_1, \dots, \bar{a}_{d+1}\} \in \mathbb{R}^d$ and their corresponding function evaluations $\{y_1 = f(\bar{a}_1), \dots, y_{d+1} = f(\bar{a}_{d+1})\}$, the* **most promising solution** *$\bar{x}^*$, subject to the edges of the simplex A, is given by $\bar{x}^* = w_{\hat{i},\hat{j}}^* \bar{a}_{\hat{i}} + (1 - w_{\hat{i},\hat{j}}^*) \bar{a}_{\hat{j}}$, where:*

$$(\hat{i}, \hat{j}) = \underset{1 \le i < j \le d+1}{\arg\min} f_{i,j}^* \qquad (2)$$

The search for $\bar{x}^*$ (from Corollary 1) is computationally easy, so this paper explores the idea of reaching the global optimum by means of promising observations $(\bar{x}^*, f(\bar{x}^*))$ in progressively smaller simplexes.

2.2 Simplex-Based Regression Tree

Algorithm 1 details a strategy for iteratively partitioning a simplex into several smaller simplexes. This strategy is also appropriate to any domain D which constitutes a polytope partitionable into a feasible number of simplexes. As a preliminary step, if the domain D is not a simplex, D is partitioned to constitute an initial simplexes collection (Line 1). After that, for each iteration: 1) A simplex A is extracted from the collection (Line 3), 2) The promising point $\bar{x}^*$ in A (Corollary 1) and its objective function evaluation $y^* = f(\bar{x}^*)$ are computed (Lines 4–5), and 3) The extracted A is bisected into two simplexes (Definition 2), and both resulting simplexes are added to the collection (Line 7). When the number of items in the simplexes collection reaches a limit n, the cycle stops.

Algorithm 1. Partition strategy

Require: An objective function $f : D \to \mathbb{R}$ and an maximum of simplexes n
1: simplexesCollection ← splitIntoSimplexes(D)   ▷ E.g. a square D into 2 triangles
2: **for** simplexesCollection.size() $< n$ **do**
3:     $A \leftarrow \{(\bar{a}_1, y_1), \dots, (\bar{a}_{d+1}, y_{d+1})\} \leftarrow$ simplexesCollection.extract()
4:     $\bar{x}^* \leftarrow$ computePromisingPoint($\{(\bar{a}_1, y_1), \dots, (\bar{a}_{d+1}, y_{d+1})\}$)   ▷ Corollary 1
5:     $y^* \leftarrow f(\bar{x}^*)$
6:     $\{A_1, A_2\} \leftarrow bisect(A, \bar{x}^*)$ ▷ Definition 2
7:     simplexesCollection.insert(A_1, A_2)
8: **end for**

The hierarchical partition produced by Algorithm 1 is recordable as a tree $\mathcal{T}$, which is an efficient tool for approximating the objective function. Formally,

Definition 3. *[6] Let $\mathcal{T}$ be a tree-structure, in which each terminal node corresponds to an item of the simplexes collection $\{A_1, A_2, \ldots, A_n\}$ produced by Algorithm 1. For any $\bar{x} \in D$, $\mathcal{T}$ constitutes a **regression tree** that can approximate the value of the objective function $f(\bar{x})$ as a random variable $Y|\bar{x} \sim Normal$ with parameters:*

$$\mu = \frac{1}{d+1} \sum_{i=1}^{d+1} f(\bar{a}_i), \quad \sigma^2 = \frac{1}{d} \sum_{i=1}^{d+1} (f(\bar{a}_i) - \mu)^2$$

where, $\{a_1, \ldots, a_{d+1}\}$ are the extreme points of the simplex A_i to which $x \in D$ belongs.

2.3 Selection Criterion for the Next Simplex to Split

A decisive aspect of Algorithm 1 is the selection of the next simplex to split. For example, a deterministic selection criterion based on the maximum Lesbegue measure λ (length, area, volume, etc.) of simplexes will produce a space-balanced tree, which is proper for exploring the space but not ideal for optimisation. To introduce an improvement by means of $\mathcal{T}$, firstly consider a random criterion based on selecting the simplex to which a realisation of the random variable $\bar{X} \sim \text{Uniform}(D)$ belongs. Formally, for any simplex $A \subset D$, $\Pr(\bar{X} \in A) = \lambda(A)/\lambda(D)$. Thus, this random criterion based on the measure λ also constitutes a space-balanced criterion.

To update the last non-informative random criterion by means of the observed data, consider a realisation of $\bar{X} \sim \text{Uniform}(D)$ whose containing simplex is A. Now, under the assumption $\bar{X} \in A$, by Definition 3, $Y = f(\bar{X})|\bar{X} \in A \sim Normal(\mu, \sigma^2)$. Then, for any $\delta \in \mathbb{R}$, $\Pr(Y = f(\bar{X}) < \delta|\bar{X} \in A)$ is known. And finally, by the Bayes theorem:

$$\Pr(\bar{X} \in A|Y = f(\bar{X}) < \delta) = \frac{\Pr(Y = f(\bar{X}) < \delta|\bar{X} \in A)\Pr(\bar{X} \in A)}{\Pr(Y = f(\bar{X}) < \delta)} \quad (3)$$

In the context of optimisation, a remarkable interpretation of the last probability is: If a new $\bar{X} \sim \text{Uniform}(D)$ is iteratively simulated until achieving the event $f(\bar{X}) < \delta$. Then, at least theoretically, the simplex A^* that maximises $\Pr(\bar{X} \in A^*|Y = f(\bar{X}) < \delta)$ is the likeliest to contain the observation $\bar{X}$ such that $f(\bar{X}) < \delta$. Therefore, if the event is not impossible, directly exploring the simplex A^* should increase the probability of achieving the event $f(\bar{X}) < \delta$.

Given $\mathcal{T}$, the search for the optimal A^* is a feasible and **deterministic** process. In Algorithm 1, maximising $\Pr(\bar{X} \in A^*|Y = f(\bar{X}) < y_{\min})$ is the criterion for selecting the next simplex A^* to split, where $y_{\min}$ is the minimal evaluation of f at the moment. This Bayesian selection criterion is a novel approach in DIRECT-type algorithms. There is no similar criterion reported either in surveys about DIRECT variations [9,17] or in recent literature focused on selection criteria of DIRECT-type algorithms [8,19].

According to [1], a probabilistic model constitutes an acquisition function if it is able to infer the most promising next observation. In Algorithm 1, after selecting a simplex to split, the next point to evaluate in f is given by Corollary 1. Therefore, the implicit model $\mathcal{T}$ constitutes an **acquisition function**.

3   Results

Two Monte Carlo experiments are performed for a collection of well-known optimisation benchmark functions whose corresponding formulæ, implementation
and feasible domains are detailed in [2]. To ensure reproducibility, the proposal is compared with R libraries for Genetic Algorithms (GA 3.2.3), Differential Evolution (DEoptim 2.2.6), Particle Swarm Optimisation (pso 1.0.4),
and DIRECT (nloptr 1.2.2). In each case, the package and its corresponding default parameters are the same than those were tested in the comparative
study [14]. DIRECT-type algorithms are focused on lower dimensions ≤ 8, for
this reason, the dimension d of the tested benchmark functions is restricted to
$2 \leq d \leq 8$.

3.1   Comparison with DIRECT

Algorithm 1 and DIRECT are deterministic. However, consider that the first step
in the DIRECT algorithm is to evaluate the centroid of the function domain $\mathbb{D}$,
where the optimum of the most of tested functions is located. Then, to ensure a
fair comparison in each run, a hypercube $D \subset \mathbb{D}$ is randomly defined, and both
algorithms perform the search in such subspace D. For every function f and
dimension d listed in Table 1, thirty Monte Carlo comparisons are performed.
Each Monte Carlo run $t = 1, 2, \ldots, 30$ consists of computing a Bernoulli random
variable B_t by the following steps:

1. Randomly define a hypercube $D \subset \mathbb{D}$ which contains the optimum.
2. Run the DIRECT algorithm for $f : D \to \mathbb{R}$ (Function direct from the R
   package nloptr [14], with default parameters). And, let y^*_{DIR} the minimum
   after $FEs = 200d$ function evaluations.
3. Run Algorithm 1 for $f : D \to \mathbb{R}$. And, let y^*_{TREE} be the minimum after
   $FEs = 200d$ function evaluations.
4. If $y^*_{TREE} < y^*_{DIR}$, i.e. the proposal is better, then the Bernoulli variable
   counts a success $B_t = 1$. Otherwise, $y^*_{TREE} \geq y^*_{DIR}$, so the current run is a
   failure $B_t = 0$.

Therefore, the sum $B = \sum_{t=1}^{30} B_t$ is a Binomial variable: $B \sim Binomial(30, \rho)$,
where $\rho = \Pr(y^*_{TREE} < y^*_{DIR})$. The statistic B is useful to perform a sign test.
Consider that, under the null hypothesis $H_0 : \rho = .5$ i.e. both algorithms are
equivalent, $1 - \Pr(7 < B < 23) \approx .05/10$ (Bonferroni correction). Therefore,

– If $B \geq 23$, then H_0 is rejected in favour of H_+ : The proposal is statistically
  better than DIRECT.
– If $B \leq 7$, then H_0 is rejected in favour of H_- : The proposal is statistically
  worse than DIRECT.

   The corresponding statistics B for each function and dimension are arranged
in Table 1. Figure 2 illustrates Table 1 as a group of series that show the evolution
of the number of success according to the dimension. In the series plot, a pair of
horizontal lines delimits the rejection region for $H_0 : \rho = .5$.

Table 1. Number of success (the proposal is better than the DIRECT algorithm) after 30 Montecarlo comparisons. The count is highlighted when the proposal statistically is **better** or *worse* than the DIRECT algorithm.

Dimension	2	3	4	5	6	7	8
Ackley	11	18	**25**	18	10	15	**23**
Cigar	*3*	**25**	**30**	**30**	21	**30**	**26**
Dixon price	18	20	**28**	23	26	28	**30**
Griewank	*3*	*3*	*5*	11	13	18	**25**
Levy	15	*6*	15	18	21	15	16
Rastrigin	10	16	20	18	13	11	20
Rosenbrock	21	**26**	13	**23**	25	**30**	**26**
Schwefel	13	18	20	**30**	20	16	20
Sphere	18	**23**	**30**	28	**30**	**30**	**26**
Zakharov	**30**	**30**	**30**	**30**	**30**	**30**	**30**
Total	142	185	216	229	209	223	242

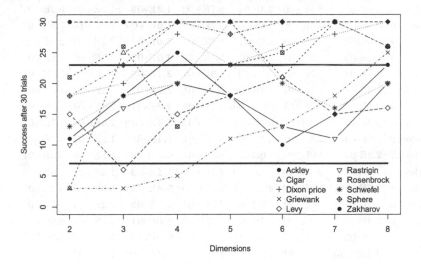

Fig. 2. Data of Table 1 plotted as series (success by dimension for each function)

3.2 Benchmark Study: Regression Tree vs Evolutionary Algorithms

To provide a proper referential context, our proposal is compared with R libraries for well-known evolutionary algorithms: Genetic Algorithms, Differential Evolution and Particle Swarm Optimisation. In each case, the package and its corresponding default parameters are the same than those were tested in the comparative study [14]. After running 30 times each algorithm with a limit of $FEs = 200d$, the best and worst evaluations for each function are listed in Table 2. The Algorithm 1 runs only once because it performs a deterministic search, its output (best evaluation computed) is included in the last column of Table 2.

Table 2. Best and worst function evaluations after running 30 times each algorithm (Genetic Algorithms, Differential Evolution and Particle Swarm Optimisation) for the listed functions with dimension $d = 2, 4, 6$. The last column contains the best function evaluation computed by the deterministic Algorithm 1. The **best** solution of each row is highlighted.

Fn Dim		GA		DE		PSO		RTree Output
		Best	Worst	Best	Worst	Best	Worst	
Ackley	2	5.5E-03	6.6E+00	1.9E-03	5.8E+00	2.0E-03	1.3E+01	**1.6E-06**
Cigar	2	2.2E+01	9.7E+07	2.9E-01	1.1E+08	2.2E+01	1.0E+10	**6.6E-05**
Dixon	2	4.2E-04	1.3E+02	2.0E-04	1.4E+02	**9.3E-05**	7.2E+04	1.2E-01
Griew	2	6.5E-02	1.3E+01	1.4E-02	1.2E+01	1.8E-02	1.8E+02	**1.8E-09**
Levy	2	9.8E-05	2.3E+00	**3.3E-07**	3.4E+00	1.9E-06	6.4E+01	1.6E-02
Rastr	2	3.5E-02	1.8E+01	1.8E-02	2.0E+01	1.8E-02	5.8E+01	**6.9E-11**
Rosen	2	3.1E-02	1.3E+03	**1.6E-04**	1.0E+03	3.3E-04	8.1E+05	9.5E-01
Schwef	2	4.9E-01	6.5E+02	9.5E-02	6.8E+02	**5.0E-03**	1.2E+03	1.2E+02
Sphere	2	2.2E-05	4.5E+00	6.4E-07	3.6E+00	2.5E-06	5.2E+01	**3.5E-13**
Zakha	2	2.3E-04	7.5E+00	**3.1E-06**	4.9E+00	4.1E-06	2.0E+02	5.8E-02
Ackley	4	2.0E-02	8.4E+00	2.3E-01	8.7E+00	**4.3E-03**	1.3E+01	5.2E+00
Cigar	4	3.0E+04	6.4E+09	1.4E+05	3.7E+09	**2.6E+02**	3.0E+10	7.5E+08
Dixon	4	1.3E-02	1.0E+04	1.5E-01	1.3E+04	**8.6E-04**	3.2E+05	2.3E+02
Griew	4	9.2E-02	5.9E+01	4.1E-01	5.1E+01	**8.0E-02**	3.6E+02	1.7E+01
Levy	4	1.7E-03	1.7E+01	1.5E-02	1.3E+01	**2.1E-05**	1.7E+02	2.1E+00
Rastr	4	2.4E-01	4.7E+01	3.3E+00	5.3E+01	**2.0E-01**	1.2E+02	1.4E+01
Rosen	4	2.0E+00	1.2E+05	6.6E+00	1.1E+05	**2.3E-01**	2.4E+06	2.6E+03
Schwe	4	2.3E+02	1.4E+03	5.7E+01	1.3E+03	**5.1E+00**	2.4E+03	9.5E+02
Sphere	4	7.5E-04	2.3E+01	3.9E-04	1.6E+01	**1.1E-05**	1.0E+02	4.7E+00
Zakha	4	2.9E-03	4.0E+01	1.0E-02	3.5E+01	**4.6E-06**	4.0E+02	3.0E+01
Ackley	6	1.1E-01	8.5E+00	1.2E+00	8.7E+00	**4.1E-03**	1.3E+01	6.8E+00
Cigar	6	1.7E+06	8.3E+09	2.1E+07	1.0E+10	**5.4E+02**	5.0E+10	3.2E+09
Dixon	6	4.2E-01	5.3E+04	2.0E+00	5.5E+04	**1.7E-02**	7.2E+05	3.5E+03
Griew	6	5.3E-01	1.0E+02	1.4E+00	1.1E+02	**1.6E-01**	5.4E+02	4.8E+01
Levy	6	1.9E-02	2.8E+01	1.9E-01	3.2E+01	**2.0E-05**	2.8E+02	8.7E+00
Rastr	6	**1.7E+00**	8.9E+01	8.6E+00	8.8E+01	4.1E+00	1.7E+02	8.3E+01
Rosen	6	4.6E+00	3.0E+05	6.8E+01	3.7E+05	**4.3E-01**	4.1E+06	3.1E+04
Schwe	6	5.1E+02	2.2E+03	2.5E+02	2.0E+03	**1.0E+01**	3.6E+03	1.4E+03
Sphere	6	3.0E-03	3.5E+01	8.5E-02	3.2E+01	**4.7E-06**	1.6E+02	1.4E+01
Zakha	6	5.1E-02	7.4E+01	2.9E-01	7.2E+01	**1.2E-05**	6.0E+02	6.7E+01

4   Discussion

Algorithm 1 vs DIRECT. In Table 1, the most of statistics do not reject the null hypothesis H_0: *Both algorithms are equivalent.* The exceptions in this regard are:

- 32 statistics (**boldtype**) in favour of H_+: *The proposal is better.*
- 5 statistics (*cursive*) in favour of H_-: *The proposal is worse.*

Therefore, Algorithm 1 is equivalent to or better than DIRECT. Furthermore, our proposal seems to be more reliable and robust to overcome dimensionality. The last conjecture is supported by the increasing total of success for higher dimensions in Table 1, or visually, by the non-negative trend of series in Fig. 2. The series with positive trend imply that the proposal overcomes dimensionality more effectively than DIRECT.

Algorithm 1 vs Evolutionary Algorithms. In Table 2, there are exceptionally good results only in dimension $d = 2$, in which the proposal is better than the other three algorithms for five functions. For the rest of rows in Table 2, the continuous interval between the worst and the best solution of each evolutionary algorithm invariably contains the optimum found by Algorithm 1. Since such empirical evidence, a practical interpretation is that the deterministic solution given by the proposal is a possible result of an evolutionary method. Although better than DIRECT, the proposal does not outperform evolutionary algorithms when the dimension increases.

5   Conclusions and Future Work

This paper presents a new optimisation algorithm based on a regression tree of the objective function. The idea of sequentially fitting a tree model seems intuitive and is, of course, not utterly novel [7,10,11]. However, the specific design of a simplex-tree based on a Brownian process is original. Furthermore, the Bayesian criterion for selecting subsets (Eq. 3) is a novel approach, not reported even in recent literature about DIRECT-type algorithms [8,9,19].

In comparison with DIRECT, the algorithm has a superior performance which becomes more evident as dimension increases. For this reason, our proposal is an excellent alternative in contexts where DIRECT is still in use. However, the presented algorithm has a mean performance compared with three popular evolutionary algorithms: Differential Evolution, Genetic Algorithms, and Particle Swarm Optimisation.

Other variants of DIRECT could become a source of room for improvement. Consider that, even recent DIRECT-type algorithms such as [8] and [19] produce some results that are not statistically different from the original DIRECT. As future work, the authors suggest hybridising those algorithms with the proposed Bayesian selection criterion. In this respect, this preliminary paper settles the bases for an extensive comparative study with other variants of DIRECT.

Disclosure of Interests. The authors have no competing interests to declare.

References

1. Archetti, F., Candelieri, A.: Bayesian Optimization and Data Science. Springer, Cham (2019). https://doi.org/10.1007/978-3-030-24494-1
2. Bäck, T.: Evolutionary Algorithms in Theory and Practice: Evolution Strategies, Evolutionary Programming, Genetic Algorithms. Oxford University Press, Oxford (1996). https://doi.org/10.1093/oso/9780195099713.001.0001
3. De Ath, G., Everson, R.M., Rahat, A.A.M., Fieldsend, J.E.: Greed is good: exploration and exploitation trade-offs in bayesian optimisation. ACM Trans. Evol. Learn. Optim. 1(1), 1–22 (2021). https://doi.org/10.1145/3425501
4. Garnett, R.: Bayesian Optimization. Cambridge University Press, Cambridge (2023)
5. Glasserman, P.: Monte Carlo Methods in Financial Engineering. Applications of Mathematics: Stochastic Modelling and Applied Probability. Springer, New York (2004). https://doi.org/10.1007/978-0-387-21617-1
6. Hastie, T., Tibshirani, R., Friedman, J.: The Elements of Statistical Learning. Springer, New York (2009). https://doi.org/10.1007/978-0-387-84858-7
7. Hutter, F., Hoos, H.H., Leyton-Brown, K.: Sequential model-based optimization for general algorithm configuration. In: Coello, C.A.C. (ed.) LION 2011. LNCS, vol. 6683, pp. 507–523. Springer, Heidelberg (2011). https://doi.org/10.1007/978-3-642-25566-3_40
8. Jia, K.E.: A new partition method for direct-type algorithm based on minimax design. J. Glob. Optim. 88(1), 171–197 (2024). https://doi.org/10.1007/s10898-023-01297-6
9. Jones, D.R., Martins, J.R.R.A.: The direct algorithm: 25 years later. J. Global Optim. 79(3), 521–566 (2020). https://doi.org/10.1007/s10898-020-00952-6
10. Kubica, B.J.: Interval Methods for Solving Nonlinear Constraint Satisfaction, Optimization and Similar Problems: From Inequalities Systems to Game Solutions. Springer, Cham (2019). https://doi.org/10.1007/978-3-030-13795-3
11. Larrañaga, P., Bielza, C.: Estimation of distribution algorithms in machine learning: a survey. IEEE Trans. Evol. Comput. 1 (2023). https://doi.org/10.1109/TEVC.2023.3314105
12. Liu, H., Xu, S., Wang, X., Wu, J., Song, Y.: A global optimization algorithm for simulation-based problems via the extended direct scheme. Eng. Optim. 47(11), 1441–1458 (2014). https://doi.org/10.1080/0305215x.2014.971777
13. Loh, W.: Classification and regression trees. WIREs Data Min. Knowl. Discov. 1(1), 14–23 (2011). https://doi.org/10.1002/widm.8
14. Mullen, K.M.: Continuous global optimization in R. J. Stat. Softw. 60(6) (2014). https://doi.org/10.18637/jss.v060.i06
15. Norkin, V.I., Pflug, G.C., Ruszczyński, A.: A branch and bound method for stochastic global optimization. Math. Program. 83(1–3), 425–450 (1998). https://doi.org/10.1007/bf02680569
16. Paulavičius, R., Chiter, L., Žilinskas, J.: Global optimization based on bisection of rectangles, function values at diagonals, and a set of lipschitz constants. J. Global Optim. 71(1), 5–20 (2016). https://doi.org/10.1007/s10898-016-0485-6
17. Rios, L.M., Sahinidis, N.V.: Derivative-free optimization: a review of algorithms and comparison of software implementations. J. Global Optim. 56(3), 1247–1293 (2012). https://doi.org/10.1007/s10898-012-9951-y

18. Salmerón, J.M.G., Aparicio, G., Casado, L.G., García, I., Hendrix, E.M.T., G.-Tóth, B.: Generating a smallest binary tree by proper selection of the longest edges to bisect in a unit simplex refinement. J. Comb. Optim. **33**(2), 389–402 (2015). https://doi.org/10.1007/s10878-015-9970-y
19. Stripinis, L., Paulavičius, R.: Lipschitz-inspired halrect algorithm for derivative-free global optimization. J. Global Optim. **88**(1), 139–169 (2024). https://doi.org/10.1007/s10898-023-01296-7

Missing Data and Their Effect on Algorithm Selection for the Bin Packing Problem

José Carlos Ortiz-Bayliss$^{(\boxtimes)}$ [ID], Anna Karen Gárate-Escamilla[ID], and Hugo Terashima-Marín[ID]

School of Engineering and Sciences, Tecnologico de Monterrey,
64849 Monterrey, Mexico
{jcobayliss,karen.garate,terashima}@tec.mx

Abstract. When multiple algorithms are available to solve a particular problem, deciding which to use may be challenging. Depending on the problem at hand and the available algorithms, choosing the wrong solver might represent significant performance losses. Machine learning has emerged as a paramount tool for implementing algorithm selectors. Regardless of their success in various applications, how incomplete information on the individual solvers' performance may affect the overall quality of the decisions remains unexplored. This work uses Neural Networks (multi-layer perceptron) to implement algorithm selectors for the one-dimensional bin packing problem. We explore situations involving missing values and their treatment to observe their impact on the algorithm selectors generated. Our results suggest that the algorithm selectors may be more sensitive to missing values than expected.

Keywords: Algorithm Selection Problem · Bin Packing Problem · Missing Values · Neural Networks

1 Introduction

Recent years have grown the interest in methods combining the strengths of 'simple' algorithms to solve challenging problems. Notably, we have observed advances related to strategies such as algorithm portfolios [2,3,10,13] and hyper-heuristics [8,9], which can broadly be considered algorithm selectors [17]. Algorithm selectors are collections of algorithms that run interchangeably, avoiding the single selection of a poor individual algorithm [10].

We have observed a trend for powering algorithm selectors with machine learning models in the past few years [11,15,19]. In this context, it is common to treat the problem as a supervised learning problem, in which a set of labeled examples is provided to train the models, and once the models are trained, they are tested on a set of unseen labeled examples. This scheme reduces the algorithm selection problem to a classification one that requires learning the

E. Mezura-Montes et al. (Eds.): MCPR 2024, LNCS 14755, pp. 34–43, 2024.
https://doi.org/10.1007/978-3-031-62836-8_4

problem features (classifier's input) that map to a suitable algorithm (classifier's output).

Missing values are around us, and they will stay there for a long time [16]. Then, it seems reasonable to think that missing values may also be present when generating algorithm selectors. However, the effect of missing values when using machine learning to produce algorithm selectors remains unexplored in the literature. Let us clarify this knowledge gap in the following lines. The rationale behind algorithm selection is to create a mapping between the problem features and one suitable algorithm from a set of available ones. Since this approach relies on supervised learning (the training requires a set of labeled examples), such training examples are usually represented as a vector containing $k + 1$ elements (the values of the k problem features and the identifier of the recommended algorithm). Producing such a vector requires at least two algorithms to solve the instance represented by such features. Only then can the best algorithm be identified. Thus, generating meaningful labels requires solving the instances with at least two algorithms. However, this may only be possible in some cases. For example, if we have four available algorithms but only the records of two of them are available for some instances in the training set. In light of this scenario, it is essential to consider the following questions: Would the missing values for the other two methods on the remaining instances affect the overall performance of the algorithm selector once it is trained? Can the missing values in the algorithms' results bias the selector towards selecting one particularly 'good' algorithm? How does it affect its capability to generalize? Would it be possible for the algorithm selectors to somehow 'resist' the effect of missing values in the data that produces the training examples? The literature has never deepened into this situation. However, it may represent an essential issue in the future since the algorithms the selectors choose from are getting better, sometimes requiring more computational resources in exchange. This additional consumption of resources may eventually become prohibitive and restrict us from getting the results of all the solvers (heuristics) to train an algorithm selector.

In this work, we explore the impact of missing values when using machine learning models as algorithm selectors. Particularly, we use multi-layer percep- trons (MLPs) as algorithm selectors, and we test our ideas on a widespread problem domain: the one-dimensional Bin Packing Problem (BPP). The BPP is a combinatorial problem in which a finite set of items with a specific length must be packed into bins, respecting a capacity constraint.

The remainder of this document is as follows. Section 2 contextualizes our work with respect to related studies. In Sect. 3, we describe our solution model. Section 4 describes the experiments conducted and analyses their main results. Finally, Sect. 5 presents the conclusion and provides potential paths for future work.

2   Background and Related Work

Machine learning has been used in the past to power algorithm selectors. In this regard, some representative works include that of Guo and Hsu [4], who explored how machine learning could be used for algorithm selection concerning

NP-hard optimization problems and tested their approach on the Most Probable Explanation Problem in probabilistic inference; Ortiz et al. [11], who proposed a framework for generating and testing algorithm selectors for Constraint Satisfaction Problems through various machine learning models; and Tornede et al. [20], who explored meta-learning to support algorithm selection for the Boolean Satisfiability Problem.

Neural networks have been used recurrently for addressing the algorithm selection problem. The earliest works on this topic include the one by Li et al. [7], who combined neural networks and logistic regression to produce problem-independent algorithms selectors. Later, Ortiz et al. [12] explored using Learning Vector Quantization (LVQ) Neural Networks to choose which heuristic to use when solving constrain satisfaction problems. Among the most recent works, we can cite the work of Mohamad et al. [1], who explored using recurrent neural networks to capture the sequential nature existing in combinatorial problems such as bin packing; and the work of Diaz et al. [6], who applied attention-based neural networks as meta-learners to enhance the performance of the mapping mechanism within the algorithm selection problem.

3   Solution Approach

Our solution approach generates algorithm selectors using neural networks—specifically, MLPs. Once trained, such perceptrons receive the problem state of an instance and recommend which algorithm to use. Because we test our approach on the BPP, the algorithms to choose from are simply heuristics.

The following lines provide insights into the main elements of our solution approach.

3.1   The Instances

We initially produced two sets of BPP instances: a training and a test set. We used the evolutionary approach proposed by Plata et al. [14] to generate instances challenging particular heuristics. Following this idea, the two sets contain various instances that allow the heuristics to exhibit opposite behaviors throughout the sets (sometimes they perform well, others do not). The training and test sets contain 100 and 400 instances, each with 20 items, a bin capacity of 64 units, and a maximum item length of 32. Although we admit that these instances may be considered small, they represent a good starting point to analyze how missing values affect the generation process of algorithm selectors through neural networks.

Starting from the training set, we gradually introduced missing values (completely at random) into the results obtained by the heuristics. In this way, we produced six versions of the training set based on the proportion of missing values introduced: NA00 (0%), NA05 (5%), NA10 (10%), NA15 (15%), NA20 (20%), and NA25 (25%). It is relevant to remind the reader that introducing missing values affects only the values of the heuristics. So, the values of the features are always complete. Once we produced the six training sets containing the different proportions of missing values (NA00 to NA25), we generated two new 'treated' versions of sets NA05 to NA25: one where only complete cases remain (any row with one or more missing values was removed) and another where the median bin usage per heuristic is used to complete missing values. These two techniques are among the most basic when dealing with missing values. Finally, for each of the sets produced, we labeled the best heuristic. At this point, the data is ready to train the networks. In total, we use 16 training sets and a test set in this work. We graphically describe such sets in Fig. 1.

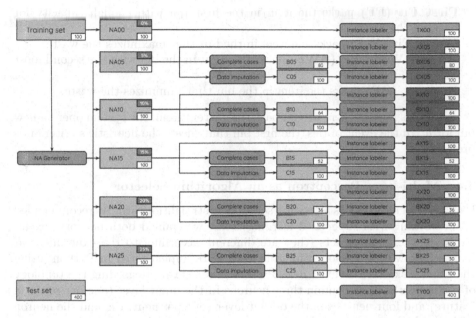

Fig. 1. Graphical depiction of the process to generate the training and test sets used in this investigation. The percentages in the top-right corners indicate the proportion of missing values contained in the corresponding set. The bottom-right numbers indicate the instances contained in the corresponding set.

3.2 Problem Characterization

This investigation deals with the one-dimensional version of the BPP. So, we can only use the length of the items to characterize the instances. For this purpose, we rely on three straightforward features related to the lengths of the items within the instance:

- **LENGTH** indicates the average length of the items within the instance. This value is normalized by dividing the actual average by 32 (the maximum length of items considered for this work).
- **SMALL** represents the proportion of 'small' items in the instance (items with a length smaller than 0.5).
- **LARGE** represents the proportion of 'large' items in the instance (items with a length larger or equal to 0.5).

We chose 0.5 as the threshold value for classifying an item as long or small based on preliminary observations. Besides, all these features lie in the range $[0, 1]$.

3.3 The Heuristics

For this work, we have considered four commonly used heuristics for the BPP [18].

- **First Fit (FF)** packs the item in the first bin with enough capacity for packing the item.
- **Worst Fit (WF)** packs the item in the bin that maximizes the waste.
- **Almost Worst Fit (AWF)** packs the item in the bin with the second most waste produced.
- **Best Fit (BF)** packs the item in the bin that minimizes the waste.

If there is no bin where we can pack the current item, the system opens a new bin for it. In the event of ties, the first bin that meets the heuristic's criterion is preferred.

3.4 Multi-layer Perceptron as an Algorithm Selector

Using neural networks as algorithm selectors is straightforward. As recommended when working with supervised learning tasks, we trained both networks exclusively on the training sets (they are different according to the experiment at hand). The MLPs developed for this work were implemented in Python, using the library `sklearn.neural_network.MLPClassifier`. Regarding the topology of the networks, they contain three neurons in the input layer (one per problem feature) and four neurons in the output layer (one per heuristic, and the neuron with the highest output value in the output layer is the one that determines the solver to use). Besides, the perceptrons have three hidden layers of 12, 10, and 6 neurons, respectively, and their corresponding biases. Although we consider that using some kind of hyper-parameter tuning strategy might improve the performance of the algorithm selectors these networks represent, we have used a straightforward parameter setting based on our previous experience. For adjusting the weights of the networks, we used the LBFGS optimizer. We used the default values in `sklearn.neural_network.MLPClassifier` for the rest of the configuration.

4 Experiments and Results

All the experiments conducted in this work focus on the impact of missing values under the most straightforward case regarding missing values, the Missing Completely at Random (MCAR) scenario. In MCAR situations, all the records of the heuristics hold the same probability of disappearing [5]. In all the experiments presented in this section, we analyze the performance of the heuristics and the algorithm selectors through boxplots.

4.1 No Treatment on Missing Values

For this first experiment, we generated the algorithm selectors without treating the missing values in the training sets. This way, we chose the heuristic with the largest bin usage for each instance. Please note that the missing values affect different heuristics for each instance. Then, if one heuristic presents a missing value for one of the instances, it cannot be considered for selecting the best heuristic for such an instance.

We generated three algorithm selectors using set TX00 (complete training set with no missing values). Besides, we produced three algorithm selectors per training set AX05 to AX25. This resulted in 18 algorithm selectors with different proportions of missing values: 0%, 5%, 10%, 15%, 20%, and 25%; three selectors for each case. The training sets in this experiment received no treatment to deal with the missing values.

To our surprise, the results of this experiment (Fig. 2) suggest that only a small proportion of missing values in the training set are sufficient to harm the resulting algorithm selector. The difference between the algorithm selectors trained with no missing values (EX1-00-01 to EX1-00-03) and the rest of the selectors is evident. We can easily observe how the IQR in the rest of the algorithm selectors increases, indicative of a larger standard deviation; hence, the results' dispersion. In summary, a small proportion of missing values, such as 5%, seems enough to prevent the neural networks from learning the mapping between features and heuristics, at least in this particular setting.

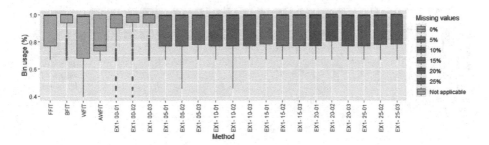

Fig. 2. Boxplot of the bin usage of the four heuristics and the 18 algorithm selectors trained on sets TX00 and AX05 to AX25 (instances with missing values in different proportions). We report the results obtained exclusively for set TY00.

Regarding algorithm selectors' performance, regardless of the different decisions taken in some instances, EX1-00-02 and EX-00-03 are statistically equivalent to BFIT, the best heuristic for the test set. This result was validated for each algorithm selector using a two-tailed Wilcoxon test on the medians of the selector and BFIT, with a 5% of significance. The null hypothesis, which states that both medians are equal, was accepted with p-values of 0.2209 and 1, respectively.

Although it is always gratifying when the selectors outperform the best individual algorithm, it is not always possible. In this study, we are aware of the limitations of the model proposed and the opportunities to improve its results. For example, choosing a different set of problem features or fixing the neural networks' parameters via a systematic procedure. Indeed, those upgrades should improve the performance of the algorithm selectors produced by the model. However, behaving as well as the best individual heuristic is not a bad result. On the contrary, it confirms that the neural network is learning to discriminate and choose a suitable heuristic for each case. In this case, BFIT is the heuristic that provides the best overall performance, and the selectors have learned to perform as such a heuristic.

4.2 Working only with Complete Cases

For this second experiment, we applied a common technique for dealing with missing values: the complete cases analysis. Thus, we removed from the training sets any instance where at least one of the results from the heuristics was missing. As expected for this procedure, the number of training examples decreased with the number of missing values in the training sets. For example, for training set B25, we lost 70% of the training data when keeping only the complete cases. We acknowledge that such a data loss is out of proportion and unacceptable in any practical application. However, in this experiment, we aim to observe the various effects of missing values and the consequences of some of the frequently used techniques to deal with them.

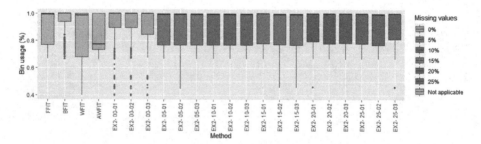

Fig. 3. Boxplot of the bin usage of the four heuristics and the 18 algorithm selectors trained on sets TX00 and BX05 to BX25 (instances that originally contained different proportions of missing values and now only complete cases remain). We report the results obtained exclusively for set TY00.

As in the previous experiment, we produced three algorithm selectors using set TX00. Additionally, we generated three algorithm selectors per training set (BX05 to BX25). As previously described, the training sets in this experiment contain only complete cases. For this reason, the sets contain only a proportion of their original counterparts NA05 to NA25, reducing the number of examples for training (see Fig. 1 for more details). Then, we tested the algorithm selectors on set TY00.

The results shown in Fig. 3 look similar to the ones from the previous experiment. The algorithm selectors trained with no missing values tend to replicate the behavior of BFIT in the test set. Based on these results, it seems complicated to appreciate a difference in the performance of the remaining algorithm selectors and their counterparts concerning the proportion of missing values from the previous experiment.

4.3 Using Data Imputation

We conducted a third and last experiment involving data imputation. Instead of keeping only the complete cases, we synthetically produced some values to fill the gaps. The process required calculating the median bin usage of each heuristic (ignoring missing values) in the corresponding training set and then using that median to fill any missing value for the heuristics. Although this approach allowed us to keep all the records, there is a price to pay: some of the values in the data are synthetically produced, and then the labels of the best heuristic per instance may change based on the number of missing values replaced (Fig. 4).

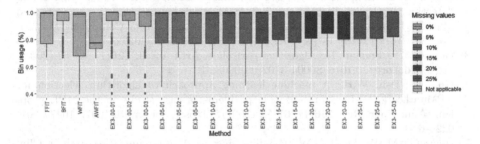

Fig. 4. Boxplot of the bin usage of the four heuristics and the 18 algorithm selectors trained on sets T00 and CX05 to CX25 (instances that originally contained different proportions of missing values but were replaced with the median of each heuristic). We report the results obtained exclusively for set TY00.

The results obtained from this experiment are similar to the previous ones. The selectors trained with TXOO (complete training set) are clearly better than the other algorithm selectors. Statistically, EX3-00-01, EX3-00-02, and EX3-00-03 are equivalent in performance to BFIT, with p-values of 0.2331, 0.1670, and 0.0555. As in previous cases, we cannot observe evident differences between the performance of the algorithm selectors produced with imputed data.

5 Conclusion

We have analyzed a few particular scenarios regarding missing values and their effect on the generation of algorithm selectors implemented as multi-layer perceptrons. Our results suggest that missing values affect the training process and the resulting selector regardless of the treatment used. An explanation for this is that a missing value (and its corresponding imputation) may alter the label of the best heuristic for an instance. On a larger picture, this can derive in contradictory cases that difficult the training. Of course, this preliminary work requires more experiments to confirm our initial observations.

We have considered some paths for future work derived from this investigation. First, we limited the scope of this work to MCAR scenarios within missing data. However, exploring other more complex scenarios, such as Missing at Random (MAR) and Missing not at Random (MNAR), is relevant [5]. Besides, other machine learning models could be used as algorithm selectors. Exploring other popular options like Logistic Regression, Support Vector Machines (SVM), and Decision Trees would be interesting and worth studying.

References

1. Alissa, M., Sim, K., Hart, E.: Automated algorithm selection: from feature-based to feature-free approaches. J. Heuristics **29**(1), 1–38 (2023). https://doi.org/10.1007/s10732-022-09505-4
2. Chalé, M., Bastian, N.D., Weir, J.: Algorithm selection framework for cyber attack detection. In: Proceedings of the 2nd ACM Workshop on Wireless Security and Machine Learning, WiseML 2020, pp. 37–42. Association for Computing Machinery, New York (2020). https://doi.org/10.1145/3395352.3402623
3. Gomes, C.P., Selman, B.: Algorithm portfolios. Artif. Intell. **126**(1), 43–62 (2001). https://doi.org/10.1016/S0004-3702(00)00081-3
4. Guo, H., Hsu, W.H.: A machine learning approach to algorithm selection for NP\mathcal{NP}-hard optimization problems: a case study on the MPE problem. Ann. Oper. Res. **156**(1), 61–82 (2007). https://doi.org/10.1007/s10479-007-0229-6
5. Heymans, M.W., Twisk, J.W.: Handling missing data in clinical research. J. Clin. Epidemiol. **151**, 185–188 (2022). https://doi.org/10.1016/j.jclinepi.2022.08.016
6. Díaz de León-Hicks, E., Conant-Pablos, S.E., Ortiz-Bayliss, J.C., Terashima-Marín, H.: Addressing the algorithm selection problem through an attention-based meta-learner approach. Appl. Sci. **13**(7) (2023). https://doi.org/10.3390/app13074601
7. Li, J., Burke, E.K., Qu, R.: Integrating neural networks and logistic regression to underpin hyper-heuristic search. Knowl.-Based Syst. **24**(2), 322–330 (2011). https://doi.org/10.1016/j.knosys.2010.10.004
8. Li, W., Özcan, E., Drake, J.H., Maashi, M.: A generality analysis of multiobjective hyper-heuristics. Inf. Sci. **627**, 34–51 (2023). https://doi.org/10.1016/j.ins.2023.01.047
9. Marcel Panzer, B.B., Gronau, N.: A deep reinforcement learning based hyper-heuristic for modular production control. Int. J. Prod. Res. 1–22 (2023). https://doi.org/10.1080/00207543.2023.2233641
10. Muñoz, M.A., Soleimani, H., Kandanaarachchi, S.: Benchmarking algorithm portfolio construction methods. In: Proceedings of the Genetic and Evolutionary Computation Conference Companion, GECCO 2022, pp. 499—502. Association for Computing Machinery, New York (2022). https://doi.org/10.1145/3520304.3528880

11. Ortiz-Bayliss, J.C., Amaya, I., Cruz-Duarte, J.M., Gutierrez-Rodriguez, A.E., Conant-Pablos, S.E., Terashima-Marín, H.: A general framework based on machine learning for algorithm selection in constraint satisfaction problems. Appl. Sci. **11**(6) (2021). https://doi.org/10.3390/app11062749
12. Ortiz-Bayliss, J.C., Terashima-Marín, H., Conant-Pablos, S.E.: Learning vector quantization for variable ordering in constraint satisfaction problems. Pattern Recogn. Lett. **34**(4), 423–432 (2013). https://doi.org/10.1016/j.patrec.2012.09.009
13. Piechowiak, K., Drozdowski, M.: Éric Sanlaville: framework of algorithm portfolios for strip packing problem. Comput. Ind. Eng. **172**, 108538 (2022). https://doi.org/10.1016/j.cie.2022.108538
14. Plata-González, L.F., Amaya, I., Ortiz-Bayliss, J.C., Conant-Pablos, S.E., Terashima-Marín, H., Coello, C.A.C.: Evolutionary-based tailoring of synthetic instances for the knapsack problem. Soft. Comput. **23**(23), 12711–12728 (2019). https://doi.org/10.1007/s00500-019-03822-w
15. Pylyavskyy, Y., Kheiri, A., Ahmed, L.: A reinforcement learning hyper-heuristic for the optimisation of flight connections. In: 2020 IEEE Congress on Evolutionary Computation (CEC), pp. 1–8 (2020). https://doi.org/10.1109/CEC48606.2020.9185803
16. Ren, L., Wang, T., Sekhari Seklouli, A., Zhang, H., Bouras, A.: A review on missing values for main challenges and methods. Inf. Syst. **119**, 102268 (2023). https://doi.org/10.1016/j.is.2023.102268
17. Rice, J.R.: The algorithm selection problem. Adv. Comput. **15**, 65–118 (1976). https://doi.org/10.1016/S0065-2458(08)60520-3
18. Silva-Gálvez, A., et al.: Discovering action regions for solving the bin packing problem through hyper-heuristics. In: 2020 IEEE Symposium Series on Computational Intelligence (SSCI), pp. 822–828 (2020). https://doi.org/10.1109/SSCI47803.2020.9308538
19. Slavchev, B., Masliankova, E., Kelk, S.: A machine learning approach to algorithm selection for exact computation of treewidth. Algorithms **12**(10) (2019). https://doi.org/10.3390/a12100200
20. Tornede, A., Gehring, L., Tornede, T., Wever, M., Hüllermeier, E.: Algorithm selection on a meta level. Mach. Learn. **112**(4), 1253–1286 (2022). https://doi.org/10.1007/s10994-022-06161-4

Statistical Evaluation of CESAMO Encoder for Pattern Preservation in Categorical Data

Eric Valdez-Valenzuela[1]([✉]), Angel Kuri-Morales[2], and Helena Gomez-Adorno[3]

[1] Posgrado en Ciencia e Ingeniería de la Computación, Universidad Nacional Autónoma de México, Mexico City, Mexico
ericvaldez@comunidad.unam.mx
[2] Instituto Tecnológico Autónomo de México, Mexico City, Mexico
akuri@itam.mx
[3] Instituto de Investigaciones en Matemáticas Aplicadas y en Sistemas, Universidad Nacional Autónoma de México, Mexico City, Mexico
helena.gomez@iimas.unam.mx

Abstract. It is common to find categorical attributes in datasets used for training Machine Learning (ML) algorithms. However, most ML models are designed to exclusively handle numerical inputs. To effectively incorporate these categorical attributes, it is necessary to convert them into numerical values. Preserving the inherent patterns and information associated with the categorical attributes is essential throughout this conversion process. Any loss of information or pattern might adversely impact the performance of ML algorithms. Several encoding techniques have been proposed to handle this conversion. This paper delves into the exploration of the CESAMO encoding technique. CESAMO encoder captures the relationships between categorical attributes and other variables using what is inferred as Pattern Preserving Codes. A statistical evaluation of this encoding technique was conducted using synthetic data, comparing its performance with other encoding methods. The experimental results demonstrate that CESAMO outperforms all the other categorical encoding techniques that were compared.

Keywords: Categorical attributes · machine learning · data preprocessing

1 Introduction

Many machine learning (ML) algorithms are designed to process only numerical attributes for analysis, with a few exceptions. Theoretical capabilities exist for tree-based model algorithms such as Random Forest and Gradient Boosting, as well as Naive Bayes, to handle both numeric and categorical data [1]. However, when implementing these algorithms with commonly used libraries like Scikit-learn [2], LightGBM [3], and XGBoost [4], there arises a need to convert categorical instances into numeric values. In real-world datasets, a blend of categorical and numerical attributes is commonly encountered. To harness the information within, categorical variables must be transformed into numerical values. It is critical that this mapping process preserves the inherent patterns within the data. Failing to do so poses a potential risk of information loss, which could adversely affect the performance of ML models.

E. Mezura-Montes et al. (Eds.): MCPR 2024, LNCS 14755, pp. 44–52, 2024.
https://doi.org/10.1007/978-3-031-62836-8_5

Converting categorical attributes into numerical ones is especially crucial in clustering problems. In this kind of problem, there is an absence of a priori information regarding a dependent variable or target. Instead, these tasks involve clustering unlabeled data into distinct groups based on inherent patterns or similarities. In such problems, the importance of categorical encoding techniques becomes particularly noteworthy since failing to preserve the underlying relations could result in entirely different or unexpected outcomes. Therefore, it is crucial to select encoders that preserve patterns while, on the other hand, do not introduce spurious patterns.

Due to its simplicity, the following encoding techniques are typically employed:

1) Ordinal or label encoding involves converting each unique category instance into an integer value. This method is appropriate when categorical instances exhibit a natural order. However, it is not recommended for nominal variables (no natural order). As highlighted in [5], applying ordinal encoding to nominal data may result in poor performance because it introduces non-existent orders among categorical instances.
2) One-hot encoding represents categorical variables as binary vectors, where each category is mapped to a unique binary value. It creates a binary matrix where each column corresponds to a distinct category, and only one element in each column is set to 1, indicating the presence of that category. As noted in [6], the drawbacks of this approach encompass: a) potential computational inefficiency, b) limited adaptability to new categories, and c) curse of dimensionality.

Other examples of unsupervised techniques include: binary encoding [7], count encoder [8], and Hashing encoder [9].

One limitation of these techniques (ordinal, one-hot, binary, count, and hashing encoders) is that they do not consider patterns that may exist between the categorical attribute and other attributes in the dataset. Nonetheless, other techniques are designed to find existing relationships through codes that preserve these patterns.

Pattern Preserving Codes
The main goal of converting categorical values into numerical codes is to preserve the underlying data patterns. Failing to achieve this could result in information loss, potentially impacting the performance of ML algorithms adversely.

Pattern Preserving Codes (PPCs) are numeric values that maintain the relationship between a chosen categorical attribute and the others. Suppose we have a set of n-dimensional tuples, denoted as U, containing a total of m elements. In this context, there exist n unknown functions of n−1 variables. We represent such a function as f_k:

$$f_k(v_1, ..., v_{k-1}, v_{k+1}, ..., v_n); k = 1, ..., n \qquad (1)$$

Let us additionally assume the availability of a method that allows us to estimate f_k (from the tuples) as F_k. Express the resultant n functions of $n-1$ independent variables as F_i, consequently:

$$F_k \approx f_k(v_1, ..., v_{k-1}, v_{k+1}, ..., v_n); k = 1, ..., n \qquad (2)$$

The difference between f_k and F_k will be represented by e_k, wherein, for attribute k and the m tuples in the dataset:

$$e_k = |f_{ki} - F_{ki}|; i = 1, ..., m \qquad (3)$$

PPCs minimize e_k across all k. This is because only those codes that uphold the relationships between variable k and the remaining $n - 1$ variables (while doing so for every variable in the collection) effectively keep the complete set of relations (i.e., patterns) present in the database.

There are encoding techniques designed to identify these PPCs, and one such method is the CESAMO algorithm [10], which stands for *Categorical Encoding by Statistical Applied Modeling*. Through numerical and statistical principles, CESAMO identifies PPCs for each categorical instance, ensuring the preservation of patterns specific to the dataset. Essentially, CESAMO's algorithm replaces categorical instances with randomly selected numerical codes, subjecting them to evaluation within an approximation function. Several numerical codes are evaluated until a statistical criterion is reached. Finally, the PPCs are determined by selecting the codes that yield the smallest error.

In this study, our main goal is to perform a quantifiable statistical assessment of CESAMO's performance and compare it with other encoding techniques. The paper is organized as follows: Sect. 2 offers a detailed overview of the methodology used to evaluate CESAMO's performance. Section 3 contains the experimental results. Finally, in Sect. 4, we present our conclusions.

2 General Methodology

There are studies [11–13] that have measured and compared the performance of different encoding techniques. While these works offer solid results indicating that certain techniques are more effective than others, their limitation lies in the lack of statistical support. In most of these studies, encoders are assessed by subjectively selecting an arbitrary number of real-world datasets. Nevertheless, for more objective conclusions, evaluations should be supported by statistical criteria.

In this study, we employed a statistically supported methodology to objectively evaluate encoding techniques.

Suppose there exists a probability distribution function that expresses the errors associated with an encoding technique. This Error Distribution (ED) encompasses all the possible errors that could be obtained when employing an encoding technique to solve a problem. The ED is characterized by its mean μ_{ED}, which, in a probability distribution, represents the central tendency or the expected value. In this work, we assessed and compared the encoding techniques based on their μ_{ED}.

The next question is *how can we determine the Error Distribution of an encoding technique?* To achieve this, we evaluate the encoders using as many datasets as necessary until a statistical criterion is met. Essentially, this criterion is based on obtaining errors until their mean normalizes. This will always occur as per the Central Limit Theorem.

Therefore, our goal was to assess CESAMO alongside other encoding techniques and compare their performance using μ_{ED}. The following sections provide a more in-depth exploration of the reasoning behind this evaluation approach, the procedures to find the μ_{ED}, and the resultant findings.

2.1 CESAMO Algorithm

CESAMO algorithm aims to identify Pattern Preserving Codes (PPCs) for each categorical attribute within a dataset. To achieve this, the algorithm randomly selects numerical values, referred to as candidate codes. These codes are evaluated using an approximation function that aims to determine the relationship between the categorical attribute and other attributes. The evaluation generally results in an error. Candidate codes are assessed until a stopping criterion is satisfied. The PPCs are defined as those that yield the smallest error when evaluated in F. Ultimately, the categorical instances are replaced by their corresponding PPCs.

Two relevant features of CESAMO merit explanation:

a) How to define the approximation function?
b) Which stopping criterion is used for determining the number of candidate codes to sample?

Concerning a), the algorithm employs a mathematical model that takes into account high-order relations. This model is based on a universal polynomial approximation:

$$F(x) = c_0 + \sum\nolimits_{i=1}^{6} c_i x^{2i-1} \tag{4}$$

In [14], it was shown that any continuous function can be represented by a linear combination of monomials, incorporating a constant and terms of odd degree. The polynomial coefficients can be determined using the Ascent Algorithm [15].

Concerning b), regardless of the error distribution, the means of the errors will converge to a Normal distribution, signifying statistical stability, and further sampling won't substantially alter the population's characterization.

2.2 Synthetic Data Generation

Determining the Error Distribution (ED) of an encoding technique requires evaluating it with datasets until a stopping criterion is met. Doing this with real-world datasets would pose a challenge, as statistical support for our results demands a large number of datasets, and we lack prior knowledge regarding the specific number needed. To address this fact, synthetic datasets were employed.

These synthetic datasets were generated using polynomial functions, incorporating both numerical and categorical attributes. To emulate characteristics commonly observed in real-world datasets, properties such as the total number of numerical and categorical attributes, size, etc., were varied within a range.

We analyzed 10 real-world datasets to determine the parameters of the polynomial functions that will generate synthetic data with characteristics similar to the real-world datasets. The polynomial parameters are shown in Table 1.

To generate the synthetic datasets, the polynomial parameters take random values in the established ranges, so that each generated dataset is different from the others.

As the purpose of these datasets is to evaluate categorical encoding techniques, categorical attributes were also added to the datasets. It was found that in real-world datasets, roughly 30% of the attributes are categorical variables.

Table 1. Polynomial parameters and ranges used to generate synthetic datasets

Parameter name	Range	Type	Description
Number of polynomial variables	[5, 34]	Integer	The count of attributes in the synthetic dataset
Variables domain	[0, 1]	Float	The range of values found in each attribute instance
Polynomial degrees	[0,11]	Integer	The max and min exponents of the polynomial
Polynomial terms	[1, 13]	Integer	The max and min terms of the polynomial
Coefficient values	[−1, 1]	Float	The constant value that will multiply each term
Number of variables in each term	[1, 5]	Integer	The max and min variables in each term
Dataset size	[1000, 3000]	Integer	The number of tuples

2.3 Categorical Encoders Evaluation

We proceeded to evaluate the encoding techniques. Our goal was to assess the encoders' ability to retain patterns in categorical attributes. Essentially, the better the encoder preserves information within categorical attributes, the more effectively ML models perform when utilizing these encoded datasets.

The synthetic datasets were transformed into a classification problem, featuring a 50%–50% distribution of positive and negative targets. Each dataset was individually processed by the encoders. Following the encoding stage, the dataset was handled by a supervised ML model.

To prevent bias in favor of a single supervised ML model during the evaluation, we employed five distinct models: a Multilayer Perceptron Neural Network (MLP), Logistic Regression (LR), Support Vector Machine (SVM), Gaussian Naive-Bayes (GNB), and XGBoost. These models were implemented using the Sklearn library.

The encoding methods under evaluation included: CESAMO, Binary, Hashing, One-hot, Ordinal, and Count encoders. All of these, except CESAMO, were implemented using the Category Encoders library [16].

We followed the next steps to assess the encoding techniques:

1. Generate a synthetic dataset using the polynomial function.
2. Apply the encoding technique to replace the categorical instances in the dataset.
3. Solve the encoded dataset with an ML algorithm, and evaluate the error.
4. Repeat steps 1, 2, and 3 until at least 36 errors are obtained.
5. Calculate and store the mean of the errors.
6. Determine if the distribution of the means of the errors is normal. If true go to step 7, otherwise repeat step 1.
7. Once the error means distribution is normal, the sampling process is stopped, and the μ_{ED} and from the ED can be determined.

In step 4, regarding the choice of a sample size of 36, this is a general rule of thumb based on the Central Limit Theorem, where the sample distribution will approach a normal distribution regardless of the population distribution as the sample size increases [17].

In step 6, to confirm if the distribution is normal, the Л Distribution was implemented.

2.4 Л Distribution

The term goodness-of-fit (GOF) refers to a statistical test that determines how well sample data fits an expected distribution. In our case, we expect a normal distribution. GOF measures the discrepancy between the observed values and those expected. There are multiple methods to determine GOF: Chi-Squared test (χ^2 test), Shapiro-Wilk test, Anderson-Darling test, and Kolmogorov-Smirnov.

The limitation of the test examples mentioned in the previous paragraph is that these focus on rejecting or not the null hypothesis based on significant evidence found. When conducting a GOF test, failing to reject the null hypothesis does not confirm that the distribution is normal. Rather, it indicates that there is insufficient evidence to reject the null hypothesis. Lack of evidence, however, does not imply confirmation of normality. In our case, we want to ensure that the distribution is normal.

This crucial distinction was overlooked in [18]. The study introduced a statistically supported method to compare algorithms, which is an early version of the one we are using in our assessment. In that early version, the Chi-Square test was employed to determine if the distribution of the error means was normal. The issue was that the Chi-Square test does not guarantee normality, leading to inaccurate results.

To circumvent this problem, the Л distribution was proposed [19]. It guarantees with a very high probability that the sample comes from a normal distribution. The foundation of Л distribution rests on answering the question *"How probable is it to compute an experimental value of Л larger than* ξ*"* for a set of data which are normally distributed?

To address this question, the sample distribution is segmented into quantiles. Each quantile varies in width to encompass the same area under the curve of the distribution. Figure 1 illustrates an example where the distribution is divided into deciles (10 quantiles).

Let Q represent the number of quantiles, O_i denotes the number of observed events in the *i-th* quantile. E_i is the number of expected events in the *i-th* quantile, and Φ is the minimum number of observations required per quantile. Also, let p denote the probability that Л exceeds ξ when data is normally distributed and there are at least Φ events in all quantiles. Then:

$$\text{Л} = \sum_{i=1}^{Q} \frac{(Q_i - E_i)^2}{E_i} \wedge [O_i \geq \Phi \, \forall \, i] \tag{5}$$

The smaller the Л is, the closer the distribution is to normality. Therefore, if $\text{Л} \leq \xi$, we know that the data is normally distributed with a probability greater than $1 - p$. The critical values ξ were determined through a Monte Carlo Simulation and are predefined. Thus, the process involves determining Л, comparing its value with ξ, and subsequently determining the probability of the sample being normal.

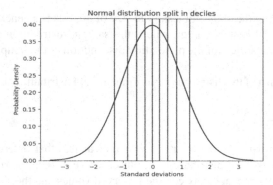

Fig. 1. Normal distribution segmented into deciles. Each decile contains 10% of the area under the curve.

3 Experimental Results

The evaluation of the encoding techniques required approximately 3,000 datasets for each combination of *encoder-MLmodel* to meet the stopping criterion. Once the Distribution of the Means of the Errors (DME) reached normality, we computed its mean μ_{DME}, and then we were able to determine the ED mean since $\mu_{ED} \approx \mu_{DME}$. The resulting values after computing μ_{ED} are presented in Table 2.

Table 2. Error Distribution means obtained after evaluating the encoding techniques.

Encoder	Error mean (μ_{ED})
CESAMO	**0.2994374188**
Binary	0.3055365472
Hashing	0.3069885601
One hot	0.3088986654
Ordinal	0.3215438146
Count	0.3572900108

As may be noticed from Table 2, CESAMO emerged as the technique with the lowest mean error. In fourth place, we have the One-Hot encoding technique, one of the most commonly used in practice.

On the other hand, the Count Encoder had the largest μ_{ED}, preceded by the Ordinal Encoder, which interestingly is also widely used in practice. Figure 2 presents a comparison of the μ_{ED} between CESAMO and the Ordinal encoder. As observed, the μ_{ED} of CESAMO is positioned to the left of the ordinal encoder mean. A lower value indicates a better technique performance.

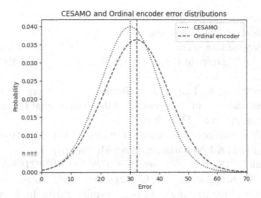

Fig. 2. Comparison of μ_{ED} (vertical lines) between CESAMO and Ordinal encoder

4   Conclusions

In this study, we conducted a statistical evaluation of CESAMO, a categorical encoding technique designed to identify Pattern Preserving Codes. Additionally, we compared its performance with other encoding techniques: Binary, Hashing, One-hot, Ordinal, and Count encoders. To provide statistical support for the results, each encoder was assessed with approximately 3,000 synthetic datasets. The metric used to compare the encoders' performances was the mean of the Error Distribution (μ_{ED}). The results demonstrated that CESAMO achieved the lowest error mean, followed by Binary encoder. Another notable finding was that Ordinal encoder, one of the most commonly used techniques, performed less effectively than the other encoders, getting the 5 position out of 6.

In summary, taking advantage of statistical and numerical principles, CESAMO emerges as a promising and effective solution for transforming categorical data into numerical values. Moreover, this study highlights the categorical encoder's crucial role in machine learning tasks, emphasizing their capacity to preserve patterns during the preprocessing of datasets containing both numerical and categorical attributes.

References

1. Kuhn, M., Johnson, K.: Feature Engineering and Selection: A Practical Approach for Predictive Models. Chapman and Hall/CRC, Boca Raton (2019)
2. Pedregosa, F., et al.: Scikit-learn: machine learning in Python. J. Mach. Learn. Res. **12**, 2825–2830 (2011)
3. Ke, G., et al.: Lightgbm: a highly efficient gradient boosting decision tree. In: Advances in Neural Information Processing Systems, vol. 30 (2017)
4. Chen, T., Guestrin, C.: Xgboost: a scalable tree boosting system. In: Proceedings of the 22nd ACM SIGKDD International Conference on Knowledge Discovery and Data Mining, pp. 785–794 (2016)
5. Hancock, J.T., Khoshgoftaar, T.M.: Survey on categorical data for neural networks. J. Big Data **7**(1), 1–41 (2020)
6. Zheng, A., Casari, A.: Feature Engineering for Machine Learning: Principles and Techniques for Data Scientists. O'Reilly Media, Inc., Sebastopol (2018)

7. Seger, C.: An investigation of categorical variable encoding techniques in machine learning: binary versus one-hot and feature hashing (2018)
8. Galli, S.: Python Feature Engineering Cookbook: Over 70 Recipes for Creating, Engineering, and Transforming Features to Build Machine Learning Models. Packt Publishing Ltd., Birmingham (2022)
9. Weinberger, K., Dasgupta, A., Langford, J., Smola, A., Attenberg, J.: Feature hashing for large scale multitask learning. In: Proceedings of the 26th Annual International Conference on Machine Learning, pp. 1113–1120 (2009)
10. Kuri-Morales, A.: Pattern discovery in mixed data bases. In: Martínez-Trinidad, J.F., Carrasco-Ochoa, J.A., Olvera-López, J.A., Sarkar, S. (eds.) MCPR 2018. LNCS, vol. 10880, pp. 178–188. Springer, Cham (2018). https://doi.org/10.1007/978-3-319-92198-3_18
11. Valdez-Valenzuela, E., Kuri-Morales, A., Gomez-Adorno, H.: Measuring the effect of categorical encoders in machine learning tasks using synthetic data. In: Batyrshin, I., Gelbukh, A., Sidorov, G. (eds.) MICAI 2021. LNCS (LNAI), vol. 13067, pp. 92–107. Springer, Cham (2021). https://doi.org/10.1007/978-3-030-89817-5_7
12. Pargent, F., Bischl, B., Thomas, J.: A benchmark experiment on how to encode categorical features in predictive modeling. Ludwig-Maximilians-Universität München, München (2019)
13. Matteucci, F., Arzamasov, V., Boehm, K.: A benchmark of categorical encoders for binary classification. arXiv preprint arXiv:2307.09191 (2023)
14. Kuri-Morales, A., Cartas-Ayala, A.: Polynomial multivariate approximation with genetic algorithms. In: Sokolova, M., van Beek, P. (eds.) AI 2014. LNCS (LNAI), vol. 8436, pp. 307–312. Springer, Cham (2014). https://doi.org/10.1007/978-3-319-06483-3_30
15. Cheney, E.W.: Introduction to Approximation Theory. McGraw-Hill Book Company, New York (1966)
16. McGinnis, W.D., Siu, C., Andre, S., Huang, H.: Category encoders: a scikit-learn-contrib package of transformers for encoding categorical data. J. Open Source Softw. 3(21), 501 (2018)
17. Forsyth, D.: Probability and Statistics for Computer Science, pp. 36–42. Springer, Cham (2018). https://doi.org/10.1007/978-3-319-64410-3
18. Kuri-Morales, A.F.: A methodology for the statistical characterization of genetic algorithms. In: Coello Coello, C.A., de Albornoz, A., Sucar, L.E., Battistutti, O.C. (eds.) MICAI 2002. LNCS (LNAI), vol. 2313, pp. 79–88. Springer, Heidelberg (2002). https://doi.org/10.1007/3-540-46016-0_9
19. Kuri-Morales, A.F., López-Peña, I.: Normality from monte carlo simulation for statistical validation of computer intensive algorithms. In: Pichardo-Lagunas, O., Miranda-Jiménez, S. (eds.) MICAI 2016. LNCS (LNAI), vol. 10062, pp. 3–14. Springer, Cham (2017). https://doi.org/10.1007/978-3-319-62428-0_1

Shortest Reducts Versus Shortest Constructs

Yanir Gonzalez Diaz[1]($\boxtimes$) (ID), José Fco. Martínez-Trinidad[1] (ID),
Jesús A. Carrasco-Ochoa[1] (ID), and Manuel S. Lazo-Cortés[2] (ID)

[1] Department of Computer Science, Instituto Nacional de Astrofísica,
Óptica y Electrónica (INAOE), 72840 Puebla, Mexico
{ygdiaz,fmartine,ariel}@inaoep.mx
[2] Graduate Division, Tecnológico Nacional de México/IT Tlalnepantla,
54070 Tlalnepantla de Baz, Mexico
manuel.lc@tlalnepantla.tecnm.mx

Abstract. This paper investigates the comparative performance of
shortest reducts and shortest constructs in supervised classification tasks
using real-life datasets from various domains, including both original
datasets and noise-distorted variations. The study evaluates the effectiveness of the shortest reducts and shortest constructs, particularly in
noisy environments. Experimental results provide insights into the relative performance of these attribute subsets and their impact on classification accuracy. The findings contribute to the understanding of the use
of shortest reducts versus shortest constructs in supervised classification
problems.

Keywords: rough sets · shortest reducts · shortest constructs ·
supervised classification

1 Introduction

In rough set theory [6], constructs [8] represent irreducible attribute subsets
that capture essential information for discerning objects belonging to different
classes while preserving intra-class similarity. Conversely, reducts [4] are irreducible attribute subsets that maintain the same discriminative ability among
classes as the entire set.

While constructs and reducts share similarities, constructs may hold an
advantage in certain situations by preserving intra-class similarity. In [8], Susmaga shows the superior performance of constructs over reducts in noisy environments. However, the number of constructs and reducts in real-world datasets
poses challenges for practical applications, necessitating the evaluation of small
subsets of contructs or reducts for classification tasks.

Supported by CONAHCYT through his doctoral scholarship.

E. Mezura-Montes et al. (Eds.): MCPR 2024, LNCS 14755, pp. 53–62, 2024.
https://doi.org/10.1007/978-3-031-62836-8_6

This study focuses on assessing the performance of the shortest reducts and the shortest constructs and their susceptibility to noise. By examining the effectiveness of these subsets of reducts or constructs, we aim to provide insights into their utility in classification tasks and their resilience to noise-induced perturbations.

The rest of the paper is organized as follows: Sect. 2 provides an overview of the basic concepts relevant to our study. Section 3 is dedicated to the experimental evaluation of the shortest constructs versus the shortest reducts in problems of supervised classification. The final section, Sect. 4, concludes the paper by summarizing the main findings, contributions, and possible future work directions.

2 Basic Definitions

In the Rough Set Theory (RST), a dataset in a supervised classification problem is represented by a decision table (DT). A decision table consists of rows and columns, where the columns represent attributes, the rows represent objects, and the cells contain the values of the attributes for each object. Formally, a decision table is denoted as the pair $DT = \langle \mathcal{O}, \mathcal{Q} \rangle$, where:

- $\mathcal{O}$ stands for a finite non-empty object set $\mathcal{O} = \{o_1, o_2, o_3, ..., o_n\}$, representing the universe of the decision table.
- $\mathcal{Q}$ stands for a finite non-empty attribute set: $\mathcal{Q} = \mathcal{C} \cup \{d\}$, where $\mathcal{C}$ denotes the set of condition attributes, and d signifies the decision attribute. Condition attributes characterize the objects, while the decision attribute defines the class of each object.

For each attribute a belonging to the set $\mathcal{Q}$, there exists a function $I_a :$ $\mathcal{O} \rightarrow V_a$, where V_a represents the set of values associated with attribute a. The function $I_a(x)$ indicates the value assigned to object x for attribute a. In simpler terms, the function I_a assigns a specific value to each object concerning a specific attribute.

In summary, a decision table in RST consists of a set of objects $\mathcal{O}$, a set of attributes $\mathcal{Q}$ (including condition attributes $\mathcal{C}$ and the decision attribute d), and information functions I_a that assign attribute values to objects for each attribute $a \in \mathcal{Q}$. This representation is commonly used in rough set-based supervised classification problems.

A decision table (DT) is considered consistent if it satisfies the following conditions:

1. For any pair of objects with the same value on the decision attribute d, there is at least one condition attribute in the set of condition attributes $\mathcal{C}$ with the same value for both objects.
2. For any pair of objects with different values on the decision attribute d, at least one condition attribute in $\mathcal{C}$ possesses different values for the two objects.

Unless specified otherwise, all mentioned decision tables are assumed to be consistent in this paper.

A reduct is a minimal subset of condition attributes that preserves the discriminatory power of the entire set of attributes in a decision table. The reducts can be defined as follows.

Definition 1. *Given a DT, a subset of attributes $\mathcal{R} \subseteq C$ is a reduct of DT if and only if $\mathcal{R}$ fulfills the following conditions:*

$$\forall_{(x,y)\in\mathcal{O}\times\mathcal{O}} [x \neq y, I_d(x) \neq I_d(y)], \exists_{a\in\mathcal{R}} I_a(x) \neq I_a(y) \tag{1}$$

$$\forall_{a\in\mathcal{R}} \exists_{(x,y)\in\mathcal{O}\times\mathcal{O}} [x \neq y, I_d(x) \neq I_d(y)], \forall_{c\in\mathcal{R}-\{a\}} I_c(x) = I_c(y) \tag{2}$$

Condition (1) guarantees that the identified reduct maintains the same discriminatory capacity for pairs of object from different classes as the entire set of attributes, ensuring consistency. Condition (2) ensures that a reduct is as small as possible in terms of its inclusion (minimality).

In [8], R. Susmaga introduces the concept of constructs, which are subsets of condition attributes. These subsets ensure the differentiation of objects belonging to different classes while retaining the same discriminatory power as the full set of condition attributes. Additionally, constructs maintain the similarity among objects within the same class, aligning with the overall discriminatory capability of the entire attribute set. The definition of constructs is as follows:

Definition 2. *Given a DT, a subset of attributes $\mathcal{A} \subseteq C$ is a construct of DT if and only if $\mathcal{A}$ fulfills the following conditions:*

$$\forall_{(x,y)\in\mathcal{O}\times\mathcal{O}} [x \neq y, I_d(x) \neq I_d(y)], \exists_{a\in\mathcal{A}} I_a(x) \neq I_d(y) \tag{3}$$

$$\forall_{(x,y)\in\mathcal{O}\times\mathcal{O}} [x \neq y, I_d(x) = I_d(y)], \exists_{a\in\mathcal{A}} I_a(x) = I_a(y) \tag{4}$$

$$\forall_{a\in\mathcal{A}} \begin{cases} \exists_{(x,y)\in\mathcal{O}\times\mathcal{O}} [x \neq y, I_d(x) \neq I_d(y)], \forall_{c\in\mathcal{A}-\{a\}} I_c(x) = I_c(y) \\ \qquad\qquad or \\ \exists_{(x,y)\in\mathcal{O}\times\mathcal{O}} [x \neq y, I_d(x) = I_d(y)], \forall_{c\in\mathcal{A}-\{a\}} I_c(x) \neq I_c(y), \end{cases} \tag{5}$$

Condition (3) signifies that a construct preserves the ability to differentiate objects from different classes. Moreover, condition (4) guarantees similarity among objects within the same class. Condition (5) ensures the construct's minimality with respect to inclusion.

Given the closeness between the concepts of constructs and reducts, algorithms designed for binary matrices can generate both. The distinction lies in how the binary matrices are built [5].

For our study any algorithm can be used, thus we employed, the algorithm outlined in [3] following the methodology of [5] to compute the shortest reducts and constructs, utilizing the respective binary matrix for each case.

3   Experimental Evaluation

In this section, our objective is to evaluate the effectiveness of using the shortest reducts/constructs in classification problems, particularly examining their performance in the presence of noise within the datasets.

The datasets utilized in the experiments are real-life datasets from the UCI Machine Learning Repository [1] and the OpenML Repository [9]. These datasets have been used extensively in diverse experiments and analyses, including research papers on the computation of reducts and constructs.

The datasets used for computing reducts/constructs are computable only for discrete condition attributes. Thus, the continuous attributes within these datasets had to undergo a process of discretization. We applied the discretization method available in Weka [2] as follow:

– weka.filters.unsupervised.attribute.Discretize -B 10 -M -1.0 -R first-last -precision 6.

Table 1 shows the fundamental characteristics of the datasets, including the name of the dataset, the number of condition attributes (the set of attributes excluding the decision attribute), the number of objects (instances), and the classes (distinct values of the decision attribute).

Table 1. Characteristics of the datasets used in the experiments.

Dataset	#Condition Attr.	#Objects	#Classes	Source
Anneal	38	898	5	OpenML [9]
Credit-g	20	1000	2	OpenML [9]
Dermatology	34	366	6	UCI [1]
Eucalyptus	19	736	5	OpenML [9]
Flags	29	194	2	UCI [1]
Ilpd	10	583	2	UCI [1]
Loan	10	614	2	OpenML [9]
Lymphography	18	148	4	UCI [1]
Mushroom	21	8124	2	UCI [1]
Soybean	35	683	19	UCI [1]
Sponge	44	76	2	UCI [1]
Student-mat	32	395	18	UCI [1]
Titanic	12	1309	2	OpenML [9]
Zoo	16	101	7	UCI [1]

The workflow of the experiment was as follows. Each dataset was randomly divided into training and testing sets, with 90% of the data allocated for training and 10% for testing purposes. Additionally, modified versions were created adding different levels of noise for each training set. For instance, considering the dataset "Anneal-train', modified versions such as 'Anneal-train-0.01', 'Anneal-train-0.02', and 'Anneal-train-0.03' were generated with 1%, 2%, and 3% random noise, respectively; i.e., 1% of all values were randomly distorted, meaning the original values were randomly replaced with other values from the appropriate domain. Similarly, in 'Anneal-train-0.02', twice the values (2%) were distorted, and so forth. This process allowed for the assessment of performance under different levels of noise.

For each training set, all the shortest reducts/constructs were computed using [3] following the methodology of [5]. Subsequently, each reduct/construct was individually used to describe the objects in the training and test sets getting a reduced dataset.

These reduced datasets were utilized to train and test a supervised classifier. The classifier employed for our experiments was Support Vector Machine (SVM) with the defaults parameters as following: kernel='rbf', gamma=0.5, and C=1.0.

A voting technique was applied using the classifiers trained with the shortest reducts/constructs to classify an object in the test set. This technique involves aggregating the predictions made by each individual classifier and selecting the class with the most votes as the final prediction.

Processing large datasets with numerous reducts/constructs can be time-consuming. Therefore, it is more practical to use only the shortest reducts/constructs instead of considering all of them [7]. We conducted a series of experiments comparing the effectiveness of the shortest reducts versus the shortest constructs.

To validate the results, we employed three additional classifiers: HistGradientBoostingClassifier, RandomForestClassifier, and DecisionTreeClassifier. However, since these classifiers yielded similar results, we opted to present only the results obtained with the SVM classifier. However, the results with the other classifiers can be seen at https://github.com/ygdiaz1202/ReductsVsConstructs.git.

3.1 Experiments with Data Sets Without Noise

The first batch of experiments involved 14 real-life datasets. The results are shown in Table 2 and include the number of the shortest reducts/constructs, the size of the shortest reducts/constructs, and the accuracy of the classifier based on the shortest reducts/constructs.

The analyzed datasets typically yield more shortest constructs than shortest reducts. Additionally, it is observed that shortest reducts tend to be smaller than the shortest constructs. Moreover, given that shortest constructs not only maintain the difference between objects from different classes but also preserve the similarity among objects within the same class. As a result, they may require additional attributes compared to reducts to fulfill this dual objective. Therefore, in general, the shortest constructs tend to be equal to or larger in size than the shortest reducts.

The accuracy achieved by shortest reducts is slightly better than that achieved on the shortest constructs, but the differences are not statistically signif-

Table 2. Results without adding noise.

Name	Shortest Reducts			Shortest Constructs		
	Number	Size	Accuracy	Number	Size	Accuracy
Anneal	24	7	0.94	14	7	0.96
Credit-g	1	2	0.72	10	15	0.72
Dermatology	1	5	0.49	41	6	0.57
Eucalyptus	28	3	0.51	1	14	0.41
Flags	1	4	0.60	13	7	0.65
German-credit	2	2	0.67	11	15	0.67
Ilpd	20	3	0.69	1	10	0.69
Loan	1	2	0.61	1	9	0.61
Lymphography	6	6	0.53	46	8	0.53
Mushroom	1	10	0.97	7	12	0.97
Soybean	90	11	0.65	86	11	0.64
Sponge	58	3	1.00	117	4	1.00
Student-mat	78	6	0.033	1	8	0.030
Titanic	1	3	0.85	2	8	0.76
Zoo	7	5	1.00	5	5	1.00

icant. This conclusion is supported by the Student two-tailed test with a p-value of 0.92. With a p-value greater than the typical significance level of 0.05, we fail to reject the null hypothesis, indicating that there is no statistically significant difference in accuracy between the using the shortest reducts and the shortest constructs.

The final remark is that despite some differences, neither the shortest reducts nor the shortest constructs exhibit any noteworthy advantage over the other option.

3.2 Experiments with Noise-Distorted Data Sets

The second group of results involve modified datasets that included some noise added to the datasets. This was done to verify whether the shortest constructs become better for classification than the shortest reducts when excessive noise distorts the proper definition of classes as in [8] with all the reducts/constructs.

The results obtained are shown in Tables 3, 4, and 5 and include the number of shortest reducts/constructs, the size of the shortest reducts/constructs, and the accuracy of the classifier based on the shortest reducts/constructs.

Results at Noise Level 1%: At noise level 1%, the t-test yielded a p-value of 0.8744. These results indicate no statistically significant difference between using the shortest reducts or the shortest constructs. Therefore, we fail to reject

Table 3. Results adding 1% of noise.

Name	Shortest Reducts			Shortest Constructs		
	Number	Size	Accuracy	Number	Size	Accuracy
Anneal-0.01	1	9	0.86	7	10	0.86
Credit-g-0.01	10	3	0.72	1	16	0.75
Dermatology-0.01	95	6	0.43	75	8	0.49
Eucalyptus-0.01	32	3	0.47	1	19	0.036
Flags-0.01	4	4	0.65	794	9	0.68
German-credit-0.01	8	3	0.67	2	17	0.67
Ilpd-0.01	10	3	0.69	1	10	0.69
Loan-0.01	1	3	0.60	1	10	0.61
Lymphography-0.01	1	6	0.60	24	9	0.53
Mushroom-0.01	1	17	0.93	1	21	0.92
Soybean-0.01	27	11	0.61	3	11	0.58
Sponge-0.01	16	3	1.00	100	5	1.00
Student-mat-0.01	3	5	0.033	262	9	0.030
Titanic-0.01	1	5	0.44	1	11	0.44
Zoo-0.01	1	9	0.91	1	9	0.91

the null hypothesis, suggesting that any observed differences could be due to random variation.

Results at Noise Level 2%: At noise level 2%, the t-test yielded a p-value of 0.8492. Similar to the previous case, these results indicate no statistically significant difference between using the shortest reducts or the shortest constructs. Thus, we cannot reject the null hypothesis, suggesting that the observed differences may be attributed to random variation.

Results at Noise Level 3%: For noise level 3%, the t-test yielded a p-value of 0.9839. Once again, these findings indicate no statistically significant difference between using the shortest reducts or the shortest constructs. Consequently, we do not reject the null hypothesis, implying that any discrepancies observed between the use of the shortest reducts/constructs may be due to random variation.

Overall, across all noise levels (1%, 2%, and 3%), the t-tests consistently indicated no significant difference in accuracy between using the shortest constructs versus the use of the shortest reducts. These results underscore the importance of considering other factors and conducting comprehensive evaluations when selecting reducts or constructs for classification tasks.

Table 4. Results adding 2% of noise.

Name	Shortest Reducts			Shortest Constructs		
	Number	Size	Accuracy	Number	Size	Accuracy
Anneal-0.02	13	10	0.81	100	11	0.81
Credit-g-0.02	1	2	0.72	3	17	0.72
Dermatology-0.02	77	6	0.49	79	8	0.49
Eucalyptus-0.02	1	2	0.034	1	19	0.034
Flags-0.02	2	4	0.60	169	8	0.60
German-credit-0.02	1	2	0.67	1	15	0.69
Ilpd-0.02	26	3	0.69	1	10	0.69
Loan-0.02	5	3	0.61	1	9	0.65
Lymphography-0.02	8	6	0.60	46	9	0.60
Mushroom-0.02	2	17	0.91	1	20	0.91
Soybean-0.02	3	11	0.62	127	12	0.67
Sponge-0.02	1	3	1.00	4	5	1.00
Student-mat-0.02	240	6	0.025	54	9	0.030
Titanic-0.02	1	4	0.56	1	12	0.63
Zoo-0.02	4	11	1.00	4	11	1.00

Table 5. Results adding 3% of noise.

Name	Shortest Reducts			Shortest Constructs		
	Number	Size	Accuracy	Number	Size	Accuracy
Anneal-0.03	3	10	0.80	21	11	0.80
Credit-g-0.03	10	3	0.72	1	17	0.72
Dermatology-0.03	84	6	0.41	5	8	0.59
Eucalyptus-0.03	36	3	0.57	1	19	0.034
Flags-0.03	22	5	0.60	166	8	0.65
German-credit-0.03	8	3	0.67	2	16	0.68
Ilpd-0.03	24	3	0.69	1	10	0.69
Loan-0.03	1	2	0.61	1	9	0.63
Lymphography-0.03	1	5	0.60	1	8	0.60
Mushroom-0.03	1	18	0.92	1	21	0.91
Soybean-0.03	6	12	0.62	1	12	0.62
Sponge-0.03	1	3	1.00	7	5	1.00
Student-mat-0.03	1	5	0.025	10	9	0.028
Titanic-0.03	13	6	0.65	1	12	0.62
Zoo-0.03	11	11	1.00	11	11	1.00

4   Conclusions

The primary aim of this paper was to conduct a comparative analysis of the effectiveness of the shortest reducts versus the shortest constructs for classification problems with datasets affected by noise.

The experiments at different noise levels (0.01, 0.02, and 0.03) revealed no statistically significant differences between the shortest reducts and the shortest constructs. The corresponding p-values were substantially greater than the typical significance level of 0.05. Consequently, we failed to reject the null hypothesis in all cases, indicating no significant difference between the means for the accuracy when the shortest reducts or the shortest constructs are used for classification tasks.

These findings suggest that, the choice between using the shortest reducts or the shortest constructs may not significantly impact the performance of the classifier.

While the experiments did not reveal a clear advantage of the use of the shortest constructs over the shortest reducts, it is crucial to consider other factors, such as computational efficiency, interpretability, and robustness in real-world applications.

In summary, while the shortest constructs did not demonstrate superiority over the shortest reducts, as it happens when using all reducts or constructs [8] is essential to conduct comprehensive evaluations and consider various factors when reducts/constructs are used for classification tasks.

References

1. Dua, D., Graff, C.: UCI Machine Learning Repository. University of California, School of Information and Computer Science, Irvine, CA (2019). http://archive.ics.uci.edu/ml
2. Frank, E., Hall, M.A., Witten, I.H.: The WEKA Workbench. Morgan Kaufmann, Burlington (2016)
3. González-Díaz, Y., Martínez-Trinidad, J.F., Carrasco-Ochoa, J.A., Lazo-Cortés, M.S.: Algorithm for computing all the shortest reducts based on a new pruning strategy. Inf. Sci. **585**, 113–126 (2022). https://doi.org/10.1016/j.ins.2021.11.037. https://www.sciencedirect.com/science/article/pii/S0020025521011592)
4. Jia, X., Shang, L., Zhou, B., Yao, Y.: Generalized attribute reduct in rough set theory. Knowl.-Based Syst. **91**, 204–218 (2016). https://doi.org/10.1016/j.knosys.2015.05.017. https://www.sciencedirect.com/science/article/pii/S0950705115002038. Three-way Decisions and Granular Computing
5. Lazo-Cortés, M.S., Carrasco-Ochoa, J.A., Martínez-Trinidad, J.F., Sanchez-Diaz, G.: Computing constructs by using typical testor algorithms. In: Carrasco-Ochoa, J.A., Martínez-Trinidad, J.F., Sossa-Azuela, J.H., Olvera López, J.A., Famili, F. (eds.) MCPR 2015. LNCS, vol. 9116, pp. 44–53. Springer, Cham (2015). https://doi.org/10.1007/978-3-319-19264-2_5
6. Pawlak, Z.: Rough sets. Int. J. Comput. Inf. Sci. **11**(5), 341–356 (1982)

7. Rodríguez-Diez, V., Martínez-Trinidad, J.F., Carrasco-Ochoa, J.A., Lazo-Cortés, M.S., Olvera-López, J.A.: A comparative study of two algorithms for computing the shortest Reducts: MiLIT and MinReduct. In: Roman-Rangel, E., Kuri-Morales, Á.F., Martínez-Trinidad, J.F., Carrasco-Ochoa, J.A., Olvera-López, J.A. (eds.) MCPR 2021. LNCS, vol. 12725, pp. 57–67. Springer, Cham (2021). https://doi.org/10.1007/978-3-030-77004-4_6

8. Susmaga, R.: Reducts versus constructs: an experimental evaluation. Electron. Notes Theor. Comput. Sci. **82**(4), 239–250 (2003)

9. van Rijn, J.N., et al.: OpenML: a collaborative science platform. In: Blockeel, H., Kersting, K., Nijssen, S., Železný, F. (eds.) ECML PKDD 2013. LNCS (LNAI), vol. 8190, pp. 645–649. Springer, Heidelberg (2013). https://doi.org/10.1007/978-3-642-40994-3_46

Diversity in Genetic Algorithms
in the Generation of School Schedules

Alejandro Moreno Martinez[1] , Victor Manuel Landassuri Moreno[1]([⊠]) ,
Asdrúbal López Chau[2] , and Saturnino Job Morales Escobar[1]

[1] Centro Universitario UAEM Valle de México, Boulevard Universitario S/N, Río San Javier,
54500 Cd, López Mateos, Atizapán de Zaragoza, Estado de México, Mexico
amorenom758@alumno.uaemex.mx, {vmlandassurim,
sjmoralese}@uaemex.mx
[2] Centro Universitario UAEM Valle de Zumpango, 55600 Zumpango de Ocampo, Mexico
alchau@uaemex.mx

Abstract. The Timetabling task is classified as a NP-complete problem; therefore, several constrains must be adjusted to generate valid timetables. In this type of problem, it is well known that the complexity of this task grows exponentially with the increasing number of variables and range of values, making it unfeasible to design schedules manually. Given their effectiveness in tackling large search spaces, Genetic Algorithms (GA) have emerged as a promising tool for addressing the Timetabling problem. Thus, an important aspect of GA is to maintain diversity among individuals during evolution, aiming to converge to an optimal solution efficiently. Therefore, this study focuses on exploring similarity techniques to measure diversity in order to improve GA individuals in timetabling generation. The obtained results demonstrate the population's evaluation performance, indicating higher accuracy with Jaccard similarity and faster evaluation with Hamming distance.

Keyword: Genetic Algorithms · School Schedules · Timetabling · Diversity

1 Introduction

Genetic Algorithms (GAs) are an Artificial Intelligence tool based on heuristics, used to potentially find adequate solutions to tasks that do not have a deterministic solution. Such tasks are typically challenging to solve manually, and there may be multiple solutions that meet the desired overall outcome (acceptable solution). Thus, GAs are based on the evolutionary principle of species, where individuals are matched with possible potential solutions to the task to be solved. The diversity of individuals within the population is crucial to ensure exploration across the search space, thereby avoiding the risk of falling into local optima. That is, a diversity metric measures the degree of difference between two individuals. If diversity is lost during evolution, it implies that similar individuals are exchanging their genes, which prevents the search space from being explored effectively. Similarly, if most of the individuals in a population are alike, it is possible

© The Author(s), under exclusive license to Springer Nature Switzerland AG 2024
E. Mezura-Montes et al. (Eds.): MCPR 2024, LNCS 14755, pp. 63–72, 2024.
https://doi.org/10.1007/978-3-031-62836-8_7

that evolution gets trapped in a local optimum. This could prevent finding an adequate solution to the problem or result in longer execution times. In such cases, there may be a greater burden on the mutation operator in the hope that an individual can reach the global optimum. To address the challenges of generating optimal school timetables, this paper investigates the importance of diversity in Genetic Algorithms (GAs). Section 2 delves into the complexities of the class schedule generation problem and its inherent challenges, highlighting the need to maintain diversity. Section 3 demonstrates how a Genetic Algorithm operates, detailing the formation of both global and local adaptability within the given task. Following this, Sect. 4 outlines four distinct methods for assessing diversity, i.e., Hamming Distance, Jaccard's Similarity Index, Euclidean Distance and Manhattan Distance. Section 5 describes the experimental setup and various preliminary settings for the GA. Section 6 presents the results obtained, and finally, Sect. 7 discusses the conclusions and outlines future work.

2 Class Schedule Generation Problem

Generating class schedules constitutes a frequent issue in the academic planning of most educational institutions. Typically, the following factors are taken into account: classrooms, subjects, teachers, scheduling (days and times), as well as student groups. Hence, it is imperative to adjust the values of these variables to prevent conflicts or inconsistencies. For example, scenarios where two groups occupy a room simultaneously or a teacher has overlapping classes. Consequently, the generation of schedules becomes a search and optimization problem. Timetable generation is an NP-complete problem, i.e., non-deterministic polynomial time problem [1], meaning it's computationally challenging to find an optimal solution. There are different techniques to address the problem of class schedule generation. Some of the techniques used are GAs [1, 2], local search algorithms [3], Linear programming through mathematical models [4] or the use of heuristic methods [5]. GA known for their ability to efficiently explore large search spaces, emerge as an ideal tool for tackling this complexity (Mohammed et al., 2017) to solve the timetabling problem. If a solution already exists (such as a timetable from previous semesters) and the requirements for the current semester remain unchanged, there is no need to seek new solutions. However, in the absence of such historical data or in the presence of new changes, adjustments are necessary to achieve an acceptable solution.

To create school schedules, it is necessary to satisfy both hard and soft constraints. Examples of hard constraints include: 1) matching the size of the classroom to the size of the group, ensuring that small groups are not assigned to large classrooms, and vice versa; 2) respecting the availability of teachers, considering their potential commitments elsewhere; and 3) taking into account the subject expertise of each teacher, as a mathematics teacher cannot be assigned to teach a social sciences class, for instance. Conversely, soft constraints may include a) assigning specific courses at earlier times, taking into consideration the cognitive aspect of students being more rested, rather than the final subjects of the day; b) another instance could be a teacher's preference towards teaching particular subjects; c) maintaining continuity in the group's schedule, thereby preventing empty hours between classes; d) limiting the number of subjects taught in the same day. It is worth noting that the soft constraints may or may not be satisfied, and yet a solution can still be considered valid, i.e., one that can be implemented in a real-world scenario and functions effectively in all considered aspects. The OR-Library set [6], designed with the objective of complying with hard constraints like teacher availability and room capacity, was chosen to test the algorithm due to its simplicity based on combinations of teachers and hours. It consists solely of data regarding classes, teachers, classrooms, and time slots. The OR-Library comprises five sets named hdtt4, hdtt5, hdtt6, hdtt7, and hdtt8. Each set includes variables corresponding to its name; for instance, hdtt4 features 4 classes, 4 teachers, and 4 classrooms, with type 4 representing the simplest level of complexity that progressively increases in the subsequent sets.

3 Genetic Algorithms

As bio-inspired algorithms, GAs incorporates concepts such as 'individuals', which represent potential solutions to the problem. These individuals are characterized by a set of genes, also known as a chromosome, which encapsulates the solution space explored by the GA. Mimicking nature, GAs leverage genetic operators like selection, crossover, and mutation to efficiently search for optimal solutions. These operators, inspired by natural processes, guide the evolution of individuals within the population, leading to increasingly better solutions. Therefore, the selection process entails selecting the fittest individuals from every generation, according to their adaptability score, derived from their respective fitness function. In GAs, an individual's "adaptability" refers to its effectiveness in solving the problem. There are several types of selection as mentioned [7]: Tournament selection, where different individuals from the population compete to determine the fittest among them, or random selection, which randomly selects individuals from the population, among others. The crossover operator on the other hand, plays a crucial role trying to improve actual solutions, by combining genes from two selected individuals (parents) to create new offspring. This process aims to inherit and potentially improve the favorable traits of both parents, leading to better solutions over generations. Various types of crossovers exist, but the most prevalent ones are single-point crossover, where a portion of the individuals are exchanged between them; and uniform crossover, where each gene of the individual may be exchanged with the other individual. Lastly, the mutation operator is responsible for randomly modifying one individual in each generation, primarily to explore the solution space by introducing greater diversity in the genetic information of individuals. For instance, [8] discusses three mutation techniques for the timetabling problem: Random Modification, wherein a random single genetic element is modified; Decreasing Probability, commencing with a high mutation probability initially, then reducing it throughout the process to avoid excessive disturbance as solutions converge; and Increasing Probability, beginning with a low mutation probability, subsequently augmenting it to preserve diversity and forestall premature convergence.

Figure 1 depicts the general diagram of a GA. The process initiates with a population of individuals, typically initialized randomly. For this study, it implies that each individual comprises the specified groups, their respective class schedules, teachers, subjects, and corresponding days and hours of instruction. Afterward, each individual's performance is assessed using an adaptation function that measures its effectiveness in solving the problem. This evaluation helps determine whether the evolution continues or if a desired level of solution quality has been achieved, based on predefined stopping criteria such as reaching a specific fitness level or completing a maximum number of generations. Stopping criteria may also include execution time or the discovery of an individual that meets all specified constraints. If the stopping criteria are not met, the selection, crossover, and mutation operators are used to generate a new population. In GAs, the generational change occurs when the newly created offspring population replaces the parent generation. Notably, GAs often includes an elitism operator to preserve the best solutions found so far. However, these operators will not be discussed in detail in this study, as the focus is on the diversity behavior of the algorithm.

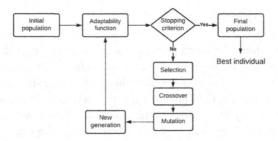

Fig. 1. General Diagram of a GA.

3.1 Adaptability Function

During the evolutionary process conducted by GAs, it is essential to determine the adaptation value (or fitness value) of each individual, i.e. the accuracy of each individual. Therefore, it is crucial to have a function that can evaluate the members of the population. Individuals will be evaluated based on the algorithm's predefined restrictions. Those that meet these restrictions will receive higher adaptability scores, while those that do not will be penalized. The evaluation criteria for individuals will vary depending on the problem. This work employs a hierarchical adaptation function, consisting of a global function and several local ones. The global adaptability function, measuring the overall performance of an individual, is determined by the sum of the local functions, as shown in Eq. 1 below.

$$Fg(i) = \sum_{x=1}^{N} fl(x) \tag{1}$$

where i represents an individual, x represents the schedule matrices, and N indicates the total number of matrices in the individual, with each matrix pertaining to a specific group within the individual. As mentioned earlier, the local adaptability function is applied to each group within the individual. This involves evaluating a series of parameters to determine the correctness of the group's schedule, as described in Eq. 2.

$$fl(x) = CHD(x) + CP(x) + DP(x) + PIM(x) + LHS(x) + LHM(x) \tag{2}$$

These local functions include CST, which checks for classes scheduled at the same time; TMG, which identifies when a teacher is assigned to multiple groups simultaneously; TA, which verifies teacher availability during the assigned time; TPS, which ensures a teacher is not assigned a prohibited subject; GHR, which confirms the group's adherence to weekly hour requirements; and SDH, which validates the subject's compliance with program-defined hours. Similarly, for each individual function (CST, TMG, TA, TPS, GHR, and SDH), any detected constraint violations will result in a penalty of adding a value of 1 to the corresponding local adaptability function. For instance, an individual presenting two teacher joints across all groups (TMG = 2) and one subject joint (CST = 1) would yield an adaptability value fl(x) = 3. Consequently, the fittest individual is characterized by low values, the goal of the GA being to minimize the occurrence of errors in the schedule.

4   Diversity in the Population

Diversity within the population refers to the genetic variation present among individuals. Maintaining this diversity across generations is crucial to avoid converging prematurely to local optima. Given the likelihood of multiple solutions to a problem, exploring a wide range of possibilities often leads to superior solutions. To assess diversity, various metrics are used to evaluate individuals. The choice of the most suitable metric depends on the individual's structure, whether it is represented as a genotype or phenotype. For instance, [9] utilized metrics such as Hamming distance, edit distance, Semi-Partial Marching (SePM), and Aggregated Mean Absolute Difference (AggM) to analyze diversity in college scheduling.

4.1   Hamming Distance

The Hamming distance measures the difference between two strings of characters of the same length. In [10]. To calculate the Hamming distance, two individuals were selected, and the differences between the same groups were compared. For example, group 1 of individual 1 was compared with group 1 of individual 2, and so on for the other groups. This process was repeated to evaluate all individuals.

Figure 2 illustrates that while the two schedules are generally similar, they exhibit differences in certain aspects. For instance, the Physics class is taught by a different teacher, and the last class of Programming 1 is scheduled on Friday instead of Wednesday. In this case, there is a difference of 3, indicating disparities across three elements. A higher difference value suggests greater diversity. However, given that other similarity measures are normalized and for comparison purposes, it was decided to normalize the Hamming distance values according to Eq. 3.

$$\text{Hamming distance} = -\frac{\text{Difference}}{\text{Total Elements}} + 1 \tag{3}$$

This clarifies that values near 0 indicate distinct individuals, while 1 implies identical individuals, similar to the Jaccard Similarity index discussed next, which shares the same value range.

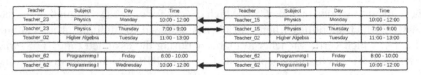

Teacher	Subject	Day	Time
Teacher_23	Physics	Monday	10:00 - 12:00
Teacher_23	Physics	Thursday	7:00 - 9:00
Teacher_02	Higher Algebra	Tuesday	11:00 - 13:00
Teacher_62	Programming I	Friday	8:00 - 10:00
Teacher_62	Programming I	Wednesday	10:00 - 12:00

Teacher	Subject	Day	Time
Teacher_15	Physics	Monday	10:00 - 12:00
Teacher_15	Physics	Thursday	7:00 - 9:00
Teacher_02	Higher Algebra	Tuesday	11:00 - 13:00
Teacher_62	Programming I	Friday	8:00 - 10:00
Teacher_62	Programming I	Friday	10:00 - 12:00

Fig. 2. Example of groups to apply the Hamming distance.

4.2 Jaccard's Similarity Index

The Jaccard index is a method of comparing two individuals by examining the number of shared elements between them relative to the total number of elements (Eq. 4).

$$J(A, B) = \frac{|A \cap B|}{|A \cup B|} \tag{4}$$

where sets A and B serve as the basis for comparison, $|A \cap B|$ represents the number of elements that are in both sets (the intersection) and $|A \cup B|$ is the total number of elements in both sets (the union). Analogous to the Hamming distance comparison, the Jaccard index (Eq. 4) will be utilized to compare sets representing group schedules. This index calculates similarity by dividing the intersection of both sets by their union. Values closer to 0 indicate very different schedules, while values closer to 1 indicate very similar or identical schedules.

4.3 Euclidean Distance

The Euclidean distance between two points is calculated as the length of the shortest straight line connecting both points.

$$E(A, B) = \sqrt{(x_2 - x_1)^2 + (y_2 - y_1)^2} \tag{5}$$

where x1 and x2 represent the coordinates points of A, and similarly y1 and y2 correspond to those of set B, E denotes the Euclidean distance between A and B.

4.4 Manhattan Distance

The Manhattan distance is calculated by adding the absolute differences of the coordinates of two points, i.e., it takes the difference in the horizontal position and adds the difference in the vertical position.

$$M(A, B) = |x_2 - x_1| + |y_2 - y_1| \tag{6}$$

where x1 and x2 are the coordinates points of point A, y1 and y2 correspond to those of set B, M is Manhattan distance between A and B. To apply Manhattan distance like Euclidean requires numeric data. In GAs with a genotype, this metric can be an alternative, yet to use it with phenotypes, it must be tailored. Hence, a numerical value needs to be generated for each teacher, subject, day, and time slot. Accordingly, Euclidean and Manhattan distances were customized by converting everyone's schedules into numerical representations, with the expectation that they may not perform well because of this modification. As a result, a list was constructed, where each entry signifies an individual's schedule, and Eqs. 7 and 8 were implemented accordingly, denoting the chosen pairings of individuals' groups.

$$dEuclidiana = \sqrt{\sum_{i=1}^{n}(x_{2i} - x_{1i})^2} \qquad (7)$$

$$dManhattan = \sum_{i=1}^{n}|x_{2i} - x_{1i}| \qquad (8)$$

5 Experimental Setup

In this work, Jaccard, Hamming Distance, Euclidean, and Manhattan distances were used to assess class schedule diversity because the GA operates directly on phenotypes, limiting the use of other metrics without transformations (e.g., using the genotype).

The parameters used for the genetic algorithm are as follows: a stopping criterion set to 10,000 generations to evaluate the algorithm's performance. Additionally, 100 individuals are employed, evolving throughout the process. The selection process involves tournament selection, where two individuals compete, and the better one is incorporated into a new list of parents. This list comprises 75% of the original population and serves to generate offspring. Uniform crossover is applied with a 70% probability of information exchange between individuals. A mutation process occurs with a 30% probability of altering any gene value. Elitism is implemented by selecting the top 10% of individuals to maintain optimal solutions across generations. Furthermore, 10 independent runs were conducted for each metric to evaluate their performance. All these parameters were set at convenient traditional values and are not intended to be optimal. However, experiments were conducted to explore how altering some of these parameters affects GA diversity.

One key finding was that choosing the number of parents has a significant impact. With fewer parents (40% of parents selected), individuals become more similar over generations due to limited genetic combinations. On the other hand, using a higher percentage of parents (60%) leads to a more diverse population. Another finding was that the number of competing offspring in the tournament selection influences diversity. With more offspring participating in the tournament (5 competing individuals), better individuals tend to be selected rapidly, leading to quick convergence toward similar solutions.

6 Results

This section details the experimental analysis of the diversity indices derived utilizing the Hamming, Jaccard, Euclidean, and Manhattan metrics. Upon executing the algorithm for 10,000 generations, the population's diversity may be observed (Fig. 3).

In Fig. 3, individuals are evaluated in pairs, comparing each with all others in the population except itself. The graphs shown display information in symmetrical triangular matrices, where the value at position (X, Y) equals that at position (Y, X) due to the same similarity between them. The axes of individuals (ordinate and abscissa axis) from 0 to 10 correspond to those selected by elitism. Rows and columns from position 11 to 100 represent the remaining population generated with crossover and mutation operators. The diagonal equals 0 as individuals are not compared to themselves. Figure 3 shows a high degree of similarity among individuals, with Jaccard similarity values ranging from 0.6 to 0.8, indicating some identical pairs. The Hamming distance suggests even higher similarity, while both Euclidean and Manhattan distances exhibit similar patterns but with results too high for clear interpretation. Based on the preceding findings, it was determined to conduct further testing while replacing the tournament selection operator by a random selection, thus eliminating any propensity towards consistently choosing the finest individuals; however, this approach carries the potential risk of introducing greater variance in the quality of the individuals, due to selecting less competent ones.

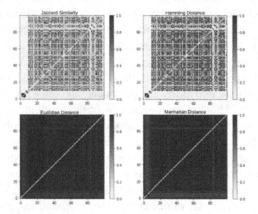

Fig. 3. Population diversity whit the four metrics.

Figure 4 shows improved diversity, particularly with Hamming Distance and Jaccard Similarity Index. Both metrics maintain significantly higher diversity after 10,000 generations compared to Fig. 3, which used tournament selection. In both figures (Figs. 3 and 4), the Euclidean and Manhattan distance metrics exhibit the poorest performance in assessing population diversity based on the similarity of individuals in the timetabling problem.

It was evaluated the algorithm's execution time after 10 independent runs, using both selection types and all metrics with the final population. Average times are shown in Table 1, where there are no major differences when comparing the metrics with the same selection method. However, Tournament selection proves to execute within fewer iterations.

As evident from the Figs. 3 and 4, the Hamming distance outperforms the Jaccard similarity index regarding efficiency in terms of time complexity, given its ability to swiftly compute the difference without needing to convert the data into sets and perform

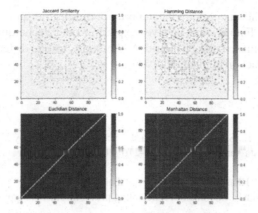

Fig. 4. Population diversity with random selection operator.

Table 1. Execution time.

Metric	Tournament selection (sec)	Random selection (sec)
Hamming distance	5731.35125	6611.59459
Jaccard similarity	5746.58997	6623.16802
Euclidian distance	5778.49072	6623.98079
Manhattan distance	5774.19334	6630.59170

intersection and union operations, which make the Jaccard Index slower in calculating the discrepancies. Despite the Hamming Distance's speed advantage over the Jaccard Index, the latter provides a more precise comparison by considering both individuals as sets.

7 Conclusions

Assessing population diversity based on the similarity of individuals, such as class schedules, offers valuable insights into observing Genetic Algorithm behavior and aids in error correction that might otherwise be challenging to identify. This study underscores the importance of selecting metrics tailored to the specific problem at hand; for instance, metrics like Manhattan or Euclidean distance may not be directly applicable and, even with modifications, may not prove useful in certain cases as expected. It is advisable to conduct various tests to determine optimal parameter values for the problem at hand. Furthermore, this research revealed the significant influence of selection operators on population diversity. After running the algorithm for 10,000 generations, it became evident that tournament selection, while effective for scheduling problems, tends to favor the best individuals, potentially leading to homogeneity over generations. In contrast, random selection can maintain diversity by accommodating individuals with varying adaptability levels. This underscores the importance of selecting an appropriate operator in algorithm design. Future work involves exploring other techniques to evaluate the feasibility and performance of each metric. Additionally, testing different operators will help assess their impact on population diversity.

References

1. Guerra, M., Pardo, E., Salas, E.: Problema del School Timetabling y algoritmos genéticos: una revision. Revista Vínculos **10**(2), 259–276 (2013). https://doi.org/10.14483/2322939X. 6478
2. Mohammed, M.A., Khanapi, M., Ghani, A., Obaid, O.I., Mostafa, S.: A review of genetic algorithm application in examination timetabling problem. J. Eng. Appl. Sci. **12**, 5166–5181 (2017)
3. Shahvali Kohshori, M., Saniee Abadeh, M.: Hybrid genetic algorithms for university course timetabling. Int. J. Comput. Sci. Issues (IJCSI) (2012)
4. González, A., Partida, D., Alcaraz, C., Benitez, E.: Aplicación de Programación Lineal para la Asignación de Horarios en una Institución Educativa Méxicana. Revista Ingeniería Industrial **15**, 135–146 (2016)
5. Abdullah, S., Turabieh, H., McCollum, B., McMullan, P.: A hybrid metaheuristic approach to the university course timetabling problem. J. Heuristics **18**(1), 1–23 (2012). https://doi.org/ 10.1007/s10732-010-9154-y
6. Beasley, J.E.: Or-Library timetabling, Homepage. http://people.brunel.ac.uk/~mastjjb/jeb/ orlib/tableinfo.html. Accessed 26 Jan 2024
7. Fang, H.-L.: Genetic Algorithms in Timetabling and Scheduling, Doctoral dissertation, University of Edinburgh (1994)
8. Neira, V.: El problema de timetabling para colegios chilenos. Solución mediante Algoritmos Genéticos, Master thesis, Conception University (2014)
9. Sakal, J., Fieldsend, J.E., Keedwell, E.: Genotype diversity measures for escaping plateau regions in university course timetabling. In: Proceedings of the 2023 Genetic and Evolutionary Computation Conference Companion, GECCO, Lisbon, Portugal, pp. 2090–2098. Association for Computing Machinery, Inc. (2023). https://doi.org/10.1145/3583133.359 6334
10. Mendoza, C., Guarda, T.: Use of genetic algorithms to solve problems in the Academic field Problem Solving Methods. In: 14th Iberian Conference on Information Systems and Technologies (CISTI), Coimbra, Portugal, pp. 1–6. IEEE (2019). https://doi.org/10.23919/ CISTI.2019.8760792.

Multiobjective Assignment of Citizens to INE Service Modules Using NSGA-II: An Efficient Optimization Approach

Edgar Jardón[ID], Marcelo Romero[ID], and José-Raymundo Marcial-Romero[✉][ID]

Autonomous University of State of Mexico, 50000 Toluca, Mexico
{ejardont,jmarcialr}@uaemex.mx
https://www.uaemex.mx/

Abstract. Efficient allocation of citizens to service modules is crucial for the National Electoral Institute (INE) of Mexico, particularly for those applying for their voter identification card for the first time. This study focuses on a multi-objective optimization approach, using the Second Generation Non-Dominated Genetic Algorithm (NSGA-II), to assign citizens from 16 municipalities in the Toluca Valley to 10 INE service modules. The involved municipalities include Almoloya de Juárez, Calimaya, Chapultepec, Lerma, Metepec, among others, and the service modules are distributed in locations such as Almoloya de Juárez, Metepec, Lerma, and more. Two objective functions are utilized: (1) Maximizing facility coverage, ensuring that the largest number of citizens is assigned to a module, subject to the capacity constraints of each module, and (2) Minimizing transportation costs by reducing the total distance citizens need to travel to reach the modules. The NSGA-II algorithm is compared to alternative optimization methods, and fuzzy logic is employed to evaluate the quality of the generated solutions. The results demonstrate that the NSGA-II-based approach outperforms alternative methods in both efficiency and solution quality, and its impact on INE practice is discussed.

Keywords: Allocation problem · Urban planning · NSGA-II

1 Introduction

Strategic decision making on resource management requires optimal solutions, due to their implementation affects the future state of various scenarios. An example is the budget decisions making and the public demand that the government implements each year, since these decisions could have a long-term impact on the quality of citizens life [8].

Therefore, it is necessary to have quality information, from reliable sources, whether they are public or private institutions that use methodologies according to current needs, since this contributes to the generation of studies for the benefit of social development. An example is the National Electoral Institute (INE),

E. Mezura-Montes et al. (Eds.): MCPR 2024, LNCS 14755, pp. 73–83, 2024.
https://doi.org/10.1007/978-3-031-62836-8_8

which is an autonomous body in Mexico and it is in charge of regulating electoral processes, citizen participation and establishing the guidelines that citizens must respect.

Such information highlights the importance of social dynamics that exist in the current environment, which demands the implementation of methods for geographical analysis, whose objective is to optimize the planning of services [1].

One of the most relevant issues for decision-makers, both in the governmental and private sectors, is the efficient allocation of clients and services. This issue becomes particularly important in contexts such as the National Electoral Institute (INE), where the proper allocation of resources and service management directly impacts citizen participation and democratic exercise [7].

In this regard, the present research focuses on addressing the specific challenge of allocating citizens from the Toluca Valley, aged between 17 and 18 years old (Table 1 shows the population of 17 and 18-year-olds per municipality in the Valley of Toluca), who are applying for their voter identification card for the first time at the INE modules closest to their homes. This population represents a significant portion of the electoral base, and their adequate access to INE services is essential to ensure the representativeness and legitimacy of electoral processes.

Table 1. Inhabitants from the valley of Toluca between 17 and 18 years old

INEGI ID	Municipality	Inhabitants
005	Almoloya de Juárez	6,748
018	Calimaya	2,645
027	Chapultepec	498
051	Lerma	6,521
054	Metepec	8,248
055	Mexicaltzingo	543
062	Ocoyoacac	2,752
067	Otzolotepec	3,684
072	Rayón	625
073	San Antonio la Isla	1,285
076	San Mateo Atenco	3,803
087	Temoaya	4,269
090	Tenango del valle	3,444
106	Toluca	32,815
115	Xonacatlán	2,122
118	Zinacantepec	8,105
	Total	**88,107**

The implementation of a resource optimization model in this context not only aims to improve the operational efficiency of the INE but also has a direct impact on the quality of life of citizens. By ensuring proper allocation of available resources, waiting times are reduced, transportation costs are minimized, and the exercise of the right to vote for this specific population is facilitated.

1.1 Solution Proposal

To ensure effective client-to-service assignments, a model based on NSGA II (Non-dominated Sorting Genetic Algorithm II) coupled with fuzzy logic will be implemented. This fusion enables multi-objective optimization, simultaneously considering criteria like maximizing service coverage, minimizing citizen travel costs, and ensuring equitable resource distribution.

NSGA-II is renowned for its efficiency in identifying optimal solutions across multiple objectives. By leveraging this approach, diverse resource allocation configurations can be explored, striking an optimal balance between criteria.

Additionally, integrating fuzzy logic enhances adaptability and robustness. It allows handling inherent uncertainties, ensuring a context-sensitive assignment process that dynamically adjusts to changing conditions.

1.2 Related Work

In this section, we will explore previous research that addresses the use of NSGA-II for service allocation. These studies demonstrate the effectiveness and advantages of using NSGA-II in similar allocation problems, highlighting its ability to obtain Pareto-optimal solutions.

The research by [3] presents NSGA-II as a fast and elitist multi-objective genetic algorithm. The study demonstrates the effectiveness of NSGA-II in solving assignment problems by providing non-dominated solutions on the Pareto front and maintaining effective diversity among them.

Similarly, [2] propose a multi-objective evolutionary algorithm based on NSGA-II for dynamic service composition. The algorithm aims to optimize multiple objectives such as cost, reliability, and latency to adapt to real-time changes and enhance the quality of service composition.

In another study, [10] propose a hybrid approach that combines NSGA-II with the search algorithm to solve the service allocation problem in cloud computing environments. The results demonstrate that the combination of these two algorithms improves the quality of solutions in terms of efficiency and user satisfaction.

In additional research conducted by [9], a multi-objective genetic algorithm based on NSGA-II is proposed to address the dynamic task allocation problem in service-oriented manufacturing systems. The results show that the proposed algorithm can find efficient solutions that balance performance and cost objectives in real-time.

These studies consistently demonstrate that NSGA-II is an efficient and effective tool for service allocation in various domains. Its ability to generate Pareto-optimal solutions and maintain diversity among solutions makes it a promising approach for addressing multi-objective assignment problems.

2 Methodology

In this section, the methodology used to design and evaluate a multi-objective assignment model based on NSGA-II is presented, with the aim of managing decision-making in the allocation of public services.

2.1 Methodological Framework

Efficient allocation of public services is crucial to improve the quality of life for the population and ensure equitable distribution of resources. In this section, a detailed guide consisting of 6 stages is provided (see Fig. 1): 1. Problem Analysis, 2. Selection of Involved Variables, 3. Possible Solution Selection for the Assignment Problem, 4. Creation of a Set of Potential Solutions, 5. Selection of the Best Solution, and 6. Final Results.

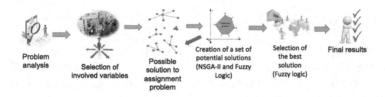

Fig. 1. Stages of the proposed methodology.

Problem Analysis. In the problem analysis stage, a comprehensive study is conducted to define the objectives, constraints, and requirements associated with decision-making in public service allocation. This involves examining the socioeconomic, geographic, and demographic context. The goal is to identify user needs, as well as challenges in service provision. Factors like population density, demand distribution, socioeconomic characteristics, and budget constraints are considered. Additionally, objectives for public service allocation are analyzed.

Selection of Involved Variables. In the variable selection stage, a detailed process identifies and selects the most relevant variables for the multi-objective optimization model in public service allocation. This steps ensures the model covers all critical aspects and considerations.

1. Accessibility and Connectivity
2. Expected Demand
3. Objectives and Constraints

Possible Solution Selection for the Assignment Problem. During the solution selection stage, a detailed analysis aims to optimize public service allocation, maximizing efficiency and effectiveness. Various techniques are used for this purpose:

1. Assignment Models
2. Workload Balancing
3. Spatial Considerations

Creation of a Set of Potential Solutions. In creating a set of potential solutions, a detailed process is undertaken to generate diverse alternatives for addressing the multi-objective optimization problem in public service allocation. This involves specific steps, such as:

1. Definition of Variables
2. Generation of Initial Solutions
3. Evaluation of Generated Solutions
4. Diversification of Solutions

Selection of the Best Solution. During solution selection, a thorough analysis is conducted to identify the optimal solution from various options. This involves evaluating and comparing potential solutions using different techniques [6].

1. Definition of Evaluation Criteria
2. Sensitivity Analysis
3. Comparison and Selection
4. Feedback from Experts and Stakeholders

Final Results. In the final results stage, the obtained results from the selection of the best solution in the multi-objective optimization process for public service allocation are presented and analyzed. This stage involves a thorough evaluation of the results and effective communication of the findings to stakeholders and decision-makers [4,5].

3 Experimentation

In this section, we present the results of applying the multi-objective assignment approach to INE service modules using NSGA-II. We outline the simulation scenarios, parameters used, and analyze the results. Additionally, we compare the application of genetic algorithms, local search, and tabu search, with comparative tables for each aspect evaluated. Furthermore, a table is included to show solution classification using fuzzy logic.

- Simulation scenarios: Three simulation scenarios were generated with the aim of covering different representative situations of the INE service module assignment problem. Each scenario was designed considering a specific distribution of the population of citizens among the municipalities of the Valle de Toluca and the capacities of the INE service modules.

  1. Equal distribution of population: In this scenario, an equal distribution of the population of citizens among the municipalities of the Valle de Toluca is assumed. This implies that the number of citizens in each municipality is approximately the same. Additionally, the capacities of the INE service modules are distributed proportionally to cover this equal distribution of the population.

  2. Unbalanced population distribution: In this scenario, an unbalanced distribution of the population of citizens among the municipalities of the Toluca Valley is considered. Some municipalities have a higher concentration of citizens in the age range of 17 to 18 years, while others have fewer citizens in this age range. The capacities of the INE service modules are adjusted to reflect this unbalanced population distribution.

  3. Scenario 3: Heterogeneous distribution of module capacities: In this scenario, a heterogeneous distribution of the capacities of the INE service modules is considered. Some modules have a higher capacity than others, reflecting situations where certain areas have a greater demand for attention than others. The distribution of the population of citizens among the municipalities remains equitable.

- Simulation parameters:

  1. Population Size: A population size of 100 individuals was configured for each simulation scenario.

  2. Crossover Rate: An 80% crossover rate was used to encourage exploration of the solution space.

  3. Mutation Rate: A mutation rate of 5% was established to maintain genetic diversity in the population.

The capacity of the service modules of the INE (within a 9-day period) is a crucial aspect to consider in the process of assigning citizens. The following table provides details on the capacity of each service module in the Valle de Toluca:

Table 2 displays the names of the service modules and their respective capacity in terms of the number of citizens that can be attended simultaneously at each module.

3.1   Model Formulation

This section presents in detail the variables, parameters, and constraints used to model the multi-objective assignment problem of citizens to INE service modules using NSGA-II. The following variables are introduced:

- n: Total number of clients (population of citizens between 17 and 18 years old).

Table 2. Attention capacity for each municipal module in a period of nine days

INEGI ID	Module	Working hours	Service desks	Attendees
005	Almoloya de Juárez	8:00–15:00	Basic +1	4,536
			Basic +1	
051	Lerma	8:00–20:00	Basic +2	10,692
			Basic +2	
054	Metepec	8:00–15:00	Basic +3	9,072
			Basic +3	
076	San Mateo Atenco	8:00–15:00	Basic +2	6,804
			Basic +1	
087	Temoaya	8:00–20:00	Basic +2	5,346
090	Tenango del valle	8:00–15:00	Basic +2	3,402
106	Toluca 1	8:00–20:00	Basic +7	28,512
			Basic +7	
106	Toluca 2	8:00–15:00	Basic +7	18,144
			Basic +7	
115	Xonacatlán	8:00–20:00	Basic +1	3,564
118	Zinacantepec	8:00–20:00	Basic +3	7,128

- m: Total number of facilities (INE service modules).
- d_{ij}: Distance between client i and facility j.
- α: Coefficient representing the transportation cost per unit distance.
- X_{ij}: Binary variable indicating if the demand of client i is assigned to facility j. Takes the value 1 if the assignment is made and 0 otherwise.

Minimizing Transportation Cost from Clients to Facilities. The Eq. 1 aims to minimize the total transportation cost from the clients (citizens) to the facilities (service modules). The transportation cost is calculated as the sum of the distance d_{ij} between each client i and the facility j, multiplied by a binary variable αX_{ij} that indicates whether client i is assigned to facility j.

$$Min\ f_1 = \sum_i^n \sum_j^m d_{ij}\alpha X_{ij} \qquad (1)$$

$$X_{ij} = \begin{cases} 1\ Customer\ demand\ (i)\ is\ assigned\ to\ facility\ (j) \\ 0 \qquad\qquad\quad Another\ case \end{cases} \qquad (2)$$

Maximize Facility Coverage, Subject to Capacity Constraints. The Eq. 3 aims to maximize the coverage of facilities, that is, to ensure that the largest possible number of clients is assigned to a facility. This is achieved by multiplying a binary variable D_{mij} that indicates whether the distance d_{ij} between client

i and facility j is less than or equal to a predefined maximum distance d_{mij}, where $d_{mij} = 6$ km. Additionally, another binary variable Y_{ij} is used to indicate whether the capacity of facility j (c_{ij}) is greater than or equal to the demand r_{ij} of the clients assigned to it.

$$Max\ f_2 = \sum_i^n \sum_j^m r_{ij} D_{mij} Y_{ij} \tag{3}$$

$$D_{mij} = \begin{cases} 1 & Si\ d_{ij} \leq d_{mij} \\ 0 & Another\ case \end{cases} \tag{4}$$

$$Y_{ij} = \begin{cases} 1 & Si\ c_{ij} \geq r_{ij} \\ 0 & Another\ case \end{cases} \tag{5}$$

4   Results Analysis

In this section, the results of the citizen assignment to the INE service modules are examined, and the benefits and limitations of each approach are analyzed.

1. Facilities Coverage: The number of citizens assigned to each service module was evaluated, considering the capacity constraints of each module. The results revealed a balanced and efficient allocation of citizens to the available modules.
2. Travel cost: The total distance traveled by citizens to reach the assigned modules was calculated. The results demonstrated a significant reduction in travel cost compared to non-optimized assignments.
3. Efficiency of the assignment: The overall quality of the obtained solutions was analyzed in terms of the satisfaction of the stated objectives. The results showed that the multi-objective assignment approach using NSGA-II generated optimal and high-quality solutions.
4. A comparison was conducted between the results obtained using the NSGA-II approach and those generated by traditional genetic algorithms, local search, and tabu search.
5. Measurements were conducted for each evaluated aspect, including facility coverage (see Table 3), transportation cost (see Table 4), assignment efficiency (see Table 5), and execution time (see Table 6).
6. Comparative tables will be presented to summarize and visualize the differences and advantages of NSGA-II in relation to the other evaluated algorithms.

The Table 3 shows that in scenarios 2 and 3, it can be observed that NSGA-II achieved a coverage of 98% and 97% respectively, while the genetic algorithms, local search, and tabu search algorithms obtained coverages lower or equal to 90%. This demonstrates that NSGA-II is the algorithm that achieves a more efficient and balanced assignment of citizens to service modules. In scenario 2, it is also observed that NSGA-II outperforms the other algorithms in terms of facility coverage. The coverage percentages for NSGA-II are 98% and 97% respectively, while the genetic algorithms, local search, and tabu search algorithms have lower coverages in both scenarios. The same case occurs in scenario 3.

Table 3. Comparison of facility coverage

Algorithm	Scenario 1	Scenario 2	Scenario 3
NSGA-II	100%	98%	97%
Genetic algorithms	100%	90%	85%
Local Search	100%	82%	78%
Tabu Search	100%	81%	76%

The Table 4 presents the comparison of travel cost. In scenario 2 and 3, NSGA-II achieved a travel cost of 5,108 m, while the genetic algorithms, local search, and tabu search algorithms had costs of 5,089 m, 5,091 m, and 5,089 m, respectively. Despite NSGA-II having slightly longer distances, it achieves greater coverage, making the solution more efficient. This same situation occurs in scenario 3.

Table 4. Comparison of transportation cost (in meters)

Algorithm	Scenario 1	Scenario 2	Scenario 3
NSGA-II	4,960.5 m	5,108 m	5,356 m
Genetic algorithms	4,965.5 m	5,089 m	5,223 m
Local Search	4,965.5 m	5,091 m	5,133 m
Tabu Search	4,965.5 m	5,089 m	5,433 m

The Table 5 presents the classification of solutions generated by NSGA-II in each simulated scenario using fuzzy logic. Quality categories such as "Optimal", "Good", "Acceptable", and "Non-optimal" were established and assigned to each solution based on the obtained results. In all scenarios, NSGA-II obtains an "Optimal" ranking in assignment efficiency. This indicates that the solutions generated by NSGA-II excel in meeting the assignment objectives, outperforming the other algorithms that receive "Good" or "Acceptable" rankings.

Table 5. Efficiency comparison of the assignment

Algorithm	Scenario 1	Scenario 2	Scenario 3
NSGA-II	Optimal	Optimal	Good
Genetic algorithms	Good	Good	Acceptable
Local Search	Acceptable	Acceptable	Acceptable
Tabu Search	Acceptable	Acceptable	Acceptable

Table 6 compares the execution times required by each algorithm (programmed in Python 3.2) to complete the assignment of citizens to the service modules in each of the simulated scenarios, using a computer with Windows 10 operating system, 6 GB of RAM, and 500 GB of SSD, Intel Core i7 10th gen. The execution time is measured in seconds and is an important metric for evaluating the efficiency and speed of the algorithms in solving the assignment problem.

Table 6. Runtime Comparison

Algorithm	Scenario 1	Scenario 2	Scenario 3
NSGA-II	210 s	235 s	256 s
Genetic algorithms	270 s	293 s	310 s
Local Search	138 s	150 s	178 s
Tabu Search	160 s	172 s	195 s

5   Conclusions and Future Work

The proposal of assigning the municipal population to the INE modules using the multi-objective optimization approach based on NSGA-II has proven to be an effective solution for the citizen assignment problem. Although this study focused on the population of the Toluca Valley, this methodology can be replicated in other areas of the country, as long as information on the capacity of each module and the population size is available.

In summary, this study presents a robust and efficient methodology that can be highly useful for the INE and other organizations facing similar assignment problems. It establishes a precedent for integrating multi-objective optimization and fuzzy logic in solving complex assignment problems. The NSGA-II based approach, evaluated using fuzzy logic, has demonstrated superior results compared to alternative methods such as traditional genetic algorithms, local search, ant colony optimization, and tabu search.

In conclusion, the presented methodology has a significant impact on the INE's practice by enabling a more efficient and effective assignment of citizens to the service modules. Furthermore, areas for future research are suggested, including the development of adaptive heuristics, the incorporation of additional decision criteria, and the application of the assignment approach in different geographical contexts. Additionally, exploring the integration of artificial intelligence and machine learning techniques to further improve assignment outcomes is recommended.

References

1. Chouksey, A., Agrawal, A.K., Tanksale, A.N.: A hierarchical capacitated facility location-allocation model for planning maternal healthcare facilities in India. Comput. Ind. Eng. **167**, 107991 (2022)
2. Coello, C.A.C., Brambila, S.G., Gamboa, J.F., Tapia, M.G.C.: Multi-objective evolutionary algorithms: past, present, and future. In: Pardalos, P.M., Rasskazova, V., Vrahatis, M.N. (eds.) Black Box Optimization, Machine Learning, and No-Free Lunch Theorems. SOIA, vol. 170, pp. 137–162. Springer, Cham (2021). https://doi.org/10.1007/978-3-030-66515-9 5
3. Deb, K., Pratap, A., Agarwal, S., Meyarivan, T.A.M.T.: A fast and elitist multi-objective genetic algorithm: NSGA-II. IEEE Trans. Evol. Comput. **6**(2), 182–197 (2002)
4. Deb, S., Dash, S.K., Mahapatra, S.S.: Sensitivity analysis in multi-objective optimization using evolutionary algorithms. In: Evolutionary Multi-Criterion Optimization, pp. 105–119. Springer, Heidelberg (2007)
5. García, J.L., Pérez, A., López, A.: Optimización de la asignación de ciudadanos a módulos de atención en el INE utilizando algoritmos genéticos. Actas del IV Congreso Internacional de Ciencias Computacionales y Sistemas (CICCS 2018), p. 139 (2018)
6. Harrison, E., Barlow, J.: Public participation in decision-making: a three-fold process. Front. Psychol. **8**, 235 (2017)
7. Pérez, B.C.Z.: Consejera Electoral del INE. Las elecciones en México 2017-2019, en perspectiva comparada, p. 10
8. Pezzica, C., Cutini, V., de Souza, C.B.: Mind the gap: state of the art on decision-making related to post-disaster housing assistance. Int. J. Disaster Risk Reduction **53**, 101975 (2021)
9. Li, F., Zhang, L., Liao, T.W., Liu, Y.: Multi-objective optimisation of multi-task scheduling in cloud manufacturing. Int. J. Prod. Res. **57**(12), 3847–3863 (2019)
10. Mousavi, S., Mood, S.E., Souri, A., Javidi, M.M.: Directed search: a new operator in NSGA-II for task scheduling in IoT based on cloud-fog computing. IEEE Trans. Cloud Comput. (2022)

Feature Engineering for Music/Speech Detection in Costa Rica Radio Broadcast

Juan Angel Acosta-Ceja[4], Marvin Coto-Jiménez[1]([✉]),
Máximo Eduardo Sánchez-Gutiérrez[2], Alma Rocío Sagaceta-Mejía[3],
and Julián Alberto Fresán-Figueroa[4]

[1] Universidad de Costa Rica, San Jose, Costa Rica
marvin.coto@ucr.ac.cr
[2] Colegio de Ciencia y Tecnología, Universidad Autónoma de la Ciudad de México,
Ciudad de México, Mexico
[3] Departamento de Física y Matemáticas, Universidad Iberoamericana, Ciudad de
México, Mexico
[4] Departamento de Matemáticas Aplicadas y Sistemas, Universidad Autónoma
Metropolitana Unidad Cuajimalpa, Ciudad de México, Mexico

Abstract. The exponential growth of audio data in radio broadcasts has generated the need for efficient tools for their manipulation and analysis to develop systems such as audio content classification and enhance user experience. In this study, we explore the application of classifiers to discriminate between speech and music in Costa Rican radio broadcasts. The main purpose is first to select the best features for classification algorithms to obtain the best classification performance in terms of computational cost. The study presents a comprehensive comparative analysis of feature-selection methods, introducing a novel proposal based on a voting mechanism that integrates various feature-selection techniques. The research contributes to refining audio content classification systems and analysis for particular accents within broadcast contexts.

Keywords: classification · feature selection · speech

1 Introduction

In recent years, there has been a significant increase in multimedia data, including video images and audio from radio and television broadcasts, as well as podcasts [1, 2]. This growth has created new demands for efficient tools to manipulate this type of data, such as transcription, summarization, description for different environments, and storage.

However, due to the sheer volume of audio data, it is impossible to create labels, descriptions, or transcriptions manually [14]. This problem has led to the emergence of audio content analysis (ACA) as a research field for extracting information directly from acoustic signals to perform tasks like classification, description, and semantic annotation [9].

E. Mezura-Montes et al. (Eds.): MCPR 2024, LNCS 14755, pp. 84–95, 2024.
https://doi.org/10.1007/978-3-031-62836-8_9

One of the primary challenges in ACA is distinguishing between music and speech, as both have distinct characteristics and applications. Furthermore, it is necessary to reduce the number of features to improve the performance and processing of data and models while accurately classifying speech and music with low delay and reduced complexity [13], given the extensive database data requiring efficient processing.

This study proposes using machine learning techniques to select features for speech/music classification of Costa Rican radio broadcasts. The goal is to reduce the number of features while maintaining or improving classification accuracy and minimizing computational costs. Two classifiers, Support Vector Machines (SVM) and K-Nearest Neighbor (KNN), are used to test for classification accuracy. Feature selection is performed using the Random Forest algorithm, as other classifiers, such as Naive Bayes, have low accuracy and high error rates for this application [9].

1.1   Related Work

Numerous recent studies have advanced the classification of speech and music, each proposing unique methodologies and feature sets. For instance, in [14], authors introduced a Spectral Peak Tracking (SPT) approach for modeling spectrogram patterns, utilizing features such as mean and standard deviation of peak traces. Another work by the same authors [15] explored phase-based features, emphasizing their potential through statistical significance tests and canonical correlation analyses.

Different sets of features have been examined, such as chromatogram textures and spectral features [16]. Their study involved transforming audio into chromatogram image representation and using uniform local binary pattern textural descriptors.

A more recent study [17] presented a convolutional neural network-based approach on Mel-spectrograms and MFCC-delta-RNN methods for separating music and speech. That research demonstrated superior results, especially in languages like Bengali, Punjabi, and Tamil. Additionally, they addressed the challenge of classifying audio segments with overlapped speech and music regions, achieving high accuracy.

Another study [18] analyzed a large set of features for speech/nonspeech discrimination, utilizing Principal Component Analysis (PCA) as the primary feature selection technique.

Our proposal employs several standard features, particularly chroma, MFCC, and many others related to energy, time, and frequency domains. We aim to enhance previous music and speech discrimination results for specific contexts by following the analysis of the studies above for particular accents and contexts but utilizing more feature selection algorithms.

1.2 Data and Feature Extraction

In this section, we will provide a description of the database utilized in this study. The database was compiled from podcasts of "Comunidad 870," a program run by the University of Costa Rica's "Radio 870." We extracted a dataset of 178 music files and 773 clean voices from this database. Notably, the file duration varies widely, with some lasting several minutes while others are only a few seconds [9].

We employed pyAudioAnalysis to extract features that cover three types of sets: Spectral and Energy Features (Energy), Mel Frequency Ceptral Coefficients (MFCC), and Chroma Vectors (Chroma) [10]. It is worth noting that pyAudio-Analysis regards these three sets of features as short-term, breaking down the input signal into short-term windows or frames and extracting features for each. Moreover, the feature extraction tool represents the signal through statistics of the short-term feature sequences extracted earlier, such as mean and standard deviation, called medium-term features. Additionally, delta features were incorporated for added information. In total, 136 features were obtained, encompassing short-term features, medium-term features, and delta functions to analyze each audio [10].

It is important to highlight that the audios are segmented, therefore, it is enough to identify voice and non-voice. This work does not consist of audio segmentation, but rather a classification work.

The remainder of this paper is structured as follows: Sect. 2 presents the Feature Selection Techniques applied to individual cases, and Sect. 3 presents the Pairwise Feature Selection techniques considered in the study. Section 4 presents the Results and Discussion, and finally, the Conclusions are presented in Sect. 5.

2 Individual Feature Selection

In machine learning, feature selection is crucial in improving model performance and efficiency by reducing dimensionality and eliminating noise or redundancy in a feature set.

The general idea of individual feature selection is to assign a score to each feature based on a specific criterion. The set of characteristics can be selected by choosing the best k characteristics or those whose score is greater than or equal to an established threshold. We define the following sets that will be used in this article.

Let $\mathcal{X} = \{\mathcal{C}_1, \mathcal{C}_2, \ldots, \mathcal{C}_m\}$ be the original feature set, and let $\mathcal{D}_i = \{d_1^{(i)}, d_2^{(i)}, \ldots, d_n^{(i)}\}$ be the data associated with feature $\mathcal{C}_i$ for each $i \in \{1, 2, \ldots, n\}$. Finally, we will say that $\overline{\mathcal{D}_i}$ is the mean of the set $\mathcal{D}_i$. For each Ci the following selection methods will be applied for $f : \mathcal{X} \to \mathbb{R}$.

2.1 Low Variance

Variance measures the degree of dispersion of data in a characteristic. A low variance (LV) implies less dispersion of data, therefore, it does not provide enough information and will be of less relevance [4]. Feature selection based on low variance is defined as follows:

$$f(\mathcal{C}_i) = \sum_{j=1}^{n} \frac{(d_j^{(i)} - \overline{\mathcal{D}_i})^2}{n},$$

(1)

2.2 Lasso

The Lasso regression operator is a technique for addressing overfitting problems and improving traditional regression models' generalization. Lasso introduces a penalty term based on the $L1$ norm of the feature weights in the linear regression [3]. Feature selection using Lasso can be defined as follows:

With a coefficient w_i, which minimizes the Lasso cost function using the following function:

$$f(\mathcal{C}_i; \lambda) = w_i,$$

(2)

where λ is the regularization parameter. The larger the value chosen for λ, the greater the penalty on feature weights w_j, and the more that will be removed.

2.3 Decision Trees

Decision trees are machine learning models for decision-making and data classification based on features [7]. The feature's position in the tree hierarchy permits selection using decision trees. Features are chosen by their level in the tree, with top-level features being the most relevant.

2.4 Principal Component Analissis (PCA)

Principal Component Analysis (PCA) is an algorithm for transforming correlated variables into uncorrelated variables called principal components, intending to reduce data dimensionality. Feature selection through PCA involves associating a vector with each original feature based on the eigenvectors of the covariance matrix. Features can be chosen by clustering the vectors and selecting the nearest vector to each centroid [5].

2.5 Mean Absolute Difference

Mean Absolute Difference (MAD) measures the disparity between the data values of a variable and its mean. Features with a higher MAD have more dispersed data, indicating greater relevance [12].

$$f(\mathcal{C}_i) = \frac{\sum |d_j^{(i)} - \overline{\mathcal{D}_i}|}{n},$$

(3)

2.6 Dispersion Ratio

The dispersion ratio (DR) is used to measure data variability. A DR close to 1 indicates low feature relevance, as it suggests that the data values are similar [6].

$$f(\mathcal{C}_i) = \frac{\overline{\mathcal{D}_i}}{\mathcal{D}_{gi}}, \tag{4}$$

were $\mathcal{D}_{gi}$ is the geometric mean of the set $\mathcal{D}_i$.

3 Pairwise Feature Selection

The methods described in this section do not assign a score to each feature; instead, they allow us to establish a relationship between pairs of features and in this case, establishes a relationship between the features and the classes.

3.1 Chi-Square Text

The Chi-Square test is used in statistics to evaluate the independence of events or variables, which consists of assigning an actual number to a pair of variables. A larger Chi-Square value commonly indicates a higher dependence between the two variables. If the expected frequency equals the observed frequency, the Chi-Square value is zero, indicating no dependence [4].

$$\chi^2(\mathcal{C}_i, \mathcal{C}_j) = \sum \frac{(f_0 - f_e)^2}{f_e}, \tag{5}$$

where f_0 is the observed frequency, and f_e is the expected frequency. It is important to note that the Chi-Square test aims to investigate the existence of a relationship between variables.

3.2 Pearson Correlation

The Pearson correlation coefficient calculates the linear relationship between two random variables. Its values range between -1 and 1. A value of 1 indicates a perfectly positive correlation, meaning that as one variable increases, the other also does. A value of -1 indicates a perfectly negative correlation, meaning that as one variable increases, the other decreases. A value of 0 suggests no linear relationship [11]. The following expression gives the coefficient:
    Where

$$\rho(\mathcal{C}_i, \mathcal{C}_j) = \frac{\mathrm{Cov}(\mathcal{D}_i, \mathcal{D}_j)}{\sqrt{\mathrm{Var}(\mathcal{D}_i) \cdot \mathrm{Var}(\mathcal{D}_j)}}, \tag{6}$$

where $\mathrm{Cov}(\mathcal{D}_i, \mathcal{D}_j)$ is the covariance, and $\mathrm{Var}(\mathcal{D}_i)$ is the variance.

4   Methodology

This study was designed to evaluate and compare different feature selection methods and their performance for KNN and SVM classifiers on a dataset. The methodological process followed is described below along with its diagram Fig. 1:

1. Application of Selection Methods: Feature selection methods were applied both individually and in pairs on the aforementioned data set.
2. Extraction of the Best Features: The best k features were extracted for each selection method, limiting the maximum number of features to 60%. In addition, a threshold was established for all characteristics, discarding those that did not reach it.
3. "Approval Vote" Criterion: This criterion was introduced to determine new sets of features from the selection methods. This criterion required a predefined number of votes to identify the best features among the algorithms. Specifically, features were selected with a minimum of 8, 7, 6 and 5 votes denoted as AV8, AV7, AV6 and AV5 respectively. These sets were considered potential and relevant selections for the analysis in terms of contributing to the classification problem.
4. Creating Training and Test Sets: Ten different training and test sets were created from the dataset, using a test set size of 30%. Subsequently, two machine learning models (SVM and KNN) were trained for each of the selection methods, and their performance information was recorded.
5. Results Averaging and Table Creation: The performance results of the models were averaged and the corresponding Tables 1, 2 were created for further analysis.

5   Results and Discussion

Each feature selection algorithm was applied to the entire feature set to facilitate the comparison in terms of the number of features and the performance of the classification algorithms, as demonstrated in Tables 1 and 2. Considering that the primary objectives are to minimize the number of features and maximize accuracy, we emphasize feature selection methods that demonstrate robust performance in terms of accuracy while achieving a significant reduction in the number of features.

It is important to note that the maximum number of features for each selection method was established after several tests, revealing that surpassing 60% decreases accuracy for all selection methods compared to using all features, as demonstrated in Tables 1 and 2. Exceeding this limit could lead to a significant loss of accuracy, an undesirable outcome for our KNN and SVM models. It is noteworthy that Tables 1 and 2 show methods with fewer features. This reduction is attributed to applying a threshold that excludes features failing to surpass it, thereby discarding them from the analysis.

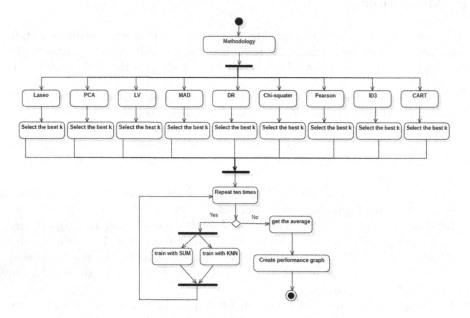

Fig. 1. Flowchart for the methodology

Table 1. Evaluation of KNN results for each feature selection method. The Energy, MFCC and Chroma columns indicate the number of features selected from each of these sets.

KNN Selection Method	Energy	MFCC	Chroma	Accuracy	Precision	Recall	F1 Score
DR	22	31	28	0.96	0.96	0.96	0.96
ID3*	4*	4*	5*	0.96*	0.96*	0.96*	0.96*
Approval voting 5	16	27	14	0.96	0.96	0.96	0.96
MAD	19	33	29	0.96	0.96	0.96	0.96
Low Variance	19	32	30	0.95	0.96	0.95	0.95
Approval Voting 7	4	4	2	0.95	0.95	0.95	0.95
Complete	32	52	52	0.95	0.95	0.95	0.95
PCA	18	31	32	0.95	0.95	0.95	0.95
Chi-Square	20	33	28	0.95	0.95	0.95	0.95
Approval voting 6	9	11	4	0.95	0.95	0.95	0.95
Pearson	18	35	28	0.95	0.95	0.95	0.95
CART	3	2	1	0.95	0.95	0.95	0.94
Approval voting 8*	3*	1*	0*	0.95*	0.95*	0.95*	0.94*
Random Forest	8	11	2	0.94	0.94	0.94	0.94
Lasso	2	3	0	0.90	0.90	0.90	0.90

Table 2. Evaluation of SVM results for each feature selection method. The Energy, MFCC and Chroma columns indicate the number of features selected from each of these sets.

SVM							
Selection Method	Energy	MFCC	Chroma	Accuracy	Precision	Recall	F1 Score
Pearson	18	35	28	0.97	0.97	0.97	0.97
Complete Data	32	52	52	0.97	0.97	0.97	0.97
MAD	19	33	29	0.97	0.97	0.97	0.97
Low Variance	19	32	30	0.97	0.97	0.97	0.97
Chi-Square	20	33	28	0.97	0.97	0.97	0.97
Approval voting 5*	16*	27*	14*	0.97*	0.97*	0.97*	0.97*
PCA	18	31	32	0.97	0.97	0.97	0.97
Approval voting 6	9	11	4	0.96	0.96	0.96	0.96
ID3	4	4	5	0.96	0.96	0.96	0.96
Random Forest	8	11	2	0.96	0.96	0.96	0.95
Approval voting 7*	4*	4*	2*	0.96*	0.96*	0.96*	0.95*
Approval voting 8*	3*	1*	0*	0.94*	0.94*	0.94*	0.93*
CART	3	2	1	0.93	0.93	0.93	0.93
DR	22	31	28	0.93	0.93	0.93	0.92
Lasso	2	3	0	0.90	0.90	0.90	0.89*

From this perspective, we consider a selection method S as a vector (a, f), where a represents its accuracy and f denotes the total number of features it contains. This representation allows us to quantify the quality of feature selection methods in terms of their performance and efficiency. Then, given two selection methods $S_1 = (a_1, f_1)$ and $S_2 = (a_2, f_2)$, we say that method S_1 is better than S_2 if $a_1 > a_2$ and $f_1 < f_2$, i.e., a method S_1 is considered better than S_2 if it achieves higher accuracy and uses a smaller number of features. This approach allows us to construct a partial ranking order that prioritizes the different selection methods, prioritizing those that maximize the accuracy and minimize the complexity of the feature set.

The best feature selection methods can be observed in Tables 1 and 2, marked with an asterisk. Based on this information, a performance graph where each point represents a selection method can be created, as shown in Fig. 4. The best results are denoted with a black star; any methods within the region bounded by the dotted lines exhibit inferior performance, either at a higher number of features or having lower accuracy. In this case, the AV8, AV7 and AV5 methods stood out as the most effective for the SVM algorithm (Fig. 2). On the other hand, AV8 and ID3 methods are the ones that stand out for KNN (Fig.3). It is important to highlight that when comparing both classification models, the AV5, AV7 of SVM-selected and AV8 of KNN-selected feature sets prevail as the better ones (Fig. 4).

From this perspective, Table 3 shows the features with the highest approval rating, i.e., those that received at least seven votes. It is important to note that the LV, MAD, DR, and Chi-Square methods selected all available features.

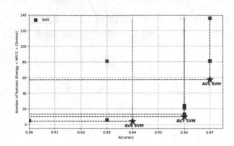

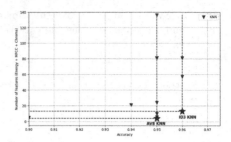

Fig. 2. Performance of the SVM selection methods.

Fig. 3. Performance of KNN selection methods.

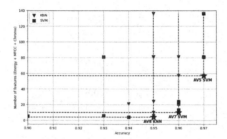

Fig. 4. Performance of the KNN and SVM selection methods.

It is relevant to note that, although the same accuracy was not achieved with all attributes in [9], in general terms superior results were observed with feature selection. The maximum performance obtained was with 84 attributes (Energy with MFCC), achieving an accuracy of 0.98, while in our case we achieved 0.96 using only 13 attributes with the ID3 algorithm and 0.95 with AV 8 for KNN. Regarding SVM, the previous study achieved an accuracy of 0.90 with 84 attributes (Energy with MFCC and Chroma), while we obtained 0.97 with AV 5, 0.96 with AV 7 and 0.94 with AV 8.

Figure 5 reveals that the features selected by a maximum of three methods are primarily associated with PCA and DR methods. When considering this in conjunction with Figurate 3 and Table 3, it becomes evident that these methods exhibited equal accuracy, even with 60% of the features. In other words, although these methods incorporate features with higher approbatory votes, a subset of these features possesses low relevance (indicated by a lower number of votes), which does not contribute significantly to the performance of the classification models.

Regarding PCA, its suboptimal performance can be attributed to its unsupervised nature, neglecting the relationship between features and the target variable. Additionally, PCA relies heavily on the K-Means algorithm for feature selection, introducing variability in results with the same dataset due to its

Table 3. Voting table of each selection method for the features with the highest evidential vote.

Feature	LV	Lasso	PCA	CART	ID3	Random Forest	MAD	DR	Chi-Square	Pearson	total
Delta Chroma 12 std	x				x	x	x	x	x	x	7
Delta MFCC 2 std	x		x			x	x	x	x	x	7
Delta MFCC 3 std	x	x				x	x	x	x	x	7
Chroma 10 Mean	x		x		x		x	x	x	x	7
Delta MFCC 1 std	x		x	x		x	x	x	x		7
Delta Spectral Centroid std	x			x	x	x	x	x	x		7
MFCC 3 Mean	x	x	x	x		x	x	x	x		8
Spectral Flux Mean	x	x	x	x	x	x	x	x	x	x	10
Energy Entropy Mean	x	x	x	x	x	x	x	x	x	x	10
ZCR Mean	x	x	x	x	x	x	x	x	x	x	10

random initialization of centroids. The initial placement of centroids may impact the algorithm's outcome, potentially converging to a local minimum rather than the global optimum.

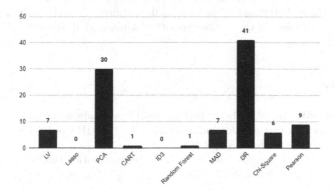

Fig. 5. Number of features chosen by the selection methods for those that were chosen only by 1, 2 or 3 methods. In total, 51 features were identified that meet this criterion.

6 Conclusion

The study's findings reveal that none of the three feature sets (Energy, MFCC, and Chroma) have significant classification relevance when used alone. Instead, to attain better results, combining features from these sets is crucial.

The Approval Voting algorithm plays a vital role in the classification models by selecting optimal attributes from various methods. These feature sets display more dispersion in their respective data, effectively reducing impurity and entropy within the dataset. Moreover, they significantly reduce the problem's dimensionality, enabling a more nuanced observation of variable dependencies. In this specific problem, the Approval Voting algorithm yields the most favorable classification results.

Future investigations should delve into a detailed analysis of MFCC and Chroma features. Results indicate a slight preference towards the initial MFCC features, highlighting their importance in speech recognition. Additionally, there seems to be a preference for later Chromas, raising questions about potential biases in the samples towards specific musical genres or male/female voices. Further exploration of these aspects could enhance our understanding of feature dynamics and their impact on classification outcomes. Also, giving different weights to each selection method is an area of opportunity to improve the Approval Voting sets.

Acknowledgments. This work was partially funded by the authors' universities and the *Consejo Nacional de Ciencia y Tecnología (CONACyT)* from México. Its contents are the responsibility of the authors and do not reflect the views of the research granting bodies. The authors were responsible for the data analysis after the extraction and linkage.

Alma Rocío Sagaceta Mejía would like to thank the support of Universidad Iberoamericana, Ciudad de México. Julián Alberto Fresán Figueroa and Juan Angel Acosta Ceja would like to thank the support of Universidad Autónoma Metropolitana, Unidad Cuajimalpa. Máximo Eduardo Sánchez Gutiérrez would like to thank the support of Universidad Autónoma de la Ciudad de México, Unidad Cuautepec. Marvin Coto Jiménez would like to thank the support of Universidad de Costa Rica, Escuela de Ingeniería Eléctrica.

References

1. Rachna, R., Mishra, M.: The growth of audio podcasts as an emergent form of streaming content category for Indian audiences. In: AIP Conference Proceedings, vol. 2523, no. 1. AIP Publishing (2023)
2. Aujla-Sidhu, G.: The power of podcasting: telling stories through sound. Radio J. Int. Stud. Broadcast Audio Media **21**(1) (2023). https://doi.org/10.1386/rjao_00077_5
3. Bukov, M., et al.: A high-bias, low-variance introduction to machine learning for physicists. Phys. Rep. **810**, 1–124 (2019)
4. Cheng, K., et al.: Feature Selection. ACM Comput. Surv. **50**(6), 1–45 (2017). https://doi.org/10.1145/3136625
5. Cohen, I.S., Lu, Y., Tian, Q., Zhou, X.: Feature selection using principal feature analysis (2007). https://doi.org/10.1145/1291233.1291297
6. Ferreira, A.J., Figueiredo, M.A.: Efficient feature selection filters for high dimensional data. Pattern Recognit. Lett. **33**(13), 1794–1804 (2012). https://www.sciencedirect.com/science/article/pii/S0167865512001870

7. Gupta, R., Priyam, A., Rathee, A., Srivastava, S.: Comparative Analysis of Decision Tree Classification Algorithms. INPRESSCO (2013). http://inpressco.com/wp-content/uploads/2013/03/Paper17334-3371.pdf
8. Ghosal, A., Dutta, S.: Speech/music discrimination using perceptual feature. In: Computational Science and Engineering: Proceedings of the International Conference on Computational Science and Engineering (Beliaghata, Kolkata, India, 4–6 October 2016). CRC Press (2016)
9. Sánchez-Solís, J., Coto-Jiménez, M.: Comparación de cuatro clasificadores para la discriminación de voz y música: un primer estudio de caso para la radiodifusión costarricense . Revista Tecnología En Marcha **35**(8), 119–127 (2022). https://doi.org/10.18845/tm.v35i8.6463
10. Giannakopoulos, T.: Pyaudioanalysis: an open-source python library for audio signal analysis. PLoS ONE **10**(12), e0144610 (2015)
11. Rincón, L.: Introducción a la probabilidad (2.a ed.). Universidad Nacional Autónoma de México, Facultad de Ciencias (2016). http://lya.fciencias.unam.mx/lars/Publicaciones/Prob1-2016.pdf
12. Simaan, Y.: Estimation risk in portfolio selection: the mean vairance model versus the mean absolute deviation model. Manage. Sci. **43**, 1437–1446 (1997)
13. Wu, Q., et al.: A combination of data mining method with decision trees building for speech/music discrimination. Comput. Speech Lang. **24**(2), 257–272 (2010)
14. Bhattacharjee, M., Prasanna, S.R.M., Guha, P.: Speech/music classification using features from spectral peaks. IEEE/ACM Trans. Audio Speech Lang. Process. **28**, 1549–1559 (2020)
15. Bhattacharjee, M., Prasanna, S.R.M., Guha, P.: Speech/music classification using phase-based and magnitude-based features. Speech Commun. **142**, 34–48 (2022)
16. Birajdar, G.K., Patil, M.D.: Speech/music classification using visual and spectral chromagram features. J. Ambient. Intell. Humaniz. Comput. **11**, 329–347 (2020)
17. Sawant, O., Bhowmick, A., Bhagwat, G.: Separation of speech & music using temporal-spectral features and neural classifiers. Evol. Intell. 1–15 (2023)
18. Redelinghuys, H., Wang, Z.: Evaluating audio features for speech/non-speech discrimination. In: 2022 First International Conference on Artificial Intelligence Trends and Pattern Recognition (ICAITPR). IEEE (2022)

Towards a Novel Approach for Knowledge Base Population Using Distant Supervision

Juan-Luis García-Mendoza[1], Davide Buscaldi[1], Lázaro Bustio-Martínez[3(✉)],
Kata Gábor[2], Haïfa Zargayouna[1], Thierry Charnois[1],
and Vitali Herrera-Semenets[4]

[1] Université Sorbonne Paris Nord, LIPN. 99 Av. Jean Baptiste Clément,
Villetaneuse, France
{garciamendoza,davide.buscaldi,haifa.zargayouna,
thierry.charnois}@lipn.univ-paris13.fr
[2] Institut National des Langues et Civilisations Orientales, 65 rue des Grands
Moulins, Paris, France
kata.gabor@inalco.fr
[3] Department of Engineering Studies for Innovation, Iberoamerican University,
Prolongación Paseo de Reforma 880, 01219 Mexico City, Mexico
lazaro.bustio@ibero.mx
[4] Advanced Technologies Application Center (CENATAV),
7a 21406, Playa, Havana, Cuba
vherrera@cenatav.co.cu

Abstract. Distant Supervision is an approach in Relation Extraction
that automatically labels a dataset using a Knowledge Base as a guide.
However, the incompleteness of Knowledge Bases poses a significant challenge, leading to incorrectly labeled sentences due to the absence of corresponding relations. This study introduces a novel approach to enhance
and complete Knowledge Bases, aiming to reduce false negatives in labeling using Distant Supervision. A key aspect of this approach is determining whether an instance expresses a specific relation. To address this,
it is proposed a novel unsupervised method based on Deep Embedding
Clustering. The experiments conducted demonstrated the effectiveness
of the proposed method, outperforming several state-of-the-art methods even when subjected to varying percentages of incorrectly labeled
instances. Furthermore, the proposed method shows promising performance in identifying relations with similar characteristics. Finally, we
evaluate various threshold levels to determine the presence of a specific
relation in an instance.

Keywords: Knowledge Base Population · Relation Extraction ·
Distant Supervision · Deep Embedding Clustering

© The Author(s), under exclusive license to Springer Nature Switzerland AG 2024
E. Mezura-Montes et al. (Eds.): MCPR 2024, LNCS 14755, pp. 96–106, 2024.
https://doi.org/10.1007/978-3-031-62836-8_10

1   Introduction

Information Extraction is recognized as a crucial process used to build and populate Knowledge Bases (KBs) [13]. KBs serve as central components in various Artificial Intelligence applications although the "degree" of intelligence in such systems is dependent on the completeness and coverage of the KBs. Thus, it becomes evident that populating the KBs with relevant entities and relations is of paramount importance in covering the problem domain.

KBs play a pivotal role in guiding the task of Relation Extraction (RE) by providing a structured and organized source of information that can be utilized to identify and classify relations between entities. An illustrative example of this concept is provided by Distant Supervision (DS), where a RE dataset is automatically labeled using the entities and relations present in the KBs. DS generally adheres to the heuristic or assumption proposed by [15], who posited that *"if two entities participate in a relation, any sentence that contains those two entities might express that relation."* One of the most significant challenges associated with automatic labeling in DS stems from the coverage and completeness of the KBs. As noted by [18], *"since the Knowledge Base is incomplete, the absence of a relation label does not necessarily imply the absence of the corresponding relation."* False negatives are primarily a result of the incompleteness of KBs.

The research presented in this paper is focused on proposing a novel approach for the automated population of KBs. This approach addresses two primary issues: Incompleteness of the KBs and False Negatives Introduced by DS. Additionally, this research makes a significant contribution by proposing a novel unsupervised method for determining whether a given instance expresses a particular relation.

2   Related Work

KBs are usually incomplete because it is not possible to cover all knowledge [14]. Furthermore, these KBs are generally built manually. Nevertheless, several authors have tried to deal with this problem in a semi-supervised [14] or supervised [21] way. However, the dataset used was constructed following the assumption proposed by [15], which introduces instances with wrong labels. In [6], an unsupervised approach is proposed to handle these instances and improve the final classification results. This approach uses classic Autoencoders [8] and Adversarial Autoencoders [12] to obtain representations that allow identifying and eliminating wrongly labeled instances.

A fundamental aspect of the approach proposed in [6] is obtaining data representations. In [5], the authors evaluated various data representations, including the Autoencoders (AE) and Adversarials Autoencoders (AAE) models from [6], which outperformed pre-trained embeddings, as well as traditional representations like bag of words and TF-IDF, in reducing noise. Additionally, there are other methods such as ProtoRE [3], Deep Embedded Clustering (DEC) [20], Ada-002 by OpenAI [16], and Instructor [19] that have been used to obtain data representations from text.

Regarding the Instructor model, it achieves the best state-of-the-art performance in text embedding benchmarks, demonstrating superior results across 70 diverse datasets [19]. The embedding process with the Instructor model involves the inclusion of both: the input text and its associated end task, and domain instructions. This marks a departure from previous embedding methods, which typically focus solely on text input. Instructor, in contrast, embeds the same input into distinct vectors tailored to specific end goals.

The approach presented by [6] for noise reduction serves as the foundational framework for the approach proposed in this research. However, this study operates under the assumption that more effective sentence representations, particularly when compared to AE and AAE, can be derived through the application of DEC. It is expected that these enhanced representations will lead to improved precision in identifying instances with correct labels. Another notable aspect of this research involves the adoption of a distinct method for each relation, as it is recommended in [6, 21].

3   Notations

To facilitate a better understanding of the theoretical foundations of this research, certain notations are introduced. Let it be:

- $\mathcal{E} = \{e_z \mid z = 1 \ldots |\mathcal{E}|\}$: Set of entities.
- $\mathcal{R} = \{r_j \mid j = 1 \ldots |\mathcal{R}|\}$: Set of labels (relations), including $\mathcal{NA}$ representing the negative class. $\mathcal{R}^\dagger = \mathcal{R}/\{\mathcal{NA}\}$.
- $\Gamma = \{(h, r, t) \mid h, t \in \mathcal{E}, r \in \mathcal{R}^\dagger\}$: Set of triplets, known as Knowledge Base.
- $\mathcal{S} = \{s_i \mid i = 1 \ldots |\mathcal{S}|\}$: Set of sentences, each containing two entities $(h_i, t_i) \in \mathcal{E}$.
- $\mathcal{X} = \{x_k \mid x_k = (s_i, r_j) \in \mathcal{S} \times \mathcal{R}^\dagger\}$: Labeled instances obtained using DS.
- $\mathcal{U} = \{x_l \mid x_l = (s_i, \mathcal{NA})\}$: Instances with $\mathcal{NA}$ relation obtained using DS.
- $C : \mathcal{S} \to \mathcal{R}^\dagger$: Classifier assigning a relation label $r_j \in \mathcal{R}^\dagger$ to a given sentence $s_i \in \mathcal{S}$.
- $f_r : \mathcal{S}_r \to \mathcal{V}_r$: Function mapping sentences to vector representations for each $r \in \mathcal{R}^\dagger$.
- $g_r : \mathcal{S}_r \xrightarrow{f_r} \mathcal{V}_r \to \mathcal{R}$: Function assigning a relation label based on the vector representation, where $g_r(s_i) = \begin{cases} r & \text{if correct}(v_i) \\ \mathcal{NA} & \text{otherwise} \end{cases}$.

4   Proposal

The proposed approach begins with a set of sentences $\mathcal{S}$, where each $s_i \in \mathcal{S}$ contains two entities $(h, t \in \mathcal{E})$ that have been identified. These sentences are labeled with the corresponding relation $(r_j \in \mathcal{R})$ using a combination of KB and DS approaches. The collection of all sentences thus annotated by the DS method collectively forms the set of instances referred to as $\mathcal{X}$. Sentences with relation

$r_j = \mathcal{NA}$ (representing cases where h and t are not related in the Knowledge Base) are added to the set of instances $\mathcal{U}$. Following the concept proposed in [6], the instances in $\mathcal{X}$ are first processed using functions f and g and then utilized in the classifier $\mathcal{C}$. Furthermore, f and g are jointly trained using sentences that belong to the same relation r (see Algorithm 1). Subsequently, the set $\mathcal{U}$ is iterated upon using the procedure formalized in Algorithm 2, as described below:

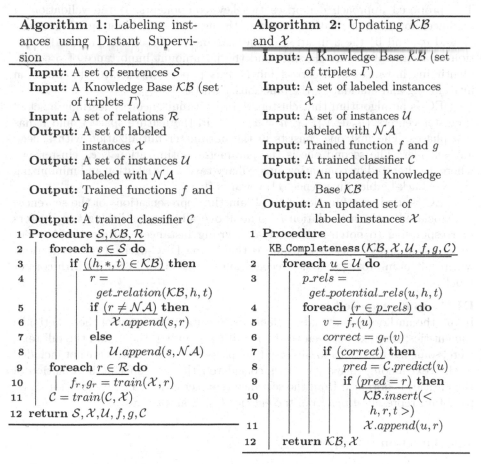

Algorithm 1: Labeling instances using Distant Supervision

Input: A set of sentences $\mathcal{S}$
Input: A Knowledge Base $\mathcal{KB}$ (set of triplets Γ)
Input: A set of relations $\mathcal{R}$
Output: A set of labeled instances $\mathcal{X}$
Output: A set of instances $\mathcal{U}$ labeled with $\mathcal{NA}$
Output: Trained functions f and g
Output: A trained classifier $\mathcal{C}$

1 **Procedure** $\mathcal{S}, \mathcal{KB}, \mathcal{R}$
2   **foreach** $s \in \mathcal{S}$ **do**
3   **if** $((h, *, t) \in \mathcal{KB})$ **then**
4        $r = $ get_relation$(\mathcal{KB}, h, t)$
5   **if** $(r \neq \mathcal{NA})$ **then**
6          $\mathcal{X}$.append(s, r)
7   **else**
8          $\mathcal{U}$.append$(s, \mathcal{NA})$
9   **foreach** $r \in \mathcal{R}$ **do**
10      $f_r, g_r = $ train$(\mathcal{X}, r)$
11    $\mathcal{C} = $ train$(\mathcal{C}, \mathcal{X})$
12 **return** $\mathcal{S}, \mathcal{X}, \mathcal{U}, f, g, \mathcal{C}$

Algorithm 2: Updating $\mathcal{KB}$ and $\mathcal{X}$

Input: A Knowledge Base $\mathcal{KB}$ (set of triplets Γ)
Input: A set of labeled instances $\mathcal{X}$
Input: A set of instances $\mathcal{U}$ labeled with $\mathcal{NA}$
Input: Trained function f and g
Input: A trained classifier $\mathcal{C}$
Output: An updated Knowledge Base $\mathcal{KB}$
Output: An updated set of labeled instances $\mathcal{X}$

1 **Procedure** KB_Completeness$(\mathcal{KB}, \mathcal{X}, \mathcal{U}, f, g, \mathcal{C})$
2   **foreach** $u \in \mathcal{U}$ **do**
3   p_rels $= $ get_potential_rels(u, h, t)
4   **foreach** $(r \in$ p_rels$)$ **do**
5        $v = f_r(u)$
6   correct $= g_r(v)$
7   **if** $(correct)$ **then**
8   pred $= \mathcal{C}$.predict(u)
9   **if** $(pred = r)$ **then**
10            $\mathcal{KB}$.insert$(< h, r, t >)$
11            $\mathcal{X}$.append(u, r)
12   **return** $\mathcal{KB}, \mathcal{X}$

- For each sentence $s_i \in \mathcal{U}$, its potential relations $r_j \in \mathcal{R}^\dagger$ are obtained using the entity types.
- Then, for each sentence $s_i \in \mathcal{U}$, their corresponding representation is obtained in a latent space $\mathcal{V}_r$ with the function f_r associated with each potential relation $r \in \mathcal{R}^\dagger$.
- For each instance s_i represented in the latent space $\mathcal{V}_r$ corresponding to a potential relation $r \in \mathcal{R}^\dagger$, the function g is employed to ascertain the correctness of the relation label.
- If, within the set $\mathcal{U}$, s_i possesses at least one correct label according to the function g, then the instance is subjected to classification by $\mathcal{C}$ to validate the label. Here, $\mathcal{C}$ can be any state-of-the-art method in DS or RE.

- If the classifier's prediction aligns with one of the labels identified as correct by g, and the triplet formed by (h, r, t) is not present in the KB, it is incorporated into the KB under the condition that it meets certain criteria.

4.1 Proposed f Function

The proposed approach comprises two key components: i) the validation of instances for a given relation, achieved through the combination of functions f_r and g_r, and ii) the utilization of the classifier $\mathcal{C}$. Given the proposed adoption of a state-of-the-art classifier and the paramount importance of precisely identifying instances with correct labels, this paper concentrates its efforts on introducing and elucidating the functions f and g.

DEC is an algorithm that clusters data by simultaneously learning a set of k cluster centers $\{\mu_n \in \mathcal{V}\}_{n=1}$, $n = 1, \ldots, k$ in the feature space $\mathcal{V}$ and it has two phases. The first one consists in the parameter initialization with a deep autoencoder. The second one is the parameter optimization (*i.e.*, clustering), where it is iterated by computing an auxiliary target distribution and minimizing the Kullback-Leibler divergence [11] towards it.

DEC is used as a function f to obtain the representations of the sentences s_i associated with each relation r_j. The above allows establishing two clusters (corresponding to potential correct and wrong instances) within the Autoencoder latent space. The expectation is that using DEC-derived representations will result in improved sentence recognition precision for instances with correct labels.

DEC input proposed.
In [5], the authors concatenate 4 elements to obtain the input of their methods: the entities, the text between the two entities including them, and the full text. Here, some modifications to this input are proposed. The entities are not included in the text among themselves. It is considered that the specific information of the entities is obtained from the sentence representation. The use of TransE [2] to obtain representations from the entities $h \in \mathcal{E}$ and $t \in \mathcal{E}$.

4.2 Function g Proposed

The function f is employed for obtaining the sentence representations. It utilizes a loss function that combines the Reconstruction Loss (rl) from the latent space of the Autoencoder and the Clustering Loss. The use of rl is proposed as function g assuming that "an instance has a correct label when its reconstruction error is lower than the average of all errors". The assumption here is that if the error in the reconstruction of an instance exceeds the average error, it indicates that its representation in the latent space did not fit correctly to the learned distribution. In the experiments section, the proposed method refers to DEC (function f) and rl (function g).

5   Experiments

The goal of the first experiment is to evaluate the precision of the proposed method in identifying instances belonging to the correct class. To achieve this, the SemEval-2010 Task 8 (SemEval2010) [7] dataset was employed. As this dataset lacks noise in the relations, instances of the $\mathcal{NA}$ class were randomly introduced into each relation.

The chosen metric for evaluation is macro-precision concerning instances in the correct class. This choice is justified because all instances in the set $\mathcal{U}$ are initially considered as incorrect instances due to the absence of a relation between their entities in the $\mathcal{KB}$. It is crucial to ensure precision when determining an instance's correctness, even when it undergoes dual validation by the classifier. This approach ensures that only instances with a high degree of confidence in their representation matching specific relations are passed to the relation classifier.

Platform. The platform used for conduct the experiments was an Intel(R) Xeon(R) Gold 6248 CPU @ 2.50GHz equipped with 2 sockets, 20 cores per socket, 80 CPUs and 256 GB of RAM. Additionally, an 8 GPUs Tesla V100-SXM2 with 32 GB of RAM was used.

Dataset. SemEval2010 dataset is used in this study because it facilitates controlled experimentation and prior knowledge of correct and wrong instances [5]. In the research carried out by [5], instances associated with the relations $\mathcal{NA}$ were considered wrong labels. This presents an advantage in comparison to the distantly labeled dataset New York Times 2010 (NYT2010), proposed by [17], where the proportions of these labels are not known in advance.

SemEval2010 has ten relations, nine positive labels without overlap [4] and "Other" label, which represents $\mathcal{NA}$. The nine positive relations are represented in a bidirectional way, becoming 18 relations, which, when adding $\mathcal{NA}$, are 19. The total of instances is 8000 and 2717 for the train and test partitions respectively. The relation $\mathcal{NA}$ is not included because it is the negative class nor "Entity-Destination(e2,e1)" because it contains a single instance.

Noise Generation. In order to evaluate the proposed method it is imperative to incorporate instances with wrong labels. These instances are introduced into each relation by means of a random selection process from the $\mathcal{NA}$ label. The number of instances to include is determined by selecting a percentage of the total instances of each positive class. In the following experiments 10% and 30% are used. For example, the relation *Product-Producer(e1,e2)* has 108 test instances, so it were added 11 and 33 wrong instances respectively.

Comparative Methods. The following methods were considered for performance comparison:

- Autoencoders and Adverarial Autoencoders [6]: These methods are used as functions f. In [6], they outperforms several representations for noise reduction. The input of these methods is obtained with LASER [1].

- ProtoRE [3]: The authors propose a method that learns predictive, interpretable and robust representations of semantic relations.
- OpenAI text embeddings (Ada-002 model) [16]: It was decided to incorporate these embeddings due to the usefulness of chatGPT and openAI in several tasks. The OpenAI endpoint is used as the function f to obtain the representations of the sentences s_i for each realtion r_j.
- Instructor [19]: This method obtains representations from an instruction where task and domain descriptions can be specified. *E.g.*: the instruction: "Represent the sentence for the relation extraction task:" is employed in the acquisition of representations for each of the instances.

In [6], an instance is determined to have a wrong label when its distance cosine or euclidean to the rest of the instances exceeds than the average. This assumption is used as function g in all the previous cases.

Proposed Method. Different configurations of function f were evaluated in order to validate the proposed method. In all cases rl (see Sect. 4.2) was used as function g.

- DEC combines the 4 input elements of the input. Two variants are evaluated in the input representation. In the first of them, LASER pretrained embeddings is exclusively employed and is referred to as DEC in the experimental context. In the second, a fusion of the LASER and TransE is employed, as proposed in Sect. 4.1, and is denoted as DEC_Transe.
- DEC using the 4 elements as independent input as explained in Sect. 4.1. The same aforementioned variants are evaluated. On one hand, the input obtained using LASER is labeled as DEC_m. On the other hand, the fusion of LASER and TransE is denoted as DEC_Transe_m.

Statistical Tests. To ensure a rigorous and unbiased evaluation of performance, it is imperative to conduct multiple replications, thereby mitigating the potential influence of random chance on our results. The determination of the number of replications, also referred to as the sample size, was carried out through power analysis [10]. The number of replications was determined using ANOVA One Way test for a desired significance level of 0.05, statistical power of $\beta = 0.95$ and assuming an effect size of Cohen's $d = 0.4$. The results was 17 repetitions per method. From the results of the replications, ANOVA One Way test is applied to know if there are significant differences between the results achieved. Finally, if there were significant differences, pairwise comparisons were made to observe which pair of methods showed differences. The two-by-two comparisons were made with t-test and Holm Correction [9]. The significance threshold was set at $p < 0.05$.

5.1 Results

Macro-precision Detecting Correct Instance. Table 1 shows the macroprecision after 17 iterations for correct and wrong labels introducing 10% of wrong instances in the test partition. It can be seen how the proposed method significantly surpasses the results of the rest of the methods and configurations. Significant differences were found (ANOVA: $F(8, 142) = 97.23, p < 2e^{-16}$) in the precision values for the correct labels. Also, the proposed method (DEC_Transe_m) presents significant differences from the other methods in pairwise comparisons with t-test.

When introducing 30% noise, the results obtained are similar (see Table 1). Significant differences (ANOVA: $F(8, 144) = 197, p < 2e^{-16}$) were found among the results of all methods. Similarly, pairwise comparisons indicate that DEC_Transe_m is statistically superior to the rest.

The results obtained by introducing both percentage values validate the assumptions of this paper regarding the improvement in the representations and identification of correct instances.

Table 1. Precision with different levels of noise.

Method	10%		30%	
	Correct class	Wrong class	Correct class	Wrong class
AE	0.967 ± 0.007	0.153 ± 0.010	0.898 ± 0.016	0.336 ± 0.011
AAE	0.902 ± 0.030	0.129 ± 0.024	0.761 ± 0.047	0.286 ± 0.053
ProtoRE	0.928 ± 0.007	0.111 ± 0.009	0.805 ± 0.012	0.275 ± 0.011
OpenAI (ada 002)	0.939 ± 0.009	0.120 ± 0.011	0.847 ± 0.014	0.289 ± 0.012
Instructor	0.955 ± 0.007	0.132 ± 0.007	0.883 ± 0.014	0.313 ± 0.012
DEC	0.903 ± 0.007	0.084 ± 0.010	0.765 ± 0.011	0.223 ± 0.010
DEC_m	0.911 ± 0.009	0.090 ± 0.011	0.764 ± 0.012	0.229 ± 0.014
DEC_Transe	0.961 ± 0.005	0.124 ± 0.005	0.895 ± 0.016	0.300 ± 0.008
DEC_Transe_m	0.979 ± 0.006	0.153 ± 0.005	0.941 ± 0.010	0.344 ± 0.009

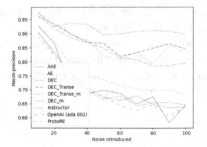
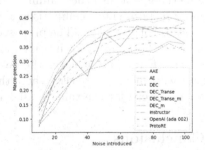

(a) Comparison using correct instances.   (b) Comparison using wrong instances.

Fig. 1. Macro-precision values for different levels of noise in the test partition.

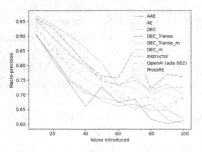
(a) Comparison using correct instances.

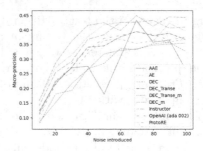
(b) Comparison using wrong instances.

Fig. 2. Macro-precision values for different levels of noise in train and test partition.

Comparison Using Various Levels of Noise Introduction in Test Partition. The performance of each method was evaluated by introducing varying percentages of noise in the test partition. These noise levels were systematically incremented by 10 steps. On one hand, Fig. 1(a) presents a comparison using macro-precision for detecting correct instances. DEC_Transe_m outperforms the other methods for all percentages except 20. Furthermore, it does not experience a significant drop in its performance. This indicates that the proposed method is capable of identifying correct instances within datasets where up to half of the instances are wrong.

On the other hand, Fig. 1(b) utilizes macro-precision for classifying incorrect instances. In this scenario, the performance of the proposed method exhibits results similar to Autoencoders for most of the introduced noise percentages. Notably, an increase in macro-precision is observed as more noise is introduced into the dataset.

Comparison Using Various Levels of Noise Introduction in Train and Test Partitions. Different percentages of noise are introduced into both the training and testing partitions. This approach enables not only the evaluation of the methods but also the training of them using noisy data.

Figure 2(a) presents a comparison of the methods in terms of macro-precision for detecting correct labels. The proposed method, DEC_Transe_m, outperforms the other methods up to an introduction of 50% noise. Beyond this point, the DEC_TransE method achieves the best results. Similarly, the same pattern is observed with incorrect labels, where the method DEC_Transe_m outperforms the others, except for the values of 0.6 and 0.8 (see Fig. 2(b)).

6   Conclusions

This study introduces an approach for enhancing and automatically completing KBs. A key aspect of this approach is determining the correctness of instances for specific relations. To achieve this, it is proposed a novel unsupervised method based on DEC, utilizing various instance elements as input.

The results demonstrate that the proposed method outperforms several state-of-the-art approaches in terms of macro-precision for detecting correct instances, even in the presence of varying noise levels. Additionally, it was conducted an evaluation to assess the impact of the threshold on macro-precision values, confirming the approach as a threshold.

As future work, it is planed to explore new architectures and input information to further enhance the detection of these instances.

Acknowledgements. This research was supported by "Laboratoire d'Excellence" Empirical Foundations of Linguistics (LabEx EFL) and the IBERO University though the Crescencio Ballesteros Trust and/or the SNI100 Fund in Support of National Researchers' Mobility. Additionally, the authors thank INAOE Supercomputing Laboratory's Deep Learning Platform for Language Technologies.

References

1. Artetxe, M., Schwenk, H.: Massively multilingual sentence embeddings for zero-shot cross-lingual transfer and beyond. Trans. ACL **7**, 597–610 (2019)
2. Bordes, A., Usunier, N., Garcia-Durán, A., et al.: Translating embeddings for modeling multi-relational data. In: Advances in Neural Information Processing Systems, pp. 2787–2795 (2013)
3. Ding, N., Wang, X., Fu, Y., et al.: Prototypical representation learning for relation extraction. In: 9th International Conference on Learning Representations, ICLR 2021, Virtual Event, Austria, 3–7 May 2021. OpenReview.net (2021)
4. Gábor, K., Zargayouna, H., Tellier, I., et al.: Exploring vector spaces for semantic relations. In: Proceedings of the 2017 Conference on Empirical Methods in NLP, pp. 1814–1823. ACL (2017)
5. García-Mendoza, J.L., Villaseñor-Pineda, L., Buscaldi, D., et al.: Evaluation of a new representation for noise reduction in distant supervision. In: Pichardo Lagunas, O., Martínez-Miranda, J., Martínez Seis, B. (eds.) MICAI 2022. LNCS, vol. 13613, pp. 101–113. Springer, Cham (2022). https://doi.org/10.1007/978-3-031-19496-2_8
6. García-Mendoza, J.L., Villaseñor-Pineda, L., Orihuela-Espina, F., et al.: An autoencoder-based representation for noise reduction in distant supervision of relation extraction. J. Intell. Fuzzy Syst. **42**(5), 4523–4529 (2022)
7. Hendrickx, I., Kim, S.N., Kozareva, Z., et al.: SemEval-2010 task 8: multi-way classification of semantic relations between pairs of nominals. In: Proceedings of the 5th International Workshop on Semantic Evaluation, pp. 94–99. ACL (2010)
8. Hinton, G.E., Salakhutdinov, R.R.: Reducing the dimensionality of data with neural networks. Science **313**(5786), 504–507 (2006)
9. Holm, S.: A simple sequentially rejective multiple test procedure. Scand. J. Stat. **6**(2), 65–70 (1979)
10. Howell, D.C.: Statistical Methods for Psychology. Cengage Learning ALL (2012)
11. Kullback, S., Leibler, R.A.: On information and sufficiency. Ann. Math. Stat. **22**(1), 79–86 (1951)
12. Makhzani, A., Shlens, J., Jaitly, N., et al.: Adversarial Autoencoders. arXiv:1511.05644v2 (2015)
13. Martinez-Rodriguez, J.L., Hogan, A., Lopez-Arevalo, I.: Information extraction meets the semantic web: a survey. Semant. Web **11**(2), 255–335 (2020)

14. Min, B., Grishman, R., Wan, L., et al.: Distant supervision for relation extraction with an incomplete knowledge base. In: Proceedings of the 2013 Conference of the North American Chapter of the ACL: Human Language Technologies, pp. 777–782. ACL (2013)
15. Mintz, M., Bills, S., Snow, R., et al.: Distant supervision for relation extraction without labeled data. In: Proceedings of the 47th Annual Meeting of the ACL, pp. 1003–1011 (2009)
16. Neelakantan, A., Xu, T., Puri, R., et al.: Text and code embeddings by contrastive pre-training. arXiv preprint arXiv:2201.10005 (2022)
17. Riedel, S., Yao, L., McCallum, A.: Modeling relations and their mentions without labeled text. In: Balcázar, J.L., Bonchi, F., Gionis, A., Sebag, M. (eds.) ECML PKDD 2010. LNCS (LNAI), vol. 6323, pp. 148–163. Springer, Heidelberg (2010). https://doi.org/10.1007/978-3-642-15939-8_10
18. Smirnova, A., Cudré-Mauroux, P.: Relation extraction using distant supervision: a survey. ACSur **51**(5), 1–35 (2018)
19. Su, H., Shi, W., Kasai, J., et al.: One embedder, any task: Instruction-finetuned text embeddings. In: Findings of the ACL, pp. 1102–1121. ACL (2023)
20. Xie, J., Girshick, R., Farhadi, A.: Unsupervised deep embedding for clustering analysis. In: International Conference on Machine Learning, pp. 478–487. PMLR (2016)
21. Xu, W., Hoffmann, R., Zhao, L., et al.: Filling knowledge base gaps for distant supervision of relation extraction. In: Proceedings of the 51st Annual Meeting of the ACL (Volume 2: Short Papers), pp. 665–670. ACL (2013)

Mapping Activities onto a Two-Dimensional Emotions Model for Dog Emotion Recognition Using Inertial Data

Eliaf Y. Garcia-Loya[1] , Mariel Urbina-Escalante[2] , Veronica Reyes-Meza[3] ,
Humberto Pérez-Espinosa[4] , and Irvin Hussein Lopez-Nava[1](✉)

[1] Centro de Investigación Científica y de Educación Superior de Ensenada, 22860
Baja California, Mexico
{eliaf,hussein}@cicese.edu.mx
[2] Doctorado en Ciencias Biológicas, Universidad Autónoma de Tlaxcala, 90070
Tlaxcala, Mexico
[3] Centro Tlaxcala de Biología de la Conducta, Universidad Autónoma de Tlaxcala,
90070 Tlaxcala, Mexico
veronica.reyesm@uatx.mx
[4] Instituto Nacional de Astrofísica, Óptica y Electrónica, 72840 Tonantzintla, Mexico
humbertop@ccc.inaoep.mx

Abstract. Understanding animal reactions is essential for the welfare of
animals, but accurately interpreting dogs' emotions, despite their bond
with humans, is challenging and often yields subjective results from
human observers. Emotions manifest through physiological changes, such
as heart rate fluctuations, or behavioral patterns, such as dog movements. In the present study, we measured and analyzed the movements
of a group of dogs during four localized activities in two dimensions of
emotion: arousal and valence. These activities (frustration, toy, abandonment, petting) were performed in natural settings while wearing the
PATITA capture device. Statistical and temporal features were derived
from acceleration signals and used to train various classification models.
An average F1-score of 0.92 ($\sigma = 0.05$) was scored when classifying the
four emotions with the ExtraTrees classifier. This work contributes to a
more accurate and consistent understanding of canine emotional states
using dog movements, which has potential applications in shelters, day-
care centers, and even homes, where dogs often spend a lot of time alone.

Keywords: Canine emotions · Emotion recognition · Emotion
classification · inertial data · inertial signals

1 Introduction

In animal welfare, understanding their reactions is critical; these reactions
include biological responses, behavioral signals, and expressions of emotional

E. Mezura-Montes et al. (Eds.): MCPR 2024, LNCS 14755, pp. 107–118, 2024.
https://doi.org/10.1007/978-3-031-62836-8_11

states. Specifically related to dogs, despite their close relationship with humans, interpreting their emotions presents a considerable challenge. Traditionally, this interpretation has relied on human observation, primarily the dogs' owner, but it often results in subjective and inconsistent outcomes.

The study of canine emotions is essential to improve animal welfare. Still, it also provides valuable information on topics such as human-dog bonding, veterinary medicine, and dog training, leading to a better understanding of the dog, which improves interaction decisions and communication strategies.

Emotions, often subjective interpretations of experiences, are crucial in understanding behavioral patterns. Common emotions such as happiness, fear, sadness, and anger are observable in humans [6] and dogs [3]. These emotional states trigger internal and external changes in dogs, manifesting physiologically through alterations in heart and respiratory rates, and behaviorally through distinct poses and movement patterns.

Emotions can be decoded in different ways, so a significant aspect is mapping these emotions onto measures or dimensions such as valence and arousal [2]. Valence captures the positivity or negativity of the emotional state, while arousal reflects the level of excitement or passivity. Using this method of mapping, we could get a deeper understanding of how emotions can be perceived, helping us interpret their emotion based on either the intensity or the type of emotion.

2   Related Work

In human and non-human animals, basic emotions such as fear, happiness, sadness, disgust, and anger are considered biologically based states essential for survival [6]. These emotions drive behaviors and improve communication intra- and inter-species. Identifying animal emotions typically involves monitoring changes in biological parameters and behaviors following negative or positive events.

Researchers have investigated various aspects of canine emotional expression using physiological measurements and behavioral observations [5]. Studies have explored physiological responses associated with emotions in dogs, revealing significant changes in heart rate in positive situations, such as being petted by a familiar person [10]. Temperature changes have also been described as a reliable measure of emotional state, Travain et al. [14] significant increases in dog eye temperature during stressful veterinary examinations.

In addition to physiological changes, researchers have also examined observable reactions such as facial expressions [11], body postures [7], and tail movements in dogs [12]. For example, Tami et al. [13] reported that bouncing, ears raised and forward, and tail wagging are commonly reported as signs of playfulness, while showing teeth and barking are perceived as aggression. Kuhne et al. [10] found that dogs also showed fewer displacement activities and more appeasement gestures such as blinking, closing both eyes, freezing, sitting, lying down, licking the nose, among others.

In machine learning (ML) for automatic classification tasks related to canine well-being, experiments concentrate on activities, emotions, or a combination of both. Activity recognition methods give insight into dogs' daily routines, with movements indicating various behaviors [9]. These methods have been used to improve the capabilities of service dogs through wearable devices, achieving high accuracy in the classification. Emotional classification, a field of growing interest, uses visual, physiological, and audio data to identify canine emotions. Studies score high accuracy using image datasets and marker analysis [7,8].

In previous research [1], Inertial Measurement Units (IMUs) were strategically placed on the base of the neck and tail base, as the waging direction of the tail meant that the dog was experiencing positive, negative, or neutral emotion. However, no explicit stimuli were mentioned to invoke the dog's emotions. Their findings showed that automatic dog emotion recognition could be correctly retrieved using commonly known ML algorithms, such as Random Forest, Support Vector Machine, K-Nearest Neighbors, and Naïve Bayes.

This study introduces a novel method for recognizing canine emotions by tracking their movement patterns in response to stimuli that elicit emotional reactions. By correlating these movements with specific emotional states and using ML models to analyze acceleration data, the research aims to provide a comprehensive and precise understanding of canine emotions.

3   Methodology

Our primary objectives in this study include the development of a new dataset acquired using a sensing and data collection tool. Secondly, we aim to use this valuable dataset for training and evaluating several ML algorithms. The complete proposed methodology is shown in Fig. 1.

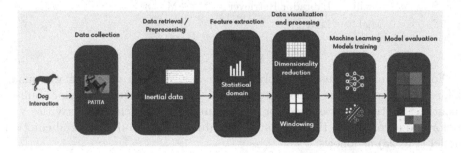

Fig. 1. Proposed methodology for automated recognition of Canine Emotions

The first steps involve collecting data by applying a structured testing protocol (Subsect. 3.1), and by using a specialized sensing device (see Subsect. 3.2). In the following steps, the collected inertial data was analyzed by feature engineering (Subsect. 3.3), and training several classification models to obtain the best model for automated recognition of dog emotions.

3.1   Data Collection

A comprehensive data collection protocol was designed to gather necessary experimental data, outlining the process for recording and analyzing dogs' emotional responses within a structured experimental setup. Our approach integrates standardized testing methodologies with systematic observation techniques. The protocol is designed to encompass a diverse sample demographic comprising medium to large-breed dogs one year and older. Selection criteria deliberately exclude dogs with medical treatment and those with sterilization or neutering procedures, ensuring a focused and representative dataset.

The protocol was approved by the Bioethics and the Academic Committees of the Postgraduate Program in Biological Sciences at the Autonomous University of Tlaxcala (UATx). Prior to execution, thorough evaluations ensured the participating canines' optimal health, nutritional status, and hygiene, and the suitability of the stimulus application environment. We collected data from 5 dogs (2 males and 3 females) ranging from 1 to 8 years old. Owners signed informed consent for their dogs to participate in this study. Behavioral tests were conducted at the dog's residence or nearby zone. The general details about the dogs' are shown in Table 1.

Table 1. General information about the dogs participating in the study.

Name	Breed	Sex	Age (years)
Sam	Border Collie	F	4
Oli	Belgian Shepherd Malinois	F	1
Lumiere	Dalmatian	M	3
Archi	Labrador Retriever	M	8
Miel	Mixed	F	3

For every capture session involving each dog, a 2-min recording was made before the stimulus was applied to capture the dog's usual behavior. Subsequently, the stimulus was used for one minute. The sequence of activities was performed according to the associated stimulus in the two-dimensional emotion model (Fig. 2a) as follows:

- **Petting** (low arousal, positive valence): The owner was instructed to remain close and gently pet continuously, pausing briefly to avoid making the dog uncomfortable.
- **Toy** (high arousal, positive valence): The owner was instructed to play with the dog using their favorite toy, object, or how he usually plays with his dog.
- **Abandonment** (low arousal, negative valence): The dog was removed from its usual living area and tied to a post or tree in the shade. The owner was instructed to secure the dog to the post and then depart from the location. This test lasted for three minutes.

- **Frustration** (high arousal, negative valence): The owner was instructed to do all the steps in preparation for a walk with his dog: taking the leash, putting the leash on the dog, moving to the nearest exit door, but standing before the door for a brief moment, before retreating from the exit and returning on repeated occasions.

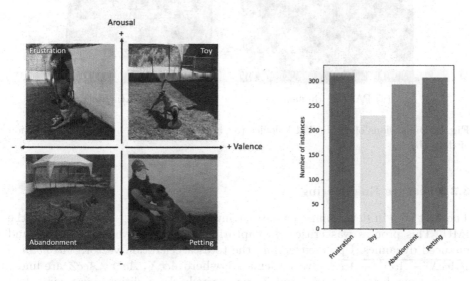

(a) Emotions organized by arousal and valence   (b) Data distribution by class

Fig. 2. Description of the emotions studied in two-dimensional model (a), and distribution of the data collected by emotion (b).

3.2 Materials

The implementation of the data collection protocol incorporates several materials, including a behavioral recording sheet, a concise owner interview, two Sony HDR-CX405 video cameras mounted on tripods, a leash, the PATITA (Portable Advanced Tracking Information Technology for Animals) device, and a smartphone equipped with the PATITA mobile application.

PATITA is an electronic device noted for its compactness and lightweight design; see Fig. 3a. PATITA proves to be particularly conducive to secure attachment to a belt placed in the stomach region (see Fig. 3b), ensuring optimal contact with the animal's skin due to minimal hair interference. The device integrates several sensors, including environmental and body temperature monitors, an optical heart rate sensor, an accelerometer, a gyroscope, and GPS.

Although PATITA can monitor various parameters, this study focuses exclusively on inertial data. The dataset collected allows for a detailed analysis of canine movement patterns, providing valuable information on locomotion, posture changes, and activity levels. We hypothesize that such metrics are particularly effective in discerning emotional states by arousal levels.

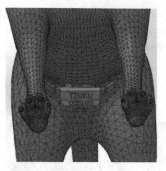

(a) PATITA dimensions   (b) PATITA attachment

Fig. 3. Dimensions of the PATITA device (a), and its placement in the stomach region of dogs (b).

3.3 Feature Engineering

The first step in developing our dataset involved extracting raw data from the IMU. This process was critical in capturing the dog movement's subtle and nuanced dynamics. Upon extraction, the total acceleration vector, $AccTotal = \sqrt{AccX^2 + AccY^2 + AccZ^2}$, was calculated; where $AccX$, $AccY$, $AccZ$ are linear accelerations for axes X, Y, and Z, respectively. In addition, gyroscope data was used to complement acceleration data, and we calculated $GyrTotal$. After retrieving all of these signals, we employed a windowing process by segmenting the eight inertial signals into 2-second windows. The number of segments per emotion is shown in Fig. 2b. We extracted 20 statistical and temporal features within these slices using Python's package TSFEL. As a result, we arranged a feature vector with a dimensionality of 320, and it was labeled according to their respective emotion, creating a mapping between the observed inertial data and the specific emotional or behavioral state it represented.

To find the optimal dimensionality for our dataset, we systematically tested various ML algorithms with decreasing dimensions. This method identified the best balance between dimensionality and performance, showing that 20 dimensions achieved high accuracy without the complexity and minimal gains of additional dimensions. Table 2 shows the features for training classification models in two ways: using all features, and only the most relevant ones.

3.4 Classification

A set of machine learning algorithms was trained across different families: Gaussian Naive Bayes (GNB), Support Vector Machines (SVM), Extra Tree (ExT), k-Nearest Neighbors (kNN), and Voting (Vot)- on a classification task using both baseline and reduced-dimensionality data. Voting is a meta-classifier that uses the other algorithms as base models. Initially, the classification was based on arousal levels, considering their potential differentiation through the dog's

Table 2. List of features extracted and selected from inertial data.

Approach	Features	From signals
All features	Abs. energy, Avg. power, ECDF, ECDF percentile, ECDF percentile count, Entropy, Histogram, Interquartile range, Kurtosis, Max, Min, Mean, MAD, Peak to peak distance, RMS, Skewness, Std. deviation, Variance:	AccX, AccY, AccZ, GyrX, GyrY, GyrZ, TotalAcc, TotalGyr
Selected features	Max:	AccX, AccZ, GyrX, GyrY, AccTotal
	Min:	AccX, AccY, AccZ, GyrX, GyrY, GyrZ, GyrTotal
	Abs. energy, Avg. power, Peak to peak distance, RMS:	GyrX, GyrZ, GyrTotal

movement rather than solely on valence. The task then shifted focus to valence, attempting to distinguish emotional states by their positive or negative nature. After analyzing arousal and valence separately, we combined both dimensions for a holistic examination of the emotional states.

4 Results

Before classifying emotions, an exploratory analysis using t-distributed stochastic neighbor embedding (t-SNE) was performed. This step facilitates the visual evaluation of data clustering and separation, providing insight into how the data points are grouped according to each emotion or dimensional space, see Fig. 4.

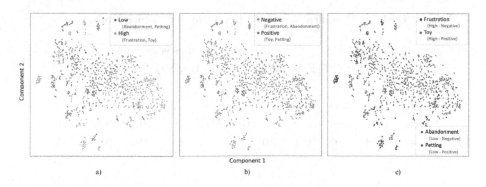

Fig. 4. Data visualization using t-SNE for arousal, valence, and the four emotions.

In analyzing arousal data, we noted clear class separation (low, high), suggesting distinct clusters. While valence data (positive, negative) showed slight separation with significant overlap among individual emotions, outdoor instances formed specific clusters. Despite imperfect separation, this suggests classification algorithms can distinguish between classes effectively.

The last step was to evaluate the performance of the classification models from different perspectives, first by focusing on the two-dimensional model separately (valence and arousal), as well as a combined analysis for all emotions. In Table 3, we report the F1 scores for arousal for two conditions: using all calculated features and feature selection. F1 scores, for valence and specific emotions are similarly detailed in Tables 4 and 5, respectively.

Table 3. Classification results (F1 score) for arousal levels.

	All features					Features selected				
	GNB	SVM	ExT	kNN	Vot	GNB	SVM	ExT	kNN	Vot
High	0.59	0.81	**0.91**	0.90	0.83	0.54	0.64	**0.93**	0.86	0.81
Low	0.75	0.85	**0.91**	0.91	0.86	0.74	0.74	**0.93**	0.87	0.84
Average	0.68	0.83	0.91	0.90	0.85	0.64	0.69	**0.93**	0.87	0.83
std dev	0.11	0.03	0.00	0.01	0.02	0.14	0.07	0.00	0.01	0.02

In the domain of arousal classification, the best model achieved F1 scores of 0.93 for distinguishing high arousal states (both frustration and toy) from low arousal (both abandonment and petting), using ExtraTrees classifier trained with relevant features. This outcome was anticipated, as it has been proven that inertial data-trained classifiers demonstrate robustness in classifying activities with varying movement levels; even 7 of the 10 classifiers achieved an average F1 score above 0.83 for this task.

Table 4. Classification results (F1 score) for valence levels.

	All features					Features selected				
	GNB	SVM	ExT	kNN	Vot	GNB	SVM	ExT	kNN	Vot
Negative	0.69	0.88	**0.95**	0.86	0.84	0.71	0.76	**0.95**	0.89	0.85
Positive	0.43	0.85	**0.94**	0.84	0.77	0.43	0.62	**0.94**	0.87	0.78
Average	0.57	0.86	0.94	0.85	0.81	0.58	0.69	**0.94**	0.88	0.81
std dev	0.18	0.02	0.01	0.01	0.05	0.20	0.10	0.01	0.01	0.05

In the realm of valence classification, the best models achieved F1 scores of 0.95 for negative emotions (both frustration and abandonment) and 0.94 for positive emotions (both toy and petting) when ExtraTrees classifier was trained with all or selected features. This notable performance emphasizes the classifier's ability to differentiate between subtle emotional nuances. The model with fewer features is favored in this case.

Remembering the main emphasis of this work is the recognition of emotions in dogs, Table 5 presents the results this time for four classes. These findings

Table 5. Classification results (F1 score) of emotions in two-dimensional model.

	All features					Features selected				
	GNB	SVM	ExT	kNN	Vot	GNB	SVM	ExT	kNN	Vot
Frustration	0.29	0.81	**0.94**	0.83	0.79	0.11	0.32	**0.94**	0.69	0.63
Toy	0.64	0.77	**0.85**	0.76	0.72	0.58	0.60	**0.84**	0.68	0.64
Abandonment	0.48	0.71	**0.93**	0.81	0.75	0.45	0.15	**0.89**	0.63	0.59
Petting	0.68	0.87	**0.95**	0.86	0.84	0.03	0.60	**0.90**	0.69	0.75
Average	0.52	0.79	0.92	0.82	0.78	0.27	0.42	0.90	0.67	0.65
std dev	0.18	0.07	0.05	0.04	0.05	0.26	0.22	0.04	0.03	0.07

align with earlier classification results, with the ExtraTrees classifiers achieving the highest F1 scores; notably, the model trained using all features outperformed slightly. Overall, the emotions of Frustration and Petting were best recognized, while Toy obtained the lowest results.

Finally, the confusion matrices presented in Fig. 5 provide a quantitative visual representation of the performance of the best classifiers for each task. ExtraTrees classifier trained with all features for the binary tasks, and the same classifier but trained with relevant features for classifying the four emotions. In the case of classifying arousal levels, the model confuses twice as many instances of low arousal with instances of high arousal. For valence, the misclassification rate is low and balanced. When analyzing the four emotions in detail, we observe that several instances of Frustration and Abandonment were misclassified as Toy; the same number of instances of Toy that the model indicated were Petting.

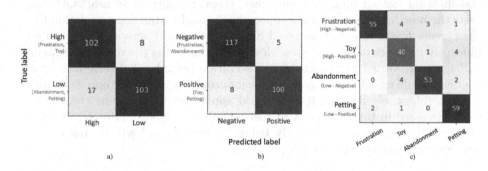

Fig. 5. Confusion matrices for best-performing algorithms: a) ExT for arousal using selected features, b) ExT for valence using selected features, c) ExT per-trial using all features.

5   Discussion

The first objective of this study was to develop a new data set using a detection and data collection tool, it is important because there are few data sets to follow dogs and recognize emotions [4], and our dataset includes the evaluation of dogs in their natural environment, carrying out everyday activities that elicit both positive and negative emotions with high and low arousal.

Our study also aimed to train and assess machine learning (ML) algorithms with our dataset, revealing distinct performances in classifying canine emotions into valence and arousal tasks. Surprisingly, valence classification (positive vs. negative states) showed higher accuracy, suggesting more consistent patterns in these emotional states, contrary to our initial expectations. This contrasts with the broader variability in arousal, where reactions to stimuli like petting or toys differ widely among dogs. Notably, the ExtraTrees algorithms stood out in accurately classifying these behaviors, highlighting ML's potential in animal behavior analysis. Yet, the performance disparity between valence and arousal underscores the necessity for further refinement of these algorithms to more accurately capture the complexities of canine emotions.

The strategic implementation of feature selection emerged as a beneficial choice, enhancing the efficiency of several models without detracting from their accuracy. By narrowing down to 20 key features, mirroring our dimensionality reduction efforts, we notably minimized the data volume required for processing. This streamlining underscores the potential to refine ML model training and classification further, particularly valuable for emotion recognition tasks. Such optimization holds promise for development in mobile applications, offering practical tools for dog trainers and owners.

Future work should aim at improving data collection methods. While valence classification yielded promising outcomes, the variability in arousal states suggests the need for a more detailed approach. Expanding the dog population from the current five is essential, as breed diversity, size, and activity levels can significantly influence emotional cues. Moreover, broadening the range of behaviors through more varied trials, extended observation periods, or diverse interaction contexts would enrich the dataset. Such enhancements would not only bolster the model's robustness but also its real-world applicability, advancing the applications discussed in this section. A further technical analysis and in-depth review of the PATITA device is currently being developed, and will be released for subsequent usage in experiments.

6   Conclusion

Our research marks a notable advancement in applying ML to decode canine emotions, showcasing the efficacy of several widely known algorithms and the strategic use of feature selection for streamlined data processing. This foundation paves the way for future explorations into a broader spectrum of emotional states, incorporating diverse data types such as physiological, visual, and even audio data to enrich our understanding and assessment of animal welfare.

The proposed methodology not only has the potential to propel the field of ML in animal behavior analysis but also establishes a precedent for future research involving alternative data sources, such as physiological signals or image data. Moving forward, we aim to broaden the scope of our research to encompass these additional data streams, promoting a more holistic approach to animal emotion recognition and further solidifying our contribution to enhancing animal welfare through technological innovation.

Acknowledgements. We thank CONAHCYT for the Master's degree grant: 1190719 the Doctoral grant 1081073, and funding CF-2019/2275. We are very grateful to the owners of the dogs who participated in this study and to Dra. Paola Castañeda Campos and Om Canin for their willingness made this research possible.

References

1. Aich, S., Chakraborty, S., Sim, J.S., Jang, D.J., Kim, H.C.: The design of an automated system for the analysis of the activity and emotional patterns of dogs with wearable sensors using machine learning. Appl. Sci. **9**(22), 4938 (2019)
2. Barrett, L.F.: Discrete emotions or dimensions? The role of valence focus and arousal focus. Cogn. Emot. **12**(4), 579–599 (1998)
3. Caeiro, C., Guo, K., Mills, D.: Dogs and humans respond to emotionally competent stimuli by producing different facial actions. Sci. Rep. **7**(1), 15525 (2017)
4. Chen, H.Y., Lin, C.H., Lai, J.W., Chan, Y.K.: Convolutional neural network-based automated system for dog tracking and emotion recognition in video surveillance. Appl. Sci. **13**(7), 4596 (2023)
5. Csoltova, E., Martineau, M., Boissy, A., Gilbert, C.: Behavioral and physiological reactions in dogs to a veterinary examination: owner-dog interactions improve canine well-being. Physiol. Behav. **177**, 270–281 (2017)
6. Ekman, P., et al.: Basic emotions. In: Handbook of Cognition and Emotion, vol. 98, no. 45–60, p. 16 (1999)
7. Ferres, K., Schloesser, T., Gloor, P.A.: Predicting dog emotions based on posture analysis using deeplabcut. Future Internet **14**(4), 97 (2022)
8. Hernández-Luquin, F., et al.: Dog emotion recognition from images in the wild: debiw dataset and first results. In: Proceedings of the Ninth International Conference on Animal-Computer Interaction, pp. 1–13 (2022)
9. Kasnesis, P., et al.: Deep learning empowered wearable-based behavior recognition for search and rescue dogs. Sensors **22**(3), 993 (2022)
10. Kuhne, F., Hößler, J.C., Struwe, R.: Emotions in dogs being petted by a familiar or unfamiliar person: validating behavioural indicators of emotional states using heart rate variability. Appl. Anim. Behav. Sci. **161**, 113–120 (2014)
11. Mota-Rojas, D., et al.: Current advances in assessment of dog's emotions, facial expressions, and their use for clinical recognition of pain. Animals **11**(11), 3334 (2021)
12. Siniscalchi, M., Lusito, R., Vallortigara, G., Quaranta, A.: Seeing left-or right-asymmetric tail wagging produces different emotional responses in dogs. Curr. Biol. **23**(22), 2279–2282 (2013)

13. Tami, G., Gallagher, A.: Description of the behaviour of domestic dog (canis familiaris) by experienced and inexperienced people. Appl. Anim. Behav. Sci. **120**(3–4), 159–169 (2009)
14. Travain, T., Colombo, E.S., Heinzl, E., Bellucci, D., Previde, E.P., Valsecchi, P.: Hot dogs: thermography in the assessment of stress in dogs (canis familiaris)-a pilot study. J. Vet. Behav. **10**(1), 17–23 (2015)

An Exploratory Study on Machine-Learning-Based Hyper-heuristics for the Knapsack Problem

José Eduardo Zárate-Aranda(iD) and José Carlos Ortiz-Bayliss(✉)(iD)

Tecnologico de Monterrey, School of Engineering and Sciences, 64849 Monterrey, Mexico
{A01630299,jcobayliss}@tec.mx

Abstract. Hyper-heuristics have risen as a recurrent method to solve combinatorial optimization problems since they use a set of heuristics selectively according to the problem state. Although many ideas have been developed to produce hyper-heuristics, a recent trend involves treating the heuristic selection problem as a classification one. This allows the introduction of machine learning elements into the hyper-heuristic process. This work explores creating hyper-heuristics using Machine Learning classifiers to solve the Knapsack Problem, a fascinating and well-studied combinatorial problem. We propose two approaches to these hyper-heuristics: a dynamical approach, where the hyper-heuristic may change heuristics throughout the whole solving process, and a static approach, where the hyper-heuristic makes one initial choice of heuristic and no further changes are allowed. Our results confirm that hyper-heuristics powered by machine learning techniques can deal with the Knapsack problem and obtain competent results. Besides, we also observed a clear superiority in the performance of the hyper-heuristics running under the static approach concerning the dynamic counterpart.

Keywords: Machine Learning · Heuristics · Hyper-heuristics · Knapsack Problem

1 Introduction

When solving an optimization problem, we have to make choices. One primary choice concerns how much we are willing to 'invest' to solve such a problem and our expectations about the solutions. For example, we may be tempted to invest a lot and use tailor-made algorithms so that the solution for one particular instance of the problem is solved in the best possible way. In other cases, we could just apply a general solver that consumes fewer resources and be satisfied with a valid solution of acceptable quality. Although there are many scenarios to explore, in this work, we focus on the one where we aim for solutions of

E. Mezura-Montes et al. (Eds.): MCPR 2024, LNCS 14755, pp. 119–128, 2024.
https://doi.org/10.1007/978-3-031-62836-8_12

acceptable quality for various instances of the problem. We are not interested in the best possible solver for one particular instance but a method capable of performing "well enough" over various types of instances of a problem.

Hyper-heuristics, or "heuristics to choose heuristics" [5], have proven suitable for the scenario described before since they create a mapping between problem states (characterized by some problem features) and suitable heuristics. In other words, they intelligently apply existing heuristics to improve the quality of the solutions. This work proposes developing hyper-heuristics to solve the Knapsack Problem. This widely studied combinatorial optimization problem remains relevant nowadays due to its many applications in different fields, such as production planning, health care, financial modeling, and computer networks [1,4,6]. Although many versions of the Knapsack Problem exist, this work explores its most straightforward version, the 0/1 KP, where each item has only two options: to be packed or left out of the solution set [1]. Since we will only refer to this version of the problem, we will simply refer to this problem as KP. The KP consists of (1) items, each with a profit and weight, and (2) a knapsack with a particular capacity. Solving the problem requires finding a subset of items that maximize the overall profit without breaking the knapsack's capacity.

As described before, we propose using a hyper-heuristic (HH) to solve the KP. The hyper-heuristic must learn when to apply one heuristic based on the problem state under exploration. Various strategies, such as ant colony optimization [8], genetic programming [7], fuzzy logic [15], and reinforcement learning [22], have already been used to generate hyper-heuristics for solving the KP or some of its variations. However, an almost unexplored trend in hyper-heuristics, used in other problem domains, treats the heuristic selection problem as a classification one. Under this perspective, the hyper-heuristic assigns a set of features to a suitable class, which is nothing but a heuristic [16,17]. To the authors' knowledge, this approach has yet to be explored for the KP.

The remainder of this document is organized as follows. Section 2 mentions the existing solution methods for the KP. Section 3 describes the solution model and its operation. Afterward, the experiments and results can be found in Sect. 4. Finally, Sect. 5 presents the conclusion and some ideas for future work derived.

2   Background and Related Work

We start this section by briefly defining the KP. The KP contains a set of items. Each item is associated with a weight and profit. When solving the KP, the objective is to select a subset of items that maximizes the total profit without exceeding the knapsack's capacity. The KP is challenging and recurrent in Combinatorial Optimization (CO) [20], and the literature is rich in methods for solving such a problem. We can broadly classify the solving methods as exact and approximation ones. Exact methods guarantee to find the optimal solution if enough time is provided. However, this is only possible in some practical (and rather) cases. Some examples of exact methods include: linear programming [2,13], branch and bound approach [11,24], dynamic programming [3,9]. As mentioned earlier, these methods can offer optimal solutions only to small-scale instances, which limits their application to practical cases. Regarding approximation methods, we can mention heuristics, metaheuristics, and hyper-heuristics. Heuristics are usually known as "rules of thumb" that use little computational resources to find an acceptable solution. Heuristics are problem-dependent; they cannot be used generically for different problems. Metaheuristics work on a higher level than simple heuristics in different problem domains, unlike simple heuristics [10]. Hyper-heuristics, on the other hand, work at an even higher level [15,18,21]. Instead of exploring the solution space, they select or generate low-level heuristics suitable for the current problem being solved. Those heuristics will be responsible for solving the problem.

3 Solution Approach

As mentioned before, our solution proposal uses some popular classifiers to produce HHs that map the problem state of a KP instance to a suitable heuristic to apply. Before describing how the hyper-heuristic model works, we introduce some vital elements of such a proposal.

3.1 The Features

This work characterizes the instances using three straightforward features. It is relevant to note that these features are dynamic. Every time an item is packed, the values for these features change for what remains of the instance.

Profit (P). This is the average profit of all the remaining items in the instance divided by the maximum profit among all the remaining items.

Weight (W). This represents the average weight of all the remaining items in the instance divided by the maximum weight among all the remaining items.

Correlation (C). It estimates the correlation between the profits and weights of the remaining items in the instance. Since correlation is calculated using the Pearson correlation coefficient, which lies in the range $[-1, 1]$, we divide it by two and add 0.5. This adjusts the range of this feature to $[0, 1]$, as with the first two features described.

3.2 The Heuristics

As in other heuristic-based works that solve the KP, deciding which item to pack next is done by applying heuristics iteratively, one item at a time. For this purpose, we have considered four heuristics, which are briefly described as follows:

Default (DEF). DEF packs the items following the order established in which they appear in the instance (no additional ordering is conducted on the items).

Minimum Weight (MINW). MINW prefers the item with the smallest weight. Then, MinW prioritizes lighter items, allowing the selection of the most lightweight items that still fit within the knapsack's capacity.

Maximum Profit (MAXP). MAXP chooses the item with the largest profit. It uses a greedy approach to fill the knapsack.

Maximum Profit per Weight (MAXPW). MAXPW prioritizes the profit-to-weight ratio. It computes each item's profit-to-weight ratio and selects the items in decreasing order. So, the objects with the highest profit-to-weight ratio are packed first.

3.3   The KP Instances

In this work, we used synthetic KP instances produced with the algorithm proposed by Plata et al. [19]. The instances are grouped into two sets: training and testing[1]. The training set contains 100 instances, while the testing set has 400. All the instances in this work have 100 items and a maximum capacity of 64 weight units. We acknowledge that these sets may seem arbitrarily chosen or small to achieve conclusive results. However, the main characteristic of the sets produced for this work is that they are 'balanced.' Thus, no heuristic is the best option when considering all the instances throughout the sets. Each heuristic is the best performer in 25% of the instances of each set. So, in each set, the instances are also grouped in four subsets: SET_DEF, SET_MAXP, SET_MAXPW, and SET_MINW, where the best performers are DEF, MAXP, MAXPW, and MINW, respectively. The rationale behind this distribution is that no single heuristic outperforms the other when considering the whole training or testing set. This makes this scenario suitable to test hyper-heuristic performance.

3.4   Performance Metrics

As in other studies where the KP is studied, the profit of the solution is used as a quality metric. The larger the profit (without exceeding the knapsack's capacity), the better the solution. To allow the comparison of various models, and address the fact that some instances may result in larger profits than others, we have normalized the results per instance. So, for each instance, the best method obtains a normalized profit of 1 and the worst method, 0. Normalization is calculated as $z = \frac{x - \min(x)}{\max(x) - \min(x)}$, where x is a vector that contains the profits obtained by different methods for a particular KP instance.

We will also use the success rate to evaluate the methods' performance along with the normalized profit. The success rate indicates the percentage of instances where a method obtains the best possible result among all analyzed methods. Although this seems similar to the concept of accuracy, commonly used in classification scenarios, the rationale behind them is different. For example, we cannot

---

[1] These instances are publicly available at https://bit.ly/3wvxPly.

use the accuracy on our four heuristics since they do not perform any classification process. Then, we calculate the proportion of instances where these heuristics obtain the best result, and we use it to compare its performance against the remaining methods.

3.5   Using Machine Learning to Power Hyper-heuristics

This work explores using ML techniques to produce hyper-heuristics that solve the KP. To do so, we assume that choosing the most suitable heuristic at a given moment can be seen as a classification problem. Under this perspective, the hyper-heuristic is a classifier that chooses the correct class (a heuristic) given a particular input vector (the normalized features that characterize the problem state).

We propose two ways to apply such a classifier in this context. We will refer to them as static and dynamic, and they work as follows.

Dynamic. A hyper-heuristic implemented under the dynamic approach can use different heuristics when solving an instance. So, for each item, the hyper-heuristic uses the problem characterization to choose a heuristic. When the hyper-heuristic applies a heuristic to the instance (an item is packed), the number of items reduces. As a consequence, the problem characterization also changes. The hyper-heuristic process repeats until it packs the last item, deciding which heuristic to apply for each item to pack throughout the solving process. The dynamic approach is the most common way hyper-heuristics have been implemented in the literature [12,14,23].

Static. A hyper-heuristic from the static approach decides which heuristic to use only once per instance when it selects the first item to pack. The selected heuristic is used repeatedly until the instance is solved (no further changes in the heuristic are allowed). This means that when the hyper-heuristic faces an instance, it only uses the problem characterization to decide which heuristic to apply for the initial state. Later, the problem characterization becomes useless since the hyper-heuristic will ignore it. Most of the works that have used ML algorithms to produce hyper-heuristics implement this approach [16].

4   Experimental Results

We used the training set described in Sect. 3.3 to train the classifiers (the hyper-heuristics). We produced five hyper-heuristics using five different machine learning techniques: k Nearest Neighbors (KNN), Logistic Regression (LR), Multi-layer Perceptrons (MLP), Random Forests (RF), and Support Vector Machines (SVM). Thus, the five hyper-heuristics considered for the analysis are KNN-HH, LR-HH, MLPC-HH, RF-HH, and SVM-HH, where the prefix indicates the ML classifier used in each case. In all cases, we used Python's Scikit-Learn to implement the classifiers. For simplicity, we used the default configuration for each algorithm.

Once the hyper-heuristics were trained, we used them to solve the instances in the test set. Thus, all the results presented from this point on correspond exclusively to the testing set.

4.1 Analysis of the Success Rate

Before analyzing the success rate, imagine a hypothetical solver who always makes the right heuristic choice. Let this method be called ORACLE. As expected, the ORACLE will always make the right choice, and its success rate will be 100%. Of course, constructing the ORACLE is only possible after running all the solvers on a particular instance and selecting the best outcome. In this case, we have solved the instances in the test set using all the heuristics. Hence, we can construct the ORACLE and use it for comparison purposes.

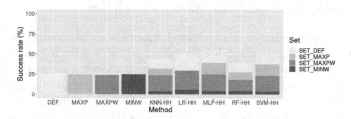

Fig. 1. Success rate of the methods under study in the testing set (the hyper-heuristics work using the dynamic approach).

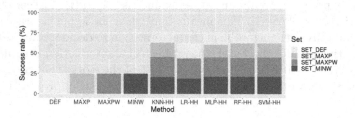

Fig. 2. Success rate of the methods under study in the testing set (the hyper-heuristics work using the static approach).

Figures 1 and 2 show the success rate of the methods studied in this work for the dynamic and static approaches, respectively. For a deeper analysis, we have shown each set's contribution to each method's success rate.

As mentioned in Sect. 3.3, the training and testing sets are composed of subsets where one heuristic is the best performer. This explains why the success rate of each of the heuristics is 25% since they obtain the best result only in their corresponding set. Regarding the dynamic approach (Fig. 1), we observed that, as expected, the hyper-heuristics obtain a better success rate than the heuristics. The best hyper-heuristic MLP-HH obtains the best result in a little more than half the instances in the test set. These results support the idea that using hyper-heuristics to solve the KP is good. When analyzing the hyper-heuristics under the static approach (Fig. 2), we observed a significant improvement in terms of the success rate concerning the hyper-heuristics running under the dynamic approach. Of course, the success rate of the heuristics remains the same since it does not depend on the approach used by the hyper-heuristic. Regardless of the outstanding behavior of the hyper-heuristics running under the static approach, they all obtain a success rate below 80%. Then, there is plenty of room for improvement in this regard.

4.2   Analysis of the Normalized Profit

In this section, we compare the performance of the methods considering the normalized profit. The higher the normalized profit, the better the method's performance. Figure 3 depicts the distribution of normalized profits of the heuristics and hyper-heuristics produced when used to solve the testing set under the dynamic approach.

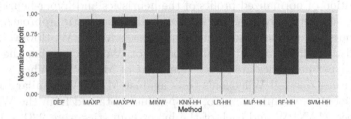

Fig. 3. Normalized profit of the methods under study in the testing set (the hyper-heuristics work using the dynamic approach).

The hyper-heuristics under the dynamic approach reduce their performance significantly. Although the medians of LR-HH, MLP-HH, and SVM-HH are larger than that of MAXPW (the best heuristic in this set), the variance in the results is larger than that of MAXPW. Comparing the means using a one-tail Wilcoxon's test fails to find enough evidence that supports the real median of any of these three hyper-heuristics (LR-HH, MLP-HH, and SVM-HH) is larger than MAXPW. In these tests, H_0 states that the real median of the normalized profits of MAXPW is larger or equal to that of the hyper-heuristic in turn. Conversely, H_1 states that the real median of the normalized profit of MAXPW is smaller than the one of the heuristics in turn. So, small p-values suggest that the corresponding hyper-heuristic outperforms MAXPW regarding the normalized profit. So, the statistical evidence is overwhelming against the idea that any of these hyper-heuristics has a real median larger than the one of MAXPW. In all the cases, the p-values of the tests for LR-HH, MLP-HH, and SVM-HH were 0.6313, 0.1791, and 0.2796, respectively. In simpler words, although LR-HH, MLP-HH, and SVM-HH are better than MAXPW in the testing set (based on the median normalized profit), there is no statistical evidence that supports that such hyper-heuristics are actually better than MAXPW.

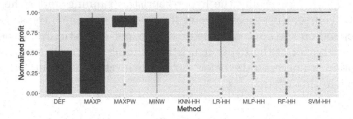

Fig. 4. Normalized profit of the methods under study in the testing set (the hyper-heuristics work using the static approach).

In the static approach, as described before, a decision is made only when packing the first item in the instance. The heuristic chosen to pack the first item is used to pack all the remaining items in the instance. Figure 4 depicts the distribution of normalized profits of the heuristics and hyper-heuristics produced when used to solve the testing set under the static approach. Among the four heuristics, the best individual performer is MAXPW. However, the five hyper-heuristics exhibit an outstanding behavior. We observe that the medians of the five hyper-heuristics are larger than that of MAXPW. When comparing the means using one-tail Wilcoxon's tests against MAXPW, similar to the one conducted for the dynamic scenario, the p-values obtained from the Wilcoxon's tests between MAXPW and each of the hyper-heuristics were 2.31×10^{-16} for LR-HH and 2.2×10^{-16} for the other hyper-heuristics. As observed, in all cases, the statistical evidence supports the idea that using ML techniques (such as the ones considered in this work) to produce hyper-heuristics for solving the KP is suitable and improves the results obtained by single heuristics.

5   Conclusion and Future Work

This work explores using ML methods to produce hyper-heuristics for solving the KP. These hyper-heuristics work in two different modes: dynamic and static. As previously stated, when using the dynamic approach, the solver selects a heuristic whenever the hyper-heuristic must pack an item. Then, we obtain a solution by applying a sequence of heuristics, not a single one. This is different from what happens in the static approach, where only one choice is made. Although the dynamic approach remains the most used regarding hyper-heuristics, our results suggest that using the static approach may be a better idea since hyper-heuristics working on such an approach (only choosing a heuristic when the search starts) obtained the best results on a sample level and a statistical one (with 5% of significance). Besides, the computational effort derived from the dynamic approach is more significant since it implies invoking the hyper-heuristic for every decision. In contrast, the static approach only requires invoking the hyper-heuristic once per instance.

Regarding future work, it seems interesting to explore other ML methods and compare their performance against other hyper-heuristic approaches, and not only against the heuristics. Besides, our results on the differences between the static and dynamic approaches should be verified in other problem domains with larger instance sets.

References

1. Assi, M., Haraty, R.A.: A survey of the knapsack problem, pp. 1–6. IEEE, November 2018. https://doi.org/10.1109/ACIT.2018.8672677
2. Best, M.J., Ritter, K.: Linear Programming Active Set Analysis and Computer Programs. Prentice Hall Englewood Cliffs, N.J., January 1985
3. Bhargava, A.Y.: Dynamic Programming, vol. 1. Manning Publications, Shelter Island, 1 edn., May 2016
4. Bretthauer, K.M., Shetty, B.: The nonlinear knapsack problem - algorithms and applications. Eur. J. Oper. Res. **138**, 459–472 (2002). https://doi.org/10.1016/S0377-2217(01)00179-5
5. Burke, E.K.: Hyper-heuristics: a survey of the state of the art. J. Oper. Res. Soc. **64**(12), 1695–1724 (2013)
6. Cacchiani, V., Iori, M., Locatelli, A., Martello, S.: Knapsack problems - an overview of recent advances. part i: Single knapsack problems. Comput. Oper. Res. **143**, 105692 (2022). https://doi.org/10.1016/j.cor.2021.105692, https://www.sciencedirect.com/science/article/pii/S0305054821003877
7. Drake, J.H., Hyde, M., Ibrahim, K., Ozcan, E.: A genetic programming hyper-heuristic for the multidimensional knapsack problem. Kybernetes **43**, 1500–1511 (2014). https://doi.org/10.1108/K-09-2013-0201
8. Duhart, B., Camarena, F., Ortiz-Bayliss, J.C., Amaya, I., Terashima-Marín, H.: An experimental study on ant colony optimization hyper-heuristics for solving the knapsack problem. In: Martínez-Trinidad, J.F., Carrasco-Ochoa, J.A., Olvera-López, J.A., Sarkar, S. (eds.) MCPR 2018. LNCS, vol. 10880, pp. 62–71. Springer, Cham (2018). https://doi.org/10.1007/978-3-319-92198-3_7
9. Eddy, S.R.: What is dynamic programming? Nat. Biotechnol. **22**, 909–910 (2004). https://doi.org/10.1038/nbt0704-909
10. Žerovnik, J.: Heuristics for np-hard optimization problems - simpler is better!? Logist. Sustain. Transp. **6**, 1–10 (2015). https://doi.org/10.1515/jlst-2015-0006
11. Kellerer, H., Pferschy, U., Pisinger, D.: Basic Algorithm Concepts, pp. 27–29. Springer, Berlin, 1 edn., October 2004. https://doi.org/10.1007/978-3-540-24777-7
12. Mischek, F., Musliu, N.: Reinforcement learning for cross-domain hyper-heuristics. In: Raedt, L.D. (ed.) Proceedings of the Thirty-First International Joint Conference on Artificial Intelligence, IJCAI-22. pp. 4793–4799. International Joint Conferences on Artificial Intelligence Organization, July 2022. https://doi.org/10.24963/ijcai.2022/664, main Track

13. Mougouei, D., Powers, D.M.W., Moeini, A.: An Integer Linear Programming Model for Binary Knapsack Problem with Dependent Item Values, vol. 10400, pp. 144–154. Springer, Cham, 1 edn., July 2017. https://doi.org/10.1007/978-3-319-63004-5_12

14. Ochoa, G., et al.: HyFlex: a benchmark framework for cross-domain heuristic search. In: Hao, J.-K., Middendorf, M. (eds.) EvoCOP 2012. LNCS, vol. 7245, pp. 136–147. Springer, Heidelberg (2012). https://doi.org/10.1007/978-3-642-29124-1_12

15. Olivas, F., Amaya, I., Ortiz-Bayliss, J.C., Conant-Pablos, S.E., Terashima-Marin, H.: A fuzzy hyper-heuristic approach for the 0-1 knapsack problem, pp. 1–8. IEEE, July 2020. https://doi.org/10.1109/CEC48606.2020.9185710

16. Ortiz-Bayliss, J.C., Amaya, I., Cruz-Duarte, J.M., Gutierrez-Rodriguez, A.E., Conant-Pablos, S.E., Terashima-Marín, H.: A general framework based on machine learning for algorithm selection in constraint satisfaction problems. Appl. Sci. 11(6) (2021). https://doi.org/10.3390/app11062749

17. Ortiz-Bayliss, J.C., Terashima-Marín, H., Conant-Pablos, S.E.: Neural networks to guide the selection of heuristics within constraint satisfaction problems. In: Martínez-Trinidad, J.F., Carrasco-Ochoa, J.A., Ben-Youssef Brants, C., Hancock, E.R. (eds.) MCPR 2011. LNCS, vol. 6718, pp. 250–259. Springer, Heidelberg (2011). https://doi.org/10.1007/978-3-642-21587-2_27

18. Pillay, N., Beckedahl, D.: Evohyp - a java toolkit for evolutionary algorithm hyper-heuristics, pp. 2706–2713. IEEE, June 2017. https://doi.org/10.1109/CEC.2017.7969636

19. Plata-González, L.F., Amaya, I., Ortiz-Bayliss, J.C., Conant-Pablos, S.E., Terashima-Marín, H., Coello Coello, C.A.: Evolutionary-based tailoring of synthetic instances for the knapsack problem. Soft Comput. 23, 12711–12728 (2019). https://doi.org/10.1007/s00500-019-03822-w

20. RASHID, M.H.: A GPU accelerated parallel heuristic for the 2d knapsack problem with rectangular pieces, pp. 783–787. IEEE (11 2018). https://doi.org/10.1109/UEMCON.2018.8796818

21. Sánchez-Díaz, X., Ortiz-Bayliss, J.C., Amaya, I., Cruz-Duarte, J.M., Conant-Pablos, S.E., Terashima-Marín, H.: A feature-independent hyper-heuristic approach for solving the knapsack problem. Appl. Sci. 11, 10209 (2021). https://doi.org/10.3390/app112110209

22. Tu, C., Bai, R., Aickelin, U., Zhang, Y., Du, H.: A deep reinforcement learning hyper-heuristic with feature fusion for online packing problems. Expert Syst. Appl. 230 (2023). https://doi.org/10.1016/j.eswa.2023.120568

23. Tyasnurita, R., Özcan, E., John, R.I.: Learning heuristic selection using a time delay neural network for open vehicle routing. In: 2017 IEEE Congress on Evolutionary Computation (CEC), pp. 1474–1481 (2017). https://api.semanticscholar.org/CorpusID:5959987

24. Zeng, Z., Xiong, C., Yuan, X., Bai, Y., Jin, Y., Lu, D., Lian, L.: Information-driven path planning for hybrid aerial underwater vehicles, April 2022

Computer Vision

Pattern Recognition of Pupillary Reflex Dynamics to Isoluminescent RGB Chromatic Stimuli

J. C. Belen-Luna[1]($\boxtimes$) (iD), C. O. González-Morán[2] (iD), V. Lima-Gómez[3] (iD), and E. Suaste-Gómez[1] (iD)

[1] Department of Electrical Engineering, CINVESTAV-IPN, Bioelectronics Section
Av. IPN #2508 Col. San Pedro Zacatenco, 07360 Mexico City, Mexico
{juancarlos.belenl,esuaste}@cinvestav.mx
[2] Centro Universitario UAEM Valle de México, Boulevard Universitario S/N Valle Escondido, Río San Javier, 54500 López Mateos, Mexico, Mexico
[3] Department of Ophthalmology, Hospital Juárez de México, Mexico City, Mexico

Abstract. In this work, the design, development and implementation of an experimental arrangement for the objective evaluation of pupillary reflex dynamics to chromatic RGB isoluminescent stimuli were carried out. The system were designed to operate in a controlled environment under scotopic conditions, surrounded by magnetic shielding. This environment allowed obtaining video-recordings of the pupillary response to RGB colors under the same luminance. Pattern recognition and processing of the pupil-frames was performed by means of artificial vision techniques. As a sample of the performance of the instrumentation developed, the graph of pupillary activity in front of a blue color for a subject is shown. As a prerequisite, a research protocol for this project was submitted and approved, since the work involved human experimentation. This research was registered under ethics committee number 007.2023.

Keywords: pupillary reflex · artificial vision · RGB

1 The Pupil

Light enters the eye through the cornea and the diameter of the incident light beam is controlled by means of the iris muscles that form the diaphragm of the eye. The opening formed in the iris is called the pupil [13]. The pupils light reflex is considered a servomechanism, because the pupil functions as a regulator of light that impacts the retina; it is part of the sympathetic and parasympathetic system [9]. Because the pupil is a limiting element in the optics of the visual system, when it changes size it controls the amount of light entering and visual functioning, since the eye has numerous optical aberrations that increase in measure with pupil dilation. Obtaining accurate pupillary area measurements requires the subject to remain completely still [19].

E. Mezura-Montes et al. (Eds.): MCPR 2024, LNCS 14755, pp. 131–140, 2024.
https://doi.org/10.1007/978-3-031-62836-8_13

For the study of pupil size it is essential to expose the eye to a luminous stimulus in a punctual way [22]. In this specific case we involve the study of pupillary reflexes and variability in pupil size. Pupillary activity is measured by an afferent (visual) and an efferent (motor; miosis-mydriasis) pathway. In miosis the pupil contracts and in mydriasis it dilates, this reaction phenomenon occurs according to the intensity of light [26]. In bright light it contracts and in the dark it dilates so the pupil diameter is given in proportion to this, generally varying between 2 and 8 mm. The size of the pupil depends on the density of the light flux, the type of light and the stimuli that surround it [8].

The pupil and its diameter are different in each person and between eyes of the same subject. Generally the average diameter is 3.5 mm with asymmetries up to 20% rarely exceeding 0.5 mm. The pupil diameter is usually larger in childhood and with increasing age becomes smaller and smaller [11]. The pupil is a good regulator of light since its responses to light are influenced by its initial size. After a contraction due to illumination a slow redilation occurs and the pupil returns to its initial size.

The pupil can only be considered a partial (and bandpass) regulator for brief changes in light [23]. The frequency response of the pupillary reflex corresponds to a low-pass filter, with a cutoff frequency of 1.5 Hz [20]. The effects on pupillary responses with interaction between the luminance components of the stimulus and color are complex and further studies are required to fully understand how these hypothesized mechanisms work [3].

2   Color Vision

The visual information that we as humans perceive is processed in the visual or occipital cortex, which is located at the back of the brain. Within the visual cortex several distinct regions provide increasingly specialized forms of processing [21]. Color vision is an illusion created by interactions of billions of neurons in the brain. In the outside world there is no color, it is created by neural programs and projected onto the outside world we see.

Color is created using two properties of light, energy and vibrational frequency, or wavelength (λ). How our brain separates these two properties and then recombines them in the perception of color is a mystery that has intrigued scientists over the centuries [7]. Visible light is part of the electromagnetic radiation spectrum. Since light behaves as a wave, its λ is the distance between consecutive wave crests.

For the exposed in [21] the visible part in the spectrum of electromagnetic radiation is between λ of the 400 to 700 nm. And according to what is detailed in [15] in the visible spectrum, the (λ) for each color is: violet (400–430 nm), blue (430–480 nm), greenish-blue(480–490 nm), bluish-green (490–500 nm), green (500–510 nm), yellowish-green (510–560 nm), yellow-green (560- 570 nm), yellow (570–580 nm), orange (580–590 nm), reddish-orange (590–620 nm) and red (620–650 nm) according to the (CIE 1978).

Color is what we see when rays of light with a particular range of λ strike the retina. For which the visual cells of the retina called cones and rods serve as light receptors that control pupillomotor activity. The cones are in charge of differentiating the λ and are located in the central part or fovea and those responsible for night vision are the rods, located on the sides of the fovea. Color vision (trichromacy) is composed of three types of receptors or cones with different spectral sensitivity each for red, green and blue. That there are exactly three types of color cones explains why we are able to construct vision of any color. On the other hand, any alteration of one or all of them produces anomalies or lack of color vision [12].

3 Pupil Detection, Pattern Recognition and Tracking

Eye tracking technology appears with the aim of tracking eye movements and detecting eye position, some of the applications in various research areas are human-computer interaction, assistive technologies, driving assistance systems, biometrics, marketing analysis and medicine to mention a few. For example, in the medical field the pupil area can be used to support a doctors decision for early detection of diabetes, with the PLR (pupil light reflex) method detecting abnormalities in the pupil area in diabetic patients [16,17]. With recent developments in video-based eye-tracking or video-oculography (VOG) technology, eye tracking has become an important tool for cognitive behavioral studies in various areas [1,5,18]. In VOG systems, video cameras are used for monitoring and recording eye of the subjects movements as the cameras record eye movements while the subject performs various tasks or interacts with visual stimuli. And then implement specialized software for data analysis.

The detection of the eye position and the tracking of its movements are performed by detecting features related to its appearance, being the pupil and its center the most important features [10]. The implementation of VOG methods in controlled environments where the users motion is limited has allowed the development of systems with high accuracy as is the case with the content of this work. Since for better pupil detection, the camera must be positioned directly in front of the eye of subjects avoiding any movement [4].

Based on what was found in [2], eye movements and pupillary area changes in response to stimuli and controlled environments can be categorized according to patterns found with the implementation of a clustering algorithm. Therefore, this research aims to correlate the pupillary reflex areas in each subject, recognizing patterns in their contractions and dilations to isoluminescent RGB stimuli. By developing an innovative approach to quantify relevant features within a carefully controlled experimental environment, an accurate and repeatable capture of pupillary activity is achieved. This provides a comprehensive quantitative understanding of the dynamics of the human visual system's response to color.

4   Instrumentation

A well elaborated methodology not only guides the execution of the experiments in an efficient way, but also supports the confidence in the results obtained. That is why, in Fig. 1 you can visualize the process diagram to be followed for the development of this research, for the recording and analysis of the dynamics of pupillary reflexes to colors. To obtain the recording of the pupillary reflexes (PR), a system was designed that allows the recording of the changes in the pupillary area based on the consensual reflex to light [20], analyzing its response according to the luminance and chromaticity of each of the three stimuli (RGB). The design was based on a VOG system [14, 16, 25] that allows us to record the right pupil of the subject for 4 s in which the stimulus is projected for a time of 10 milliseconds, this process is repeated for 3 occasions for each RGB color. In Fig. 2 it is observed that the distance D1 (eye-stimulus) is 30 cm, the distance D2 (eye-camera lens) is 8 cm and the distance D3 (stimulus-camera lens) is 8 cm. The recording sequence is not repeated on more occasions due to the eye fatigue that could be generated to the subject, thus avoiding erroneous results. In front of the camera lens there is a 1.63 cm diameter infrared (IR) LED ring to illuminate the pupil in the penumbra, without affecting its response to stimulation. The IR ring is used for a minimal amount of time during recording to avoid damage to the subjects eye.

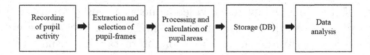

Fig. 1. Process diagram for methodology development.

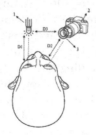

Fig. 2. Consensual pupil reflex, (1) LED RGB, (2) camera, (3) IR ring.

To control the necessary sequence, an electrical circuit was developed, through which the RGB LED is turned on by pressing the switch corresponding to each color, likewise the IR ring has another switch connected to the power supply that allows turning it on and off at will for the correct focus on the recording of the pupil, the sequence of work to obtain the video recordings is programmed in the Arduino IDE 2.2.1 and the components with their respective connections can be seen in Fig. 3. For the analysis of the pupillary response, in this particular case we used a Canon camera, model EOS Rebel T3i with the adaptation of a Sigma Macro 1:2.8 f = 50 mm lens. The manipulation software used to obtain the recordings is the EOS Utility. For the above, the characteristics of the pupil recording are the capture of 60 frames per second (fps) with an HD quality 1280×720 pixels and an ISO light sensitivity of 3200. On the other hand, for the projection of the stimulus and the recordings, a controlled environment was developed where the Goldmann perimeter is placed inside a magnetically shielded room (Faraday cage) under scotopic conditions. Each of the components that integrate the system for the recording of the PR to the colors can be seen in Fig. 4. In Fig. 5, an approach to the Goldmann perimeter is observed, which inside has a movable base with $2°$ of freedom which contains a support base for the camera and stimulus. As well as a background illumination calibrated with a photometer model IL1400 at 1.03 cd/m^2 to maintain the pupil size in an intermediate diameter, neither fully contracted nor fully dilated. On the outside, there is an ophthalmological support with an adjustable base for the user to support their chin and forehead. In addition, the stimulus inside is a 1 W ultra-bright LED diode of the RGBW type, calibrated with the IL1400 photometer in its red, green and blue colors at the same luminance of 93.19 in cd/m^2, the stimulus has a diffusion filter in front, followed by a biconvex lens for its projection and the background illumination is achieved with the fragments of a white light LED strip powered at 12 V.

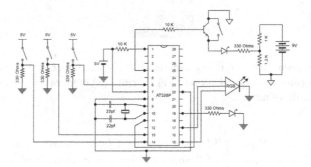

Fig. 3. Electrical diagram of the components that integrate the control system.

5   Experimental Results

Once the recordings of the subject are obtained, the collected videos are defragmented by means of a programming algorithm which obtains only the frames that contain information of the pupil shots (pupil-frames). Since in each of the three tests with each of the three colors, there is a pause for pupil size recovery and the camera obtains dark images for 6 s, during which time the IR is

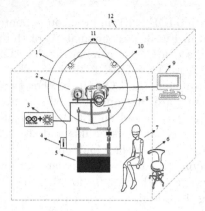

Fig. 4. (1) Goldmann perimeter, (2) stimulus, (3) control system, (4) DC source, (5) ophthalmological support, (6) adjustable bench, (7) subject, (8) IR ring, (9) PC, (10) camera, (11) background illumination, (12) Faraday cage.

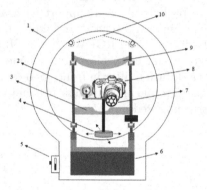

Fig. 5. (1) Goldmann perimeter, (2) stimulus, (3) chin support, (4) movable base, (5) DC source, (6) ophthalmological support (7) IR ring, (8) camera, (9) forehead support, (10) background illumination.

turned off. Regularly the pupil-frames captured for each color add up to a total of 720 fps, having a sequence of 3 shots of the stimulus with a recording of 4 s ($60fps \times 4sec \times 3shots = 720fps$).

It is worth mentioning that the number of pupil-frames is not the same for each subject since sometimes, although it is requested to avoid blinking this does not always work, so the pupil-frames contaminated with the eyelid are discarded manually. Due to the above, in the ideal scenario we would have 720 fps in each of the 3 colors with a sequence of 3 shots for each color on a single subject, which would result in a total of 2160 fps ($720fps \times 3colors = 2160fps$).

Once this is achieved, the process to follow is shown in Fig. 6 where the first element is the recording file, based on which the algorithm that extracts the fps that make up the video is worked, also in this block the fps are processed according to a selection with the condition of containing a minimum value of significant pixels (threshold value), those pupil-frames that do not meet the condition are discarded, storing only those that do meet it in the folder. Once this block in the folder is finished, we proceed to a manual selection of pupil-frames classified as not necessary, since if the subject blinked during the recording the pupil-frames are not processable and likewise if they contain a minimum of the threshold value which means that the pupil-frames is very dark. Afterwards, having achieved the above, we have a folder with the total number of pupil-frames that will be processed in the next algorithm.

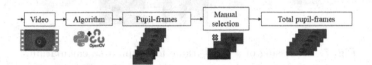

Fig. 6. Processes for obtaining pupil-frames.

Then, based on [6,24] the pupil-frames that are in the folder are processed by the algorithm which starts by applying the resizing of the pupil-frames, followed by the conversion to grayscale, then to improve the contrast an equalization is applied, followed by a smoothing to reduce the noise in the image, continuing with the brightness adjustment to modify the luminous intensity, then the thresholding for the segmentation that follows and once segmented proceeds to the hole filling so that the edge detection is applied exclusively to the part of the pupil and suppress its execution in the small segments present in the IR ring, therefore the adjustment of the ellipse is performed at the edge of the pupil detected and the calculation of the ellipse area ends with the detection of the pupil area. The above process can be visualized in Fig. 7.

Also in Fig. 8, the processes that integrate the second programming block are shown, for which all the pupil-frames are resized, followed by the treatment of the images by means of artificial vision techniques for the calculation of the pupil area for all its contractions and dilatations with respect to the stimulation during the test. Each of the areas is stored in a database (DB) in Excel file for further analysis and/or graphing.

Consequently, Fig. 9 shows the patterns of pupillary dynamics for a subject in response to the color blue, for which the values of the areas can be used to extract significant characteristics in response to different color stimuli. Such as the change of size, shape, speed of contraction and dilation, among others. The graph shows the pupil constrictions and dilations for S4 during the experimental protocol. The dotted lines mark the time of stimulation, based on this we infer that the latency time for each reaction is the same. The next stage of this research, having validated the compliance in obtaining the pupil-frames with the system developed here, is the generation of a extensive database for the analysis and classification in the interpretation of the features extracted

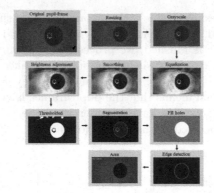

Fig. 7. Processing of a pupil-frame for pupil area calculation.

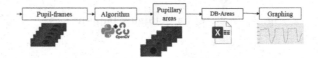

Fig. 8. Processes for the treatment of pupil-frames and their results.

with machine learning techniques. This will allow the comparison of pupillary responses between different subjects and the evaluation of the consistency of the pupillary reflex within the same subject, as well as the comparison in front of different colors.

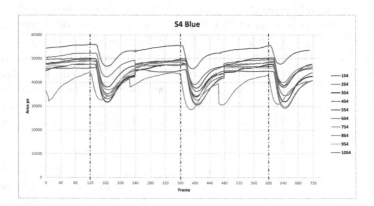

Fig. 9. Pupillary reflex of a subject during ten repetitions to the color blue. (Color figure online)

6   Conclusions and Future Work

The development of this innovative VOG system has made it possible to accurately capture pupillary activity in a controlled environment for each of the

RGB colors. Plotting the obtained pupillary reflex areas for a subject with the color blue demonstrates that the instrumentation developed meets the objective. Based on the results so far, we assume that the subject's pupillary reflex is similar and with the use of machine learning techniques we will validate or refute this inference. It is important to note that the repeatability of the tests can be effectively scaled to a significant level of individuals, thanks to the rigorous control of all variables and elements involved during the recordings. The next step in this research will involve the recording of subjects with different genders and ages, in order to build a extensive database. Subsequently, a thorough processing and analysis of the data (pupil-frames) will be carried out, comparing them with the results obtained from the pupillary reflexes to color stimuli for each subject. This approach will allow the classification of patterns in pupillary activity, which will be fundamental for the identification of significant trends in relation to responses to color stimuli. In addition, it is intended to find their correlation with visual evoked potentials.

References

1. Attard-Johnson, J., Ó Ciardha, C., Bindemann, M.: Comparing methods for the analysis of pupillary response. Behav. Res. Methods **51**, 83–95 (2019). https://doi.org/10.3758/s13428-018-1108-6
2. Balaban, C.D., Kiderman, A., Szczupak, M., Ashmore, R.C., Hoffer, M.E.: Patterns of pupillary activity during binocular disparity resolution. Front. Neurol. **9** (2018). https://doi.org/10.3389/fneur.2018.00990
3. Carle, C.F., James, A.C., Maddess, T.: The pupillary response to color and luminance variant multifocal stimuli. Invest. Ophthal. Vis. Sci. **54**(1), 467–475 (2013). https://doi.org/10.1167/iovs.12-10829
4. Fuhl, W., Kübler, T., Sippel, K., Rosenstiel, W., Kasneci, E.: ExCuSe: robust pupil detection in real-world scenarios. In: Azzopardi, G., Petkov, N. (eds.) CAIP 2015. LNCS, vol. 9256, pp. 39–51. Springer, Cham (2015). https://doi.org/10.1007/978-3-319-23192-1_4
5. Fuhl, W., Santini, T., Kasneci, G., Kasneci, E.: Pupilnet: convolutional neural networks for robust pupil detection. CoRR **abs/1601.04902** (2016). http://arxiv.org/abs/1601.04902
6. Gonzalez, R.C..R.E.W.: Digital Image Processing. Pearson, London (2009)
7. Gouras, P.: Color Vision. University of Utah Health Sciences Center, Salt Lake City (UT) (1995). http://europepmc.org/books/NBK11537
8. de Groot, S.G., Gebhard, J.W.: Pupil size as determined by adapting luminance*. J. Opt. Soc. Am. **42**(7), 492–495 (1952). https://doi.org/10.1364/JOSA.42.000492
9. Heed, A.F.: ADLER'S Physiology of the eye Clinical Application. The C. V Mosby Company, seventh edition edn. (1981)
10. Larumbe-Bergera, A., Garde, G., Porta, S., Cabeza, R., Villanueva, A.: Accurate pupil center detection in off-the-shelf eye tracking systems using convolutional neural networks. Sensors **21**(20) (2021). https://doi.org/10.3390/s21206847
11. Leon-Sarmiento, F.E., Prada, D.G., Gutiérrez, C.: Pupila, pupilometría y pupilografía. Acta Neurol Colomb **24**(4), 188–197 (2008)
12. Malacara, D.: Color vision and colorimetry: theory and applications (2011)
13. Marín, M.C.P.: Óptica fisiológica. Editorial Complutense (2006)

14. Pinheiro, H.M., da Costa, R.M.: Pupillary light reflex as a diagnostic aid from computational viewpoint: a systematic literature review. J. Biomed. Inform. **117**, 103757 (2021). https://doi.org/10.1016/j.jbi.2021.103757
15. Rodríguez Guzmán, D., Zúñiga López, A., Suaste Gómez, E.: Respuestas pupilares a estímulos cromáticos en el espectro de 400 nm a 650 nm, en el estado estable. Revista mexicana de física **51**(4), 365–370 (2005)
16. Sánchez, A.S., Suaste, E., Villarreal, E.: Isoluminant chromatic high speed video-oculography to study the dynamic of the pupillary response. In: Braidot, A., Hadad, A. (eds.) VI Latin American Congress on Biomedical Engineering CLAIB 2014, Paraná, Argentina 29, 30 & 31 October 2014. IFMBE Proceedings, vol. 49, pp. 465–467. Springer, Cham (2015). https://doi.org/10.1007/978-3-319-13117-7_119
17. Sari, J.N., Hanung, A.N., Lukito, E.N., Santosa, P.I., Ferdiana, R.: A study on algorithms of pupil diameter measurement. In: 2016 2nd International Conference on Science and Technology-Computer (ICST), pp. 188–193 (2016). https://doi.org/10.1109/ICSTC.2016.7877372
18. Sharma, S., et al.: Factors influencing the pupillary light reflex in healthy individuals. Graefe's Archive Clin. Exp. Ophthalmol. **254**, 1353–1359 (2016). https://doi.org/10.1007/s00417-016-3311-4
19. Stark, L.: Stability, oscillations, and noise in the human pupil servomechanism. Proc. IRE **47**(11), 1925–1939 (1959). https://doi.org/10.1109/JRPROC.1959.287206
20. Stark, L., Sherman, P.M.: A servoanalytic study of consensual pupil reflex to light. J. Neurophysiol. **20**(1), 17–26 (1957)
21. Stone, J.V.: Vision and Brain: How we Perceive the World. MIT Press, Cambridge (2012)
22. Suaste-Gomez, E., Guzman, M.C.M.D.A.R., Druzgalski, C.: Pupillary responses to chromatic stimulus. In: Rogowitz, B.E., Pappas, T.N. (eds.) Human Vision and Electronic Imaging V. vol. 3959, pp. 709 – 719. International Society for Optics and Photonics, SPIE (2000). https://doi.org/10.1117/12.387202
23. Sun, F., Stark, L.: Pupillary escape intensified by large pupillary size. Vision. Res. **23**(6), 611–615 (1983). https://doi.org/10.1016/0042-6989(83)90066-4
24. Vázquez Romaguera, T., Vázquez Romaguera, L., Castro Piñol, D., Vázquez Seis-dedos, C.R.: Pupil center detection approaches: a comparative analysis. Computación y Sistemas **25**(1), 67–81 (2021)
25. Villamar, L.A., Sánchez, A.S., Suaste, E.: Methodology to determinate pupillary responses based in high speed videoculography in clinical eye applications. AIP Conf. Proc. **1310**(1), 162–165 (2010). https://doi.org/10.1063/1.3531597
26. Wiechers, D.E.G.: Exploración de los reflejos pupilares. McGraw-Hill Education, New York, NY (2015), accessmedicina.mhmedical.com/content.aspx?aid=1117580925

On the Minimal Perimeter Polygon for Digital Objects in the Triangular Tiling

Petra Wiederhold[✉][iD]

Centro de Investigación y de Estudios Avanzados (CINVESTAV-IPN), Avenida I.P.N. 2508, Col. San Pedro Zacatenco, 07360 Ciudad de México, México
petra.wiederhold@cinvestav.mx, pwiederhold@gmail.com

Abstract. The present work proposes an algorithm to determine the minimum perimeter polygon (MPP) of digital objects given as edge-adjacency-connected sets of tiles, in the plane tiling of regular triangles. As input data, it uses a canonical boundary path of tiles obtained via boundary tracing. The MPP algorithm finds the ordered sequence of vertices of the MPP frontier, being the shortest polygonal curve which visits the entire boundary. It relies on the construction and iterative restriction of cones of visibility through boundary tiles. The algorithm is illustrated by examples, and a correctness proof is outlined for digital objects with simple boundary paths, that is, whose boundaries are digital Jordan curves.

Keywords: minimum perimeter polygon · triangular tiling · boundary tracing for triangular pixels · relative convex hull · geodesic convex hull

1 Introduction

The triangular and hexagonal plane tilings have received much attention for 2D digital image modelling, as alternative to the tiling of squares which may be identified with the pixels in the digital plane $(c\mathbb{Z})^2$. For example, triangular pixels are used to develop digital distance functions and geometrical transformations [2,13], to design digital topological spaces and skeletonization algorithms [2,3,7, 11,13], to study convexity properties [15], and, for data visualization [10]. This article considers the plane tiling of equilateral triangles as support of digital images, the pixels are triangle tiles, all of the same size, the objects of interest are represented as edge-adjacency-connected sets of tiles.

The *minimum perimeter polygon (MPP)* was defined in the 1970 s in [14,15], where pixels were identified with polygonal tiles in plane tilings, and, where the MPP was shown to be a compact and useful representation of digital objects which describes their convexity and concavity features. Such properties were later studied in more detail for objects of square pixels with simple boundaries, for example in [8,9,12]. It was proved in [17] that for objects of square pixels, the MPP perimeter is a multigrid convergent perimeter estimator for any compact simply connected set $S \subset \mathbb{R}^2$ whenever its frontier is a smooth Jordan curve.

E. Mezura-Montes et al. (Eds.): MCPR 2024, LNCS 14755, pp. 141–154, 2024.
https://doi.org/10.1007/978-3-031-62836-8_14

In this regard, the MPP frontier is the minimal length Jordan curve which circumscribes $J^-(S)$ - the Inner Jordan digitization of S, but lies inside $J^+(S)$ - the Outer Jordan digitization of S [8,17]. It is relevant in [8,17] that $J^+(S)$ corresponds to a 4-connected object in $(c\mathbb{Z})^2$ whose boundary is a simple 4-path, also called digital Jordan 4-curve [8].

The MPP in [17] was studied in relation to the *relative convex hull*, also known as *geodesic hull* [18], of A with respect to B, where A, B both are simple polygons in $\mathbb{R}^2$ such that A lies in the interior of B. For the special application to Jordan digitizations based on square pixels, the MPP from [17] coincides with the MPP due to [14,15] which, at its origin, is more general and uses a distinct digitization. It was proved in [15] that under certain suppositions, for a subset C of a polygonal tiling M, the MPP of C coincides with the relative convex hull of a special subset of $|C|$ with respect to $|C|$ (denoting the point set union of all tiles belonging to C), but the involved sets are not necessarily simple polygons.

The first algorithm for determining the MPP vertices for digital objects represented by sets of general polygonal tiles, was proposed in [15], the restrictions imposed there are satisfied, for example, for rectangular and triangular tilings. There was an earlier algorithm with a similar strategy in [14] developed for rectangular tiles. The algorithms from [14,15] are many cited in the literature, including in modern textbooks such as [4,5,8], where adaptations to simple 4-contours are suggested to approximate objects. The recent work [19] showed that the algorithms from [14,15] and their adaptations used in [4,5,8], all are failing, and that their mathematical foundation is erroneous, even for square and rectangular tilings. A new MPP algorithm which use the correct ideas of previous works but avoids their errors, was proposed in [19] for sets of rectangular tiles.

The present work considers the MPP for digital objects given as edge-adjacency-connected sets of triangle tiles which have simple boundary paths. Such objects are a special kind of regular and normal complexes due to [14,15]. We propose an algorithm to calculate the MPP vertices, illustrate it by examples, and present the main ideas of a correctness proof. Our algorithm adapts the strategies from [19] to the triangular tiling. It uses as input a boundary path obtained by boundary tracing which is similar to known methods of contour finding for 4-connected objects of square pixels, and, relies on the iterative construction of cones of visibility through forthcoming tiles. We also propose an algorithm to perform the boundary tracing for edge-adjacency-connected subsets of triangles tiles, which generates so-called canonical boundary paths.

In the remaining, Sect. 2 resumes preliminaries, Sect. 3 introduces the MPP for objects in polygonal tilings due to [14,15]. Section 4 treats boundary paths generated by boundary tracing, and presents an algorithm for this. Section 5 proposes an MPP algorithm for objects with simple boundary paths, shows examples, and outlines a correctness proof.

2   Preliminaries

Let $\mathbb{Z}$ denote the set of integers, $\mathbb{R}^2$ the Euclidean plane with standard topology where fr means the topological frontier, int the interior, and d the Euclidean metric. For $p, q \in \mathbb{R}^2$, $\overline{pq}$ is the straight line segment from p to q. If $p \neq q$, $\overrightarrow{pq}$ is the directed straight line segment from p to q. All formulae refer to the standard Cartesian coordinate system in $\mathbb{R}^2$.

A *polygonal curve* is a closed curve $\gamma = f([0, 1])$ in $\mathbb{R}^2$, with a continues function $f : [0, 1] \subset \mathbb{R} \rightarrow \mathbb{R}^2$, $f(0) = f(1)$, where there exist $n \in \mathbb{N}$ and t_1, $t_2, \cdots, t_n$ with $t_0 = 0 < t_1 < \cdots < t_n = 1$ such that each $f([t_{i-1}, t_i])$, $i \in \{1, 2, \cdots, n\}$, is a straight line segment. The sum of lengths of all its straight line segments gives the finite *length* of γ. A point $f(t_i) \in \gamma$ ($1 \leq i \leq n - 1$) is a *vertex* of γ if $f(t_i) \notin \overline{f(t_{i-1})f(t_{i+1})}$. A closed curve $\gamma = f([0, 1])$ is called *simple curve* or *Jordan curve* if f is injective on $[0, 1)$. A *simple polygon* is defined as compact connected subset of $\mathbb{R}^2$ whose frontier is a Jordan polygonal curve. A simple polygon has no hole, has at least three vertices, and, its frontier does not touch itself.

More generally, a *weakly simple polygonal curve* γ may touch itself or trace back on itself, but does not transversely cross itself [18], then γ encloses *weakly simple polygon* P, and any vertex of γ is a *vertex* of P. Even a single point p is considered as a weakly simple polygonal curve having the unique vertex p, as well as a segment $\overline{pq}$ for distinct $p, q \in \mathbb{R}^2$, the cyclic vertex sequence (p, q) determines that curve. By a *polygon* we mean a compact subset of $\mathbb{R}^2$ which is a weakly simple polygon, this includes the special case of a simple polygon.

We assume Jordan curves and weakly simple polygonal curves always being traced in counterclockwise sense. Then a polygon can be uniquely represented as cyclic sequence of its vertices $(p_1, p_2, \cdots, p_k)$, where $p_i \notin \overline{p_{(i-1 \bmod k)}p_{(i+1 \bmod k)}}$ for all $i \in \{1, \cdots, k\}$. The vertices of a simple polygon are all distinct, which is not necessarily true for a weakly simple polygon. The *perimeter* of a polygon P given by the cyclic sequence $(p_1, p_2, \cdots, p_k)$ of vertices, equals the sum of lengths of the segments $\overline{p_i p_{i+1}}$, $1 \leq i \leq k - 1$, and of the segment $\overline{p_k p_1}$. Specially, the polygon $P = \overline{pq}$ has perimeter $2d(p, q)$, a polygon being a single point has perimeter zero.

The orientation of a point triple $p_1 = (x_1, y_1)$, $p_2 = (x_2, y_2)$, $p_3 = (x_3, y_3) \in \mathbb{R}^2$ can be described by $D(p_1, p_2, p_3) = x_1 y_2 + y_1 x_3 + x_2 y_3 - x_3 y_2 - x_2 y_1 - x_1 y_3$. In a right-hand Cartesian coordinate system, $D(p_1, p_2, p_3) < 0$ if and only if p_3 lies on the right of $\overrightarrow{p_1 p_2}$, (p_1, p_2, p_3) forms a *right turn*. $D(p_1, p_2, p_3) > 0$ means that p_3 lies on the left of $\overrightarrow{p_1 p_2}$, (p_1, p_2, p_3) forms a *left turn*. $D(p_1, p_2, p_3) = 0$ characterizes *collinearity*: p_1, p_2, p_3 belong to the same straight line segment which may be degenerated to a point. For consecutive points p_1, p_2, p_3 in a cyclic sequence of curve points of a polygonal curve γ traced in counterclockwise sense, p_2 is called *convex* if $D(p_1, p_2, p_3) > 0$ (left turn), and *concave* if $D(p_1, p_2, p_3) < 0$ (right turn). When a weakly simple polygonal curve γ is counterclockwisely traced, the polygon P enclosed always lies on the left of (or on) γ, whereas $(\mathbb{R}^2 \setminus P)$ lies strictly on the right.

3   Minimum Perimeter Polygon for Objects in Triangular Tilings

A *polygonal tiling* is a family of convex polygons in the plane, named *tiles*, where each of them has non-empty interior, their union covers the plane, their interiors are pairwise disjoint, and, any $p \in \mathbb{R}^2$ is the centre of some open disc which intersects only a finite number of tiles [6]. The intersection of any two tiles, either is empty, or is a non-zero length straight line segment named an *edge* of the tiling, or is a point which is a vertex of at least one of these tiles.

By a *triangular tiling* $\mathcal{M}$ we mean a polygonal tiling in $\mathbb{R}^2$ whose tiles all are equilateral triangles of the same size, and where any edge is an entire side of some tile. Hence, any two tiles which intersect each other, share a side, or, share a vertex. Each edge is a common side of exactly two tiles, and each vertex is the common vertex of three tiles. Let the tiling be positioned as shown in Fig. 1, where the tiles form rows parallel to the x-axis. In this article, when not more specified, let $\mathcal{C}$ be a finite non-empty subset of $\mathcal{M}$, and, denote its point set union by $|\mathcal{C}| = \bigcup \mathcal{C} = \{p \in \mathbb{R}^2 : p \in T \text{ for a tile } T \in \mathcal{C}\} \subset \mathbb{R}^2$.

Two distinct tiles which share an edge, are called *(edge-) adjacent* or *neighbors*. The adjacency relation generates the *adjacency graph* $G(\mathcal{M})$, graph theory provides paths and connectivity: a *path* is a sequence of tiles $(t_1, t_2, \cdots, t_k)$ such that t_i is neighbor of t_{i+1} for each $i = 1, 2, \cdots, n-1$, it is *closed* if also t_k is neighbor of t_1. A set $A \subset \mathcal{M}$ is *(edge-adjacency-) connected* if any two tiles of A are connected via a path in A. If A has at least two tiles, $T \in A$ is an *end tile* if T is adjacent to exactly one other tile of A.

Each tile of $\mathcal{M}$ has three neighbors, hence it has valence 3 as node of $G(\mathcal{M})$. The tiles of $\mathcal{M}$ are of two types: upright and inverted triangles. Since all neighbors of an upright triangle are inverted triangles, and vice versa, the tiles in any path alternately are upright and inverted triangles.

A *regular path* $(t_1, t_2, \cdots, t_k)$ in $\mathcal{C}$ is defined to satisfy that $t_{i-1} \neq t_{i+1}$ for each $2 \leq i \leq k-1$ (and $t_{k-1} \neq t_1$, $t_k \neq t_2$, for a closed path) [14]. Analogous to the well-known *simple 4-curves*, also called *Jordan digital curves* [8], a *simple path* is a closed path whose each element has exactly two neighbors in this path. Clearly any simple path is regular, but not vice versa.

Following [14,15], the set of tiles of $\mathcal{C}$ that meet $fr(|\mathcal{C}|)$, is called the *boundary* $\mathcal{B}(\mathcal{C})$ of $\mathcal{C}$. Any closed path consisting exactly of all tiles of $\mathcal{B}(\mathcal{C})$, is named a *boundary path* of $\mathcal{C}$. Note that $\mathcal{B}(\mathcal{C})$ is a uniquely defined set, but $\mathcal{C}$ may have several boundary paths with distinct properties, even $\mathcal{B}(\mathcal{C})$ may be not connected then $\mathcal{C}$ has no boundary path. The set $core(\mathcal{C}) \subset \mathbb{R}^2$ given as the point set union of all tiles of $\mathcal{C}$, all edges belonging to tiles of $\mathcal{C}$, and all vertices of tiles of $\mathcal{C}$, whenever all these do not meet $fr(|\mathcal{C}|)$, is called the *core* of $\mathcal{C}$.

Definition 1. *(from [14, 15]) Let $\mathcal{C}$ be a finite non-empty subset of a triangular tiling $\mathcal{M}$, and $P \subset \mathbb{R}^2$ a polygon. Then $\mathcal{C}$ is called an **image** of P, and P is called a **preimage** of $\mathcal{C}$, if $P \subseteq |\mathcal{C}|$ and $T \cap P \neq \emptyset$ for each tile $T \in \mathcal{C}$. Any polygon that has shortest perimeter among all polygons which are preimages of $\mathcal{C}$, is called a **minimum perimeter polygon (MPP)** of $\mathcal{C}$.*

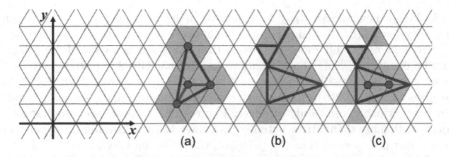

Fig. 1. A triangular tiling positioned as aligned to the Cartesian coordinate system. (a) and (b) present the same set C (shaded grey), (a) shows its core in red and its MPP frontier in blue. C is also an image of the polygon drawn in (b). The latter polygon is also a preimage of the set of tiles shown in (c) which has a smaller core. (Color figure online)

Now let C be a finite non-empty subset of a polygonal tiling. C is named **regular** if it has a regular boundary path, and $fr(|C|)$ is a Jordan curve [14], then C is (edge-adjacency-) connected and has neither end tiles nor holes. In [15], C is called **normal** if it has no end tile, and $|C|$ is simply connected in $\mathbb{R}^2$. Clearly, any regular set is normal. A normal set not necessarily is (edge-adjacency-) connected, it may present *cut points* whose deletion disconnects $|C|$. The set of tiles in Figs. 1(a)(b) is regular and normal, but its boundary has no simple boundary path. The set in Fig. 1(c) is not normal, it is not edge-adjacency-connected and has several end tiles.

The existence and uniqueness of the MPP was proved for regular subsets of rectangular tilings in [14], and for normal subsets of polygonal tilings where the union of each two adjacent tiles is convex [15]. Lemma 1 applies facts of Theorem 3.10 and Corollary 4.3 from [15] to subsets of triangular tilings. Due to Theorem 4.1 of [15], for any points a, b in a polygon B, there is a unique polygonal shortest path, called *geodesic* in B, which connects a and b. For two polygons $A \subseteq B$, A is called *convex relative* to B if A contains each geodesic in B which connects points a, b from A. The **relative convex hull** of A with respect to B is the intersection of all sets which contain A and are convex relative to B.

Lemma 1. *Any regular subset C with at least two tiles, of a triangular tiling, has a uniquely determined MPP which coincides with the relative convex hull of core(C) with respect to $|C|$. In particular, the MPP contains core(C) and is contained in $|C|$.*

For this article, define an **object** as any finite non-empty edge-adjacency-connected subset of a triangular tiling. Now suppose that an object C has a simple boundary path, then it has no end tile, and, it is easy to see that C is regular. If C has only one tile, C does not have a simple boundary path. If C has at least two tiles, it is easy to see that the lack of end tiles forces C to contain at least 6 tiles. The smallest such object has exactly 6 tiles having a common vertex and forming a hexagon, it will be denoted by C_{Hex}, see Fig. 2(a).

Adding a new tile to C_{Hex} to construct a larger object C with a simple boundary path $\beta(C)$, the edge-adjacency-connectivity and the lack of end tiles force to add more and more tiles such that always a hexagon of type C_{Hex} must be completed. Note that C contains neither one-tile-thin parts where $\beta(C)$ passes twice, nor two-tiles-thick parts where $\beta(C)$ passes "near from itself", as the objects in Figs. 2(b)(e). The latter means that $core(C)$ does not contain thin parts which consist only of edges. Figures 2(c)(d) show the smallest such objects with more than 6 tiles, actually they have 13 tiles, forming three pairwise overlapping hexagons of type C_{Hex}. Hence, the following is obtained:

Lemma 2. *Any object C which has a simple boundary path, in a triangular tiling, is a union of hexagons of type C_{Hex}. If C has more than six tiles, the core of C is a connected union of triangles.*

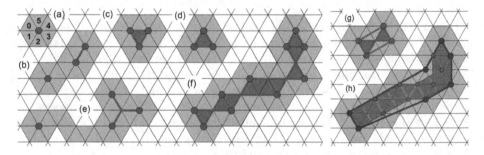

Fig. 2. Regular objects with core frontiers drawn red, the tiles contributing to the core are illuminated yellow in (a)–(g). (a), (c), (d), (f) show objects with simple boundary paths, the core in (a) is a point which coincides with the MPP. The objects (b),(e) do not have simple boundary paths, their cores are disconnected. (g), (h) show the extension of the core used in the proof of Lemma 3: for each two tiles contributing to the core but sharing only a vertex, the other vertices are connected by the line segments drawn green, to generate a rectangle, joining all these rectangles to the core creates a simple polygon, drawn yellow in (h), which contains the core but is contained in the MPP, the MPP frontier is depicted blue in (h). (Color figure online)

Lemma 3. *If C is an object having more than six tiles and a simple boundary path, in a triangular tiling, then the MPP of C is a simple polygon, where any concave MPP vertex is a concave vertex of $fr(|C|)$, and any convex MPP vertex is a convex vertex of $core(C)$.*

Proof. The affirmed property was proved in [16,17] for the relative convex hull of E with respect to F, if E, F are simple polygons and $E \subset int(F)$.

If C is an object with more than six tiles and having a simple boundary path, C is regular, its frontier is a Jordan curve, hence $B = |C|$ is a simple polygon. If the tiles contributing to the core form an edge-adjacency-connected set, then

$A = core(\mathcal{C})$ is a simple polygon and $A \subset int(B)$. Otherwise, there are tiles contributing to the core which touch each other only at a vertex, such as for the objects (f), (g) in Fig. 2. Then, the core can be extended as follows: for each two tiles which contribute to the core but shares only a vertex, the other vertices are connected by straight line segments as shown in Fig. 2(g), this generates a rectangle. Let $Ext(A)$ be the union of $core(\mathcal{C})$ with all these rectangles, see the set drawn yellow in Fig. 2(h). It is easy to see that $Ext(A)$ is a simple polygon with $core(\mathcal{C}) \subset Ext(A) \subset int(B)$, the convex vertices of A coincide with the convex vertices of $Ext(A)$, and the MPP of $\mathcal{C}$ coincides with the relative convex hull of $Ext(A)$ with respect to B. Hence the results from [17] can be applied to the sets A and B. □

4   Canonical Boundary Paths from Boundary Tracing

Boundary tracing, also called *contour tracing*, is a standard method in digital image processing to find the frontier of an object. For 4- and 8-connected objects in $\mathbb{Z}^2$, it is described, for example, in [4,5,8]. In [19], boundary tracing was generalized to edge-adjacency-connected subsets of rectangular tilings.

Now consider a triangular tiling $\mathcal{M}$, an object $\mathcal{C} \subset \mathcal{M}$ with at least two tiles, and a finite set $\mathcal{N}$ with $\mathcal{C} \subset \mathcal{N} \subset \mathcal{M}$ and such that the *background tiles* from $(\mathcal{N} \setminus \mathcal{C})$ fully surround the object $\mathcal{C}$. Similar as known for other neighborhood graphs, we use the *Freeman chain code* to represent paths in $G(\mathcal{N})$, see Fig. 3. For any tile $T \in G(\mathcal{N})$, the movement direction from T to each of its neighbors T', is coded by a number $f(T, T') \in \{0, 1, 2\}$. Since any path has alternately upright and inverted triangles, a path can be uniquely reconstructed from its Freeman chain code, whenever the type of the starting tile is known.

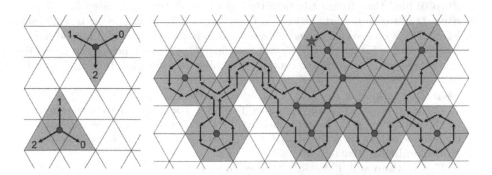

Fig. 3. Left: Freeman code for the edge-adjacency in the triangular tiling. Right: a regular set of tiles with its canonical boundary path. Due to Algorithm 1, that path starts at the leftmost tile of the top row, it is an upright triangle marked by a star in the figure, its Freeman chain code begins as $(2, 0, 2, 2, 1, 2, 1, 1, 1, 2, 2, 2, 1, \cdots)$.

Boundary tracing starts with finding a first boundary tile. One option is to find the leftmost tile T_0 of the top row of $\mathcal{C}$, as included in Algorithm 1, clearly

$T_0 \in \mathcal{B}(\mathcal{C})$. This can be done by scanning $\mathcal{N}$ on horizontal rows from the left to the right. Then T_0 has a left neighbor in the same row which belongs to the background: if T_0 is an upright triangle and $f(T_0, q) = 1$, or, if T_0 is an inverted triangle and $f(T_0, q) = 2$, then $q \notin \mathcal{C}$. For each last boundary tile T_n found, Algorithm 1 determines the Freeman code $b = f(T_n, T_{n-1})$, then inspects the tile T' in direction $(b+1) \mod 3$, if T' belongs to $\mathcal{C}$ then it is the next boundary tile found. Otherwise, the tile T' in direction $(b+2) \mod 3$ is inspected, it is the next boundary tile if it lies in $\mathcal{C}$. If not, the tile T' in direction $(b+3) \mod 3$ belongs to $\mathcal{C}$ and is the next boundary tile. The last case only occurs if T_n is an end tile of $\mathcal{C}$.

Algorithm 1 works for any edge-adjacency-connected set $\mathcal{C} \subset \mathcal{M}$ with at least two tiles and such that $|\mathcal{C}| \subset \mathbb{R}^2$ has no hole. It determines a uniquely defined boundary path $\beta(\mathcal{C}) = (T_0, T_1, T_2, \cdots, T_k)$ such that, when boundary tracing would be continued, the next tiles found would be, again, $T_{k+1} = T_0, T_{k+2} = T_1$. Step 2 will found T_0, again, when boundary tracing is finished, but this may happen also if the boundary path touches itself at T_0, the end condition test distinguishes between both situations. Since each Freeman code from Fig. 3 generates a counterclockwise order of the neigbors around a tile, the resulting boundary path counterclockwisely traces the boundary. The uniqueness of $\beta(\mathcal{C})$ is valid up to shiftings of that cyclic sequence.

Algorithm 1. Boundary tracing for a finite edge-adjacency-connected set $\mathcal{C}$ in a triangular tiling, where $\mathcal{C}$ has at least two tiles, and $|\mathcal{C}| \subset \mathbb{R}^2$ has no hole.

Input: A finite subset $\mathcal{N}$ of a triangular tiling, an object $\mathcal{C} \subset \mathcal{N}$ which is surrounded by tiles from the background $(\mathcal{N} \setminus \mathcal{C})$.

Output: List $\beta(\mathcal{C})$, a boundary path of $\mathcal{C}$.

1: **Step 0:** Find the leftmost tile T_0 of the top row of $\mathcal{C}$, then go to Step 1.
2: **Step 1:** Initialize the list $\beta(\mathcal{C}) := (T_0)$. Set $b := 1$ if T_0 is an upright triangle, set $b := 2$ if T_0 is an inverted triangle. Then perform iteratively $b := (b+1) \mod 3$. For each b, check whether the tile T' that satisfies $f(T_0, T') = b$, belongs to $\mathcal{C}$. While this is false, b is augmented to continue searching for a tile of $\mathcal{C}$. If $T' \in \mathcal{C}$, add T' to $\beta(\mathcal{C})$ (it becomes $\beta(\mathcal{C}) = (T_0, T_1)$), then go to Step 2.
3: **Step 2:** Determine $b := f(T_n, T_{n-1})$ for the current list $\beta(\mathcal{C}) = (T_0, T_1, T_2, \cdots, T_n)$. Then perform iteratively $b := (b+1) \mod 3$. For each b analyse whether the tile T' satisfying $f(T_n, T') = b$, belongs to $\mathcal{C}$. While $T' \notin \mathcal{C}$, b is increased to continue searching for a tile of $\mathcal{C}$. If $T' \in \mathcal{C}$, proceed to the End Condition Test.
4: **End Condition Test:**
5: **if** $T' \neq T_0$ **then** add T' to $\beta(\mathcal{C})$, then go to Step 2.
6: **else** (now $T' = T_0$) add T' to $\beta(\mathcal{C})$. Then run Step 2 with the current list $\beta(\mathcal{C})$ only to obtain a new next boundary tile $T' \in \mathcal{C}$. Then,
7:     **if** $T' = T_1$ **then** remove the last tile from $\beta(\mathcal{C})$, then STOP.
8:     **else** add T' to $\beta(\mathcal{C})$, then go to Step 2.
9:     **end if**
10: **end if**

Definition 2. *Let* $\mathcal{C} \subset \mathcal{M}$ *be an object in a triangular tiling* $\mathcal{M}$, *such that* $\mathcal{C}$ *has at least two tiles and* $|\mathcal{C}| \subset \mathbb{R}^2$ *has no hole. Any boundary path* $b = (t_0, t_1, \cdots, t_k)$ *of* $\mathcal{C}$ *which, up to appropriate shifting of the cyclic sequence* b, *coincides with* $\beta(\mathcal{C})$ *determined by the boundary tracing Algorithm 1, is called the* **canonical boundary path** *of* $\mathcal{C}$.

As consequence of the performance of Algorithm 1, the canonical boundary path $\beta(\mathcal{C}) = (\beta_0, \beta_1, \cdots, \beta_k)$ traces the boundary in counterclockwise sense. For a regular object, visiting the tiles β_i in the order due to $\beta(\mathcal{C})$, corresponds to trace the Jordan curve $fr(|\mathcal{C}|)$ in counterclockwise sense, where it leaves $|\mathcal{C}|$ on the left and $(\mathbb{R}^2 \setminus |\mathcal{C}|)$ on the right. If $\mathcal{C}$ is regular then $\beta(\mathcal{C})$ is also regular: $\beta_{i-1} \neq \beta_{i+1}$ for all $0 \leq i \leq k$. Figure 3 shows an example of a regular object whose canonical boundary path is not simple.

5 MPP Algorithm for Objects with Simple Boundary Paths, in a Triangular Tiling

Algorithm 2 uses as input data the canonical boundary path $\beta(\mathcal{C}) = (\beta_0, \beta_1, \cdots, \beta_t)$ which is supposed to be simple, and, β_0 is assumed as the leftmost tile T_0 of the top row of $\mathcal{C}$. The list $\beta(\mathcal{C})$ should also provide data about the vertices of each tile β_i, to calculate the end points x_i, y_i of each edge $e_i = \beta_i \cap \beta_{i+1}$.

Algorithm 2 constructs a polygon P whose vertices are vertices of the tiles of $\beta(\mathcal{C})$. Each x_i in Line 4 lies on the right of $\overrightarrow{b_i b_{i+1}}$ if b_i denotes the centre point of β_i, and y_i lies on the left of $\overrightarrow{b_i b_{i+1}}$, the same applies to x_k, y_k in Line 14 with b_k. Clearly $x_i, x_k \in fr(|\mathcal{C}|)$, and $y_i, y_k \in fr(core(\mathcal{C}))$ since $\beta(\mathcal{C})$ is simple.

In Line 1, the first polygon vertex m_1 is determined. From each polygon vertex $m = m_n$, $n \geq 1$, provided by some $\beta_z \in \beta(\mathcal{C})$, the next polygon vertex is found with the help of a cone of visibility through the forthcoming tiles. The cone rooted at m is initialized in Lines 6–7 by its right border $\overrightarrow{mp}$ and left border $\overrightarrow{mq}$ with $p = x_i$, $q = y_i$, being the right and left end points of $e_i = \beta_i \cap \beta_{i+1}$ where i is the first index larger than z such that x_i and y_i are distinct from m. The cone is updated in Lines 10–11 after inspecting each β_k: $p = x_k$ is updated if x_k restricts or confirms the right border, $q = y_k$ is updated if y_k restricts or confirms the left border. The condition of Line 9 requires that m, y_k, x_k form a right turn, or, are collinear, and that x_k, y_k do not both lie on the same side strictly outside the cone. Note that in Line 10, x_k is ignored if it lies strictly outside the cone on the right, the same in Line 11: y_k is ignored if it lies strictly outside the cone on the left. Lines 9–11 guarantee that (m, p, q) well-defines the cone, and that $\overrightarrow{mp}$ and $\overrightarrow{mq}$ belong to the union of corresponding tiles, from β_z up to the tile which provides p or q. A new polygon vertex is found if the while condition in Line 9 is not satisfied, then the boundary performs at β_k an essential movement to the left, or to the right, which makes find a convex or concave new polygon vertex in Lines 17–19.

150   P. Wiederhold

Algorithm 2. computes the ordered list of MPP vertices, for an object $\mathcal{C}$ with at least six tiles whose canonical boundary path is simple, in a triangular tiling.

Input: canonical boundary path $\beta(\mathcal{C}) = (\beta_0, \beta_1, \cdots, \beta_t)$ (counterclockwise tracing), β_0 is the leftmost tile in the top row of $\mathcal{C}$.
Output: List MPP of MPP vertices.

1: Determine the lower right corner point m of β_0.
2: $m_1 := m$, initialize the list $MPP = (m_1)$, $i := 0$, $n := 1$.
3: **if** $i > t$ **then** STOP **endif**
4: Determine the end points x_i (right) and y_i (left) of the edge $e_i = \beta_i \cap \beta_{i+1}$.
5: **if** $(m \neq x_i$ and $m \neq y_i)$ **then**
6:     $p := x_i$ (initial right cone border $\overrightarrow{mp}$)
7:     $q := y_i$ (initial left cone border $\overrightarrow{mq}$)
8:     $k := i$
9:     **while** $(m, y_k, x_k$ form a right turn or are collinear, and x_k, y_k do not both lie on the same side strictly outside the cone) **do**
10:        Update the right cone border:
           if $(m, p, x_k$ form a left turn or are collinear) **then**
           $(p := x_k$ and $z_p := k)$ **endif**
11:        Update the left cone border:
           if $(m, q, y_k$ form a right turn or are collinear) **then**
           $(q := y_k$ and $z_q := k)$ **endif**
12:        $k := k + 1$ (continue with the same cone)
13:        **if** $k > t$ **then** STOP, **endif**
14:        Determine the end points x_k (right) and y_k (left) of $e_k = \beta_k \cap \beta_{k+1}$.
15:     **end while**
16:     (A new MPP vertex is found:)
17:     **if** $(m, p, x_k$ form a right turn or are collinear) **then** $(m := p$ and $z := z_p)$ **endif**
18:     **if** $(m, p, x_k$ form a left turn) **then** $(m := q$ and $z := z_q)$ **endif**
19:     $n := n + 1$, add the point $m_n = m$ to the list MPP.
20:     $i := z + 1$ (continue searching with β_{z+1})
21:     Go to Line 3.
22: **end if**
23: $i := i + 1$
24: Go to Line 3.

Example 1: $\beta(\mathcal{C}) = (\beta_0, \beta_1, \cdots, \beta_5)$ is the input list for Algorithm 2 to process the object of Fig. 2(a). Lines 1–2 give $m = y_0$ which is the common vertex of the six tiles, and the initial list $MPP = (y_0)$. Since $m = y_0 = y_1 = y_2 = y_3 = y_4 = y_5$, i is stepwise augmented but the condition of Line 5 never is satisfied, we get $i = 6$ and arrive to Line 3 with $6 > 5$ which stops the algorithm. It returns the final list $MPP = (y_0)$ representing the MPP, a polygon being a single point.

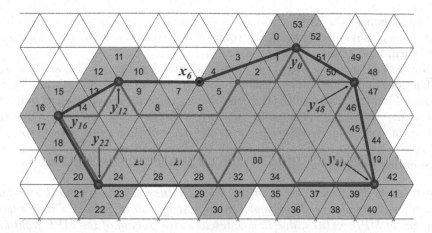

Fig. 4. Each β_k in the canonical boundary path of the shown object is represented by the number k within the tile, the core frontier is drawn red, the MPP frontier in blue, the MPP vertices are marked. (Color figure online)

Example 2: For the object of Fig. 4, the input list indicates $t = 53$. Algorithm 2 first finds $m_1 = m = y_0 = y_1$. The tile β_1 provides the initial cone with $p = x_1$ (right border) and $q = y_1$ (left border). Then $x_2 = x_1$ but $q = y_2 = y_3 = y_4$ restricts the cone, $x_3 = p$ confirms the cone (lies on the cone border), $p = x_4 = x_5 = x_6$ restricts the cone, y_5 is ignored since it lies outside the cone on the left, $q = y_6 = y_7$ confirms the cone, $x_7 = x_8$ is ignored (outside the cone on the right), and $y_8 = q$ restricts the cone. Then (m, y_9, x_9) forms a left turn, also both x_9, y_9 lie outside the cone on the left, this violates the condition of Line 9, Line 17 provides $m = m_2 = p = x_6$, $z = 6$.

Restarting with $m = x_6$, $i = 7$, β_7 gives the initial cone with $p = x_7 = x_8 = x_9$ (right border) and $q = y_7$ (left border). Then y_8 and y_9 restrict the cone which becomes a ray, it is confirmed by $y_{10} = y_{11} = y_{12} = q$. In the sequel, x_{10}, x_{11}, are ignored (outside the cone on the right), also $y_{13}, y_{14} = y_{15}$ (outside the cone on the left), but $x_{12} = x_{13} = x_{14}$ and x_{15} confirm the cone. Since both x_{16}, y_{16} lie outside the cone on the left, Line 18 gives $m = m_3 = q = y_{12}$, $z = 12$.

To restart, $i = 13$, the initial cone is given by $p = x_{13} = x_{14}$, $q = y_{13}$. It is restricted by $y_{14} = y_{15} = y_{16} = q$, confirmed by x_{15} and restricted by $x_{16} = p$. Then (m, y_{17}, x_{17}) forms a left turn, violating the condition of Line 9, Line 18 gives $m = m_4 = q = y_{16}$, $z = 16$.

Beginning with $i = 17$ and $m = y_{16} = y_{17}$, $p = x_{18}$ and $q = y_{18}$ define the initial cone which stepwise is restricted until becoming a ray with $p = x_{22}$, $q = y_{22}$. Then (m, y_{23}, x_{23}) forms a left turn, Line 18 gives $m = m_5 = q = y_{22}$.

The next initial cone given by $m = y_{22}$, $p = x_{24}$, $q = y_{24}$ is subsequently restricted and transformed into a ray with $p = x_{28}$, $q = y_{28} = y_{29} = y_{30} = y_{31}$. Then x_{29}, x_{30} are ignored but $x_{31} = x_{32} = x_{33} = x_{34}$ confirm the cone, y_{32}, y_{33} are ignored, $y_{34} = y_{35} = y_{36}$ confirm the cone, $x_{35}, x_{36} = x_{37}$ are ignored,

$y_{37} = y_{38}$ confirm the cone, $x_{38} = x_{39}$ are ignored, $y_{39} = y_{40} = y_{41} = q$ confirm the cone, x_{40} is ignored but $x_{41} = p$ confirms the cone. Then (m, y_{42}, x_{42}) forms a left turn, Line 18 gives $m = m_6 = q = y_{41}$.

Now $i = 42$, $m = y_{41} = y_{42}$, the initial cone is defined by $p = x_{43}$ and $q = y_{43}$. Restrictions and confirmations lead to $p = x_{46}$ and $q = y_{46} = y_{47} = y_{48} = q$, x_{47} is ignored but $x_{48} = p$ confirms the cone, (m, y_{42}, x_{42}) forms a left turn, resulting in $m = m_7 = q = y_{48}$. Then, since $m = y_{48} = y_{49}$, $p = x_{50}$, $q = y_{50}$ define the next initial cone. Finally we get $p = x_{53}$, $q = y_{53}$, but then i is increased to yield $i = 54 > t$, the algorithm stops to return the final list $MPP = (m_1, m_2, \cdots, m_7)$ representing the MPP.

Theorem 1. *For any object C with at least six tiles, whose canonical boundary path $\beta(C)$ is simple, in a triangular tiling, Algorithm 2 computes the ordered sequence of MPP vertices, due to counterclockwise tracing of the MPP frontier.*

Idea of Proof: Let C be an object in a triangular tiling, $\beta(C) = (\beta_0, \beta_1, \cdots, \beta_t)$ its simple canonical boundary path, γ the frontier curve (counterclockwisely traced) of the MPP of C, and P the polygon determined by Algorithm 2.

By Lemma 2, C is a union of hexagons C_{Hex}. The smallest case is the object C_{Hex} whose MPP consists of a single point, which is correctly computed by Algorithm 2 in Example 1. Now suppose that C has more than six tiles. Then C has at least 13 tiles, see Fig. 2, the core contains at least one tile, and the MPP of C has at least 3 vertices.

By Lemma 3 and results from [16,17], γ is the shortest Jordan curve which surrounds $core(C)$ and does not leave $|C|$. To see that Algorithm 2 determines exactly that curve, first observe that Algorithm 2 opens a new cone from each last found polygon vertex m_n provided by some β_z, and later, finds the next vertex m_{n+1} from some β_j. In Line 10, it does not update the right cone border if x_k lies strictly outside the cone on the right, and, y_k is ignored in Line 11 if it lies strictly outside the cone on the left. As result of construction, $\overline{m_n m_{n+1}} \subset \beta_z \cup \beta_{z+1} \cup \cdots \cup \beta_j$, which implies that $fr(P)$ visits all boundary tiles and does not leave the boundary. Since tracing the canonical boundary path $\beta(C)$ always leaves the object C on the left, $fr(P)$ is a Jordan curve which surrounds $core(C)$ and does not leave $|C|$.

The leftmost tile β_0 of the top row of C is an upright triangle belonging to an object C_{Hex} included in C, m_1 is the centre point of this hexagon and belongs to $fr(core(C))$. The curve γ approaches m_1 from the right (and, eventually, from below), goes through m_1, and then continues in some direction downwards, below the horizontal straight line which contains m_1. As result, m_1 is a convex vertex of γ, hence the vertex m_1 of P, is an MPP vertex.

The main step of the proof considers any vertex m_n, $n \geq 1$, of P, supposes that m_n is an MPP vertex, and proves that the next MPP vertex a coincides with the next polygon vertex m_{n+1} of P. For this, the cone rooted at m_n has to be analysed. The vertex m_n is provided by a tile β_z, the initial cone determined by $p = x_i \in fr(|C|)$ and $q = y_i \in fr(core(C))$, for some $i \geq z + 1$, is one of the sextants rooted at m_n, but is restricted to $30°$ by x_{i+1} or y_{i+1}. After eventual further updating, for some $k > i$, β_k is the first tile which does not satisfy the condition of Line 9. Then the cone goes through all tiles $\beta_z, \beta_{z+1}, \cdots, \beta_{k-1}$, and m_{n+1} is provided by β_j with $i \leq j < k$. In that situation, a boundary movement to the left (then $m_{n+1} = y_j$ is convex) or to the right (then $m_{n+1} = x_j$ is concave), is detected at β_k. The idea is to show that there is no straight line from m_n to reach the tile β_{k+2}, or β_{k+3}, hence γ traced from m_n to this tile needs m_{n+1} as next vertex after m_n, which implies $a = m_{n+1}$.

As result, all vertices of P are MPP vertices. Analysing the ending of Algorithm 2 reveals that the list of vertices of P coincides with the complete list of MPP vertices. ⊔⊓

6   Conclusions

This article studies properties of the MPP of digital objects in the triangular tiling, given as edge-adjacency-connected sets of tiles having simple boundary paths, and proposes an algorithm to compute the ordered sequence of MPP vertices. Our MPP algorithm uses the nature of the object given as collection of tiles, specially, it takes advantage of the canonical boundary path. Tracing the boundary path, certain backtracking is performed each time a next polygon vertex is found. A time complexity analysis is pendant for a future journal paper, as well as a detailed correctness proof, also for more general objects such as regular complexes due to [15].

Future work include the comparison with other MPP algorithms, and the exploration of applications. The algorithm from [15] was a previous MPP algorithm specifically for objects in the triangular tiling, but it was shown as failing in [19]. By Lemma 1, the MPP is a relative convex hull of $A = core(\mathcal{C})$ with respect to the simple polygon $B = |\mathcal{C}|$, the MPP frontier is a certain shortest polygonal curve. Solutions for geodesic hull and shortest path problems from Computational Geometry, such as those from [1,18], could be adapted to determine the MPP for our objects. Nevertheless, A and B are not given as input data in our MPP problem, these sets first have to be determined, Lemma 3 indicates that it would be sufficient to calculate certain vertices of A and B. Applications of the MPP for objects made from triangle tiles, may include to study convexity properties, and to develop multigrid convergent curve length estimators such as done in [16,17] for objects of square tiles.

Acknowledgements. The authors feel grateful to the reviewers for their revision and suggestions which improved the manuscript.

References

1. An, P., Hoai, T.: Incremental convex hull as an orientation to solving the shortest path problem. Int. J. Inf. Electron. Eng. **2**(5), 652–655 (2012)
2. Avkan, A., Nagy, B., Saadetoglu, M.: Digitized rotations of 12 neighbors on the triangular grid. Ann. Math. Artif. Intell. **88**, 833–857 (2020)

3. Deutsch, E.: Thinning algorithms on rectangular, hexagonal, and triangular arrays. Commun. ACM **15**(9), 827–837 (1972)
4. Gonzalez, R., Woods, R.: Digital Image Processing (Global Edition), 4th edn. Pearson Education Limited, USA (2018)
5. Gonzalez, R., Woods, R., Eddins, S.: Digital Image Processing using Matlab, 3rd edn. Gatesmark Publishing LLC, USA (2020)
6. Grünbaum, B., Shephard, G.: Tilings and Patterns. W.H. Freeman and Company, USA (1978)
7. Kardos, P., Palágyi, K.: Topology preservation on the triangular grid. Ann. Math. Artif. Intell. **75**, 53–68 (2015). https://doi.org/10.1007/s10472-014-9426-6
8. Klette, R., Rosenfeld, A.: Digital Geometry - Geometric Methods for Digital Picture Analysis. Morgan Kaufmann Publisher, USA (2004)
9. Lachaud, J., Provencal, X.: Two linear-time algorithms for computing the minimum length polygon of a digital contour. Discret. Appl. Math. **159**, 2229–2250 (2011). https://doi.org/10.1016/j.dam.2011.08.002
10. Nagy, B.: Diagrams on the hexagonal and on the triangular grids. Acta Polytechnica Hungarica **19**(4), 27–42 (2022)
11. Nagy, B.: A khalimsky-like topology on the triangular grid. In: Brunetti, S., et al. (eds.) Proceed. DGMM 2024, pp. 150—162. Springer, Switzerland (2024). https://doi.org/10.1007/978-3-031-57793-2_12
12. Roussillon, T., Sivignon, I.: Faithful polygonal representation of the convex and concave parts of a digital curve. Pattern Recogn. **44**, 2693—2700 (2011). https://doi.org/10.1016/j.patcog.2011.03.018
13. Saha, P., Rosenfeld, A.: Local and global topology preservation on locally finite sets of tiles. Inf. Sci. **137**, 303–311 (2011)
14. Sklansky, J., Chazin, R., Hansen, B.: Minimum perimeter polygons of digitized silhouettes. IEEE Trans. Comput. **21**(3), 260–268 (1972). https://doi.org/10.1109/TC.1972.5008948
15. Sklansky, J., Kibler, D.: A theory of nonuniformly digitized binary pictures. IEEE Trans. Syst. Man Cybern. **6(9)**, 637—647 (1976). https://doi.org/10.1109/TSMC.1976.4309569
16. Sloboda, F., Stoer, J.: On piecewise linear approximation of planar Jordan curves. J. Comput. Appl. Math. **55**, 369–383 (1994). https://doi.org/10.1016/0377-0427(94)90040-X
17. Sloboda, F., Zatco, B., Stoer, J.: On approximation of planar one-dimensional continua. In: Klette, R., Rosenfeld, A., Sloboda, F. (eds.) Advances in Digital and Computational Geometry, pp. 113–160. Springer, Singapore (1998)
18. Toussaint, G.: Computing geodesic properties inside a simple polygon. Revue d'Intelligence Artificielle **3**(2), 265–278 (1989)
19. Wiederhold, P.: Computing the minimal perimeter polygon for sets of rectangular tiles based on visibility cones. J. Math. Imaging Vis., 1–30 (2024)

3BUGS: Representing Building Geometries Extracted from Point Clouds

José L. Silván-Cárdenas[(✉)] [iD], Josafat Guerrero-Íñiguez,
and José M. Madrigal-Gómez

Centro de Investigación en Ciencias de Información Goeespacial,
Contoy 137, Col. Lomas de Padierna Tlalpan, 14240 Mexico City, Mexico
{jsilvan,jmadrigal}@centrogeo.edu.mx
https://www.centrogeo.org.mx/areas-profile/jsilvan

Abstract. A template for representing basic building forms, termed 3BUGS, is proposed and demonstrated in a workflow fed with dense point clouds. The template describes building primitives using transformed rings for building geometry specification. Its major features include: 1) independent specification of constituent parts of primitives, namely, floor, walls, and roof; 2) specification of common floor shapes (rectangular, round, and polygonal); 3) vertical and non-vertical walls; 4) standard and arbitrary roof shapes; 5) manual and automated production of primitives and 6) supports the level of detail 2 (LoD2) of the CityGML standard. Preliminary tests have shown that the 3BUGS can be efficiently used for building representations and some transformations without making the geometry explicit.

Keywords: Point clouds · Building modeling · Level of detail · Procedural generation · 3D cadastre

1 Introduction

The advent of drones and the advances in computer vision methods has made possible the generation of colored dense point clouds from oblique aerial photography in a virtually automated way, competing in accuracy and cost-benefit with LiDAR technology [9,13,17,19]. However, the problem of 3D object reconstruction is, in most cases, still not automated and a human modeller is always needed to define spatial and semantic relations [20,22]. Hence, point clouds shifted the problem from photographic interpretation to point cloud analysis for extracting objects that can be represented and managed within a 3D geographic information system (GIS). The transition from flat, 2D data, to 3D databases not only implies an increase in the complexity of the representation, but also entails an increase in details that change more frequently and that demands a greater update rate. Hence the importance of developing technologies that enable the automatic generation of 3D geometries of buildings and other urban elements also increased. This, in turn, requires the conceptualization and systematization of the types of objects that must be represented in computer systems [14].

© The Author(s), under exclusive license to Springer Nature Switzerland AG 2024
E. Mezura-Montes et al. (Eds.): MCPR 2024, LNCS 14755, pp. 155–165, 2024.
https://doi.org/10.1007/978-3-031-62836-8_15

An example of such systematization is the CityGML standard, an open data model for storing and exchanging of urban models, that defines a basic set of attribute entities and relationships in a 3D city model [6]. Currently, it is the urban model with greater relevance for 3D city modeling [12]. In its latest specification, CityGML considers up to 5 levels of detail (LoDs), so that LoD0 only considers the floor plan of the buildings, LoD1 models of blocks are proposed but without details on roofs, LoD2 contemplates models with greater detail on walls and roofs, LoD3 includes details of architectural exteriors such as doors and windows, while LoD4 extends the interior model, generating constructions that can be used for indoor navigation [2]. Depending on the generation technique and available preliminary information (e.g., oblique photographs, orthophotos, digital surface models, airborne LiDAR point clouds, etc.), existing building extraction methods may produce different LoDs and data models that may or may not be compliant with the CityGML standard [1]. Furthermore, most building extraction methods have so far emphasized the production of the geometry rather than its representation in a compact and consistent way for a given LoD.

This article describes a general template for representing primitives of buildings compliant with the LoD2 of CityGML, which can be though as an intermediate representation between point clouds and building geometries. The overall proposed building modeling workflow is schematically presented in Fig. 1, where boxes represent data transformations, and arrows represent data flows. This paper focuses on describing those with continuous lines. The core of this approach is the specification of buildings as complexes of building primitives which are described in Sect. 3. The manual and procedural levels of production are presented in Sect. 4. A number of examples are provided in Sect. 5 and major conclusions are presented in Sect. 6. In the following Sect. 2, we briefly describe the data used for this study.

2   Photogrammetric Point Clouds

Photogrammetric point clouds were generated for several building complexes of varying shapes using two different unmanned aerial vehicles (UAVs) from DJI Inc. (Phantom 4 Advance and Inspire V1). Low oblique photographs with 80% front overlap and 70% side overlap were acquired on a double grid flight pattern with a flight height of 50–70 m above terrain and a camera orientation of 70° forward. The point cloud generation was carried out using the Pix4D software with the standard procedure. Since positional accuracy was not a major concern for the tests reported, ground control points (GCP) where measured only for the building of CentroGeo. Furthermore, because the root mean square error of distances measured in the point cloud with GCPs (1.5 cm) and those without GCPs (13 cm) complied with the required precision by the Mexican norm [7]. It is also important to note that assessing the effects of several data acquisition configurations was beyond the scope of the present study. The reader is referred to reference [19] for a comprehensive evaluation of flight configurations for cadastral mapping.

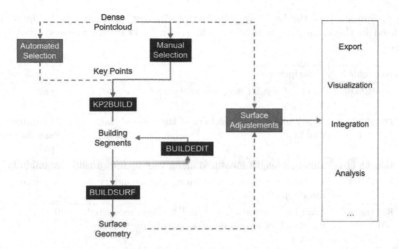

Fig. 1. Conceptual workflow of the building modeling.

3   3BUGS Template Development

Primitives are the simplest building components for which the geometry is specified through a set of relevant parameters[1]. Their geometry is conceived as composed of polygon rings (or simply rings) that are similar to the bottom ring, so that the number of rings can be variable, but the number of vertices per ring remains fixed for a given primitive. This has the advantage that it allows surfaces to be represented as matrices that are easily handled with programming languages such as MATLAB and Python, and they can also be easily triangulated. Each row in the coordinate matrix defines a ring that is a transformed version of the base ring, with the transformation parameters encoded as shift parameters. Because of that, this representation is here referred to as the "Transformed RIngs for BUilding Geometry Specification" (TRIBUGS or 3BUGS for short). Table 1 describes the attributes of the general template.

Each primitive is composed of three parts: floor, walls, and roof, each of which is specified independently to keep the model compact and flexible. The floor is the footprint of the building primitive and comprises the LoD0 specification. It is specified with the `BaseShape` parameter, and can take one of three possible shapes: rectangular ('`rect`'), elliptical ('`round`'), or polygonal ('`polyg`'). `Points` represent `NumPoints` vertices of a polygon in local coordinate system which must be specified only for polygonal bases, whereas they are internally generated for other shapes only when geometry is made explicit. The floor also carries the location (`XLoc`, `YLoc` and `ZLoc`), 2-d size (`Length`, `Width`), and orientation (`RotAngle`) of the building primitive, which are used for transforming from local (x, y, z) to global (X, Y, Z) coordinate systems.

---

[1] The specification of spatial relationships among primitives of the same building is not addressed in this article.

Table 1. Summary of the building primitives template specification. * The attribute name used in the code and, if available, in parenthesis is the math symbol used in formulae.

Parts	Attribute*	Description	Default value
Floor	BaseShape	Name of a valid base shape: 'rect', 'round', or 'polyg'	'rect'
	Points (x_b, y_b)	$N \times 2$ matrix with vertices of the base of the building	Mandatory if BaseShape is 'polyg'
	Length (L)	Building length measured along the main direction	Mandatory
	Width (W)	Building width measured along the secondary direction	Mandatory
	RotAngle (ϕ)	Building orientation on the XY-plane measured counterclockwise in degrees with respect to the X-axis	0
	NumPoints (N)	Number of vertices of the round base	32, used only if BaseShape is 'round'
	XLoc (X_{loc})	X-coordinate of primitive location	0
	YLoc (Y_{loc})	Y-coordinate of primitive location	0
	ZLoc (Z_{loc})	Z-coordinate of primitive location	0
Walls	Height (H)	Height of the walls measured along the z coordinate	Mandatory
	WallsShift	Percentages of Length, Width, and Height of the top ring(s) shift(s) with respect to the floor ring	[0 0 100]
Roof	RoofShape	A valid roof shape: 'flat', 'shed', 'gabled', 'hipped', 'tented', 'flattop', 'half-hip', 'gablet', 'gambrel', etc. or 'userdefined'	'flat'
	RoofExtent	Whether the roof extension is based on the walls or the base. Valid values are 'floor' and 'walls'. It has an effect only if WallsShift is specified	'floor'
	RoofHeight	Roof height. Some roofs require two heights, in which case the parameter must be a vector of length 2	Depends on RoofShape
	RoofShift $(\alpha, \beta, \gamma,$ $\alpha', \beta'\gamma', \delta)$	Shifts of roof rings with respect to the roof base. In general, it is an $M \times 3$ matrix for symmetrical horizontal roofs, an $M \times 4$ one for symmetrical sloped, an $M \times 5$ one for non-symmetrical horizontal roofs, an $M \times 6$ one for non-symmetrical and sloped, or an $M \times 7$ one for an arbitrarily tilted roof type	Mandatory if RoofShape is 'userdefined'
All	Parts	Indicates the parts that are included in the polyhedron. Specified as a combination of 'floor', 'walls', and 'roof' concatenated with a '+'	'floor +walls +roof'
	Colors	A 3×1 vector (indexed color) or a 3×3 matrix (RGB color) indicating the color of the base, walls, and roof	[0 0 0; 0.5 0.5 0.5; 1 0 0]

Without any additional specification, walls are understood as vertical extrusions of the base ring by `Height` units. Nonetheless, 3BUGS allows specifying inclined walls, walls that extend beyond the roof, or even broken walls. This is done by specifying a number of shift parameters in the `WallsShift` attribute that are similarly interpreted to the parameters for `RoofShift` described bellow. The roof part is the cover of a primitive that can be specified in one of two ways: 1) through a valid `RoofShape` and, optionally, its `RoofHeight` or 2) by directly specifying the `RoofShift` parameters. The former way uses a predefined library of roof shapes where shift parameters have been fixed. Such a library considers common roof types used in previous building reconstruction studies [5, 8, 15, 27]. The simplest roof model is the flat roof, which can be used for a LoD1 model, otherwise LOD2 models are attained (see Fig. 2 for examples of roof types).

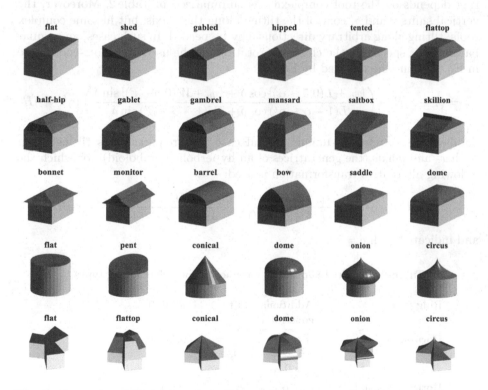

Fig. 2. Examples of library based roofs on rectangular, round, and polygonal bases.

Shift Parameters. Both walls and roofs rings are specified with 2 to 6 shift parameters:

$$(\alpha, \beta, \alpha', \beta', \gamma, \gamma') \quad \text{s.t.} \quad \alpha + \alpha' \leq 1, \quad \beta + \beta' \leq 1 \tag{1}$$

where equality holds only for the top-most closing ring. These parameters encode the translations and scalings of shifted rings with respect to a based ring. Specifically, the roof ring coordinates associated to the base coordinates (x_b, y_b, z_b) are given by:

$$x_r = (1 - \alpha - \alpha')x_b + (\alpha - \alpha')L/2 \tag{2}$$

$$y_r = (1 - \beta - \beta')y_b + (\beta - \beta')W/2 \tag{3}$$

$$z_r = (1 + \gamma)H + \left(\frac{x_b + L(0.5 - \alpha)}{L(1 - \alpha - \alpha')}\right)H \tag{4}$$

Note that the scaling and translations do not depend on the number of vertices in the bases, so the displacement parameters are exactly the same for rectangular, round, or polygonal footprints. Furthermore, the number of free parameters per ring depends on the roof complexity as summarized in Table 2. Moreover, the vertical shifts γ and γ' control the tilting along the x-axis, but in some complex roofs, tilting along arbitrary directions may be needed. In such cases, an angular parameter δ specifying the clockwise rotation can be used and the z-coordinate in Eq. (4) must be replaced by Eq. (5):

$$z_r = (1 + \gamma)H + \left(\frac{[x_b + L(0.5 - \alpha)]\cos\delta + [y_b + W(0.5 - \beta)]\sin\delta}{L(1 - \alpha - \alpha')\cos\delta + W(1 - \beta - \beta')\sin\delta}\right)(\gamma' - \gamma)H \tag{5}$$

Saddle roofs comprise a unique special case that requires rings tilting along both x- and y-axis (the generatrices of an hyperbolic paraboloid), for which the following alternative transformation is used:

$$z_r = (1 + \gamma)H + \left(\frac{x_b + L(0.5 - \alpha)}{L(1 - \alpha - \alpha')} - \frac{y_b + W(0.5 - \beta)}{W(1 - \beta - \beta')}\right)(\gamma' - \gamma)H \tag{6}$$

and indicated with $\delta = \infty$.

Table 2. Required RoofShift parameters for different ring types.

Ring type	Additional shift constraints	RoofShift
Horizontal	$\alpha = \alpha' = \beta = \beta' = 0.5$, $\gamma = \gamma' = 0$, $\delta = 0$	$(50, 50, 0)$
Horizontal symmetric	$\alpha = \alpha', \beta = \beta'$, $\gamma = \gamma', \delta = 0$	$100 \times (\alpha, \beta, \gamma)$
Sloped symmetric	$\alpha = \alpha', \beta = \beta', \delta = 0$	$100 \times (\alpha, \beta, \gamma, \gamma')$
Horizontal asymmetric	$\gamma = \gamma', \delta = 0$	$100 \times (\alpha, \beta, \gamma, \alpha', \beta')$
Sloped asymmetric	$\delta = 0$	$100 \times (\alpha, \beta, \gamma, \alpha', \beta', \gamma')$
Sloped with rotation	none	$100 \times (\alpha, \beta, \gamma, \alpha', \beta', \gamma', \delta)$
Bi-sloped	$\delta = \infty$	$100 \times (\alpha, \beta, \gamma, \alpha', \beta', \gamma', \infty)$

4   Building Generation

Building primitives are meant to be generated automatical-, manual-, and programmatically. Here we briefly describe the last two methods which correspond to the boxes labelled **KP2BUILD** and **BUILDEDIT** in Fig. 1.

4.1   Manual Building Modeling

The first method uses manual selection of the so-called key points which convey the necessary information for computing the primitive parameters. Figure 3 shows the key points for a flat roof (P1–P4), a tented roof (P1–P5), a hipped roof (P1–P6), and a flattop roof (P1–P7) on a rectangular floor. These points can be interactively selected from the point cloud while primitive is being generated. The editing process can continue defining more and more points, where each roof ring is defined with 3 points, or less if it is the last one. In each case, only the first two points will correspond to roof vertices, while the third one defines a distance. If the roof shape is specified in advance, the fifth point defines the roof height and edition ends. A similar procedure is followed for a round base, with the only difference that the first two vertices define the principal axes of the ellipse and the third vertex defines the semi-minor axis length. For a polygonal base, the roof shape must be specified in advance, and the first $n-2$ points define the vertices of a 2-d polygon of the floor, the point $(n-1)$ defines the height, and the n-th point defines the height of the roof.

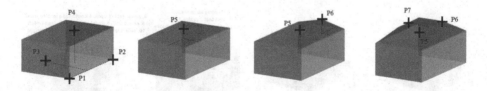

Fig. 3. Examples of key points for flat, tented, hipped, and flattop roofs on a rectangular floor.

4.2   Procedural Building Modeling

The second method is based on a procedural language developed for editing a given layer of building primitives, by means of a list of instructions of the form: <edit cmd> [<target>] [<transf cmd> <transf cmd2> ...], where <edit cmd> specifies one of the edit command described in Table 3. The <target> value can be directly specified from the building identifiers (e.g., the index of the primitive in the array), a designated 'alias' field used for identification, or a selection command. The transformation commands <transf cmd> <transf cmd2> ... correspond to basic commands that alter the attributes of one or more building primitives which are applied sequentially and cumulatively. Examples include move, align, mirror, and update, which can be combined with relative location commands in order to specify a position from a selection or from the <target> primitive. Description of such transformation and selection commands is omitted due to length constraints. It suffices to say that such transformations do not require explicit geometry generation so that they can fully operate on the template level. Figure 4 shows a coding example for creating a two-storeys building out of a rectangular base that only represents the floor and walls (Parts = 'floor+walls'). The lines 2–5 make copies, relocation and resizing of the rooms, whereas lines 6–10 define roofs types and roof height.

Table 3. Language commands to generate and/or edit building primitives.

Command	Description
create	A wrapping of KP2BUILD that can be used to create a new layer from a set of key points. No <target> and <transf cmd> values are required. The input layer must be the set of key points
delete	Delete the specified <target> primitives from the input layer. Does not require transform commands <transf cmd>
copy	Copy the <target> primitives from the input layer and set the copy as the input to subsequent <transf cmd> commands
select	Select the <target> primitives from the input layer and set them as the input to subsequent <transf cmd> commands

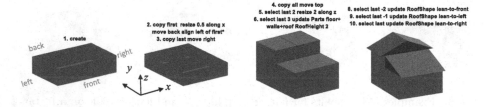

Fig. 4. Example of the procedural generation of a building with interior walls.

5   Results and Discussion

Figure 5 shows some examples of modelled buildings with their corresponding pointcloud to the left. The top-left panel shows the CentroGeo complex that was modelled using 143 key points for generating 20 primitives with square base. Some cantilevered roofs made use of the rotation parameter as some roof inclinations did not follow orientation of the local coordinates. The bottom-left panel shows the model of a church in Xochimilco, CDMX, which illustrates the use of polygonal and round bases, as well as the use of library-based roofs. The top-right panel shows the model of the Library of the Science and Technology

Park in Yucatan, using a total of 9 primitives, some o which exemplify the capabilities of the template for representing curved and inclined walls. Lastly, the bottom-right panel shows the complex of National Institute for Geography and Statistics located in Aguascalientes. This model was generated using the procedural method, with 27 macro instructions operating initially on two primitives. In addition to exploiting the similarity between the components of buildings, the procedural generation leverages the spatial relationships among primitives, allowing greater precision in the definition of locations, sizes, and orientations. Compared to other abstract building model specifications [4,25], the proposed 3BUGS approach uses simple, yet high-level objects to describe building components, and is compatible with both manual and procedural building generation methods. Moreover, using the shift parameters to encode transformations from a base polygon ring, makes this representation appealing for contour-based methods of building reconstruction [10,11,24,26].

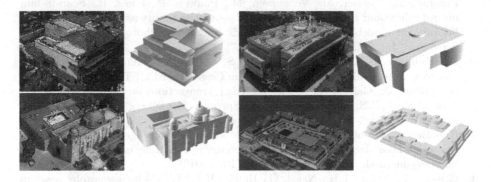

Fig. 5. Examples of modelled buildings based on point clouds.

6   Conclusions

A general template, called 3BUGS, was proposed as a model for representing the geometry of building primitives extracted from dense point clouds. The use of the template was demonstrated through the modeling of real and simulated buildings using both manual and procedural generation methods. The latter was based on a macro-language that exploits the spatial relationship of building primitives and enables the generation of repetitive building complexes, thus reducing the number of key points needed and increasing the accuracy of location, size, and orientation of primitives. Unlike most procedural modeling methods [16,21,23], in the proposed approach the production rules do not require an explicit representation of building geometry as all of them operate fully at the template level. Nonetheless, the initial shapes may be generated through manual editing which require converting from explicit geometries (points) to the template level. A workflow was proposed that envisions the automated key point identification from point clouds that is still under development. Parameter optimization from initial building models is also being investigated and preliminary works have addressed the problem of labelling the point cloud with the nearest facet [18], which is also relevant in product assessment tasks [3].

Acknowledgements. This study was funded by the project 268773 "Evaluación de técnicas avanzadas de percepción remota para la extracción de la geometría de un catastro tridimencional" of the CONACyT-INEGI Sectorial Fund.

References

1. Biljecki, F., Ledoux, H., Stoter, J.: An improved LoD specification for 3d building models. Comput. Environ. Urban Syst. **59**, 25–37 (2016)
2. Biljecki, F., Ledoux, H., Stoter, J., Vosselman, G.: The variants of an LoD of a 3d building model and their influence on spatial analyses. ISPRS J. Photogramm. Remote. Sens. **116**, 42–54 (2016)
3. Bonduel, M., Bassier, M., Vergauwen, M., Pauwels, P., Klein, R.: Scan-to-bim output validation: Towards a standardized geometric quality assessment of building information models based on point clouds. Int. Arch. Photogrammetry Remote Sens. Spat. Inf. Sci. **42**(2W8), 45–52 (2017)
4. Edelsbrunner, J., Krispel, U., Havemann, S., Sourin, A., Fellner, D.W.: Constructive roofs from solid building primitives. In: Gavrilova, M.L., Tan, C.J.K., Iglesias, A., Shinya, M., Galvez, A., Sourin, A. (eds.) Transactions on Computational Science XXVI. LNCS, vol. 9550, pp. 17–40. Springer, Heidelberg (2016). https://doi.org/10.1007/978-3-662-49247-5_2
5. Gooding, J., Crook, R., Tomlin, A.S.: Modelling of roof geometries from low-resolution lidar data for city-scale solar energy applications using a neighbouring buildings method. Appl. Energy **148**, 93–104 (2015)
6. Gröger, G., Kolbe, T.H., Nagel, C., Häfele, K.H.: OGC city geography markup language (CityGML) encoding standard (2012). www.opengis.net/spec/citygml/2.0
7. INEGI: norma técnica para la generación, captación e integración de datos catastrales y registrales con fines estadísticos y geográficos. on line (2012). https://www.snieg.mx/Documentos/Normatividad/Vigente/Norma_Tecnica_Datos_Catastrales.pdf, Accessed 06 Dec 2021
8. Kada, M., McKinley, L.: 3d building reconstruction from lidar based on a cell decomposition approach. Int. Arch. Photogrammetry Remote Sens. Spat. Inf. Sci. **38**(Part 3), W4 (2009)
9. Khanal, M., Hasan, M., Sterbentz, N., Johnson, R., Weatherly, J.: Accuracy comparison of aerial lidar, mobile-terrestrial lidar, and UAV photogrammetric capture data elevations over different terrain types. Infrastructures **5**(8), 65 (2020)
10. Lafarge, F., Descombes, X., Zerubia, J., Pierrot-Deseilligny, M.: Structural approach for building reconstruction from a single DSM. IEEE Trans. Pattern Anal. Mach. Intell. **32**(1), 135–147 (2008)
11. Li, M., Nan, L., Smith, N., Wonka, P.: Reconstructing building mass models from UAV images. Comput. Graph. **54**, 84–93 (2016)
12. Machl, T.: Minutes of the international OGC, sig 3d and tum workshop on requirements for CityGML 3.0. In: International OGC, SIG 3D and TUM Workshop on Requirements for CityGML, vol. 3, pp. 1–28 (2013)

13. Maslikhova, L., Hahulina, N., Sambulov, N., Akimova, S.: Analysis and comparison of technologies of survey of buildings and structures for the purpose of obtaining a 3d model. In: IOP Conference Series: Materials Science and Engineering, vol. 753, p. 032061. IOP Publishing (2020)
14. McGlinn, K., Wagner, A., Pauwels, P., Bonsma, P., Kelly, P., O'Sullivan, D.: Interlinking geospatial and building geometry with existing and developing standards on the web. Autom. Constr. **103**, 235–250 (2019)
15. Milde, J., Brenner, C.: Graph-based modeling of building roofs. In: 12th AGILE International Conference on Geographic Information Science, vol. 20 (2009). https://agile-online.org/conference_paper/cds/agile_2009/agile_cd/pdfs/137.pdf
16. Müller, P., Wonka, P., Haegler, S., Ulmer, A., Van Gool, L.: Procedural modeling of buildings. In: ACM SIGGRAPH 2006 Papers, pp. 614–623 (2006)
17. Noor, N.M., Abdullah, A., Hashim, M.: Remote sensing UAV/drones and its applications for urban areas: a review. In: IOP Conference Series: Earth and Environmental Science, vol. 169, p. 012003. IOP Publishing (2018)
18. Silván-Cárdenas, J.L.: On labelling pointclouds with the nearest facet of triangulated building models. In: Vergara-Villegas, O.O., Cruz-Sánchez, V.G., Sossa-Azuela, J.H., Carrasco-Ochoa, J.A., Martínez-Trinidad, J.F., Olvera-López, J.A. (eds.) MCPR 2022. LNCS, vol. 13264, pp. 269–279. Springer, Cham (2022). https://doi.org/10.1007/978-3-031-07750-0_25
19. Stöcker, C., Nex, F., Koeva, M., Gerke, M.: High-quality UAV-based orthophotos for cadastral mapping: Guidance for optimal flight configurations. Remote sensing **12**(21), 3625 (2020)
20. Thomson, C., Boehm, J.: Automatic geometry generation from point clouds for BIM. Remote Sens. **7**(9), 11753–11775 (2015)
21. Vanegas, C.A., Aliaga, D.G., Benes, B.: Building reconstruction using Manhattan-world grammars. In: 2010 IEEE Computer Society Conference on Computer Vision and Pattern Recognition, pp. 358–365. IEEE (2010)
22. Werbrouck, J., Pauwels, P., Bonduel, M., Beetz, J., Bekers, W.: Scan-to-graph: Semantic enrichment of existing building geometry. Autom. Constr. **119**, 103286 (2020)
23. Whiting, E., Ochsendorf, J., Durand, F.: Procedural modeling of structurally-sound masonry buildings. In: ACM SIGGRAPH Asia 2009 papers, pp. 1–9 (2009)
24. Wu, B., et al.: A graph-based approach for 3d building model reconstruction from airborne lidar point clouds. Remote Sens. **9**(1), 92 (2017)
25. Xiong, B., Jancosek, M., Elberink, S.O., Vosselman, G.: Flexible building primitives for 3d building modeling. ISPRS J. Photogramm. Remote. Sens. **101**, 275–290 (2015)
26. Yi, C., et al.: Urban building reconstruction from raw lidar point data. Comput. Aided Des. **93**, 1–14 (2017)
27. Zheng, Y., Weng, Q.: Model-driven reconstruction of 3-d buildings using lidar data. IEEE Geosci. Remote Sens. Lett. **12**(7), 1541–1545 (2015)

Front-to-Bird's-Eye-View Transformation for Autonomous Vehicles: A Class Imbalance-Based Approach

Daniel A. Martinez-Barba[1]([⊠])(iD), Luis M. Valentin-Coronado[1,3](iD),
Israel Becerra[2,3](iD), Sebastián Salzar-Colores[1](iD), and Carlos Paredes-Orta[1,3](iD)

[1] Centro de Investigaciones en Óptica, 37150 Guanajuato, León, Mexico
{danielmtz,luismvc,sebastian.salazar,cparedes}@cio.mx
[2] Centro de Investigación en Matemáticas, A.C., Apartado, Colombia
israelb@cimat.mx
[3] Consejo Nacional de Humanidades Ciencias y Tecnologías,
03940 Ciudad de México, Mexico

Abstract. Developing efficient and safe autonomous navigation systems for self-driving vehicles requires an accurate representation of the environment. Bird's Eye View (BEV) provides a top-down view environment representation valuable for decision-making and path-planning. In this study, we explore the use of deep learning-based models to output BEV representations directly from front-perspective images, addressing challenges such as class imbalance. We design a synthetic dataset, test various loss functions, and propose a layer-based data augmentation strategy. The experimentation results and the discussion cover implemented deep learning models, data augmentation, and class weighting methods for loss training functions.

Keywords: Bird Eye View · Perspective transform · Deep learning · Autonomous Vehicles

1 Introduction

Efficient and safe autonomous navigation systems for self-driving vehicles require careful design of three main blocks: perception, planning, and control. The environmental perception stage is crucial, influencing the functioning of subsequent stages. Thus, relying on artificial intelligence algorithms is often necessary to implement the perception stage effectively. Implementing artificial intelligence algorithms to fuse sensor data and generate environment representations improves overall system efficiency and decision-making accuracy [12]. Vision-based bird's eye view (BEV) is widely employed in applications such as urban planning, surveillance, and autonomous vehicle navigation, offering a valuable tool for gaining insights into large areas and optimizing various processes that benefit from a holistic view [6]. There are several approaches to performing this perspective transformation. Classic geometric operations have been used to perform front-to-BEV transformations by means of the intrinsic and extrinsic parameters of the camera [3,5]. However, recently, deep learning-based algorithms have outperformed geometric transformation approaches [6]. Several notable examples of these techniques include Generative Adversarial Networks (GAN) [14], Variational Autoencoders (VAE) [9], and Vision Transformer-based architectures [7]. Implementations of deep learning (DL)-based front-to-BEV perspective transformations in autonomous driving come with various challenges. One of the most significant is accurate ground truth generation for model training. Although autonomous driving datasets [8] such as Cityscapes, Kitty, NuScenes, and Argoverse, provide labeled sensor data for object and lane detection and semantic segmentation, they do not offer any ground truth for perspective transformation. Hence, in some works, the authors have estimated or even generated their own BEV maps from sensor data. For example, Florea et al. [2] developed a methodology to fuse sensor data into 3D BEV. Another example is the work of Roddick and Cipolla [11], who developed an algorithm to fuse and transform features (such as LiDAR data and object masks from annotated images) from NuScenes and Argoverse toolkits to produce 2D BEV representations to train their proposed pyramid occupancy network. On the other hand, Zhou et al. [14] used paired (front-top) images extracted from a videogame to train a GAN-based perspective transform model. Additionally, an alternative to producing objective ground truth for perspective transform models is to utilize simulation tools such as Gazebo, Unity, or Unreal Engine, where every aspect of the driving environment can also be controlled.

In this work, we explore some of the intricacies of transforming front camera perspective images (RGB) into semantically segmented bird eye's view representations. Training, evaluation, and comparison of two end-to-end state-of-the-art deep learning models are presented. Furthermore, to overcome the challenges of limited data, we propose and explore a data augmentation methodology enabled by the features of the CARLA open-source simulator for autonomous vehicle research [1]. Experiments on the interaction between deep learning models, data augmentation methods, and weight balancing of semantic segmentation and their effects are discussed.

2   Methodology

This section provides an overview of the description of the data set, as well as the deep learning-based models that were implemented.

2.1   Dataset

We have developed a dataset of 1,300 images from 13 scenes sourced from two maps, which were used for training and testing DL-based models. These scenes are characterized by their diverse scenery, encompassing a range of architectural styles and lighting settings. The scenes were generated on defined routes, where a variable number of vehicles and pedestrians were spawned on the route's roads and walkways. A variety of vehicle (type, size, color) and pedestrian (model, size, pose) 3D models were utilized. Including such a variety is intended to increase the robustness of the proposed methodology. Each sample in the dataset consists of two images, one of a front perspective view in RGB and the other of a top view in semantic format, both of which have a 1024 × 1024 pixels size. The top view images have been labeled across five semantic classes, namely non-drivable and drivable space, sidewalk, vehicle, and pedestrian. We decided to choose these specific classes based on our assessment that they could encompass a stable detection baseline for navigation. Figure 1 shows a representative example of the dataset elements, including the color code for the semantic classes.

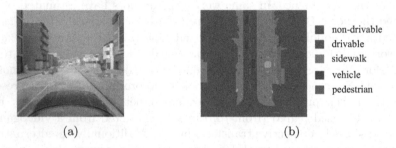

Fig. 1. Dataset representative sample. (a) Front perspective view. (b) Top segmented map and its class identifier and corresponding color.

Following the labeling of top-view images, a digital image processing step is systematically carried out. The entire process is visually described in Fig. 2. Initially, the image is resized; however, this step can lead to undesirable effects such as vehicle deformation and loss of information in pixels related to pedestrians. To address these issues, an opening morphological operation (erosion plus dilation) is executed.

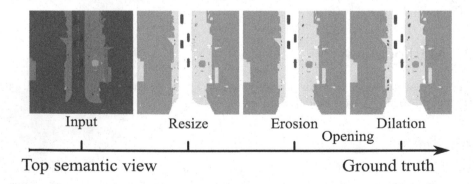

Fig. 2. Ground truth generation pipeline.

2.2 Layers-Based Data Augmentation

We propose a layer-based data augmentation (LbDA) method to increase the dataset information. Unlike conventional data augmentation techniques that generate new synthetic data by applying various transformations, LbDA involves the selective inclusion or exclusion of different object layers, such as buildings, pedestrians, and vehicles, from traffic scenes. Consequently, the dataset is made up of three types of layers. The first type, referred to as *layers-none*, displays only roads. The second type, known as *layers-all*, showcases static objects such as buildings, poles, and fences, among others. Finally, the third type, called *traffic*, includes dynamic objects such as pedestrians and vehicles, thus extending the *layers-all* type. With this approach, new features are expected to be introduced that can enhance the performance of front-to-top view mapping. In Fig. 3, augmented samples are depicted.

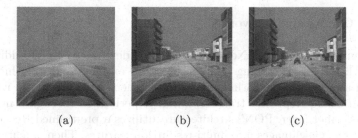

(a)   (b)   (c)

Fig. 3. Layers-based data augmentation examples, where (a), (b), and (c) show the layers *layers-none*, *layers-all*, and *traffic*, respectively.

2.3 Models

Two state-of-the-art deep learning approaches have been implemented to perform front-to-BEV perspective transformation: the Variational Encoder-Decoder and the Pyramid Occupancy Network. Model selection was based on an assessment of balance between real-time performance and accuracy, as well as model uniqueness.

Variational Encoder-Decoder

The Variational Encoder-Decoder (VED) is a neural network architecture designed to learn efficient data representations [9]. The main feature of the VED is that the encoder and decoder are not deterministic functions but probabilistic models. The encoder maps input data to a probability distribution in the latent space, typically following a Normal distribution. The encoder's output includes both the mean and the variance of this distribution, capturing the uncertainty or variability in the latent representation. Then, the decoder samples from this

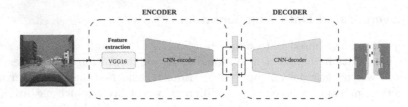

Fig. 4. Variational Encoder-Decoder's architecture.

latent space distribution to generate reconstructions of the input data. In Fig. 4, the VED architecture is shown.

In this work, the implemented VED takes as input $256 \times 512 \times 3$ front camera image and outputs a 200×196 semantic map.

Pyramid Occupancy Network

The Pyramid Occupancy Network (PON), developed by Roddick and Cipolla [11], is a deep learning architecture that extracts multi-resolution features from a monocular RGB image and maps them into a semantic BEV representation. This perspective transformation is performed through a multiscale dense transformer layer. PON's architecture utilizes a pre-trained Resnet-50 [4] to encode front-view images into multi-resolution features. Then, a feature pyramid contextualizes the high-resolution features with spatial information from the lower pyramid layers. Subsequently, a dense multiscale transformer maps the contextualized features into the BEV space. Finally, a top-down network predicts the semantic labels for the BEV representation. The structure of the PON network is depicted in Fig. 5.

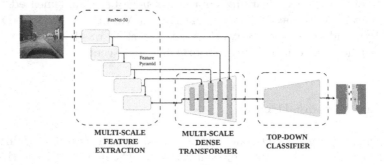

Fig. 5. Pyramid Occupancy Network's architecture [11].

Training

The dataset has been subdivided into three subsets for training and testing the models. These subsets are denoted as training, validation, and test, respectively. The subset of images utilized for the training of DL models consists of 1,000 images, with 90% allocated to training and 10% for validation purposes. The remaining 300 dataset images (images of three scenes from a different map never before seen) are dedicated to testing the models. Models have been trained for 100 epochs with an Adam optimizer. Additionally, to address the imbalanced condition of the dataset during the training process, four loss functions have been implemented: cross-entropy (CE), inverse frequency cross-entropy loss ($InvCE$), square root of the inverse frequency cross-entropy loss ($SqrtInvCE$), and $RecallCE$. Table 1 shows their definitions.

Table 1. Loss functions.

Name	Definition	Description
CE	$-\sum_{c=1}^{C} N_c \log(P^c)$	Measures the performance of the model.
$InvCE$	$-\sum_{c=1}^{C} N \log(P^c)$	Measures the performance of the model assigning appropriate weights to the classes based on their frequency.
$SqrtInvCE$	$\sqrt{InvCE}$	Square root of the $InvCE$.
$RecallCE$	$-\sum_{c=1}^{C} \left(\frac{FN_c}{FN_c + TP_c} \right) N_c \log(P^c)$	Regular cross entropy loss weighted by class-wise false negative rate

C : number of classes. N_c : number of pixels belonging to class "c". N : total number of pixels. P^c : geometric mean confidence of class "c". FN_c and TP_c: false negative, true positive values.

3   Results and Discussion

The following experiments were conducted using both the VED and PON deep learning models.

3.1   Weighted Loss-Based Models Performance

The performance of the VED and PON models in transforming the front view to BEV was evaluated using the built dataset. In this experiment, instead of following a data augmentation approach to balancing the data, a "weighted data" strategy has been adopted through the loss function (see Table 1).

Table 2. Performance of the VED and PON models using a different weighted loss function.

Method	Variational Encoder-Decoder					mIoU
	IoU					
	non-drivable	drivable	sidewalk	vehicle	pedestrian	
CE	0.6640	0.6100	**0.8241**	0.0000	0.0000	0.4196
InvCE	0.6500	**0.8161**	0.7774	0.4171	0.0534	0.5429
SqrtInvCE	**0.6962**	0.7434	0.7980	**0.5390**	**0.068**	**0.5691**
RecallCE	0.5505	0.6486	0.7752	0.0920	0.0000	0.4133
Method	Pyramid Occupancy Network					mIoU
	IoU					
	non-drivable	drivable	sidewalk	vehicle	pedestrian	
CE	**0.7071**	0.8465	0.8515	0.4763	0.0000	0.5763
InvCE	0.6504	0.8382	0.8098	0.5035	0.0737	0.5752
SqrtInvCE	0.6761	0.8472	**0.8551**	**0.5600**	**0.0870**	**0.6051**
RecallCE	0.6920	**0.8515**	0.8462	0.4629	0.0040	0.5714

The results of the validation, according to the implemented loss function, are presented in Table 2. The Intersection over Union (IoU) and mean Intersection over Union (mIoU) [10] have been used as evaluation metrics.

According to Table 2, the performance of the VED model is significantly impacted by the choice of the weighted loss function. The overall performance of the VED model is best achieved with the *SqrtInvCE* loss function. On the contrary, the choice of the weighted loss function has less impact on the performance of the PON model. Nevertheless, similar to the VED model, the best overall result for the PON model is obtained when using the *SqrtInvCE* loss function as indicated in the *mIoU* column. In general, inverse frequency weighting methods seem to have better performance on perspective transform and semantic segmentation, contrasting to Tian's *et al.* results on semantic segmentation [13], where *RecallCE* outperformed weighting methods such as inverse frequency, focal loss, softiou, among others.

3.2 Model Performance with the Layered Map Augmentation Method

Data augmentation is a widely recognized technique that is employed to enhance the performance of deep learning models. In this study, as mentioned in Sect. 2.2, a layer-based data augmentation (LbDA) is proposed in contrast to the classical data augmentation technique. The proposed technique aims to improve semantic segmentation and perspective transform performance by augmenting map layers, as objects present or absent from the original scenes may significantly impact the results. To evaluate the efficacy of the LbDA technique, three different approaches were employed to train the models. The first approach was the

"Non-augmented" method, which utilized the original nine scenes (*traffic* layer configuration). The second approach was the "classic" method, which incorporated traditional data augmentation methods such as Gaussian blur and vertical flip in the *traffic* layer configuration. Lastly, the third approach was the LbDA method, which employed the "layers-none", "layers-all", and "traffic" map layers defined in Sect. 2.2. Both classic and layer-based augmented datasets had three times more training samples.

Models were trained for 100 epochs with Adam optimizer and $SqrtInvCE$ weight loss.

Table 3. Data augmentation performance.

Method	Variational Encoder-Decoder					
	IoU					mIoU
	non-drivable	drivable	sidewalk	vehicle	pedestrian	
Non-augmented	0.6962	0.7434	0.7980	0.5390	0.068	0.5691
Classic	0.7994	**0.8819**	0.8316	**0.5750**	0.0768	0.6330
LbDA	**0.7998**	0.8777	**0.8521**	0.5586	**0.0895**	**0.6356**
Method	Pyramid Occupancy Network					
	IoU					mIoU
	non-drivable	drivable	sidewalk	vehicle	pedestrian	
Non-augmented	0.6761	0.8472	0.8551	0.5600	**0.0870**	0.6051
Classic	0.8036	0.9123	0.8865	0.5895	0.05167	0.6487
LbDA	**0.8105**	**0.9182**	**0.9070**	**0.5993**	0.0580	**0.6586**

As presented in Table 3, Classic and LbDA data augmentation approaches exhibit improvements in IoU and mIoU metrics compared to the Non-augmented approach, regardless of the model used. In particular, the Classic and LbDA models have improved between 4% and 6% with respect to the non-augmented approach. On the other hand, and similar to the weighting-methods experiment, the VED model is more affected by augmentation than PON. In summary, augmentation methods improved overall performance for all classes, though less significantly under challenging classes such as vehicle and pedestrian. LbDA exhibited a slight improvement over the classic, at least on the validation split, composed of unseen scenes from the same map during the training process.

3.3 Generalization of the Models on Unseen Scenarios

As mentioned in Sect. 2.3, a subset of 300 images of previously unseen scenarios was used to evaluate the generalization capacity of the models. These new scenarios introduce complexity, as they require the models to predict perspective transformation based on images from a completely different city. The variability of lighting, weather, and architectural conditions in this new city adds additional complexity, which is challenging for model predictions. Tests have been conducted using the trained models under the three proposed data augmentation techniques. From the results shown in Fig. 6, it can be observed that models trained using augmented methods tend to perform better. Specifically, the PON model is slightly better, with an average mIoU of 0.426 (between all three approaches), than the VED, which obtained an average of 0.4163 mIoU. However, VED exhibited the highest individual mIoU (0.461) among all trained approaches. In terms of individual class, the models employed encountered difficulties in accurately identifying the pedestrian class. This issue was likely due to the input image size, as well as the class's fewer pixel count. However, the VED model consistently outperformed the PON model in this class. In contrast, the drivable class was the best-classified class regardless of the model and data augmentation technique implemented.

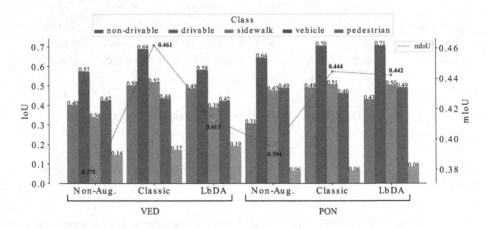

Fig. 6. Testing models generalization performance.

4   Conclusions and Future Work

In this work, an overview of a popular approach utilized in autonomous vehicles for environmental perception is presented, which involves transforming the front-view perspective into a bird's-eye view perspective. The study showcases the implementation and testing of two state-of-the-art deep learning architectures, namely the variational encoder-decoder [9] and the pyramid occupancy network [11], to transform monocular RGB images into semantically segmented bird's-eye view maps. A synthetic front view and bird's-eye view dataset were created using the CARLA autonomous vehicle research simulator [1]. Furthermore, a layer-based data augmentation method was introduced to enhance the dataset. Experiments were conducted to test the performance of the VED and

PON models, which involved training the models using a weighted loss function. Additionally, a common data augmentation technique was compared with the introduced data augmentation method, showing that the proposed method is capable of yielding better performance for certain models. Finally, the generalization ability of the models was tested using data from an unseen map, achieving a good performance for classes such as drivable surfaces.

In future work, we will extend our dataset, including more variability. In addition, we will explore the inclusion of elements such as attention blocks in the networks' architecture.

References

1. Dosovitskiy, A., Ros, G., Codevilla, F., Lopez, A., Koltun, V.: Carla: an open urban driving simulator. In: Conference on Robot Learning, pp. 1–16. PMLR (2017)
2. Florea, H., Petrovai, A., Giosan, I., Oniga, F., Varga, R., Nedevschi, S.: Enhanced perception for autonomous driving using semantic and geometric data fusion. Sensors **22**(13), 5061 (2022)
3. Garnett, N., Cohen, R., Pe'er, T., Lahav, R., Levi, D.: 3d-lanenet: end-to-end 3d multiple lane detection. In: Proceedings of the IEEE/CVF International Conference on Computer Vision, pp. 2921–2930 (2019)
4. He, K., Zhang, X., Ren, S., Sun, J.: Deep residual learning for image recognition. In: Proceedings of the IEEE Conference on Computer Vision and Pattern Recognition, pp. 770–778 (2016)
5. Justs, D.J., Novickis, R., Ozols, K., Greitans, M.: Bird's-eye view image acquisition from simulated scenes using geometric inverse perspective mapping. In: 2020 17th Biennial Baltic Electronics Conference (BEC), pp. 1–6. IEEE. (2020). https://doi.org/10.1109/BEC49624.2020.9277042
6. Li, H., et al.: Delving into the devils of bird's-eye-view perception: a review, evaluation and recipe. IEEE Trans. Pattern Anal. Mach. Intell. (2023)
7. Li, Z., et al.: Bevformer: learning bird's-eye-view representation from multi-camera images via spatiotemporal transformers. In: Avidan, S., Brostow, G., Cissé, M., Farinella, G.M., Hassner, T. (eds.) ECCV 2022. LNCS, vol. 13669, pp. 1–18. Springer, Cham (2022). https://doi.org/10.1007/978-3-031-20077-9_1
8. Liu, M., Yurtsever, E., Zhou, X., Fossaert, J., Cui, Y., Zagar, B.L., Knoll, A.C.: A survey on autonomous driving datasets: Data statistic, annotation, and outlook
9. Lu, C., van de Molengraft, M.J.G., Dubbelman, G.: Monocular semantic occupancy grid mapping with convolutional variational encoder-decoder networks. IEEE Robot. Autom. Lett. **4**(2), 445–452 (2019)
10. Rezatofighi, H., Tsoi, N., Gwak, J., Sadeghian, A., Reid, I., Savarese, S.: Generalized intersection over union: a metric and a loss for bounding box regression. In: Proceedings of the IEEE/CVF Conference on Computer Vision and Pattern Recognition, pp. 658–666 (2019)
11. Roddick, T., Cipolla, R.: Predicting semantic map representations from images using pyramid occupancy networks. In: 2020 CVF Conference on Computer Vision and Pattern Recognition, CVPR, pp. 13–19. IEEE (2020)
12. Saval-Calvo, M., Medina-Valdés, L., Castillo-Secilla, J.M., Cuenca-Asensi, S., Martínez-Álvarez, A., Villagrá, J.: A review of the Bayesian occupancy filter. Sensors **17**(2), 344 (2017)

13. Tian, J., Mithun, N.C., Seymour, Z., Chiu, H.P., Kira, Z.: Striking the right balance: Recall loss for semantic segmentation. In: 2022 International Conference on Robotics and Automation (ICRA), pp. 5063–5069. IEEE (2022)
14. Zhou, T., He, D., Lee, C.H.: Pixel-level bird view image generation from front view by using a generative adversarial network. In: 2020 6th International Conference on Control, Automation and Robotics (ICCAR), pp. 683–689. IEEE (2020). https://doi.org/10.1109/ICCAR49639.2020.9107991

Evaluating the Effectiveness of an AI Model with Transfer of Learning in the Educational Attendance Record

Sebastián Azamar-Avilés[1], Martín Granados-Reyes[1], José Ambrosio-Bastián[2] (iD),
and Zizilia Zamudio-Beltrán[2](✉) (iD)

[1] Facultad de Ingeniería, Universidad La Salle, 06140 Ciudad de México, Mexico
{sebastian.azamar,martingranados}@lasallistas.org.mx
[2] Vicerrectoría de Investigación, Universidad La Salle, 06140 Ciudad de México, Mexico
{jose.ambrosio,zizilia.zamudio}@lasalle.mx

Abstract. This paper presents a proposal for the development of a web application that applies Artificial Intelligence (AI) and transfer of learning to improve the roll call process in school classrooms. The final application is based on a system for facial recognition that uses a proprietary database for student identification. In addition, all photos used in the process are considered to have the necessary concessions and rights for this purpose. The implementation of AI algorithms and the creation of a customized database allow us to simplify and streamline attendance registration in an efficient and accurate way. The results obtained with the proposal developed in this study show an acceptable performance since the proper recognition of people individually, housed within the database, is achieved, which confirms the validity of this innovative solution. This proposal highlights the potential of AI in the optimization of administrative tasks in the educational system, offering an innovative solution to facilitate the process of roll call in classrooms, step by step. Finally, it is important to note that, although the work was developed for the educational system, it can be extended to any type of sector that requires keeping an accurate record of people's attendance.

Keywords: Artificial intelligence · transfer of learning · facial recognition · assistance · data augmentation

1 Introduction

The growing relevance of technology and artificial intelligence (AI) has sparked a revolution in various domains of our contemporary society. The adoption of automation and the deployment of advanced algorithms are radically redefining traditional processes in a broad array of sectors. Notably, the educational sector has participated in this shift, witnessing how emerging technologies reconfigure the approach to everyday challenges. The scientific community has expressed an increasing interest in educational tools enhanced with smart technology, acknowledging their potential to deeply transform pedagogical methods and learning approaches [1].

© The Author(s), under exclusive license to Springer Nature Switzerland AG 2024
E. Mezura-Montes et al. (Eds.): MCPR 2024, LNCS 14755, pp. 177–187, 2024.
https://doi.org/10.1007/978-3-031-62836-8_17

Artificial intelligence has enabled the emergence of a range of tools and solutions aimed at optimizing efficiency and enriching the educational quality. From adaptive learning platforms to automated assessment systems, technology has proven to be effective in boosting the educational process.

In this landscape, automation and AI are revolutionizing administrative methods, including classroom attendance recording. Traditional approaches, often reliant on manual processes, are confronted with challenges such as human error and significant time loss [2]. The implementation of intelligent solutions, such as AI-driven facial recognition and learning transfer, promises to surpass these limitations, offering efficient and precise alternatives. This innovation not only simplifies administrative processes but also facilitates a more integrated educational experience, aligned with the current technological demands [3].

The adoption of AI in the educational sector has facilitated the development of adaptive tools that significantly enhance the teaching and learning process. Noteworthy research in the references [4–7] demonstrates how AI can personalize the learning experience, automate administrative tasks, and provide predictive analytics on student performance, transforming the educational system towards greater accessibility and efficiency.

The use of facial recognition, powered by AI, extends to various applications, from the implementation of classifier algorithms for the secure identification of individuals [8], to its application in public transportation systems for identifying lost or suspicious persons [9]. The significance of facial recognition has been proven across multiple domains, including workforce management, public safety, and device activation, showcasing the efficiency of systems based on artificial neural networks for facial recognition, as observed in specific implementations in Ecuador [10]. Furthermore, the feasibility of using cost-effective hardware along with big data processing to enhance security and access control has been demonstrated in [11], while [12] explores a surveillance system based on facial recognition through deep neural networks.

Additionally, the management of attendance through applications has proven its applicability in various areas, from automating the attendance control of administrative and teaching staff [13, 14], to the integration of attendance systems with payroll using biometric technology in Ecuador [15, 16]. The effectiveness of these digital solutions in improving administrative processes has been extensively proven, including specific applications for student attendance developed with general technologies [17–21], Bluetooth [22, 23], and IoT-based [24].

Specifically, facial recognition for school attendance, employing AI tools, has shown significant progress in the security and automation of educational processes. The implementation of effective facial recognition systems, utilizing AI to identify attendances at distances of up to 5 m [25], or using IoT for attendance management in conjunction with web servers and APIs [26], highlights innovation in this field. Moreover, systems that employ Haar cascade detection in OpenCV [27], or proposals for automating attendance registration through facial recognition integrated into ERP web applications [28], illustrate the diversity of approaches and technologies applied to this purpose.

The main contribution of this paper is the development of a web-based facial recognition system for classroom attendance management. This system, which uses pre-trained artificial intelligence models and a proprietary database through transfer learning, simplifies the attendance pass process and could be used as a security system inside educational facilities, taking care of data confidentiality in an ethical framework, offering significant improvements to the management of educational systems.

The article is organized as follows: Sect. 2 introduces the database construction for the system. Training through transfer learning is presented in Sect. 3. Section 4 describes the development of the web application. Section 5 is dedicated to presenting the results obtained with the complete system for attendance taking. Finally, Sect. 6 outlines the conclusions and future work.

2   Database Construction

To initiate the proposed methodology of this study, it is imperative to establish a robust database that serves as the foundational cornerstone for the model's learning process. To construct an accurate and efficient database, a Python script named *Data_collection.ipynb* has been developed. Utilizing the capabilities of the OpenCV library, this script executes a loop to capture 400 images via the device's camera (Fig. 1). Considering 6 individuals for testing, the database amasses a total of 400 images. These images are specifically targeted at capturing the most pertinent facial features for facial recognition purposes. Upon completion of this acquisition phase, the images are methodically stored in a designated folder, prepared for the subsequent model training phase.

Fig. 1. Sample of the photos saved with the script.

The successful capture of these images was facilitated by leveraging an open source.xml code, *"haarcascade_frontalface_default.xml"*. True to its nomenclature, this code employs *haar cascade* functions to effectively isolate and capture the critical frontal facial features, thus enhancing the dataset's relevance and utility for facial recognition algorithms. The general process for data collection can be seen in Fig. 2.

3   Training Through Transfer Learning

The training process was conducted using a *Jupyter* notebook hosted on *Google Colaboratory*. The model employs transfer learning with the *VGG16* architecture to facilitate feature detection and image recognition within the dataset.

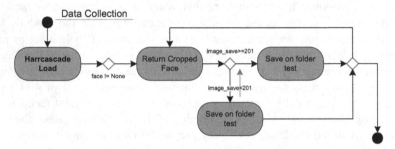

Fig. 2. Data Collection Diagram.

Opting for the transfer learning technique was a strategic decision aimed at leveraging the pre-existing knowledge of a model proficient in a similar domain (image recognition) to enhance our model's capability in executing its designated task (facial recognition). Among the plethora of renowned pre-trained models, such as *MobileNetV2, Inception-ResNetV2*, and *EfficientNet*, the *VGG16* model was selected (Fig. 3) due to its superior performance in our evaluations.

```
IMAGE_SIZE = (224, 224)

vgg16 = VGG16(input_shape=IMAGE_SIZE + (3,), weights='imagenet', include_top=False)
```

Fig. 3. *VGG16* model.

Figure 4 provides a detailed representation of the learning transfer model implemented in this study. The figure offers a comprehensive overview of the various components and processes involved.

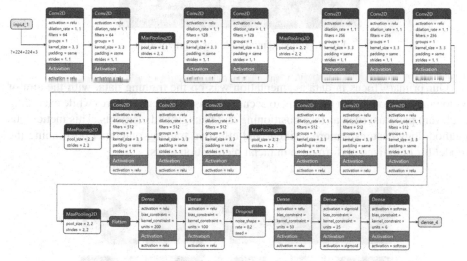

Fig. 4. Detailed model.

In Fig. 5, we present a structural view of the learning transfer model, offering a detailed insight into its architecture and components.

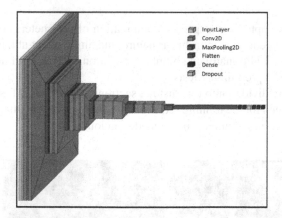

Fig. 5. Structure of the model.

To enhance the model's image detection capabilities, we employed data augmentation techniques (Fig. 6). This method serves to enrich the dataset with additional distinctive features as shown in the Fig. 7, thereby streamlining the model's training and detection tasks.

```
train_datagen = ImageDataGenerator(rescale=1/255.,
                                   brightness_range=[0.5, 1.5],
                                   rotation_range=40,
                                   shear_range=0.2,
                                   zoom_range=0.2,
                                   horizontal_flip=True,
                                   width_shift_range=0.2,
                                   height_shift_range=0.2,
                                   fill_mode='nearest'
                                   )
```

Fig. 6. Implemented code for augmentation.

Our primary focus in data augmentation was on the training data, with the aim of endowing the model with the ability to accurately discern facial features while excluding irrelevant patterns, such as face positioning and background elements. This meticulous methodology ensures a more resilient and effective training outcome, positioning the model for optimized performance in facial recognition tasks.

Fig. 7. Processing examples with *imaginedatageneration*.

For training, we opted for a specific combination of parameters (Fig. 8). The *relu* function was chosen due to its non-linear nature, making it adept at handling the complexity of the data. Additionally, the number of neurons was determined based on the results obtained from preliminary tests.

The samples are divided into two distinct sections: 'Train' and 'Test'. The first 200 images are designated for the training set, while the subsequent 200 images are allocated to the testing set, both assignments being made randomly.

```
x = Flatten()(VGG16.output)
x = Dense(200, activation='relu')(x) #200
x = Dense(100, activation='relu')(x) #100
x = Dropout(0.2)(x)
x = Dense(50, activation='relu')(x) #50
x = Dense(25, activation='sigmoid')(x) #25
prediction = Dense(len(folders), activation='softmax')(x)
```

Fig. 8. Custom final layers.

The model comprises a total of 19,759,069 parameters, with 5,044,381 of these being trainable and 14,714,618 designated as untrainable (Fig. 9). This underscored reliance on transfer learning underscores our utilization of pre-existing knowledge.

Model: "model"

Layer (type)	Output Shape	Param #
input_1 (InputLayer)	[(None, 224, 224, 3)]	0
block1_conv1 (Conv2D)	(None, 224, 224, 64)	1792
block1_conv2 (Conv2D)	(None, 224, 224, 64)	36928
block1_pool (MaxPooling2D)	(None, 112, 112, 64)	0
block2_conv1 (Conv2D)	(None, 112, 112, 128)	73856
block2_conv2 (Conv2D)	(None, 112, 112, 128)	147584
block2_pool (MaxPooling2D)	(None, 56, 56, 128)	0
block3_conv1 (Conv2D)	(None, 56, 56, 256)	295168
block3_conv2 (Conv2D)	(None, 56, 56, 256)	590080
block3_conv3 (Conv2D)	(None, 56, 56, 256)	590080
block3_pool (MaxPooling2D)	(None, 28, 28, 256)	0
block4_conv1 (Conv2D)	(None, 28, 28, 512)	1180160
block4_conv2 (Conv2D)	(None, 28, 28, 512)	2359808
block4_conv3 (Conv2D)	(None, 28, 28, 512)	2359808
block4_pool (MaxPooling2D)	(None, 14, 14, 512)	0
block5_conv1 (Conv2D)	(None, 14, 14, 512)	2359808
block5_conv2 (Conv2D)	(None, 14, 14, 512)	2359808
block5_conv3 (Conv2D)	(None, 14, 14, 512)	2359808
block5_pool (MaxPooling2D)	(None, 7, 7, 512)	0
[illegible]	[illegible]	[illegible]
dense (Dense)	(None, 200)	5017800
dense_1 (Dense)	(None, 100)	20100
dropout (Dropout)	(None, 100)	0
dense_2 (Dense)	(None, 50)	5050
dense_3 (Dense)	(None, 25)	1275
dense_4 (Dense)	(None, 6)	156

Total params: 19,759,069
Trainable params: 5,044,381
Non-trainable params: 14,714,688

Fig. 9. Total model parameters.

Once the model was trained, it was exported to a.*h5* format for attachment to the web page that was used as the interface for image recognition.

4 Development of Web Application

The primary objective of this database is to establish a facial recognition system tailored for student identification, thereby aiding educators across all academic levels in seamlessly conducting attendance procedures in a streamlined, automated, and expeditious manner. This endeavor was realized through the development of a web-based platform, utilizing *ReactJs* to optimize user interface components and ensure optimal performance when deployed on a hosting service. Furthermore, leveraging *TensorFlow* libraries facilitated the integration of pre-trained model weights into the application framework. As students traverse through the device camera's field of view, the system accurately detects their presence and promptly displays their corresponding name, facilitating efficient roll call management. Figure 12.a illustrates the main screen interface of the developed application.

5 Results

Following multiple training sessions, we achieved a remarkable training accuracy of 99.35% and a test accuracy of 98.15%, indicating our model's high precision and a minimal margin of error. The accuracy and losses of the model can be seen represented in Fig. 10.

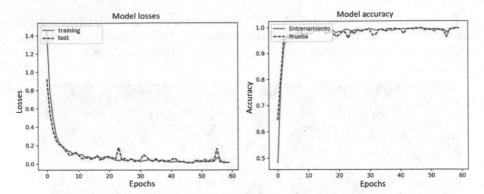

Fig. 10. Performance curves of the model.

Figure 11 shows the confusion matrix generated by the implemented model, delineating the ratio of accurately classified data relative to the total dataset. This matrix delineates the distribution of classification errors, facilitating a comprehensive understanding of misclassifications among the six students in the database. The results obtained demonstrate a notably high rate of accurate identification among the students.

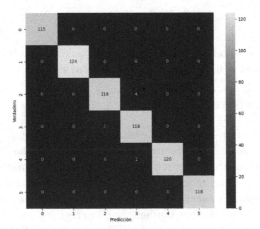

Fig. 11. Confusion matrix generated.

The web page has a simple interface with an easy-to-use switch that activates the camera for quick student recognition, as illustrated in Fig. 12.b. Photos are processed using the TensorFlow library, and the pre-loaded model handles the prediction. After processing, the label is displayed in the app. The application is also compatible with mobile devices, as shown in Fig. 12.c.

a) Web application developed

b) Web application camera

c) Responsive view

Fig. 12. Web application.

6 Conclusions and Future Work

The system proposed in this study has showcased its proficiency in bolstering educational system management by automating classroom attendance registration via an AI-powered web application. Leveraging model learning transfer, particularly in high-performing image classification tasks, enables the implementation of precise and efficient solutions through the customization of the network's final layers. The use of frameworks and libraries specialized in pattern recognition, image processing and computer vision facilitate the identification of participants through facial recognition.

As future work, the model should be optimized to reduce its computational complexity and make inferences in less time. Standardize the capture of images of the participants. Improve the user interface of the web application and generate a data privacy policy and ethical handling of information. Development of low-cost intelligent systems for access to restricted areas using IoT cards. Moreover, it is important to consider images of faces with overlapping objects, such as glasses or face shields. Although no such cases were analyzed in this study, a preliminary test indicated that the system functions correctly even with partial face obstructions. However, it is anticipated that with a larger database and retraining of the network, the identification process could be enhanced significantly. This improvement, along with its efficacy, still needs to be confirmed through further testing.

Disclosure of Interests.   The authors have no competing interests to declare that are relevant to the content of this article.

References

1. Forero-Corba, W., Negre Bennasar, F.: Techniques and applications of Machine Learning and Artificial Intelligence in education: a systematic review. [Técnicas y aplicaciones del Machine Learning e Inteligencia Artificial en educación: una revisión sistemática]. RIEDRevista Iberoamericana de Educación a Distancia **27**(1), 209–253 (2024). https://doi.org/10.5944/ried.27.1.37491

2. Nuño-Maganda, M.A., Hernández-Almazán, J.A., Hernández-Mier, Y., Polanco-Mortagón, S.: Sistema de análisis de asistencia a clases en línea. In: Archundia Sierra, E. (ed.), Desafío de la Investigación en Tecnologías para la Educación, pp. 180–194. Editores Literarios
3. Peñaherrera Acurio, W.P., Cunuhay Cuchipe, W.C., Nata Castro, D.J., Moreira Zamora, L.E.: Implementación de la Inteligencia Artificial (IA) como Recurso Educativo. RECIMUNDO **6**(2), 402–413 (2022). https://doi.org/10.26820/recimundo/6.(2).abr.2022.402-413
4. Berrones Yaulema, L.P., Salgado Oviedo, S.A.: La aplicación de la inteligencia artificial para mejorar la enseñanza y el aprendizaje en el ámbito educativo. Esprint Investigación **2**(1), 52–60 (2023). https://doi.org/10.61347/ei.v2i1.52
5. Rivas, A.: Nicolás Buchbinder e Ignacio Barrenechea (2023). El futuro de la inteligencia artificial en educación en América Latina, España, ProFuturo/OEI
6. Jara, I., Ochoa, J.M.: Usos y efectos de la inteligencia artificial en educación. Banco Interamericano de Desarrollo (Grupo BID) (2020). https://doi.org/10.18235/0002380
7. Macías Morales, Y.: La tecnología y la Inteligencia Artificial en el sistema educativo (Tesis de maestría). Universitat Jaume I, Departament d'Administració d'Empreses i Màrqueting, Castelló. Espanya (2021). http://hdl.handle.net/10234/195263
8. Karpiuk, N., Klym, H., Vasylchychyn, I.: Facial recognition system based on the Haar cascade classifier method. In: 2023 24th International Conference on Computational Problems of Electrical Engineering (CPEE), Grybów, Poland, pp. 1–4 (2023). https://doi.org/10.1109/CPEE59623.2023.10285310
9. Villanueva, U.R., Goñi Delión, J.C., Larroca, F.P.: Reconocimiento de expresiones faciales y características personales como herramienta para identificar personas en un sistema de transporte público. Ingeniería Industrial Esp. 261–277 (2022). https://doi.org/10.26439/ing.ind2022.n.5811
10. Ibarra-Estévez, J., Paredes, K.: Redes neuronales artificiales para el control de acceso basado en reconocimiento facial. Revista PUCE **106** (2018). https://doi.org/10.26807/revpuce.v0i106.140
11. Portal Díaz, J., Siles Siles, I., Puig Contreras, E., Sánchez, A.: Aplicación de técnicas de inteligencia artificial para reconocimiento facial en sistemas de seguridad en ambientes de intranet. Mare Ingenii **4**(1), 20–32 (2022). https://doi.org/10.52948/mare.v4i1.682
12. Pulugu, D., Anusha, P., Srivastava, R.R., Kalaivani, R., Pal, S.: Machine learning-based facial recognition for video surveillance systems. J. Image Video Proc. **14**(2) (2023). https://ictactjournals.in/paper/IJIVP_Vol_14_Iss_2_Paper_8_3149_3154.pdf
13. Amelia, A., Solikhah, M.: Web-based employee attendance information system on CV. Syntax Corporation Indonesia. Jurnal Indonesia Sosial Teknologi **4**(12), 2436–2442 (2023). https://doi.org/10.59141/jist.v4i12.824
14. Chamba, D.: Desarrollo de una Aplicación Web para el Control de Asistencia del Personal Docente y Administrativo del IST Primero De Mayo. Ecuadorian Sci. J. **5**(3), 112–124 (2021). https://doi.org/10.46480/esj.5.3.148
15. Arias, P.S., Jaqueline, F.: Aplicación web de control de asistencia integrado al rol de pagos para el personal docente, administrativo y de servicio, a través de un sistema biométrico para el Instituto Tecnológico Superior República del Ecuador (2014)
16. Urquiza Moreno, D.G., Vallejo Alcivar, J.A.: Desarrollo de una aplicación web para la gestión de roles de pago y control de asistencia del personal de la empresa Andrés Arturo Coka Cía. Ltda (Tesis de Licenciatura). Universidad Politécnica Salesiana, Guayaquil, Ecuador (2018). https://dspace.ups.edu.ec/bitstream/123456789/16409/1/UPS-GT002380.pdf
17. Márquez, L., Lara, Y.A., Ángulo, F.: Prototipo de control de acceso a aulas y registro automático de asistencia. Revista Colombiana de Tecnologías de Avanzada **2**(26) (2017). https://doi.org/10.24054/16927257.v26.n26.2015.2397
18. Alrowaily, M.A.: Utilizing beacon technology for the development of a smart attendance system. Int. J. Adv. Appl. Sci. **9**(6), 26–35 (2022). https://doi.org/10.21833/ijaas.2022.06.004

19. Jacksi, K., Ibrahim, F.J., Ali, S.: Student attendance management system. Scholars J. Eng. Technol. (SJET) (2018)
20. Geethanjali, T.M., Maheshwari, S.B.N., Vaishnavi, R.: Students attendance management system. Int. J. Sci. Res. Devel. **8**(1) (2020). ISSN: 2321-0613
21. Kumar, R., Lodha, K., Jucker, M., Mathur, S., Sanadhiya, S., Singh, S.: Attendance management system. Int. Adv. Res. J. Sci. Eng. Technol. **10**(2) (2020). https://iarjset.com/wp-content/uploads/2023/06/IARJSET-ICMART-3.pdf
22. Lodha, R., Gupta, S., Jain, H., Narula, H.: Bluetooth smart based attendance management system. Procedia Comput. Sci. **45**, 524–527 (2015). https://doi.org/10.1016/j.procs.2015.03.094
23. Lee, D.: Bluetooth-based smart attendance system. Int. J. Eng. Adv. Technol. (IJEAT) **9**(3), 3851–3854 (2020). https://doi.org/10.35940/ijeat.C6280.029320
24. Shekhar, J., Zerihun, D., Haile, M.A., Shifaw, B.: Automated classroom monitoring with IOT and virtuino app. Int. J. Adv. Res. IT Eng. **8**(3), 1–17 (2019). https://garph.co.uk/IJARIE/Mar2019/G-2496.pdf
25. Tovar, L.C., Echavez, M.E.: Universidad de Cartagena, Colombia, Martelo, R.J., Universidad de Cartagena, Colombia. Diseño e implementación de un sistema de biometría facial para el control de acceso en instituciones de educación superior. Revista Espacios **41**(44) (2020). https://doi.org/10.48082/espacios-a20v41n44p26
26. Nguyen, V.D., Khoa, H.V., Kieu, T.N., Huh, E.-N.: Internet of things-based intelligent attendance system: framework, practice implementation, and application. Electronics **11**, 3151 (2022). https://doi.org/10.3390/electronics11193151
27. AlRababah, A.A., Besoul, K.A., Bazi, A.G., AlSlimi, A., Arishi, I.: Facial recognition system implementation for managing techniques of student attendance. Int. J. Appl. Sci. Res. **6**(6) (2023). https://www.ijasr.org/paper/653a5117ecf36.pdf
28. Mayuri, M., et al.: Automated attendance using face recognition and automated marking in ERP system. Int. J. Res. Appl. Sci. Eng. Technol. (IJRASET) **11**(V), 6309–6314 (2023). https://doi.org/10.22214/ijraset.2023.52288

Multimodal-Attention Fusion for the Detection of Questionable Content in Videos

Arnold Morales[1]([✉]), Elaheh Baharlouei[2], Thamar Solorio[2], and Hugo Jair Escalante[1]

[1] Computer Science Department, Instituto Nacional de Astrofísica, Óptica y Electrónica, Puebla, Mexico
{arnold.morales,hugojair}@inaoep.mx
[2] Computer Science Department, University of Houston, Houston, USA
{ebaharlo,solorio}@cs.uh.edu

Abstract. We address the problem of questionable content filtering from videos, in particular, we focus on the detection of comic mischief. Attention-based models have been proposed to approach this problem, mostly relying on hierarchical cross-attention (HCA) for fusing multimodal information. While competitive performance has been obtained with such solutions, it is unclear whether the hierarchical mechanism is the best choice for this type of model. We explore in this paper the use of an alternative mechanism called parallel cross-attention (ParCA). Also, we propose the use of gated multimodal units (GMU) for fusing multiple multimodal attention mechanisms, besides the traditional concatenation. Experimental results show that the combination of parallel cross-attention and the use GMU improves considerably the performance of the reference model based on HCA.

Keywords: Multimodal cross-attention · Comic mischief detection · Gated multimodal units

1 Introduction

The widespread of multimodal information throughout diverse platforms and apps has boosted the amounts of multimodal data being generated. Large portion of this information consists of videos depicting content of questionable nature. This represents a potential risk to users which can be exposed to inappropriate or harmful content. Therefore, methods for the identification of this type of content are highly needed. Among all the categories of questionable content, comic mischief detection has been recently approached by the community [4]. In a comic mischief video, questionable content (violence, adult content, or sarcastic material) is combined with a humorous context, making it even more disruptive. According to psychologists, when something such as violence is presented in a serious context (such as war), it has a less disruptive effect than when it is presented in a pleasant and humorous context [6].

The detection of comic mischief often relies on subtle nuances of facial expressions, body language, and linguistic tone that can be better deciphered by integrating multiple modalities. Thus, unlike straightforward textual or visual content, comic elements are multifaceted and rely on an interplay between language, imagery, and context [16,19]. The working hypothesis here is that by taking advantage of multimodal information, which includes textual elements, visuals, and contextual details, we will better understand the antics intended in comics. The use of multimodal information becomes imperative in this context, as it not only enriches the analysis of comic mischief but also ensures more accurate interpretation, leading to a deeper understanding of the interplay between multimodal elements in comic content [5].

In this paper, we approach the problem of detecting questionable content in video with Multimodal Attention Based Models (MABMs). Baharlouei et al. have recently shown that MABMs comprise an effective solution to this task [4]. In particular, the authors showed that a single-head Hierarchical-Cross-Attention (HCA) based model effectively leverages multimodal information for predicting comic mischief. While effective, it is unclear whether fusion mechanisms alternative to HCA can perform better for this task. Likewise, the use of multiple heads in such MABM has not been explored. Accordingly, in this paper, we study the effectiveness of a novel *parallel cross-attention* (ParCA) mechanism to combine multimodal information in MAMBs. Additionally, we explore a new way of merging multiple multimodal attention mechanisms via gated multimodal units (GMU) [2]. Moreover, the performance of these models is explored with single-headed and multi-headed variants of MABMs.

An empirical evaluation in a dataset for comic mischief detection shows that the proposed ParCA betters captures the interaction among multiple modalities within an attention head. Also, fusion based on GMU resulted in better performance than when standard approaches (e.g., concatenation) were considered. Interestingly, our study on the use of multi-head attention showed mixed results. The main contributions of this paper are: a comparative study if HCA and the proposed ParCA mechanisms for learning multimodal cross-attention for comic mishcief detection and a new way to combine information from multiple multimodal attention mechanisms based on GMU for comic michief detection.

2   Related Work

This section reviews related work on questionable content detection and multimodal cross-attention mechanisms.

2.1   Analyzing Questionable Content

Mahsa Shafeo et al. propose a scheme based on multimodal deep learning that addresses the problem of classifying questionable content in movie trailers utilizing LSTMs and contextual attention [20]. A GMU was used to combine multimodal information from video clips. Similarly, Qian-Hua focuses on violence detection in videos using visual and audio information. They use MABMs with standard cross-attention in pairs [17]. Tianshan et al. [15] propose a MAMB for real-time anomaly detection in videos implementing a two-stage process. Only the video modality is considered in this work. Dong-Lai [23] proposes a MABM based on label refinement and multimodal fusion for violence detection in videos. Audio and video modalities were considered with a pairwise cross-attention mechanism. Recently Baharlouei, et al. describe a MABM implementing a three-modal hierarchical variant of cross-attention for comic mischief detection [4]. A new dataset is introduced and an extensive evaluation of the proposed method is reported. Authors show that multimodal information combined with HCA resulted in better performance than baselines, and state-of-the-art models including recent MABMS/transformers.

2.2   Multimodal Cross-Attention

Multimodal representation learning and fusion aim to generate a unified representation of multiple modalities that facilitates automatic analysis tasks by constructing classifiers or other models. In the context of attention-based models, multimodal attention mechanisms associated to different modalities are combined, expecting that the fusion captures information about the interaction of modalities. A basic approach is to concatenate individual representations features to obtain a final representation [1,14,18,22]. Although this is a straightforward strategy, given that the nature of the data for each modality is different, their statistical properties are generally not shared across modalities [21], requiring the predictor to model complex interactions between them.

Instead, other leverage on cross-attention to have a contextualized representation of each modality given the information of the others (see Sect. 4.1). Syed, A. et al. [24] proposed a multimodal transformer with dual attention, where they used co-attention to capture complex dependencies across different modalities. Moreover, the hierarchical cross-attention has been explored [8,9,12,25] in order to capture hierarchical intra- and inter-modal correlation. Despite the effectiveness of these methods, they consider only two modalities, which are not appropriate tasks involving more modalities.

To the best of our knowledge, the only work considering cross-attention of more than two modalities is that of Baharlouei, et al. [4]. There, authors apply three times HCA that is later combined via concatenation. While effective, it is not clear if HCA is the best way to combine multimodal information. Likewise, it remains unexplored the use of alternative ways to combine the outputs of these attention mechanisms.

In this work, we explore the use of a novel alternative cross-modal mechanism and use a GMU for fusing its outputs instead of straightforward concatenation. We show that the proposed schema outperforms the standard approach in the detection of comic mischief from videos.

3   Comic Mischief Dataset

For our experimental evaluation we rely on a subset of the comic mischief dataset introduced by Baharlouei et al. [4]. Such a dataset contains 1-minute clips obtained from YouTube videos that were crawled, segmented, and manually labeled. By curating a diverse range of videos that encompass these distinct forms of comedic expression, the comic mischief dataset provides a valuable resource for studying and analyzing the multifaceted nature of humor in online content. The dataset is labeled according to the following categories:

- **Gory humour:** is centered around gruesome or macabre elements. It often includes exaggerated violence, blood, or graphic imagery for comedic effect.
- **Slapstick humour:** is characterized by physical comedy, often involving exaggerated and humorous physical actions, gestures, or mishaps. It relies on visual gags, pratfalls, and absurd or exaggerated physical movements to generate laughter.
- **Mature humour:** is comedy that contains content or themes intended for mature audiences. It often includes jokes or references that touch upon taboo subjects, such as sexuality, politics, social issues, or dark humor.
- **Sarcasm:** is a form of humour that involves the use of irony, mocking, or taunting remarks to convey humor or to express a contradictory meaning. It relies on the delivery of statements that are opposite to what is actually meant, often with a dry or sharp tone.

(a) Gory Humour   (b) Slapstick Humour

(c) Mature Humour   (d) Sarcasm Humour

Fig. 1. Examples of the considered comic mischief categories in cartoons

Figure 1 shows screenshots from clips associated with the considered humor categories. The dataset is challenging for several reasons, including the multifaceted nature of comedic expression across categories and the fact that different categories can be expressed/distinguished by different information modalities (e.g., for detecting *Sarcasm* and *Mature* language and audio information could be more useful than visual one; while for detecting *Slapstick* humor, visual information could be more useful). The working hypothesis of our work and previous approaches is that by effectively leveraging multimodal information (image, audio, and text) one can develop competitive solutions for this task.

Table 1 shows the number of samples available for each of the categories and for different partitions for developing and evaluating our methods. Please note that this is a multi-label classification task, that is, each clip may contain humor from more than one category. Also, please note that in previous work the binary classification task of distinguishing a video containing any comic mischief category or not has been studied. Accordingly, in this work, we perform experiments for both classification tasks.

Table 1. Samples per partition and per category: Mature Humour (MH), Slapstick Humour (SH), Gory Humour (GH) and Sarcasm (S).

	MH	SH	GH	S	None	All
Train	222	166	86	374	307	1007
Validation	24	18	6	48	31	113
Test	35	19	11	41	30	113

4 Multimodal Attention-Head Fusion

This section describes the proposed cross-attention mechanisms and the usage of a GMU for combining them. Before that, we describe the base multimodal attention-based model (MABM) for comic mischief detection that we consider.

4.1 Reference Model

As a base model, we consider a simplified version of the model proposed in [4], a generic diagram is shown in Fig. 2. We describe this simplified model with both approaches, binary classification task, and multi-task model. The so-called, HIerarchical Cross-attention model with CAPtions (HICCAP) implements a hierarchical cross-attention (HCA) to combine embeddings of multiple modalities. It is divided in several stages that are described next.

Feature Extraction. In the initial stage of HICCAP, feature encoding is performed for each modality. To encode textual information, they utilize the BERT model, which effectively captures contextual embeddings and semantic representations of the text [11]. For audio feature extraction, they use the VGGish pretraiinned network, a deep convolutional neural network specifically designed for audio analysis, which extracts informative audio features citevgg. Similarly,

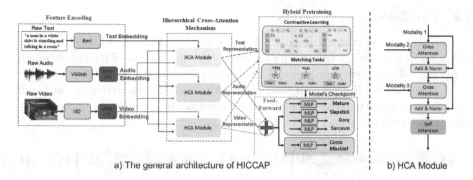

a) The general architecture of HICCAP   b) HCA Module

Fig. 2. (a) HICCAP general architecture. (b) The hierarchical attention model implemented in [4]. Image taken from [4].

for video modality, they utilize the I3D (Inflated 3D ConvNet) network, a powerful architecture for video analysis that captures spatio-temporal features [7]. Additionally, to capture sequential information in both the audio and video modalities, they incorporate an LSTM network, enabling the modeling of temporal dependencies.

Hierachical Cross-Attention (HCA) Mechanism. Once the involved modalities have been encoded with descriptors, a hierarchical cross-attention (HCA) mechanism is adopted (Fig. 2b). Three HCA modules are incorporated into HICCAP, each performing cross-attention at multiple levels to harness the attention across all three modalities, rather than solely focusing on pairwise attention. HCA facilitates the exploration of complex relationships and dependencies within the multimodal data, ultimately enhancing the overall fusion and understanding of the combined modalities. The model concatenates the contextualized outputs of the three HCA mechanisms before classification.

Pretraining and Classification. For the classification stage, following the original method, two tasks are considered: binary and multi-label classification. In the binary task, the objective is to determine whether a video clip contains comic mischief or not. To accomplish this, a multilayer perceptron (MLP) model is adopted. On the other hand, the multi-label classification aims to classify clips into four distinct categories of comic mischief. To tackle this task, a separate MLP is employed for each class, implementing a multi-task learning approach [10]. This allows the model to simultaneously learn and classify the different categories of comic mischief, leveraging the shared information across tasks to enhance the overall performance.

In [4] the model is pretrained using contrastive learning and multimodal matching tasks. For this work we decided to evaluate the performance of the model when trained from scratch, this is to reduce the number of factors that may have an impact on the modeling process.

4.2 Parallel Cross-Attention

The proposed ParCA mechanism, depicted in Fig. 3a, aims to enhance the representation of a modality concerning the two other modalities. This enhancement is performed with two multimodal cross-attention mechanisms that are then fused, see Fig. 3a. ParCA comprises two sub-blocks: cross-attention and self-attention. Cross-attention calculates the attention in parallel for modality $\mathbf{m_1}$ taking modalities $\mathbf{m_2}$ and $\mathbf{m_3}$ (Eq. 1).

$$\mathbf{x}_{\mathbf{m_1}}^2 = \mathrm{softmax}\left(\frac{Q_{\mathbf{m_1}}K_{\mathbf{m_2}}^{\top}}{\sqrt{d_k}}\right)V_{\mathbf{m_2}}, \quad \mathbf{x}_{\mathbf{m_1}}^3 = \mathrm{softmax}\left(\frac{Q_{\mathbf{m_1}}K_{\mathbf{m_3}}^{\top}}{\sqrt{d_k}}\right)V_{\mathbf{m_3}} \quad (1)$$

In Eq. 1, $\mathbf{x}_{\mathbf{m_1}}^2$ is the representation of modality $\mathbf{m_1}$ based on $\mathbf{m_2}$, and $\mathbf{x}_{\mathbf{m_1}}^3$ the representation based on $\mathbf{m_3}$. Then we employ a residual connection [13] around the first sub-block, followed by layer normalization [3] for both outputs. The last sub-block takes the outputs and passes them through standard self-attention to further enhance the representation of the modality and make it more suitable for classification. The outputs of these enhanced attention mechanisms are combined with a fusion technique.

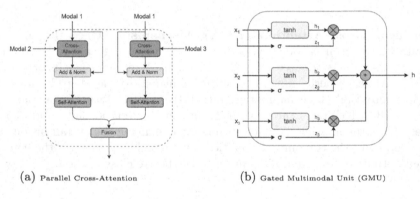

(a) Parallel Cross-Attention   (b) Gated Multimodal Unit (GMU)

Fig. 3. a) The proposed ParCA mechanism, consists of two sub-blocks: cross-attention and self-attention. b) The model of GMU for more than two modalities.

For the fusion we adopted the classical concatenation and sum techniques. Additionally, we propose the use of a GMU [2] for learning the relevance from each of the paths of cross-attention. A GMU learns the importance of the information from each modality and aims to fuse only the most relevant aspects. Using a GMU involves the derivation of an intermediate representation by amalgamating data from diverse modalities. Figure 3b illustrates the architecture of a GMU, where each x_i denotes a feature vector linked to modality i. Each feature vector is input to a neuron with a tanh activation function, aiming to encode an internal representation feature specific to the modality. For every input modality, x_i, there exists a gate neuron (σ), responsible for regulating the impact of the feature computed from x_i (represented as z) on the overall output of the unit. Upon receiving a new sample, the gate neuron associated with modality i processes input feature vectors from all modalities to determine the contribution of the modality i to the internal encoding of the given input sample.

This weighting mechanism acknowledges that not all modalities contribute equally, as there may be instances where the audio does not correspond to the visual elements or the dialogue in a video. Such discrepancies between modalities can lead to conflicts or inconsistencies in the information they provide. We repeat this process to obtain the representations for modalities m_2 and m_3, respectively. ParCA is finally incorporated into the reference model replacing the HCA mechanism.

5   Experiments and Results

In this section, we present the results obtained in both binary and multiclass tasks. We use a subset of the Comic Mischief dataset as mentioned in Sec. 3. We split this subset into three partitions: train (80%), validation (10%) and test (10%), see Table 1. To ensure fair comparisons, we use the same metrics used in the reference work [4]: F1-measure of the positive (comic mischief) in the binary task and macro F1-measure for the multilabel task.

The training of models involves the utilization of the Adam optimizer with a learning rate set at $2e - 5$ and a batch size of 16. In this study, we employ 5 distinct random weight initialization choices for all experiments, and the mean performance based on these random initializations is presented in the subsequent results. The model undergoes 25 epochs for binary tasks and 40 epochs for multi-task scenarios, as it was observed that the validation performance reaches saturation within these epoch limits.

5.1   Evaluation of Detection Performance

Tables 2 and 3 show the results obtained by the different variants we tried for the binary and multilabel tasks, respectively. In both tables we compare the performance of the reference model implementing the standard HCA [4] with 1 (first row) and 8 (second row) heads with alternatives of the HICCAP model implementing our ParCA mechanism (rows 3 and on). The latter variants use different fusion strategies for ParCa, namely: concatenation (ParCACon), sum (ParCASum), and the proposed fusion based on GMU (ParCAGMU). Also, we report the performance of models using a single attention head as in the reference [4] and multi head models with 8 heads (we tried other numbers of heads but results did not vary considerably).

From Table 2, it can be seen that overall the reference model with ParCA mechanism outperformed the standard HICCAP by 3.21% (absolute) in terms of F1 measure when using the GMU fusion in the binary task. This shows the effectiveness of the proposed mechanism in modeling multimodal interaction. There are only two results out of 6 that did not improve the reference model.

In terms of the fusion strategy, GMU obtained consistently better results than sum and concatenation. Interestingly, adding multiple attention heads into the reference model improved its performance by almost 2%, but adding more layers to the models based on ParCA did not result in a consistent improvement.

Table 2. Binary classification results. F1-Score is reported.

F1-Score Binary-Task		
Method	Num.Heads	F1
HICCAP (Baseline)	1	0.7978
HICCAP	8	0.8126
HICCAP - ParCACon	1	0.7874
HICCAP - ParCASum	1	0.8009
HICCAP - ParCAGMU	1	**0.8335**
HICCAP - ParCACon	8	0.8012
HICCAP - ParCASum	8	0.7898
HICCAP - ParCAGMU	8	0.8146

Regarding the multilabel task, Table 3 shows that this time better results in Macro F1 were obtained with the multi-head version of the HICCAP with ParCA mechanism. This result suggests that multimodal interactions are more complex for this problem, requiring of more attention heads to better model the problem. Also, please note that different variants obtained the best results in each class.

Table 3. Multi-class classification results. F1-Score for each class and Average Macro-F1 across all classes are reported.

F1-Score Multi-Task						
Method	Num. Heads	Mature	Gory	Slasptick	Sarcasm	Macro
HICCAP (Baseline)	1	0.6191	0.1769	0.3853	0.7411	0.4806
HICCAP	8	0.5910	0.1831	**0.4859**	0.7388	0.4997
HICCAP - ParCACon	1	0.6197	0.1917	0.3957	0.7455	0.4882
HICCAP - ParCASum	1	**0.6480**	0.2814	0.1118	0.1400	0.2953
HICCAP - ParCAGMU	1	0.5790	0.2829	0.3152	0.7486	0.4814
HICCAP - ParCACon	8	0.5717	0.2942	0.3611	0.7391	0.4915
HICCAP - ParCASum	8	0.6250	0.2095	0.3828	0.7395	0.4892
HICCAP - ParCAGMU	8	0.5677	**0.3190**	0.4797	0.7147	**0.5203**

Summary, experimental results reveal that the proposed ParCA mechanism results in better performance when compared to the HCA implemented in [4]. We show that the fusion of attention mechanisms using GMU consistently resulted in better performance. Finally, empirical evidence suggest that adding multiple attention heads does not necessarily result in better performance.

5.2   Qualitative Analysis

In this section, we analyze the values of the $z-$values used in the HICCAP-ParCAGMU model. These values reflect the relevance between pairs of modalities combined with PaCAR across all of the samples in the training set. Tables 4 show such values for the binary task.

Table 4. Analysis of z values according to their importance in ParCA module for Binary Task.

Analysis of z values in binary task			
	Principal modality		
Secondary Mod	Text	Audio	Image
Text	–	0.4975	0.4887
Audio	0.5216	–	0.5372
image	0.4897	0.5004	–

From this table it can be observed that relevance is not symmetrical, therefore the order in which the ParCA mechanism is fed with modalities matters. On the other hand, we can see that the multimodal interactions that have more relevance for the binary task are Image— >Audio (0.5372) and Text— >Audio (0.5216). Suggesting that Audio is the most critical modality for distinguishing videos with comic mischief from the rest.

6   Conclusions

We proposed in this paper a novel Parallel cross-attention (ParCA) mechanism for learning cross-modal attention in problems where more than two modalities are included. ParCA enhances the representation of each modality via parallel cross-attention with other modalities. The outputs of ParCA are fused and fed to the predictive part of a MABM. We evaluated the performance of our method in the task of comic mischief detection and obtained better results than a state-of-the-art model for the task.

The proposed ParCA mechanism outperformed HCA in the detection of comic mischief, suggesting our proposed mechanism better captures the interaction across modalities. Also, the use of a GMU outperformed the standard approach for the fusion of multimodal attention mechanisms. Finally, the usefulness of adding multiple heads into the reference model was not clear.

For future work, we would like to study this weighted fusion mechanism in the attention heads of MABMs. Additionally, we would like to explore more questionable content datasets, such as violence detection and hate speech detection.

References

1. Anwar, A., Kanjo, E., Anderez, D.O.: Deepsafety: multi-level audio-text feature extraction and fusion approach for violence detection in conversations. CoRR **abs/2206.11822** (2022). https://doi.org/10.48550/arXiv.2206.11822
2. Arevalo, J., Solorio, T., Montes-y Gomez, M., González, F.A.: Gated multimodal networks. Neural Comput. Appl. **32**, 10209–10228 (2020)
3. Ba, J.L., Kiros, J.R., Hinton, G.E.: Layer normalization (2016)
4. Baharlouei Elaheh, S.T.: Labeling comic mischief content in online videos. In: LREC-COLING. vol. In press (2024)
5. Baltrušaitis, T., Ahuja, C., Morency, L.P.: Multimodal machine learning: a survey and taxonomy. IEEE Trans. Pattern Anal. Mach. Intell. **41**(2), 423–443 (2018)
6. Blackford, B.J., Gentry, J., Harrison, R.L., Carlson, L.: The prevalence and influence of the combination of humor and violence in super bowl commercials. J. Advert. **40**(4), 123–134 (2011)
7. Carreira, J., Zisserman, A.: Quo vadis, action recognition? a new model and the kinetics dataset. In: proceedings of the IEEE Conference on Computer Vision and Pattern Recognition, pp. 6299–6308 (2017)
8. Chen, X., Kang, B., Wang, D., Li, D., Lu, H.: Efficient visual tracking via hierarchical cross-attention transformer. In: Karlinsky, L., Michaeli, T., Nishino, K. (eds.) ECCV 2022. LNCS, vol. 13808, pp. 461–477. Springer, Cham (2022). https://doi.org/10.1007/978-3-031-25085-9_26
9. Chen, X., Yan, B., Zhu, J., Wang, D., Yang, X., Lu, H.: Transformer tracking. In: Proceedings of the IEEE/CVF Conference on Computer Vision and Pattern Recognition, pp. 8126–8135 (2021)
10. Crawshaw, M.: Multi-task learning with deep neural networks: a survey (2020)
11. Devlin, J., Chang, M.W., Lee, K., Toutanova, K.: Bert: Pre-training of deep bidirectional transformers for language understanding (2019)
12. Dutta, S., Ganapathy, S.: Hcam–hierarchical cross attention model for multi-modal emotion recognition. arXiv preprint arXiv:2304.06910 (2023)
13. He, K., Zhang, X., Ren, S., Sun, J.: Deep residual learning for image recognition (2015)
14. Kiela, D., Bottou, L.: Learning image embeddings using convolutional neural networks for improved multi-modal semantics. Proceedings of the Conference on Empirical Methods in Natural Language Processing (EMNLP-14), pp. 36–45 (2014)
15. Liu, T., Zhang, C., Lam, K.M., Kong, J.: Decouple and resolve: transformer-based models for online anomaly detection from weakly labeled videos. IEEE Trans. Inf. Forensics Secur. **18**, 15–28 (2023)
16. Ngiam, J., Khosla, A., Kim, M., Nam, J., Lee, H., Ng, A.Y.: Multimodal deep learning. In: Proceedings of the 28th International Conference on Machine Learning (ICML-11), pp. 689–696 (2011)
17. Pang, W.F., He, Q.H., Hu, Y.J., Li, Y.X.: Violence detection in videos based on fusing visual and audio information. In: ICASSP 2021 - 2021 IEEE International Conference on Acoustics, Speech and Signal Processing (ICASSP), pp. 2260–2264 (2021)
18. Pei, D., Liu, H., Liu, Y., Sun, F.: Unsupervised multimodal feature learning for semantic image segmentation. In: The 2013 International Joint Conference on Neural Networks (IJCNN), pp. 1–6 (2013)

19. Poria, S., Cambria, E., Howard, N., Huang, G.B., Hussain, A.: Fusing audio, visual and textual clues for sentiment analysis from multimodal content. Neurocomputing **174**, 50–59 (2016)
20. Shafaei, M., Smailis, C., Kakadiaris, I., Solorio, T.: A case study of deep learning-based multi-modal methods for labeling the presence of questionable content in movie trailers. In: Proceedings of the International Conference on Recent Advances in Natural Language Processing (RANLP 2021), pp. 1297–1307. INCOMA Ltd., Held Online (sep 2021)
21. Srivastava, N., Salakhutdinov, R.R.: Multimodal learning with deep Boltzmann machines. In: Pereira, F., Burges, C., Bottou, L., Weinberger, K. (eds.) Advances in Neural Information Processing Systems, vol. 25. Curran Associates, Inc. (2012)
22. Suk, H.I., Shen, D.: Deep learning-based feature representation for AD/MCI classification. In: Mori, K., Sakuma, I., Sato, Y., Barillot, C., Navab, N. (eds.) Medical Image Computing and Computer-Assisted Intervention - MICCAI 2013. LNCS, pp. 583–590. Springer, Heidelberg (2013). https://doi.org/10.1007/978-3-642-40763-5_72
23. Wei, D.L., Liu, C.G., Liu, Y., Liu, J., Zhu, X.G., Zeng, X.H.: Look, listen and pay more attention: fusing multi-modal information for video violence detection. In: ICASSP 2022 - 2022 IEEE International Conference on Acoustics, Speech and Signal Processing (ICASSP), pp. 1980–1984 (2022)
24. Zaidi, S.A.M., Latif, S., Qadir, J.: Cross-language speech emotion recognition using multimodal dual attention transformers (2023)
25. Zhang, L., Zhang, X., Pan, J.: Hierarchical cross-modality semantic correlation learning model for multimodal summarization. In: Proceedings of the AAAI Conference on Artificial Intelligence, vol. 36, pp. 11676–11684 (2022)

Optimization of Color Dominance Factor by Greedy Algorithm for Leaves and Fruit Segmentation of Tomato Plants

Juan Pablo Guerra Ibarra$^{(\boxtimes)}$ ⓘ and Francisco Cuevas de la Rosa ⓘ

Centro de Investigaciones en Óptica A.C., Guanajuato, León 37150, Mexico
{juangi,fjcuevas}@cio.mx

Abstract. The cultivation of agricultural products destined for human consumption has played a crucial role in the advancement of societies. Consequently, the cultivation of land is facilitated by the integration of various technological advancements into tillage processes. The implementation of different areas of research and technologies have created what is called precision agriculture. In general, precision agriculture systems take information from different sources, which in most cases requires a process of filtering the information. When the source of the information is images, the filtering process in many cases requires a segmentation process to label the pixels of interest. In this work, we present a proposed *Greedy Algorithm* that seeks to highlight the color dominance present in the leaves and fruits of tomato plants to perform a segmentation process using two α parameters to optimize. Applying the $\alpha_1 = 3.2$ and $\alpha_2 = 2.6$ factors that emphasize color dominance obtained by the metaheuristic algorithm, the performance metrics *Accuracy, Precision, Recall, F1-Score* and *IoU* were used, achieving an average of 86% in fruit segmentation and 91% in leave segmentation.

Keywords: Segmentation · Greedy Algorithm · Precision Agriculture · Computer Vision · Color Dominance

1 Introduction

According to United Nations data [6], the global population is projected to reach approximately 10 billion people by the year 2050. This demographic forecast suggests significant challenges ahead for various food production activities, particularly agriculture [1, 26].

The use of modern technology in crop fields have generated what is called *Precision Agriculture* (*PA*), with the objective of increasing agricultural productivity [7, 23]. It encompasses a set of technologies that combine sensors, algorithms of *Artificial Intelligence* (*AI*) especially those of *Computer Vision* (*CV*) and optimization algorithms [1, 15, 25].

CV methods have been developed to support agricultural activity in tasks such as the estimation of fruit quality [2, 21], recognition of pests [19, 20], improvement of irrigation systems [28] and nutrient deficiency detection [13]. Xu [35] reported a method for extracting color and textures characteristics of the leaves of tomato plants, which is based on histograms and Fourier transforms. Wan [32] proposed a procedure to measure the maturity of fresh supermarket tomatoes through the development of a threshold segmentation algorithm based on the RGB color model. Tian [31] used an improved k-means algorithm based on the adaptive clustering number for the segmentation of tomato leaf images. Castillo [3] reported a color index-based thresholding method for background and foreground segmentation of plant images utilizing two color indexes about the green color of the plants. Lin [16] proposed a detection algorithm based on color, depth, and shape information for detecting cylindrical fruits. Lu [17] presented a method for segmentation of plants from background in color images, which consists of the unconstrained optimization of a linear combination of RGB color model component images to enhance the contrast between plant and background regions. Kirk [14] estimated the amount of foliage present in images of cereal crops at early stages of phenological development. Wang [33] proposed a method to segment rice plants from the background of the image based on subtracting the value of the green channel from the value of the red channel for the pixels of the image. Jeon [12] implemented computational methods to detect weeds in uncontrolled light conditions. Yadav [36] measured the amount of chlorophyll using CV algorithms. Philipp [24] performed a segmentation comparisons using different color models. In [18], Menesatti proposed the use of technique to predict the nutritional status of orange leaves utilizing visible-near infrared portable spectrophotometer. Fan [5] developed a method for segmenting apples combining local image features and color information through a pixel patch segmentation method based on a gray-centered RGB color model.

In certain stages of their processes, some methods incorporate segmentation techniques, with one of the most prevalent approaches being the utilization of thresholding values. These are usually determined by the researcher's experience without optimization procedures, which carries the risk of falling into local minima. The use of different algorithms for optimization problems has developed considerably in recent years. The main characteristic of this type of algorithms is their flexibility and robustness. This allows their use in a wide universe of problems that require some kind of optimization [15]. Different metaheuristic algorithms have been used in agriculture to optimize different processes such as irrigation schemes [8,9], fertilization [4,22,27], location of water reservoirs [11,34] and determination of crop health status [29]. The *Greedy Algorithm (GA)* is the one that taking the local optimal solution can generate a global optimal solution. Normally this algorithm is used in problems where the minimum or maximum of an objective function is to be found.

This paper presents the use of the GA algorithm to optimize the segmentation performed by a Color Dominance algorithm [10] to segment the pixels of the leaves and fruits of tomato plants.

2 Method

2.1 Color Dominance Algorithm Segmentation

This algorithm is carried out in two stages, The first one is based on the Eqs. 1 and 2 for the leaves and the fruits, respectively.

$$
h(x,y) = \begin{cases} f(x,y) \; if \; (f_G(x,y) \geq f_R(x,y)) \; and \; (f_G(x,y) \geq f_B(x,y)) \\ 0 \qquad in \qquad another \qquad case \end{cases}, \quad (1)
$$

$$
j(x,y) = \begin{cases} f(x,y) \; if \; (f_R(x,y) \geq f_G(x,y)) \; and \; (f_R(x,y) \geq f_B(x,y)) \\ 0 \qquad in \qquad another \qquad case \end{cases}. \quad (2)
$$

where $h(x,y)$ contains the pixels that are filtered from $f(x,y)$ with dominance of the green color channel over the other two and $j(x,y)$ contains the pixels with dominance of the red color channel for $\forall x = 0,1,2,...,M$ and $\forall y = 0,1,2,...,N$.

The second stage of the segmentation is based on the determination of four thresholds, based on the Eqs. 3, 4 for the leaves and 5, 6 for the fruits.

$$
U_G^R(x,y) = \frac{h_G(x,y)}{M_G} * \sigma_G^R * \alpha_1, \qquad (3)
$$

$$
U_G^B(x,y) = \frac{h_G(x,y)}{M_G} * \sigma_G^B * \alpha_1, \qquad (4)
$$

$$
U_R^G(x,y) = \frac{j_R(x,y)}{M_R} * \sigma_R^G * \alpha_2, \qquad (5)
$$

$$
U_R^B(x,y) = \frac{j_R(x,y)}{M_R} * \sigma_R^B * \alpha_2. \qquad (6)
$$

where $U_G^R(x,y)$ and $U_G^B(x,y)$ are the thresholds used to detect leaves, and $U_R^G(x,y)$ and $U_R^B(x,y)$ are utilized to find the fruit region. M_G and M_R are the highest values of the green and red color channels in $h(x,y)$ and $j(x,y)$, respectively. σ_G^R, σ_G^B, σ_R^G, and σ_R^B correspond to the standard deviations of the Δ_G^R, Δ_G^B, Δ_R^G, and Δ_R^B values, respectively. Finally, α is a factor utilized to control the thresholds.

The image $h_F(x,y)$ with the pixels that make up the leaves filtered from $h(x,y)$ and the image $j_F(x,y)$ with the pixels that make up the fruits filtered from $j(x,y)$ $\forall x = 0,1,2,...,M$ and $\forall y = 0,1,2,...,N$ is obtained with:

$$
h_F(x,y) = \begin{cases} h(x,y) \; if \; (\Delta_G^R(x,y) > U_G^R(x,y)) \; and \; (\Delta_G^B(x,y)) > U_G^B(x,y))) \\ 0 \qquad in \qquad another \qquad case \end{cases},
$$

$$
(7)
$$

$$j_F(x,y) = \begin{cases} j(x,y) \ if \ ((\Delta_R^G(x,y) > U_R^G(x,y)) \ and \ (\Delta_R^B(x,y) > U_R^B(x,y))) \\ 0 \quad in \quad another \quad case \end{cases} .$$

(8)

For more information on the Color Dominance segmentation method, see the following reference [10].

2.2 Metrics Performance

It is essential to measure the performance of the segmentation performed by algorithm. In this work, the following metrics were used: *Accuracy, Precision, Recall, F1-Score* [30] and *IoU* [37]. Four fundamental concepts must be defined: *True Positives (TP), True Negatives (TN), False Positives (FP)* and *False Negatives (FN)*, as defined by the confusion matrix illustrated in Fig. 1.

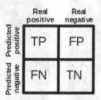

Fig. 1. Confusion matrix.

The metric *Accuracy* signifies the total number of correctly classified elements (pixels) relative to the total number of classifications made by the model, as defined by the equation:

$$Accuracy = \frac{TP+TN}{TP+TN+FP+FN}.$$

(9)

Precision, another metric, indicates the total number of true positives in relation to the number of predicted positives, defined by the equation:

$$Precision = \frac{TP}{TP+FP}.$$

(10)

The *Recall* metric reflects the number of true positives classified by the model relative to the total number of positive classifications, defined as:

$$Recall = \frac{TP}{TP+FN}.$$

(11)

F1-Score combines *Precision* and *Recall*, defined by:

$$F1 - Score = 2 * \frac{precision * recall}{precision + recall}.$$

(12)

Lastly, *IoU* measures the ratio of true positives to the total number of correctly classified items, defined by

$$IoU = \frac{TP}{TP+FP+FN}.$$

(13)

2.3   Dataset

The data set used for this work contains digital images of tomato plants grown under semi-hydroponic conditions in greenhouses, which is available for download at the following link https://www.kaggle.com/datasets/andrewmvd/tomato-detection. The data set has a total of 895 images, from the original set of images, 100 were randomly selected, an example of which is shown in Fig. 2a). The labeling of pixels of interest in a particular class is a further process used to evaluate the performance of the algorithms. The selected images were labeled using the *Computer Vision Annotation Tool (CVAT)*, which is available at the following web site https://www.cvat.ai/. The Fig. 2b) shows the mask of Fig. 2a).

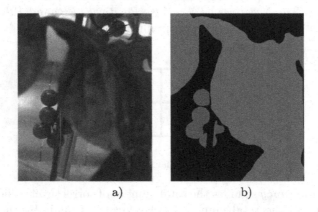

a)   b)

Fig. 2. Example of image and its mask truth ground.

2.4   Greedy Algorithm Proposed

The purpose of the *GA* is to optimize the alpha parameters used in the Eqs. 3, 4 for the leaves and 5, 6 for the fruits. The general algorithm scheme is described in following Algorithm.

$\alpha \leftarrow 2$
$AVG \leftarrow Calculation\_AVG\_metrics(\alpha)$
$AVG\_P \leftarrow 0$
while $AVG \geq AVG\_P$ **do**
    $\alpha_2 \leftarrow \alpha + 0.3$
    $AVG_P \leftarrow Calculation\_AVG\_metrics(\alpha_2)$
    if $AVG\_P >$AVG **then**
        $AVG \leftarrow$AVG_P
        $\alpha \leftarrow \alpha_2$
    end if
end while

3   Results

The greedy algorithm was run several times until the local convergence point was reached finding a lower average metric result than the current one. Figure 3 shows the results of the averages of greedy algorithm optimization.

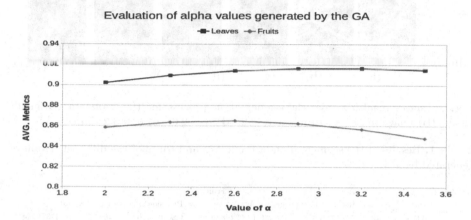

Fig. 3. Average efficiency for segmentation with the different values of α.

The values of $\alpha = 3.2$ and $\alpha = 2.6$ are those with which the highest average metric values were achieved in the segmentation of leaves and fruits, respectively. The Fig. 4 and 5 displays the result generated by different α values when segmenting the leaves and fruits of tomato plants, respectively (Table 1).

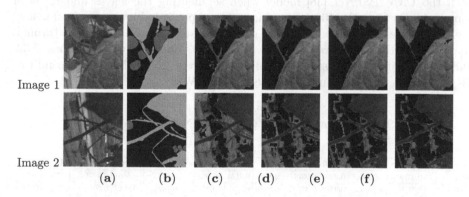

Fig. 4. Images resulting from the segmentation process for the leaves. (a) Original image, (b) Image mask, (c) Result of $\alpha = 2$, (d) $\alpha = 2.6$, (e) $\alpha = 3.2$, (f) $\alpha = 3.5$.

3.1   Comparison with CNN PSPNet Segmentation

In the current state of the art regarding segmentation algorithms, those based on deep learning exhibit a large number of implementations. The results obtained

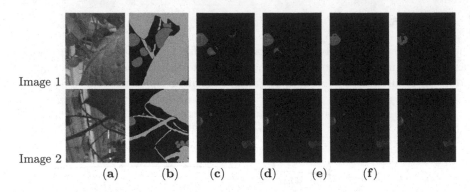

Image 1

Image 2

(a)   (b)   (c)   (d)   (e)   (f)

Fig. 5. Images resulting from the segmentation process for the fruits. (a) Original image, (b) Image mask, (c) Result of $\alpha = 2$, (d) $\alpha = 2.6$, (e) $\alpha = 3.2$, (f) $\alpha = 3.5$.

Table 1. Results of the segmentation of the leaves and fruits of the different α values generated by *GA*.

α value	Leaves						Fruits					
	Accuracy	Precision	Recall	F1-Score	IoU	Avg.	Accuracy	Precision	Recall	F1-Score	IoU	Avg.
2	0.9117	0.8743	0.9658	0.9098	0.8494	0.9022	0.9826	0.8040	0.9185	0.8397	0.7476	0.8585
2.3	0.9199	0.8904	0.9599	0.9166	0.8599	0.9093	0.9836	0.8276	0.9038	0.8469	0.7567	0.8637
2.6	0.9257	0.9030	0.9533	0.9210	0.8662	0.9138	0.9837	0.8473	0.8861	0.8491	0.7590	0.8650
2.9	0.9298	0.9133	0.9456	0.9231	0.8691	0.9162	0.9833	0.8647	0.8638	0.8466	0.7542	0.8625
3.2	0.9319	0.9216	0.9364	0.9231	0.8687	0.9164	0.9826	0.8800	0.8378	0.8396	0.7437	0.8567
3.5	0.9323	0.928	0.9256	0.9214	0.8655	0.9147	0.9815	0.8946	0.8078	0.8278	0.7278	0.8479

with the *CNN PSPNet* [38] model when segmenting the leaves and fruits of tomato plants from the 100 selected images are presented and compared below.

Table 2 presents the outcomes of optimized segmentation achieved through the *GA* algorithm. The first row showcases results obtained with α values of 3.2 and 2.6 for leaf and fruit segmentation, respectively. Meanwhile, the second row displays segmentation results produced by *PSPNet*.

Table 2. Comparison of GA and CNN PSPNet results.

alpha value	Leaves						Fruits					
	Accuracy	Precision	Recall	F1-Score	IoU	Avg.	Accuracy	Precision	Recall	F1-Score	IoU	Avg.
GA	0.9319	0.9216	0.9364	0.9231	0.8687	0.9164	0.9837	0.8473	0.8861	0.8491	0.7590	0.8650
PSPNet	0.9146	0.8509	0.9319	0.8759	0.8019	0.87504	0.9595	0.7921	0.8284	0.8013	0.6856	0.81338

4   Conclusions and Upcoming Work

While greedy algorithms may not be the most efficient in terms of execution time, optimization based on color dominance can significantly improve the computational efficiency of these algorithms for tomato plant leaf and fruit segmentation.

The combination of these has been shown to provide higher accuracy in the segmentation of leaves and fruits of tomato plants compared to conventional and other deep learning methods. Another aspect to mention is that the methodology used can be easily adapted to segment the foliage and fruits of other types of crops, which makes it versatile and applicable in a variety of agricultural scenarios by using the greedy algorithms to adapt the α values to optimize the results.

The way in which the value of the α factor was modified leaves an infinite number of possible intermediate values that could optimize the overall outcome of the segmentation process. Therefore, the exploration of different metaheuristic algorithms such as genetic algorithms, ant colony and simulated annealing to name a few is essential to try some other optimization alternatives.

Acknowledgments. It is important to thank the Institutions that made the development of this work possible by allocating resources of different kinds to carry it out, such as: Consejo Nacional de Humanidades, Ciencia y Tecnologías, Centro de Investigaciones en Óptica A.C. and Instituto Tecnológico de Estudios Superiores de Zamora.

References

1. Awasthi, Y.: Press "a" for artificial intelligence in agriculture: a review. Int. J. Inform. Vis. **4**(3), 112–116 (2020). https://doi.org/10.30630/joiv.4.3.387
2. Bhargava, A., Bansal, A.: Fruits and vegetables quality evaluation using computer vision: a review. J. King Saud Univ. Comput. Inf. Sci0 **33**(3), 243–257 (2021). https://doi.org/10.1016/j.jksuci.2018.06.002
3. Castillo-Martínez, M., Gallegos-Funes, F.J., Carvajal-Gámez, B.E., Urriolagoitia-Sosa, G., Rosales-Silva, A.J.: Color index based thresholding method for background and foreground segmentation of plant images. Comput. Electron. Agric. **178**(July), 105783 (2020). https://doi.org/10.1016/j.compag.2020.105783
4. Cropper, W.P., Comerford, N.B.: Optimizing simulated fertilizer additions using a genetic algorithm with a nutrient uptake model. Ecol. Model. **185**, 271–281 (2005). https://doi.org/10.1016/j.ecolmodel.2004.12.010
5. Fan, P., et al.: A method of segmenting apples based on gray-centered RGB color space. Remote Sens. **13**(6), 1–17 (3 2021). https://doi.org/10.3390/rs13061211, https://www.mdpi.com/2072-4292/13/6/1211
6. FAO: Our approach | Food Systems | Food and Agriculture Organization of the United Nations (2023). http://www.fao.org/food-systems/our-approach/en/
7. Gebbers, R., Adamchuk, V.I.: Precision agriculture and food security. Science **327**(5967), 828–831 (2010). https://doi.org/10.1126/science.1183899
8. Gharsallah, O., Nouiri, I., Lebdi, F., Lamaddalena, N.: Use of the genetic algorithm for the optimal operation of multi-reservoirs on demand irrigation. System **2**, 217–227 (1995)
9. González Perea, R., Camacho Poyato, E., Montesinos, P., Rodríguez Díaz, J.A.: Optimization of irrigation scheduling using soil water balance and genetic algorithms. Water Resour. Manage **30**(8), 2815–2830 (2016). https://doi.org/10.1007/s11269-016-1325-7
10. Guerra Ibarra, J.P., Cuevas, F.J.: Segmentation of leaves and fruits of tomato plants by color dominance. AgriEngineering, 1846–1864 (2023). https://doi.org/10.3390/agriengineering5040113

11. Ines, A.V.M., Honda, K., Das Gupta, A., Droogers, P., Clemente, R.S.: Combining remote sensing-simulation modeling and genetic algorithm optimization to explore water management options in irrigated agriculture. Agric. Water Manag. **83**(3), 221–232 (2006). https://doi.org/10.1016/j.agwat.2005.12.006

12. Jeon, H.Y., Tian, L.F., Zhu, H.: Robust crop and weed segmentation under uncontrolled outdoor illumination. Sensors **11**(6), 6270–6283 (2011). https://doi.org/10.3390/s110606270

13. Kaur, G., Engineering, C.: Automated nutrient deficiency detection in plantsâĂŕ: a. Palarch's J. Archaeol. Egypt **17**(6), 5894–5901 (2020)

14. Kirk, K., Andersen, H.J., Thomsen, A.G., Jørgensen, J.R., Jørgensen, R.N.: Estimation of leaf area index in cereal crops using red-green images. Biosys. Eng. **104**(3), 308–317 (2009). https://doi.org/10.1016/j.biosystemseng.2009.07.001

15. Kumar, M., Husain, M., Upreti, N., Gupta, D.: Genetic algorithm: review and application. SSRN Electron. J. **2**(2), 451–454 (2020). https://doi.org/10.2139/ssrn.3529843

16. Lin, G., Tang, Y., Zou, X., Xiong, J., Fang, Y.: Color-, depth-, and shape-based 3D fruit detection. Precision Agriculture **21**(1), 1–17 (2020). https://doi.org/10.1007/s11119-019-09654-w

17. Lu, Y., Young, S., Wang, H., Wijewardane, N.: Robust plant segmentation of color images based on image contrast optimization. Comput. Electron. Agric. **193**(January), 106711 (2022). https://doi.org/10.1016/j.compag.2022.106711

18. Menesatti, P., et al.: Estimation of plant nutritional status by Vis-NIR spectrophotometric analysis on orange leaves [Citrus sinensis (L) Osbeck cv Tarocco]. Biosyst. Eng. **105**(4), 448–454 (2010). https://doi.org/10.1016/j.biosystemseng.2010.01.003

19. Mukti, I.Z., Biswas, D.: Transfer learning based plant diseases detection using ResNet50. In: 2019 4th International Conference on Electrical Information and Communication Technology, EICT 2019, pp. 1–6. Institute of Electrical and Electronics Engineers Inc. (2019). https://doi.org/10.1109/EICT48899.2019.9068805

20. Nanehkaran, Y.A., Zhang, D., Chen, J., Tian, Y., Al-Nabhan, N.: Recognition of plant leaf diseases based on computer vision. J. Ambient Intell. Humanized Comput. **1**(0123456789), 1–18 (2020). https://doi.org/10.1007/s12652-020-02505-x, https://link.springer.com/10.1007/s12652-020-02505-x

21. Nyalala, I., et al.: Tomato volume and mass estimation using computer vision and machine learning algorithms: cherry tomato model. J. Food Eng. **263**(July), 288–298 (2019). https://doi.org/10.1016/j.jfoodeng.2019.07.012

22. Olakulehin, O.J., Omidiora, E.O.: A genetic algorithm approach to maximize crop yields and sustain soil fertility. Net J. Agric. Sci. **2**(3), 94–103 (2014)

23. Patrício, D.I., Rieder, R.: Computer vision and artificial intelligence in precision agriculture for grain crops: a systematic review. Comput. Electron. Agric. **153**, 69–81 (2018). https://doi.org/10.1016/j.compag.2018.08.001, https://linkinghub.elsevier.com/retrieve/pii/S0168169918305829

24. Philipp, I., Rath, T.: Improving plant discrimination in image processing by use of different colour space transformations. Comput. Electron. Agric. **35**(1), 1–15 (2002). https://doi.org/10.1016/S0168-1699(02)00050-9

25. Pierce, F.J., Nowak, P.: Aspects of precision agriculture. Adv. Agron. **67**, 1–68 (1999)

26. Ray, P.P.: Internet of things for smart agriculture: technologies, practices and future direction. J. Ambient Intell. Smart Environ. **9**(4), 395–420 (2017). https://doi.org/10.3233/AIS-170440

27. Sharma, D.K., Jana, R.K.: Fuzzy goal programming based genetic algorithm approach to nutrient management for rice crop planning. Int. J. Prod. Econ. **121**, 224–232 (2009). https://doi.org/10.1016/j.ijpe.2009.05.009, www.elsevier.com/locate/ijpe

28. Smith, R., Baillie, J., McCarthy, A., Raine, S., Baillie, C.: Review of precision irrigation technologies and their application. National Centre for Engineering in Agriculture Publication 1003017/1, USQ, Toowoomba. **1**(November) (2010)

29. Sulistyo, S.B., Woo, W.L., Dlay, S.S.: Regularized neural networks fusion and genetic algorithm based on-field nitrogen status estimation of wheat plants. IEEE Trans. Ind. Inf. **13**(1), 103–114 (2017). https://doi.org/10.1109/TII.2016.2628439

30. Taheri, M., Lim, N., Lederer, J.: Balancing Statistical and Computational Precision and Applications to Penalized Linear Regression with Group Sparsity. Dept. Comput. Sci. Dept. Biostatistics Med. Inf. 233–240 (2016). http://arxiv.org/abs/1609.071

31. Tian, K., Li, J., Zeng, J., Evans, A., Zhang, L.: Segmentation of tomato leaf images based on adaptive clustering number of K-means algorithm. Comput. Electron. Agric. **165**(August), 104962 (2019). https://doi.org/10.1016/j.compag.2019.104962

32. Wan, P., Toudeshki, A., Tan, H., Ehsani, R.: A methodology for fresh tomato maturity detection using computer vision. Comput. Electron. Agric. **146**(January), 43–50 (2018). https://doi.org/10.1016/j.compag.2018.01.011

33. Wang, Y., Wang, D., Zhang, G., Wang, J.: Estimating nitrogen status of rice using the image segmentation of G-R thresholding method. Field Crops Res. **149**, 33–39 (2013). https://doi.org/10.1016/j.fcr.2013.04.007

34. Wardlaw, R., Bhaktikul, K.: Application of a genetic algorithm for water allocation in an irrigation system. Irrig. Drain. **50**(2), 159–170 (2001). https://doi.org/10.1002/ird.9

35. Xu, G., et al.: Use of leaf color images to identify nitrogen and potassium deficient tomatoes. Pattern Recogn. Lett. **32**(11), 1584–1590 (2011). https://doi.org/10.1016/j.patrec.2011.04.020

36. Yadav, S.P., Ibaraki, Y., Gupta, S.D.: Estimation of the chlorophyll content of micropropagated potato plants using RGB based image analysis. Plant Cell, Tissue Organ Cult. **100**(2), 183–188 (2010). https://doi.org/10.1007/s11240-009-9635-6

37. Yu, J., et al.: Learning generalized intersection over union for dense pixelwise prediction. In: Meila, M., Zhang, T. (eds.) Proceedings of the 38th International Conference on Machine Learning. Proceedings of Machine Learning Research, vol. 139, pp. 12198–12207. PMLR (2021). https://proceedings.mlr.press/v139/yu21e.html

38. Zhao, H., Shi, J., Qi, X., Wang, X., Jia, J.: Pyramid scene parsing network. In: Proceedings - 30th IEEE Conference on Computer Vision and Pattern Recognition, CVPR 2017 **2017-Janua**, pp. 6230–6239 (2017). https://doi.org/10.1109/CVPR.2017.660

A Robust Content Identification System for Picture-In-Picture Attack Detection Using Trainable Background Removal and Perceptual Hashing Functions

Kevin Saúl Gómez-Molina[1]([✉]), Jesús Fonseca-Bustos[2],
and Claudia Feregrino-Uribe[2]

[1] Escuela Nacional de Estudios Superiores, Morelia, Michoacan, Mexico
gomosak@outlook.es
[2] Instituto Nacional de Astrofísica, Óptica y Electrónica, Puebla, Puebla, Mexico

Abstract. This paper addresses copyright infringement in multimedia distribution with a model for identifying modified images, especially targeting PiP (Picture in Picture) attacks, which involve embedding and altering images in various ways. The model uses a three-step approach: first, detecting images of interest with a fine-tuned YOLOv5 model; second, employing the U2Net model from the rembg tool for background removal; and finally, applying perceptual hashing for compact hash code extraction. This methodology not only enhances security against unauthorized distribution but also aids in intellectual property protection. The model demonstrates high accuracy and reliability, with impressive F1 scores, making it an effective solution for copyright enforcement and digital media protection against complex manipulations.

Keywords: Picture-in-Picture · Image detection · Perceptual hashing function

1 Introduction

Content identification systems detect unathorized usage of multimedia content, which is crucial for copyright protection. However, the identification of images subjected to Picture in Picture (PiP) attacks is a prevalent issue in contemporary scenarios [7]. PiP refers to a technique where one image or video is embedded within another, often manipulated image into a primary one for deceptive purposes. These manipulations can include resizing, rotating, or brightness adjustment to blend the secondary image seamlessly into the primary image. Detecting PiP attacks is challenging, as the embedded images are designed to be difficult to identify without sophisticated image analysis techniques, thus simpler methods are needed.

At present, there is a noticeable scarcity of effective algorithms specifically designed to counteract PiP attacks. In response to this challenge, we have

E. Mezura-Montes et al. (Eds.): MCPR 2024, LNCS 14755, pp. 210–219, 2024.
https://doi.org/10.1007/978-3-031-62836-8_20

endeavored to designed and implemented a robust solution comprising three stages, each strategically deployed in different phases. In the initial phase, we employ YOLOv5 (You Only Look Once), a widely-used object detection algorithm, to pinpoint and extract the region of interest within the host image. This region of interest encapsulates the pertinent elements that are potentially impacted by the PiP attack. YOLOv5's efficiency in accurately identifying objects allows us to precisely delineate the areas that require further analysis.

Moving on to the second phase, our approach involves refining the identification process by isolating the identified region of interest in the attacked image. This isolation is achieved by meticulously eliminating the background, a technique known to enhace data quality and improve model performance, particularly in the context of fashion data, as referenced in [5]. By focusing solely on the core elements of the image that are susceptible to manipulation during a PiP attack, the objective is not only to enhance the accuracy of the identification but also to streamline the subsequent analysis.

In the third step we conduct the comparison and identification process, using perceptual hashing algorithms. These algorithms generate unique identifiers or "hashes" for the isolated regions of interest. By comparing these hashes, we can rapidly assess the similarity between different images, enabling a more efficient and expedited identification of potential PiP attacks. Perceptual hash functions aim to create very similar hashes for very similar input files. The similarity between any two hashes is defined through a distance metric, and different perceptual hash functions may require the use of different distance metrics [4].

The paper is organized as follows: in Sect. 2, we present related work and relevant perceptual hashing algorithms, and in Sect. 3 we present or proposal. Section 4 presents our experiments and results, and finally Sect. 5 discusses our conclusions.

2   Related Work

In the realm of digital image analysis, particularly in the detection of sophisticated manipulations like PiP attacks, perceptual hashing function play a pivotal role. Perceptual hashing, a key technique in this domain, is subject to the inherent challenge of balancing false positives and negatives, where dissimilar input files may produce identical or similar hashes and vice versa. This complexity underscores the need for a nuanced approach in selecting hash functions, each tailored to specific attributes of an image. Perceptual hashing, also known as fuzzy hashing, robust hashing, or locality-sensitive hashing, carries the risk of false positives and negatives. This means dissimilar files might generate similar or identical hash values, and vice versa. While these terms are conceptually similar and often used interchangeably, they technically differ from one another in process and application [4].

Perceptual hashing has many applications, and different works have been proposed in the literature. In particular, four algorithm are a common choice for its efficiency identifying structural similarities or differences:

- **aHash (Average Hash)** [1]: aHash is known for its simplicity and speed, making it highly effective in capturing the basic structure of an image. It is ideal for processing images quickly while still maintaining a focus on structural elements. This hash function plays a crucial role in rapidly analyzing large volumes of images, efficiently identifying structural similarities or differences. The hashing process starts by significantly reducing the image size to a uniform 8×8 pixel square, ensuring the hash remains consistent across variations in size and aspect ratio. The image is then converted to grayscale, simplifying the color scheme from three channels to one. An average color value is computed from these grayscale tones. The hash is created by comparing each pixel's tone to the average, setting each of the 64 bits in the hash based on this comparison. Finally, these bits are assembled into a 64-bit integer, forming a compact and consistent representation of the image for comparison purposes.

- **pHash (Perceptual Hash)** [1]: pHash is employed for its ability to capture perceptual aspects of images, making it sensitive to content changes. This quality allows it to discern subtle differences in image content that other hashes might overlook. pHash's strength lies in its sensitivity to the perceptual elements of the images, which is essential in detecting nuanced content alterations. The pHash process begins by resizing the image to a larger scale than Average Hash, typically 32×32 pixels, mainly to facilitate the Discrete Cosine Transform (DCT) computation. The image is converted to grayscale to simplify calculations. A 32×32 DCT is computed, isolating frequencies and scalars, but only the top-left 8×8 section is retained, representing the lowest frequencies, is retained. The average of these low-frequency DCT values is calculated, excluding the first term to avoid skewing from solid colors. The hash is formed by comparing each DCT value against this average, setting 64 bits to represent whether they are above or below this mean. This method captures the rough relative scale of the frequencies compared to the average, resilient to certain image adjustments. The 64 bits are then set into a 64-bit integer for the final hash value.

- **wHash (Wavelet Hash)** [8]: wHash, based on wavelet transforms, is used for its robustness against scaling and rotation. This is particularly crucial for PiP attack analysis where images might be altered in these ways. wHash's capability to remain effective despite such transformations makes it a valuable tool in maintaining the integrity of image analysis in varied scenarios. Discrete Wavelet Transformation (DWT) is another form of frequency representation. The popular DCT and Fourier transformations use a set of *sin cos* functions as a basis: sin(x), sin(2x), sin(3x), etc. In contrast, DWT uses one single function as a basis but in different forms: scaled and shifted. The basis function can be changed and this is why we can have Haar wavelet, Daubechie-4 wavelet etc. This scaling effect gives us a great "time-frequency representation" when the low frequency part looks similar to the original signal.

- **Colorhash** [6]: Colorhash is specifically chosen for its ability to capture the color distribution within an image. This feature is key in detecting color manipulations in PiP attacks, identifying changes in color schemes that may indicate a potential security threat. Colorhash's focus on color attributes adds an additional layer of analysis, crucial for a comprehensive examination of image alterations.

In the article "Content-based Image Retrieval using Perceptual Image Hashing and Hopfield Neural Network" [9] focuses on using perceptual hashing for image retrieval, integrating it with Hopfield Neural Networks for enhanced performance. This method emphasizes the retrieval of similar images from large databases using hash values that capture perceptual features of images. By applying these hash functions to the isolated regions of interest, our system can thoroughly analyze and compare various aspects of the images, thereby enhancing the overall accuracy and effectiveness of the PiP attack detection process. It's worth noting that there are currently no papers proposing similar algorithms, making this approach novel in the field.

3 Methodology

The proposed system is designed to effectively detect and analyze PiP attacks in digital images. The primary objective is to identify areas of interest within an image, where a secondary image has been embedded into a primary one. The proposed system processes various types of digital images, with a particular focus on digital images that are susceptible to PiP manipulations and have copyright concerns.

3.1 System Description

The proposed system integrates advanced object detection algorithms, sophisticated hash functions, and image processing techniques. It starts by using the YOLOv5 algorithm for precise object detection, isolating regions of interest. Subsequently, it applies a series of hash functions to these regions, comparing them to known image hashes for detection and analysis of PiP alterations. Our system operates through three distinct stages, as illustrated in Fig. 1. It begins with the ROI Detection Stage, where it identifies media content, using YOLOv5 within the scene that might be relevant for PiP attacks, focusing on potential manipulated regions. Following this, the system isolates these identified areas in the Background Removal and Image Processing, allowing for a more targeted and efficient analysis. The process culminates in the Image Comparison and Analysis Stage, where these isolated regions are compared against the original images. This comparison, using perceptual hash function, is crucial for identifying any discrepancies that indicate PiP attacks, ensuring precise and effective identification.

Detection Techniques. In our approach, detection is conducted using YOLOv5. We trained our model with a dataset that was split into validation and training sets. This training enables the model to accurately identify regions

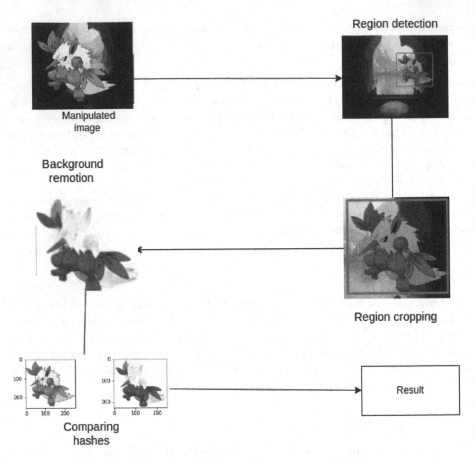

Fig. 1. Proposed Algorithm to Detect PiP Attacks

of interest within images. The output from the detection process includes the image marked with a bounding box, indicating the area where the interest image is likely located. Alongside the visual output, a text file is generated, containing the coordinates of this bounding box. This combination of visual and textual data is crucial for subsequent analysis stages.

Background Removal and Image Processing. In the proposed system, after the YOLOv5 algorithm identifies potential regions of interest in an image, these areas undergo a process of background removal and image processing. This step is crucial for isolating the suspected PiP regions from the rest of the image. Techniques employed include advanced image segmentation methods to separate foreground elements (the regions of interest) from the background using the rembg library [5], which utilizes the pretrained U2net model, to eliminate the background of images. This model can be retrained with custom data for enhanced performance. This isolation ensures that subsequent analysis and comparison focus exclusively on relevant regions, enhancing the accuracy of the detection process.

Image Comparison and Analysis. In this stage, the hash values of the protected images are systematically compared with those of the suspected PiP-attacked images. To determine the most effective hash function for our purposes, we conduct a comparison involving the analysis of hash values generated by aHash, pHash, wHash, and colorhash. This analysis seeks to identify any similarities or discrepancies among these hash values. For this comparison, we use the F_1 *score*. The closeness of these hash values, as measured by the Hamming distance, indicates the degree of similarity between the compared images [10]. The Hamming distance measures the distance for binary strings, like hash values, it's simply the number of bit positions in which the two bits are different. It's a simple yet effective way to quantify the similarity or difference between two sequences. For instance, in image hashing, a smaller Hamming distance between hash values suggests a higher likelihood that the region in the attacked image corresponds to one of the processed images. Conversely, larger Hamming distances imply less similarity, suggesting the image might not be subjected to a PiP attack. This systematic and multi-faceted comparison using Hamming distance is crucial for accurate PiP attack detection.

4   Experiments and Results

4.1   Data Building

The images used were obtained from Kaggle [3] and various websites. We collected 810 images of Pokemon and 140 background images. The goal is to create a dataset by combining these images, aiming to simulate a copyright enforcement context where a content creator needs protection.

To ensure the algorithm's correctness, we implemented a validation process by splitting the images before constructing the dataset. We randomly selected 25% images of interest and an equal percentage of host images, separating validation and training images.

The dataset construction involved embedding each image of interest into a ten randomly chosen background images, with a precaution to avoid using the same image more than once for each Pokémon. Subsequently, we determined random coordinates within the host image. The image of interest was then resized to no more than 80% of the host image's size, rotated within a range of $(-6, +6)$ degrees, and had its brightness adjusted within a range of 0.5 to 1.5, the intensity was chosen based on human identification of the image. This was done in an effort to imitate real PiP attacks before incorporating the altered image into the host. The resulting images were saved, accompanied by a text file in YOLOv5 format containing the coordinates of the interest image. Furthermore, the images were uniquely named in anticipation of their future use.

The same technique was applied to unknown files, contributing to the creation of a second dataset named the "unknown dataset." This dataset is designated for use in the testing stage, not only for detection testing but also in the overall model evaluation.

4.2   Image Detection Model Training

Before training, we divided all the images intended for the training dataset into training and validation sets, following a 66–33 proportion. This division process was carried out utilizing the *scikit-learn* library [2]. Training detection models requires careful consideration. In initiating training, we meticulously organized the data and experimented with key parameters to optimize our model. We explored different image sizes, ranging from 256×256 to 640×640 pixels, to balance processing speed and detail capture. The number of epochs was varied, starting from 10 and extending up to 100, to gauge the impact on model performance and overfitting. Batch sizes were also tested, beginning with smaller batches of 8 and 32, allowing us to assess the learning process and memory requirements. These experiments were crucial in fine-tuning the training process for optimal accuracy and efficiency. We conducted experiments and adjusted the training parameters until we achieved a satisfactory mean Average Precision (mAP50) of 0.995. This was attained using a batch size of 32, an image size of 640×640, and 10 epochs of training.

Detection is performed on the "unknown dataset" by running the YOLOv5 model over it. We extract images where all Pokémon are detected, complete with a drawn bounding box and a text file containing the coordinates of the box. YOLOv5's detection is necessary to focus all efforts of identification on the area of interest, eliminating parts of the attacked image that do not contain the information we are seeking. While this process may yield some false positives, we choose not to eliminate them, as we rely on the hash function to fulfill its role in accuracy. The subsequent steps involve preparing these images for comparison with the originals.

4.3   Cutting Data

To effectively isolate specific sections of an image where the object of interest is located, we rely on the capabilities of YOLOv5 (You Only Look Once). Upon completion of this analysis, YOLOv5 can generate a text file that details the coordinates of these detected objects. This file is invaluable as it provides precise location data for each object within the image.

With these coordinates in hand, we turn to the Python Imaging Library (PIL), a versatile library in Python used for opening, manipulating, and saving many different image file formats. Utilizing PIL, we can accurately target and extract the specific sections of the image that correspond to the coordinates provided by YOLOv5. This process involves carefully cropping these areas from the larger image.

This methodical approach ensures that we focus solely on the relevant parts of the image, significantly enhancing the efficiency of our analysis. This targeted extraction is particularly crucial in applications where precision and accuracy in image analysis are paramount.

4.4   Background Removal

We explored various techniques such as segmentation, but ultimately, we discovered a simple approach using the "rembg" [5] library, which employs a Convolutional Neural Network (CNN) to eliminate the background.

Through experimentation with different models, we considered the possibility of training our own model in the future using the images in this dataset. Currently, we utilize the U2net model, and although the best results are not guaranteed after background removal, we achieved satisfactory outcomes.

4.5   Comparing Hashes

To validate the performance of different perceptual hashing functions, we compare the performance of aHash, pHash, wHash and colorhash for this task. These were applied to images identified by YOLOv5, which were then cropped and had their background removed. For each image of interest, we computed its hash value. These hash values were then compared to the hash of the interest image. The image with the closest hamming distance to the attacked image was identified as the most similar. However, if the distance between the hash of the attacked image and all the hashes of the interest images exceeded a predefined threshold specific to each hash function, the algorithm classified the attacked image as unrecognized. This approach ensures a balance between accuracy and computational efficiency in detecting PiP attacks.

4.6   Results

The YOLOv5 object detection algorithm exhibited superior performance with an F1 score of 0.9819, highlighting its robustness in accurately identifying relevant image regions. Among the hash functions, dHash emerged as the most effective with an F1 score of 0.724, recall of 0.7588 and presicion of 0.6925, demonstrating its proficiency in capturing perceptual similarities in images. aHash showed commendable performance, achieving F1 scores of 0.4666 recall of 0.4630 and presicion of 0.4702, pHash also showed F1 score of 0.5858 recall of 0.5945 and presicion of 0.5775. However, wHash and colorhash recorded lower F1 scores of 0.3858 recall of 0.3678 and presicion of 0.4056 and F1 0.1497 recall of 0.1233 and presicion of 0.1906, suggesting a reduced effectiveness in this specific application. These results are crucial for understanding the strengths and limitations of each algorithm in PiP attack detection, each with a specific identification threshold: aHash has a threshold of 47.02, pHash at 57.75, wHash at 40.56, and colorhash at 19.06. These thresholds provide a benchmark for evaluating the performance and accuracy of each algorithm in detecting PiP attacks.

5   Conclusion

This study introduced a robust content identification model. Through the implementation of advanced techniques such as YOLOv5 for object detection and the evaluation of various hash functions (aHash, pHash, wHash, and colorhash), the system demonstrated significant proficiency in the identification manipulated images. The results indicated that YOLOv5 was highly effective in accurately detecting regions of interest, achieving an impressive F1 score of 0.9819. Among the hash functions, pHash showed the highest effectiveness in perceptual similarity detection whit $F1 - score$ of 0.745. The lower performance of wHash and colorhash suggests room for further optimization in these areas. This research contributes to the evolving field of digital image manipulation detection, providing a foundation for future enhancements and adaptations in combating PiP attacks. The system's adaptability and efficiency mark a significant step forward in protecting digital content integrity.

One of the primary limitations we encountered during our research was the absence of previous studies with comparable methodologies that could serve as benchmarks for evaluating our results. The specificity and novelty of the method used complicated direct comparisons with other studies, as no previous research addressing the same problem with a similar approach was identified. This suggests that our approach may offer a unique and valuable perspective, although it also implies the need to develop our own criteria for validating and evaluating the obtained results. In addition, it is important to note that in the future we are considering the possibility of evaluating this work with other types of multimedia content, which could further enrich the experience and understanding of the subject.

References

1. Looks like it. https://www.hackerfactor.com/blog/index.php?/archives/432-Looks-Like-It.html. Accessed 25 Jan 2024
2. Scikit-learn. https://scikit-learn.org/stable/. Accessed 26 Jan 2024
3. Pokemon Images Dataset (2020). https://www.kaggle.com/datasets/kvpratama/pokemon-images-dataset
4. Overview of perceptual hashing technology (2022). https://www.ofcom.org.uk/__data/assets/pdf_file/0036/247977/Perceptual-hashing-technology.pdf. Accessed 25 Jan 2024
5. Liang, J., Liu, Y., Vlassov, V.: The impact of background removal on performance of neural networks for fashion image classification and segmentations (2023)
6. Ali, N.H.M., Mahdi, M.E.: Detecting similarity in color images based on perceptual image hash algorithm. IOP Conf. Ser. Mater. Sci. Eng. **737**(1), 012244 (2020). https://doi.org/10.1088/1757-899x/737/1/012244
7. Chen, H., Jiang, Z., Yuan, J.: Picture in picture detection for mobile captured digital video. In: 2022 2nd International Conference on Computation, Communication and Engineering (ICCCE), pp. 70–73 (2022). https://doi.org/10.1109/ICCCE55785.2022.10036215

8. Petrov, D.: Wavelet image hash in python (2016). https://fullstackml.com/wavelet-image-hash-in-python-3504fdd282b5. Accessed 25 Jan 2024
9. Sabahi, F., Ahmad, M.O., Swamy, M.N.S.: Content-based image retrieval using perceptual image hashing and hopfield neural network. In: 2018 IEEE 61st International Midwest Symposium on Circuits and Systems (MWSCAS), pp. 352–355 (2018). https://doi.org/10.1109/MWSCAS.2018.8623902
10. Xia, M., Li, S., Chen, W., Yang, G.: Chapter five - perceptual image hashing using rotation invariant uniform local binary patterns and color feature. Adv. Comput. **130**, 163–205 (2023). https://doi.org/10.1016/bs.adcom.2022.12.001, https://www.sciencedirect.com/science/article/pii/S0065245822000857

Medical Applications of Pattern Recognition

Detection of Depression Symptoms Through Unsupervised Learning

Octavio Mendoza Gómez⬤, Mireya Tovar Vidal(✉)⬤,
and Meliza Contreras González⬤

Faculty of Computer Science, Benemerita Universidad Autonoma de Puebla,
72570 Puebla, Mexico
octavio.mendozag@alumno.buap.mx,
{mireya.tovar,meliza.contreras}@correo.buap.mx

Abstract. An increase in the decline of mental health in student populations has been observed since 2019. The objective of this study is to characterize the depression levels in university students from the Computer Science area of BUAP. The CES-D Scale was used and unsupervised algorithms K-Means, AGNES and DKM were applied for the grouping and characterization of the depression levels. The results show the symptoms that lead to a specific depression case.

Keywords: Mental health · Unsupervised learning · Deep learning

1 Introduction

Mental health is an issue of increasing importance in the current society. According to the World Health Organization (WHO), mental health is a state of well-being that enables people to deal with the stress of life, develop all their abilities, be able to learn and work adequately and contribute to the enhancement of their community. However, nearly a billion people, including 14% of adolescents around the world, were affected by a mental disorder in 2019 [12,13].

People with serious mental disorders die on average 10 to 20 years before the general population, mostly from preventable physical diseases. Moreover, the stigmatization, discrimination and violation of human rights of people with mental disorders are very common in society and in the care systems throughout the world [12].

Focusing on young adults, the mental health of college students has become an issue of increasing importance. In the last years, low levels of emotional well-being have been identified in some segments of the population, especially worsened by the effects of the COVID-19 pandemic [12,13].

Several factors that impact depression have been identified. These include excessive work and poor academic performance, sociodemographic factors such as age, sex, origin, year of study, type of work activity, family group, as well as sleep quality, poor physical shape, and poor nutrition. Also, it has been observed that the highest number of depressive disorders is present in women between 18 and 25 years [12,13].

In March 2022, the Ministry of Universities and the Ministry of Health of Spain set up a working group to perform a detailed diagnosis on the mental health status of university students, in which they observed that more than 50% have perceived the need for psychological support for recent mental health issues during the last quarter of academical year [12].

The study includes proposals to enhance the emotional well-being of students in universities, such as encouraging meeting spaces between students and professors or improving the communication of specific services to support mental health [13].

Despite the rising prevalence of mental disorders, only a small percentage of the people who needed it had access to effective, affordable and quality mental health care. Therefore, it is vital that educational institutions and decision-makers implement effective strategies to address the mental health of university students [15].

With the development of technology, machine learning has begun to be applied in the study of mental health in university students. Machine learning is a branch of artificial intelligence that allows computers to learn without being explicitly programmed certain rules [18,19].

In machine learning algorithms, data is used to learn and improve with experience. Machine learning is split into two main categories: supervised learning and unsupervised learning, the last will be used in this investigation [10].

In the health sector, machine learning is used for a variety of applications, such as disease diagnosis, health outcomes estimation and treatments adaptation. It has applications from discovering patterns in patient data and predicting those who have a larger risk of developing a specific disease [18].

In this research, it's proposed the recognition of patterns that belong to different type of depression cases most common over a College student population. To achieve such task, there will be an implementation of clustering algorithms with similar behavior but different approach of creating clusters.

The article has the following structure: in Sect. 2, the works whose research is related to this work will be presented. Section 3 where the methodology of the solution as well as the necessary theory to understand it will be presented. In Sect. 4, the results obtained from the proposed solution will be shown and finally the conclusions will be shown. It will end with Sect. 5 of the final conclusions and the future work will be discussed.

2   Related Work

The research conducted has as background works where the application of machine learning algorithms to the study of mental health is exposed. In this section we will present works that apply different machine learning algorithms to the study of mental health, as well as the different methodologies they use and their application of clustering algorithms.

In [2] three subgroups of college students who use a mental health application during the COVID-19 pandemic are identified. The findings suggest that these subgroups are unique and have different mental health care objectives. The study emphasizes the need to customize mental health applications to improve user engagement.

In the work [1] wearable sensors and machine learning are used to detect mental disorders in children. Data from 84 participants were analyzed during mood induction tasks. Latent clusters were found in the data, which were more related to gender than to age. The case studies indicated that high impairment and diagnostic subtypes could explain the most behaviorally distinctive children. More research is required to improve the features and modeling approaches.

The work presented in [3] proposes a method to visualize the laminar structure of the human cortex using magnetic resonance imaging (MRI) and machine learning. This method, which combines several techniques, allows exploring the variations in the cortical layers. The results show that the cortical layers produce distinct signatures in the MRI and that the method can distinguish them automatically. A good agreement with the histological segmentation was observed and the importance of T2 in the cortical differentiation was highlighted. The study suggests that the method could be used in vivo studies.

The research [4] presents a method to classify mental stress into three categories using neurophysiological features and unsupervised learning. Four participants were recruited for an experiment, and the K-means algorithm was applied to the collected data to create three clusters representing stress levels. The results showed a good consistency of the clusters and allowed identifying which cluster corresponds to which stress level.

The authors of the work [9] review the clustering patterns of diet, physical activity and sedentary behavior in young people, and their impact on health. 172 clusters were identified, classified as healthy, unhealthy and mixed. The unhealthy clusters, associated with worse health outcomes, were prevalent in low socioeconomic status families.

The work [7] proposes an improved k-means algorithm to analyze the mental health education of university students. The algorithm improves the selection of the initial centroids and determines the optimal number of groups. It is applied to several data sets to test its effectiveness and accuracy. The work also explores the theory of self-determination and the intervention design.

The authors of the work [8] propose to apply fuzzy clustering analysis to the mental health of university students. It presents an improved method based on the firefly algorithm and performs comparative experiments, demonstrating that the proposed algorithm has a better performance. The study also analyzes the factors that affect the mental health of university students.

In the work [6] the researchers use various machine learning algorithms to identify the mental health state of an individual. A questionnaire was designed and unsupervised learning techniques were applied to extract group labels. The authors suggest directions for future work.

The research conducted in the work [5] presents a method to identify clinical subtypes of Alzheimer's disease using electronic health records. The method discovers five clusters with different clinical profiles and demonstrates that unsupervised learning can be used to identify subtypes of heterogeneous conditions.

In this work, unsupervised learning will be implemented, using clustering algorithms K-means, AGNES and DKM, to separate a data set into groups depending on the type of depression that each record has. A metric will be presented for these three algorithms to know how correct their functioning is and the comparison of the groups created.

3   Solution Proposal

In this section, the methodology that was followed to carry out the research presented in this work will be presented.

3.1   Data Collection

A 27-question survey was created to assess general characteristics, emotions, and physical sensations in 115 computer science students across the semester. The survey incorporates the CES-D scale to identify potential depression risks. Details of the CES-D scale follow.

CES-D Scale

The **Center for Epidemiological Studies Depression Scale** (CES-D) is a tool for assessing depressive symptoms in adults. It uses 20 questions to gauge symptom frequency over the past week [14]. Symptoms are scored from 0 (not present) to 3 (present most of the time), with total scores ranging from 0 to 60 - higher scores indicate more severe symptoms. While not a replacement for clinical evaluation, the CES-D helps identify those at risk of depression who may need further evaluation [15].

3.2   Exploratory Data Analysis

Exploratory data analysis (EDA) is a set of statistical techniques whose objective is to explore, describe and summarize the nature of the data and understand the relationships existing between the variables of interest, maximizing the understanding of the data set [17].

EDA is a prerequisite for data processing, as it allows to explore, understand and evaluate the quality of the data before performing any analysis. This type of analysis is useful to identify possible errors, reveal the presence of outliers, check the relationship between variables and perform a descriptive analysis of the data using graphical representations and summaries of the most significant aspects [17].

3.3   Implementation of Unsupervised Learning Algorithms

The objective of the proposed methodology is to find the patterns followed by the CES-D scale data to determine the case of depression that the members of the sample population may have. This leads to the proposal of implementing unsupervised learning algorithms, mainly clustering algorithms, to recognize such patterns.

The clustering algorithms proposed in the methodology belong to different types of clustering but have a similar clustering style in such a way that they will generate groups with similar behavior between them.

To generate the unsupervised learning models, the Python [22] programming language will be used in which the algorithms proposed in this research will be implemented and are the following:

K-Means Clustering

The K-means clustering algorithm is an unsupervised machine learning method that is used to group data into k distinct groups [11].

In this type of clustering algorithms, it is necessary to calculate the optimal number of groups beforehand and there are many methods that allow to perform this task, in this research the elbow method will be used [20].

Agnes Clustering

The Agnes clustering algorithm is an unsupervised machine learning method that is used to group data into clusters.

The Agnes clustering algorithm is an example of agglomerative hierarchical clustering. In this type of clustering, the clusters are merged based on their similarity. The algorithm starts with each data point as an individual cluster and then merges the closest clusters at each step [11].

DKM Clustering

A differential K-means clustering algorithm (DKM) is an unsupervised machine learning method that is used to compress deep neural network (DNN) models for efficient inference on devices. DKM is a k-means clustering layer that can be integrated into the architecture of a deep neural network. DKM uses k-means clustering to group the weights of the deep neural network into k groups and then assigns each weight to its closest group [16].

3.4   Silhouette Coefficient

The silhouette coefficient is a measure of cluster consistency. It ranges from -1 to +1, with high values indicating good cluster matching and low or negative values suggesting inappropriate clustering configuration. It's calculated using the mean intra-cluster distance (a) and the mean nearest-cluster distance (b) for each sample, as follows:

$$silhouette\ coefficient = \frac{(b-a)}{\max(a,b)} \qquad (1)$$

A silhouette width over 0.7 is "strong", over 0.5 is "reasonable", and over 0.25 is "weak". However, high values are hard to achieve with increasing data dimensionality. The silhouette score is best for convex-shaped clusters and may not perform well with irregular shapes or varying sizes [21].

4   Results

In this section, the results obtained from the application of the methodology presented in Sect. 3 will be presented, the results will be presented graphically and these graphs will be explained for a better understanding.

4.1   Survey Application

To collect the data for the algorithms Google forms were used for the application of the designed survey with CES-D scale, where each question was placed as a field to be answered freely for the convenience of the students.

Fig. 1. Google forms survey

A survey conducted via Google form (Fig. 1) at the semester's start yielded a dataset of 216 useful records out of 217. The dataset, initially with 28 attributes including data capture time, will be reduced to 27 attributes for analysis. The next step is exploratory data analysis to identify atypical or empty data and understand the dataset's behavior.

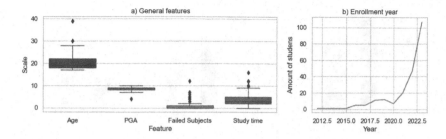

Fig. 2. General features

4.2 Exploratory Data Analysis

In exploratory data analysis, we seek to know the behavior of the data, thanks to this we can recognize atypical or empty values and replace them if necessary.

Figure 2 shows the university student data, with most students from similar study years, primarily 2023, and ages between 18 and 20. The grade point average (PGA) score is between 8 and 10, with overdue subjects and study time under 5. Figure 3 presents student symptom data, divided into physical symptoms (Fig. 3a) and personal behavior (Fig. 3b), as per the CES-D scale.

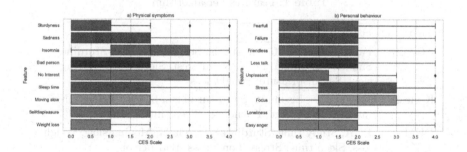

Fig. 3. CES-D symptoms

Figure 3 highlights common symptoms in the population. Dominant physical symptoms include insomnia and loss of interest in activities, while stress and short focus are dominant personal behavior symptoms. These symptoms, present at the semester's start, impact the clustering process, as will be seen in the experimental results.

4.3 Experimental Results

The clustering algorithms in Sect. 3.3 aim to categorize the dataset into three groups representing mild, moderate, and severe depression. The results, including the number of groups, will be graphically displayed. For the K-means algorithm, the group count was pre-calculated using the elbow method [20].

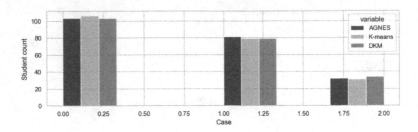

Fig. 4. Obtained clusters

In Fig. 4, the proposed algorithms create similar but not identical clusters. For mild depression cases (0–0.25), K-means gathered more population, while AGNES and DKM had similar clusters. In moderate depression cases (1.00–1.25), DKM and K-means had similar clusters, but AGNES's was larger. For severe depression cases (1.70–2.00), the largest cluster was from DKM, followed by AGNES, and the smallest from K-means.

Despite creating similar clusters, the algorithms used different methods and considered different features, as listed in Table 1.

Table 1. Features per algorithm

Algorithm	Features
AGNES	Failed subjects, Marital status, Sex, Study time, Sturdiness, Sadness, Insomnia, PGA, No interest, Sleep time, Moving slow, Self displeasure, Weight loss
K-means	Weight loss, Insomnia, Sex, Sturdiness, Stress, Sadness, No interest, PGA, Age, Friendless, Sleep time, Failure
DKM	PGA, Study time, Sturdiness, Insomnia, Moving slow, Weight loss, Sleep time, Stress, Loneliness, Bad person

Each algorithm has a different pattern of features that they use to create the clusters, but there are some features that are shared between all the algorithms which are:

- Weight loss
- Insomnia
- PGA
- Stress
- Sleep time

The main pattern of each depression case will have this features. As every algorithm has a different set of features, it's required to measure the performance of each algorithm. In Sect. 3.4 we proposed the silhouette coefficient [21] for this task, in Table 2 will present the obtained measure values.

Table 2. Silhouette coefficient per algorithm

Algorithm	AGNES	K-means	DKM
Silhouette coefficient	0.62054	0.59128	0.60143

As shown in Table 2 we can see how the values are between reasonable and strong, this may be because of the high dimensionality. As mention in Sect. 3.4 it's difficult to achieve higher values, this can be solved by a dimension reduction process for a future job.

5 Conclusions

In conclusion, the unsupervised learning models proposed in this research (K-means, AGNES and DKM) are capable of performing the three desired groups and recognizing the main attributes that give belonging to each group. In the same way, they can recognize the pattern of symptoms that lead to each case and allow observing the evolution between cases as the symptoms change throughout the semester.

A future work will be the study of a larger population and the addition of a dimentionality reduction process to have greater silhouette coefficient. Both of this actions will make a big change in the solution proposal as they may improve the behavior of some clustering algorithms.

Acknowledgments. The authors would like to thank Benemerita Universidad Autonoma de Puebla. The present work was funded by the research project 00082 at VIEP-BUAP 2024 and by the Consejo Nacional de Humanidades de Ciencia y Tecnologia (CONAHCYT) with scholarship number 1126315.

References

1. Loftness, B., et al.: Toward digital phenotypes of early childhood mental health via unsupervised and supervised machine learning (2023)
2. Shvetcov, A., et al.: Machine learning identifies a COVID-19-specific phenotype in university students using a mental health app. Internet Intervent. (2023)
3. Kundu, S., et al.: Mapping the individual human cortex using multidimensional MRI and unsupervised learning. Brain Commun. (2023)
4. Bhowmik, M., Al Bhuyain, N., Reza, M., Imtiaz Khan, N., Islam, M.: Neurophysiological feature based stress classification using unsupervised machine learning technique. In: Hossain, S., Hossain, M.S., Kaiser, M.S., Majumder, S.P., Ray, K. (eds.) Proceedings of International Conference on Fourth Industrial Revolution and Beyond 2021. LNNS, vol. 437, pp. 603–614. Springer, Singapore (2022). https://doi.org/10.1007/978-981-19-2445-3_42
5. Alexander, N., Alexander, D., Barkhof, F., Denaxas, S.: Using unsupervised learning to identify clinical subtypes of Alzheimer's disease in electronic health records. Stud. Health Technol. Inform. 499–503 (2020)

6. Srividya, M., Subramaniam, M., Natarajan, B.: Behavioral modeling for mental health using machine learning algorithms. J. Med. Syst. 88 (2018,4)
7. Lei, J.: An analytical model of college students' mental health education based on the clustering algorithm. Math. Probl. Eng. 1–11 (2022)
8. Tang, Q., Zhao, Y., Wei, Y., Jiang, L.: Research on the mental health of college students based on fuzzy clustering algorithm. Secur. Commun. Netw. 1–8 (2021)
9. Alosaimi, N., Sherar, L., Griffiths, P., Pearson, N.: Clustering of diet, physical activity and sedentary behaviour and related physical and mental health outcomes: a systematic review. BMC Public Health **23** (2023)
10. James, G., Witten, D., Hastie, T., Tibshirani, R., Taylor, J.: An Introduction to Statistical Learning with Applications in Python. Springer, Cham (2023). https://doi.org/10.1007/978-3-031-38747-0
11. Zollanvari, A.: Machine Learning with Python: Theory and Implementation. Springer, Cham (2023). https://doi.org/10.1007/978-3-031-33342-2
12. Sustancias (MSD), S. Informe mundial sobre salud mental: Transformar la salud mental para todos. World Health Organization (2022). https://www.who.int/es/publications/i/item/9789240050860. Accessed 17 Jan 2024
13. WHO Salud mental del adolescente. World Health Organization (2021). https://www.who.int/es/news-room/fact-sheets/detail/adolescent-mental-health. Accessed 17 Jan 2024
14. González-Forteza, C., Jiménez-Tapia, J., Lira, L., Wagner, F.: Undefined. Salud Pública De México, pp. 292–299 (2008)
15. Vergara, K., Díaz-Cárdenas, S., Gonzalez, F.: Síntomas de depresión y ansiedad en jóvenes universitarios: prevalencia y factores relacionados. Rev. Clínica Med. Familia 14–22 (2014)
16. Cho, M., Vahid, K., Adya, S., Rastegari, M.: DKM: differentiable K-means clustering layer for neural network compression (2022)
17. Zheng, A., Casari, A.: Feature Engineering for Machine Learning: Principles and Techniques for Data Scientists. O'Reilly Media (2018)
18. Dias Maia, C., Nobre, C., Gomes, M., Zárate, L.: Using machine learning to identify profiles of individuals with depression. In: Anais Do Symposium On Knowledge Discovery, Mining And Learning (KDMiLe), pp. 105–112 (2023)
19. Felice, M., Deroche, A., Trupkin, I., Chatterjee, P., Pollo-Cattaneo, M.: Predictive modeling for detection of depression using machine learning. In: Florez, H., Leon, M. (eds.) ICAI 2023. CCIS, vol. 1874, pp. 47–57. Springer, Cham (2023). https://doi.org/10.1007/978-3-031-46813-1_4
20. Dangeti, P.: Statistics for Machine Learning, pp 313–314. Packt Publishing (2017)
21. Bonnin, R.: Machine Learning for Developers. Packt Publishing (2017)
22. Ramalho, L.: Fluent Python. O'Reilly Media (2022)

The Role of California Fires in Predicting Valley Fever

Nathalie Valenzuela and Mario Bañuelos[✉][iD]

California State University, Fresno, Fresno, CA 93740, USA
mbanuelos22@csufresno.edu

Abstract. Valley Fever is a non-communicable disease caused by the fungus *Coccidioides*. Coccidioidomycosis is caused by two *Coccidioides* fungi found in soil, *C. immitis* and *C. posadasii* . This soilborne disease spreads when dry ground is broken up, such as during construction projects or natural disasters. When soil is disturbed, the fungi become airborne, and infect the host when their spores are inhaled. Due to their hot and arid climate, the Central Valley counties of Fresno, Kern, Kings, Madera, and Tulare have the greatest reports.

Previous studies have focused on the effects of temperature and precipitation, but have not included the potential impact of wildfires on the spread of this disease. Moreover, this is the first neural network approach proposed for predicting the case rates of this disease. In our research, we explore two different datasets that contain information about California fires and Valley Fever cases in California. We aim to quantify the impact of fires on the number of cases using a variety of deep learning approaches but only discuss the long short-term memory approach. Being able to predict the number of cases by quantifying the effect of environmental factors to help reduce the number of cases is one intended outcome. Knowing where the cases are being reported allows us to raise consciousness of the illness, so that people can better protect themselves.

Keywords: Valley Fever · Endemic Disease Time-series · Long Short-Term Memory

1 Introduction

1.1 Valley Fever Background

The two soil-found *Coccidioides* fungi, *Coccidioides immitis*, and *Coccidioides posadasii*, are the causes behind the disease, Coccidioidomycosis, also known as Valley Fever. The transmission of this disease, which is distributed through the soil, can occur when dry ground is disturbed, as can happen during construction or natural disasters. When the fungal spores are inhaled, the host can become infected through the respiratory system [16]. Since the symptoms of Valley Fever are similar to those of other respiratory illnesses, it is easy to misdiagnose it. Each year, approximately 20,000 cases are reported in the United States, and

E. Mezura-Montes et al. (Eds.): MCPR 2024, LNCS 14755, pp. 233–242, 2024.
https://doi.org/10.1007/978-3-031-62836-8_22

the number of cases is growing [3]. The southwest of the United States and some parts of South America have favorable soil conditions for the fungus to grow.

Arthroconidia are infectious propagules created by the fragmentation of hyphae that can rapidly spread from one host to another. The arthroconidia could live in your lungs and then infect you, causing symptoms 7 to 21 days later [14]. Inhaling just 10 arthroconidia of *C. immitis* or *C. posadasii* could result in infection [4,12]. Individuals 65 and older, as well as those under the age of 25, are at a higher risk of contracting the disease [14]. It typically presents as a mild, self-limited respiratory sickness or pneumonia but can also cause severe, widely spread disease and, in rare cases, result in death [6]. Approximately 60% of infected persons do not show symptoms, while the remaining 40% do. Within that 40%, 25% of people experience flu-like symptoms, including coughing, sneezing, fever, and muscular aches [16]. The remaining 15% get severely sick and experience pneumonia-like symptoms like pleurisy and thicker sputum. As a result, medicines and bed rest are necessary. Approximately 0.5–1%, of these cases—a tiny percentage—have the infection spread to the skin, bones, or meninges, which can be fatal [9,16].

Changes in the environment should have an impact on how quickly humans contract an infection. For instance, a colder and wetter rainy season should promote the development of *C. immitis*; windy conditions may promote the fungus spread; and hot, arid summers may suppress any competing organisms, promoting *C. immitis* survival and increasing the risk of infection. The fungus may thrive and spread extensively in the newly replenished, nutrient-rich soil due to the limited competition. The majority of reports happened in the dry, hot summer and fall months, especially following a wet winter [14]. The months with the most cases are frequently in the summer and early fall in California, where August and September get very little rain. Because of this, we expect data from past months would be predictive of future case rates.

According to the Centers for Disease Control and Prevention, the number of Valley Fever cases in California has increased [3]. It is anticipated that the endemic region would expand steadily until it includes more of the western United States [10]. Among the causes that could be contributing are improved reporting and surveillance systems and the reporting of mild cases that may not have been previously reported [14]. Additionally, cases must be reported to local health departments, and diagnostic procedures are now more reasonably priced. More cases are being reported as a result. Learning about Valley Fever is crucial for several reasons, such as public health knowledge, local awareness, and prevention. By increasing awareness, the effect of the fungal disease on people and communities can be reduced. It has been easier to understand where and among which demographic groups the rates have historically been the highest because of the availability of these surveillance data at the regional level, and it has also shown where rates are sharply increasing [6]. The results of this analysis had an impact on how a statewide awareness campaign for Coccidioidomycosis was planned so that the messaging, which included social media, TV, and radio segments, focused not only on the general public in the areas associated with the highest rates but also in areas where Coccidioidomycosis is increasing at the fastest rate. Anyone who visits, resides in, or works in an area where the fungus is prevalent in the environment, is at risk of contracting Valley Fever [2]. Figure 1 illustrates the incidence of Valley Fever cases rates reported within the period spanning from September 2006 to December 2015, encompassing the counties of Fresno, Kern, Merced, Madera, Tulare, and Kings.

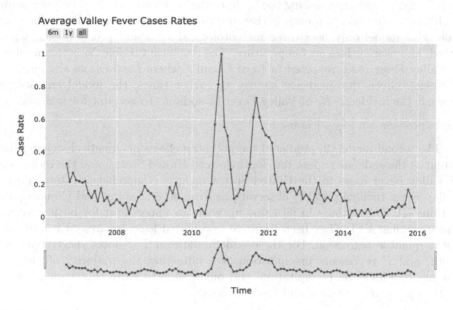

Fig. 1. This figure illustrates the monthly Valley Fever case rate from September 2006 to December 2015.

1.2 Previous Models

As we investigate the current state of Valley Fever research, it is worth acknowledging the groundwork laid by previous models and investigations that have impacted our approaches to prevention and diagnosis. Previous models use a generalized auto-regressive moving average (GARMA) model to predict the number of cases. These models use a moving average and an error correcting term to predict the future. They use a Poisson assumption for the number of VF cases and Akaike Information Criterion (AIC), which measures how well the data matches an estimated statistical model, to further refine their model and is summarized as

$$\log \lambda_t = 0.21 - 0.23 \sin\left(\frac{2\pi t}{52}\right) + 0.12 N_{t-1} + 0.07 N_{t-2} + 0.05 N_{t-4} + 0.06 N_{t-26},$$

$$(1)$$

as well as multiple linear quantile regression equations, which include:

$$VFI = \beta_1 T + \beta_2 P = (6.57)T + (-0.12)P. \tag{2}$$

The first approach (1) using the natural logarithm serves as the link function of the generalized linear model that uses weather influences to forecast incidence in the λ_t function, focusing on the rate of the Poisson function of occurrences [16]. The constant representing the background incidence is 0.21. The maximum likelihood estimation approach is then used to estimate the model's coefficients [16]. This model only uses three meteorological variables: precipitation, wind speed, and near surface air temperature. The response variable N_t is the number of Valley Fever cases reported in Kern County, where t represents the number of weeks. Given the incidence history at earlier times, the model enables to forecast the incidence N_t of Valley Fever at some t. To account for seasonality, the expression $\sin\left(\dfrac{2\pi t}{52}\right)$ is used.

The second model (2) predicted the potential effects of climate change on the extent of the endemic region, the Southwestern United States, and the incidence of Valley Fever cases in the United States using a comprehensive database of Valley Fever Incidence (VFI) observations from several states and climate projections [1]. The authors in [8] came up with an upper limit for both existing and upcoming VFI. They used iterative reweighted least squares with multiple linear quantile regression. For these endemic states, T denotes yearly temperature, and P represents precipitation. We note that the majority of current models only focus on precipitation, and our goal is to move this work forward by incorporating new data and frameworks [8].

1.3   Environmental Data

To further investigate the role of environment factors on this disease, two distinct set of data were analyzed. The first dataset is from the Office of the State Fire Marshal's (OSFM) California Incident Data and Statistics Program (CalStats) data warehouse [7]. The data includes details on each solitary fire reported across the state between September 2006 to December 2021.

Each row contains a fire report and incident details, such as the date, county, location, name of the fire, value of the total loss, the area burned (in acres), the type of incident, the number of people hurt, including bystanders and firefighters, and the reason for the fire. For both datasets, we were primarily interested in investigating fire report data from the Central Valley counties of Fresno, Kings, Madera, Mariposa, Merced, San Joaquin, Tulare, and Tuolumne. We examined the causes of the fires throughout the counties. We focus on the fires classified as vegetation because firefighters need to remove vegetation, which causes soil disruption. This results in spores being released to the air. Specifically, we concentrate our work on six specific fire causing factors: arson, smoking, debris burning, lightning, playing with fire, and camping. As a result, a dataset of 16,539 rows and 7 columns was generated.

The second dataset, which had been processed and cleaned, contains information on the total monthly case count of Valley Fever [1]. It includes the monthly case count from the states of Arizona, California, and Nevada from 2000 to 2015. However, when it comes to Central Valley counties, the California fire dataset only contains information on Fresno, Kern, Merced, Madera, Tulare, and Kings (see Fig. 2). The inclusion of fires in neighboring counties could potentially have an impact on the number of cases, which is why we included them in our analysis. Having fire data only for California, we limit our study to Valley Fever rate predictions in the state.

Fig. 2. California counties included in Coccidioidomycosis and fire analysis are highlighted in a crosshatch green pattern. Fire data from green (with horizontal lines) and Coccidioidomycosis from green (with diagonal lines) counties are included in creating our models and predictions. (Color figure online)

Using the second dataset, we computed the case rate, which is defined as

$$\text{case rate} = \frac{\text{\# of case count in a county}}{\text{population in the county}}.$$

Subsequently, we proceeded to perform data normalization. Normalizing data serves the purpose of enhancing the comparability of input importance, making it a crucial step in data analysis. This is important especially for neural network models [11]. Failure to normalize can introduce bias into our models' predictions, especially with larger datasets. By normalizing, we ensure that every feature contributes equally to the analysis, resulting in having all of the columns in the final data frame to be normalized with the `MinMaxScaler` package [15]. This rescales the original data values in the 0 to 1 range,

$$X_{std} = \frac{x - x_{min}}{x_{max} - x_{min}},$$

where x is the input value, x_{min} is the minimum of the input value, and x_{max} is the maximum input value. Then, we aggregated fire causes and acres burned by month, converted the daily data to monthly data, and combined datasets spanning from 09/2006–12/2015. Table 1 highlights an example of the processed data used for one specific county.

Table 1. First five rows of normalized monthly level data, with fire causes used for VF case rate prediction in Fresno County.

Y-M	Arson	Smoking	Debris	Lightning	Playing w Fire	Campfire	Fresno
2006-09	0.0347	0.00173	0.0069	0.00	0.00	0.00	0.458
2006-10	0.0579	0.00520	0.0006	0.136	0.0149	0.0049	0.363
2006-11	0.0197	0.0160	0.0069	0.0001	0.0372	0.0463	0.415
2006-12	0.00148	0.0118	0.00	0.00226	0.105	0.00	0.329
2007-01	0.00	0.0143	0.0069	0.00	0.0007	0.0102	0.518

2   Methods

Deep learning is a machine learning subfield that focuses on training artificial neural networks. It is worth mentioning that deep learning continues to improve, with development of new advancements and architectures [5]. This approach is adequate for modeling complex relationships in data. To handle the sequential data, we investigated three distinct approaches: Neural Networks (NN), Recurrent Neural Networks (RNNs), and Long Short-Term Memory (LSTM) models. These models have the capacity for learning from data, which enables them to identify patterns and forecast outcomes [17].

We utilize the mean squared error (MSE) to calculate the average of the squared differences between the actual and the predicted values of the VF rates, which is defined as:

$$\text{MSE} = \frac{1}{N} \sum_{i=1}^{N} (y_i - \hat{y}_i)^2,$$

where y_i is the data point value, $\hat{y}_i$ is its predicted value, and N is the total number of data points in the dataset.

We incorporated Python's `torch` library to create our models [13]. We divided our data into two sets: training and testing data. We trained with 80% of the time (in months) since 2006 and tested with the remaining 20%. We incorporated a total of six inputs, each of which served as a catalyst for the start of a fire.

2.1   Long Short-Term Memory Approach

The model's long-term memory is represented by the cell state, unaffected by the weights and biases. Their absence prevents the gradient from vanishing or exploding, allowing long-term memories to pass through the unrolled units. Additionally, the weights are impacted by the hidden state, which stands for short-term memory. Utilizing the sigmoid and tanh activation functions, LSTM will use two routes to produce predictions. The sigmoid function guarantees an output between 0 and 1. If the output is zero, it informs the network to forget everything; otherwise, if it is one, it will remember the information. While the tanh function values of new information will be between -1 and 1, if the value is negative, it is subtracted from the cell state, and if it is positive, it is added to the current timestamp. The percentage of long-term memory that is remembered is determined by the first gate, also referred to as the forget gate. The input gate, which is the second gate, employs both activation functions to calculate the percentage of potential memory that will be retained and the potential long-term memory. The last gate evaluates the percent potential memory to remember and potential short-term memory recognition using both activation functions and predicts the output.

Hyperparameters play a crucial role in influencing the behavior and performance of the model. The input dimensions (6) represent the six fire causes. The output dimension of 1 is the final prediction for the VF case rate. To prevent the model from overfitting, we use a dropout rate of 0.20, which refers to a hyperparameter regulating the rate at which neurons in a layer are deactivated randomly when training. A learning rate of 0.01, 32 hidden dimensions, and 2 layers were also used. Our experimental design is summarized in Fig. 3.

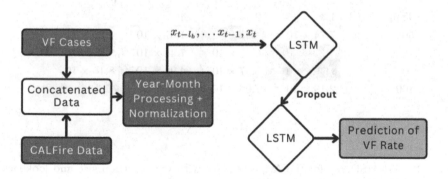

Fig. 3. Experimental diagram of proposed data processing and LSTM model for predicting VF case rates, where the input $x_t \in \mathbb{R}^6$ represents the present time and l_b represents the lookback period, the number of previous months used to predict the next time x_{t+1}.

3   Results

For our experimental approaches, we considered various pairings of training/testing dataset sizes and lookback periods. The lookback, l_b, period represents the data range considered (in months) when making predictions. Our model used four different lookback periods: 1, 2, 4, and 8 months. From the 112 monthly observations, the training/testing dataset size splits considered were 50/62, 70/42, 90/22, and 100/12 to train/test the LSTM model. This approach was applied to all six counties as well as the average VF case rates, and the MSE loss values were reported. This lets us explore the four training/testing sizes to assess their impact on the predictions.

In this section, we consider and discuss the test MSE for the average of the counties and Fresno county case rates. Tables 2 and 3 summarize these results. For each combination, the entry that has been highlighted displays the MSE values that are the smallest, indicating the accuracy and consistency of the predictions. It is clear from both tables that the lookback period of 1 month consistently yielded the lowest MSE up to a train size of 90. For a train size of 100, a lookback period of 8 months resulted in the lowest test MSE. For the training data, all the lowest MSE values in the lookback of eight months.

Even though our approach appears to not generalize on the test data, the authors feel that the results are promising and warrant further exploration because Valley Fever cases are often underreported and misdiagnosed. We are also encouraged by that fact the test predictions for each county vary, predictions for the average case rates capture the qualitative pattern observed (see Fig. 4).

Table 2. Test MSE loss for the Fresno case rates with varying train size and lookback, l_b, period. The lowest MSE is highlighted for each training size.

Train size/ l_b	1	2	4	8
50	7.74×10^{-2}	5.55×10^{-2}	1.07×10^{-1}	1.25×10^{-1}
70	5.69×10^{-2}	6.77×10^{-2}	7.44×10^{-2}	9.35×10^{-2}
90	4.18×10^{-2}	5.37×10^{-2}	4.98×10^{-2}	8.16×10^{-2}
100	2.19×10^{-2}	7.06×10^{-2}	8.69×10^{-2}	1.14×10^{-2}

Table 3. Test MSE loss for the Avg case rates with varying train size and lookback, l_b, period. The lowest MSE is highlighted for each training size.

Train size/ l_b	1	2	4	8
50	3.64×10^{-2}	5.75×10^{-2}	8.15×10^{-2}	9.35×10^{-2}
70	2.24×10^{-2}	5.64×10^{-2}	3.86×10^{-2}	4.73×10^{-2}
90	1.55×10^{-2}	2.86×10^{-2}	4.45×10^{-2}	5.01×10^{-2}
100	1.14×10^{-2}	5.79×10^{-2}	5.77×10^{-2}	3.57×10^{-3}

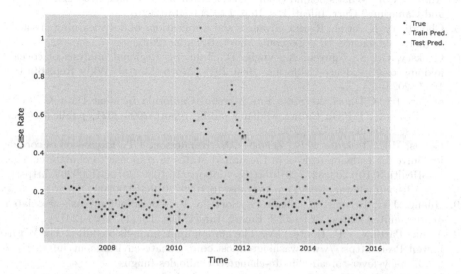

Fig. 4. Valley Fever case rates for true values (blue), train predictions (red), test predictions (green) with a train size of 70 and $l_b = 8$. (Color figure online)

4   Conclusion

Using environment data related to fire, we implemented a long short-term memory (LSTM) models to predict Valley Fever case rates. We noticed qualitative and accurate predictions for the average case rates. Reporting for Valley Fever has recently improved because there is still a lot of underreporting since it is similar to other diseases, and that may be one of the reasons why the models are not as accurate as they could be. Although the individual county predictions could be improved, this is the first implementation of such models to this data since previous models have not considered fire incidents to predict disease rates.

Acknowledgments. This study was supported by the College of Science and Mathematics at California State University, Fresno.

Disclosure of Interests. The authors have no competing interests to declare that are relevant to the content of this article.

References

1. Valley Fever Case Database. Regents of the University of California (2018). https:// github.com/valleyfever/valleyfevercasedata. Accessed 30 Aug 2022
2. Valley Fever (Coccidioidomycosis). https://www.cdc.gov/fungal/diseases/ coccidioidomycosis/index.html. Accessed 13 June 2023
3. Valley Fever (Coccidiomycosis) Awareness. https://www.cdc.gov/fungal/features/ valley-fever.html. Accessed 16 Jan 2023

4. Ampel, N.M.: What's behind the increasing rates of coccidioidomycosis in Arizona and California? Curr. Infect. Dis. Rep. **12**, 211–216 (2010)
5. Choudhary, K., et al.: Recent advances and applications of deep learning methods in materials science. NPJ Comput. Mater. **8**(1), 59 (2022)
6. Cooksey, G.L.S., Nguyen, A., Vugia, D., Jain, S.: Regional analysis of coccidioidomycosis incidence-California, 2000–2018. Morb. Mortal. Wkly Rep. **69**(48), 1817 (2020)
7. of Forestry, C.D., of the State Fire Marshal California Incident Data & Statistics Program, F.P.O.: Calfire wildland public report 2000-2021, public Records Request R004495-062722 (2022)
8. Gorris, M.E., Treseder, K.K., Zender, C.S., Randerson, J.T.: Expansion of coccidioidomycosis endemic regions in the united states in response to climate change. GeoHealth **3**(10), 308–327 (2019)https://doi.org/10.1029/2019GH000209, https://agupubs.onlinelibrary.wiley.com/doi/abs/10.1029/2019GH000209
9. Huang, J.Y., Bristow, B., Shafir, S., Sorvillo, F.: Coccidioidomycosis-associated deaths, united states, 1990–2008. Emerg. Infect. Dis. **18**(11), 1723 (2012)
10. Joshua Partlow, V.P., Houte, C.V.: The human limit: an invisible killer. The Washington Post. https://www.washingtonpost.com/climate-environment/interactive/2023/valley-fever-spread-climate-change-coccidioides-fungus/
11. Kotsiantis, S.B., Kanellopoulos, D., Pintelas, P.E.: Data preprocessing for supervised learning. Int. J. Comput. Sci. **1**(2), 111–117 (2006)
12. Lewis, E.R., Bowers, J.R., Barker, B.M.: Dust devil: the life and times of the fungus that causes valley fever. PLoS Pathog. **11**(5), e1004762 (2015)
13. Paszke, A., et al.: Pytorch: an imperative style, high-performance deep learning library. In: Advances in Neural Information Processing Systems, vol. 32 (2019)
14. Pearson, D., Ebisu, K., Wu, X., Basu, R.: A review of coccidioidomycosis in California: exploring the intersection of land use, population movement, and climate change. Epidemiol. Rev. **41**(1), 145–157 (2019)
15. Pedregosa, F., et al.: Scikit-learn: machine learning in Python. J. Mach. Learn. Res. **12**, 2825–2830 (2011)
16. Talamantes, J., Behseta, S., Zender, C.S.: Statistical modeling of valley fever data in Kern County, California. Int. J. Biometeorol. **51**, 307–313 (2007)
17. Yu, Y., Si, X., Hu, C., Zhang, J.: A review of recurrent neural networks: LSTM cells and network architectures. Neural Comput. **31**(7), 1235–1270 (2019)

Recognition of Leukemic Retinopathy Using Knowledge of Diabetic Retinopathy

Edgar Gilberto Platas-Campero⬛, Raquel Díaz Hernández(✉)⬛,
and Leopoldo Altamirano Robles⬛

Instituto Nacional de Astrofísica, Óptica y Electrónica, Puebla, Mexico
raqueld@inaoep.mx

Abstract. Leukemic retinopathy is an ocular manifestation associated with leukemia and is considered a key indicator for early diagnosis and treatment of the disease. However, the study of this pathology faces a challenge due to the scarcity of images, making it difficult to develop and train deep learning models for its classification. A dual transfer learning methodology is used to take advantage of the knowledge gained from a well-documented disease such as diabetic retinopathy and apply it to leukemic retinopathy, a less studied disease. First, transfer learning by fine-tuning is implemented on several Convolutional Neural Networks (CNN), including Compact, ResNet-18, AlexNet, RegNet, VGG16, InceptionV3, and EfficientNetV2, using diabetic retinopathy images. Then, the CNN model with the best result for diabetic retinopathy detection is subjected to a second transfer learning process but with a feature-extraction approach using leukemic retinopathy images. The results show that EfficientNetV2 achieved an accuracy of 82.14% in tests using diabetic retinopathy images. Similarly, this model demonstrated an accuracy of 93.33% when testing for leukemic retinopathy. This approach represents a significant advance in identifying leukemic retinopathy, showing the advantages of transfer learning in data-limited scenarios and the benefit of using knowledge of similar diseases to enrich the study of less documented pathologies.

Keywords: Deep Learning · Dual Transfer Learning · Diabetic Retinopathy · Leukemic Retinopathy

1 Introduction

Leukemia is considered a malignant disorder characterized by the excessive proliferation of abnormal leukocytes and their accumulation in the bone marrow and peripheral blood, causing diseases such as neutropenia, thrombocytopenia, anemia, and damage to organs such as the spleen, lymph nodes, liver, eyes, etc. At the eye level, it is known as leukemic retinopathy.

Leukemic retinopathy is characterized by the infiltration of abnormal leukocytes into the retina, causing a variety of retinal manifestations [1, 2], such as tortuous and dilated retinal veins, white-center hemorrhages, intraretinal hemorrhages, cotton-wool spots, Roth spots and cotton-wool exudates. This condition is significantly prevalent in patients with leukemia in several studies [3–9].

© The Author(s), under exclusive license to Springer Nature Switzerland AG 2024
E. Mezura-Montes et al. (Eds.): MCPR 2024, LNCS 14755, pp. 243–252, 2024.
https://doi.org/10.1007/978-3-031-62836-8_23

In addition to the clinical manifestations already described, it is essential to highlight the early appearance of leukemic retinopathy in patients with leukemia, which often precedes other symptoms. Recent studies [10–13] have shown that specific retinal lesions may be early indicators of leukemia, emphasizing the importance of early ophthalmologic diagnosis in these cases. Another notable finding is the higher incidence of leukemic retinopathy in patients with acute myeloblastic leukemia compared to those with acute lymphoblastic leukemia [14, 15], so early detection through regular ophthalmologic examinations and analysis of retinal images may play a crucial role in the identification and treatment of leukemia.

It should be noted that at the time of this review, no studies that used deep learning to detect leukemia retinopathy were identified. This lack highlights an important area of opportunity.

To train a deep learning model, it is essential to have a large set of images of leukemic retinopathy, so a search was made in different sources that offer a wide variety of fundus images showing ocular lesions such as diabetic retinopathy, myopia, optic disc edema, glaucoma, cataracts, among others. This search returned the following datasets: "Retinal Fundus Multi-Disease Image Dataset" (RFMiD) [16] covers 45 different fundus diseases or pathologies. Similarly, RFMiD2.0 [17] extends this classification to 49 categories, including common and rare diseases and normal images. In turn, the "Brazilian Multilabel Ophthalmological Dataset" (BRSET) [18] considers 14 different categories. On the other hand, "Ocular Disease Intelligent Recognition" (ODIR) [19] identifies eight types of ocular diseases. MuReD [20] studies 20 eye diseases or conditions. Finally, DR-HAGIS [21] focuses on four specific diseases.

However, despite this exhaustive search of specialized databases, none contained images specific to leukemic retinopathy. This absence presents an obstacle to training deep learning models focused on classifying this particular form of retinopathy. Given this challenge, transfer learning is considered a potential solution. Transfer learning is a technique that allows knowledge to be leveraged, reducing dependence on large data sets or limited data availability while minimizing the effort required for data collection. This technique has been successfully applied to the diagnosis of diabetic retinopathy through transfer learning [22–25]; the results of these investigations reached accuracies above 80%, representing a significant advance in computer-aided diagnosis.

Inspired by previous advances, tests were performed on different pre-trained CNN models (Compact, ResNet-18, AlexNet, RegNet, VGG16, InceptionV3, and EfficientNetV2) using leukemic retinopathy datasets, both in their original (48 training samples) and extended (127 training samples) form. In both cases, they faced the problem of overfitting due to the limited data available for this condition.

Faced with this situation, we adopted a dual transfer learning strategy. This approach is designed explicitly for leukemic retinopathy and takes advantage of previous knowledge from the study of diabetic retinopathy. First, a CNN model is selected and trained with diabetic retinopathy data through a fine-tuning process. Then, in a second transfer phase, the feature-extraction approach is applied to leukemic retinopathy images. The results highlight the benefit of using transfer learning in data-constrained contexts and the ability to improve results by leveraging knowledge from similar diseases.

The main contributions of this paper are:

- To present the application of a method using deep learning techniques for non-invasive diagnosis of leukemia from retinal lesions in fundus images.
- A procedure is proposed for transferring knowledge acquired in the diagnosis of diabetic retinopathy and adapting it to the diagnosis of leukemic retinopathy in settings where data are scarce or difficult to obtain.

2   Related Work

In this section, we review several studies that focus on applying dual transfer learning in the context of medical imaging.

First, we have Gao et al. [26], who implemented a Dual Transfer Learning (DSTL) method to address the challenges of EEG signal classification for Brain-Computer Interfaces (BCI). DSTL combines Euclidean Alignment (EA) and Transfer Component Analysis (TCA) in the preprocessing and feature extraction stages. This approach has been shown to improve classification accuracy in several transfer paradigms and to reduce the dependence on large training sets. On the other hand, Mukhlif et al. [27] introduced a Dual Transfer Learning (DTL) approach to improve medical image classification; this method was applied to four pre-trained models (VGG16, Xception, ResNet50, and MobileNetV2) on two datasets: skin cancer ISIC2020 and breast cancer ICIAR2018, the results showed a significant improvement in the accuracy of all models, particularly highlighting the Xception model in skin and breast cancer classification. Finally, Matos et al. [28] present a classification method for breast cancer histopathology images using double transfer learning; they use the Inception-v3 model, pre-trained with ImageNet to extract features from the images and an SVM classifier trained on a colorectal cancer dataset to filter and remove irrelevant patches. The method outperforms the state-of-the-art for most magnification factors in the breast cancer dataset. In conclusion, the comprehensive review of current studies demonstrates the benefits and potential of dual transfer learning in image processing and analysis.

3   Characteristics of the Dataset Used

3.1   Dataset

To carry out this research, on the one hand, the APTOS dataset [29] was used, which contains 3662 images of diabetic retinopathy, obtained by fundus photography, in PNG format, distributed as follows: in category 0, there are 1805 images in category 1, there are 370 images, in category two there are 999 images, in category three there are 193 images and, finally, in category four there are 295 images.

On the other hand, in the case of images related to leukemic retinopathy, a review was conducted to search for images showing this condition; 47 images were obtained and extracted from different portals dealing with this disease [11–15, 30].

3.2   Distribution of the Dataset

In the case of the diabetic retinopathy image set, an initial imbalance in the distribution of classes was observed. The number of images in specific categories was adjusted to address this situation and achieve a more balanced distribution in the dataset. The final distribution was as follows: 2113 images were assigned to the training phase, 303 were given to the validation phase, and 320 were given to the test phase.

As for the images of leukemic retinopathy, a total of 47 images corresponding to this condition and 52 images of healthy patients were used; the distribution for the evaluation phases was as follows: 15 images for the test phase, 69 for the training phase, and 15 for the validation phase. It is important to note that all images of healthy subjects were obtained from the Diabetic Retinopathy (resized) set [31].

3.3   Comparison of Lesion Characteristics in Retinopathies

The classification of retinal lesions is critical to the diagnosis and treatment of both diabetic and leukemic retinopathies, highlighting lesions such as microaneurysms, hemorrhages, exudates, and, in some cases, leukemic infiltrates. Table 1 presents a comparative analysis between lesions observed in diabetic retinopathy and leukemic retinopathy conditions, illustrating the distinctive characteristics of lesions in both conditions. This table allows direct visualization of the differences and similarities in the fundus images for each type of retinopathy.

Despite similarities in the manifestations of diabetic and leukemic retinopathy, there are essential differences in the onset, progression, and specific lesions observed that help to differentiate the type of retinopathy.

Table 1. Lesions associated with (A) diabetic retinopathy [32, 33] and (B) leukemic retinopathy [34–36].

	Microaneurysms	Hemorrhages	Exudates	Roth's spots	Infiltrates Foveal
A				There are no submitted	There are no submitted
B					

4   Proposed Methodology

4.1   General Outline of the Proposal

The methodology proposed in this research involves performing several tests with diabetic and leukemic retinopathy images to evaluate the effectiveness of transfer learning. Several (CNN) models previously trained on ImageNet were selected, retrained, and evaluated on the specific datasets.

A scheme consisting of three fundamental tests was designed. The first test aims to evaluate the effectiveness of transfer learning when only leukemic retinopathy images are used and to determine whether this technique allows for disease classification even when a limited number of leukemic retinopathy specific images are available.

The second test involves retraining the selected models using the transfer learning technique, applying a fine-tuning approach with diabetic retinopathy images. This process involves partially freezing the internal layers of the model and modifying the final layers to adapt them to the study's specific context. After this adaptation, the modified model is saved for later use. This intermediate step aims to take advantage of a more extensive and similar data set to strengthen the training in the face of data sparsity, as with leukemic retinopathy.

Finally, the third test focuses on applying leukemic retinopathy, using the model already adapted for diabetic retinopathy. This step involves a feature-extraction strategy that freezes all model layers except the classifier. The latter undergoes a new training process with the leukemic retinopathy dataset. This procedure allows us to take advantage of the features previously learned from the diabetic retinopathy dataset, enabling us to obtain satisfactory results in the classification of leukemic retinopathy, even with limited data availability.

4.2 Transfer Learning

Transfer learning is a machine learning technique that allows a model designed for one task to be adapted to a second related task, which is particularly useful in medical domains where data may be limited [37]. There are two main approaches to transfer learning: fine-tuning and feature-extraction.

In fine-tuning, the weights of the last layers of a pre-trained network and the added classifier are adjusted. This approach is suitable for larger datasets that are like the original training set of the network, allowing adaptation to new features.

On the other hand, feature-extraction uses a pre-trained network on a large dataset, freezes its layers, and adds a new classifier trained on the new dataset. This method is ideal for smaller datasets, as it avoids overfitting and takes advantage of previously learned general features.

Regarding adjusting the parameters of the last modified layer, in terms of the classifier, the architecture proposed by Chilukoti et al. [24] was followed during the transfer learning process in both approaches. The only modification introduced concerned the number of categories to be classified in the output layer, adapting them specifically to the cases of diabetic retinopathy and leukemic retinopathy.

4.3 Performance Metrics

Several metrics have been selected to evaluate the performance of the deep learning model using a classification approach that provides different perspectives on its performance. Accuracy offers an overview of the performance by measuring the proportion of correct predictions. Precision evaluates the model's ability to limit false positives, while Recall measures its ability to identify positive instances correctly. Finally, the F1 score provides a balanced assessment of accuracy and sensitivity, particularly useful in unbalanced classes.

4.4 Integration of the Pre-trained Model in the Proposed Solution

In this research, a variety of pre-trained models were used in ImageNet, including AlexNet, ResNet18, RegNetZD32, InceptionV3, Enhanced, VGG16, Compact and EfficientNetV2 [38], using Halcon [39], Medicmind [40], and Python tools. These models were used in a transfer learning context to evaluate their performance on image classification tasks for diabetic and leukemic retinopathy.

5 Results

In the first test of the study, the performance of various models for leukemic retinopathy was evaluated using two classes: 'Healthy' and 'LR'. Tests were conducted with and without data augmentation. In the non-augmented set, the EfficientNet-V2 model achieved 100% Accuracy, with similar results in Precision, Recall, and F1-Score. Similarly, in tests with data augmentation (127 samples), the Enhanced, AlexNet, and ResNet18 models also reached 100%. These results suggest a tendency towards overfitting.

In the second test, diabetic retinopathy images were used, and transfer learning with a fine-tuning approach was applied to different CNN models. The results obtained in this test with each model are shown in Table 2.

Table 2. Comparative table with other models using diabetic retinopathy images.

Models	Accuracy	Precision	Recall	F1-Score
InceptionV3	52.24%	52.87	50%	55.79%
RegNet	52.24%	52.87%	59.04%	55.79%
AlexNet	72.25%	78%	72%	73%
Compact	77.19%	77.20%	77.31%	77.10%
ResNet-18	77.81%	77.47%	78.01%	77.65%
VGG16	79%	79.6%	80.4%	80.4%
EfficientNetV2	**82.14%**	**83%**	**82%**	**82%**

Among all the CNN models evaluated, EfficientNetV2 stood out by achieving the highest level of accuracy on the test set, with 82.14%, as shown in Table 3.

In addition, Fig. 1 shows in detail how loss and accuracy behaved throughout the training and validation process by epoch, providing insight into the performance of EfficientNetV2 during the second test.

As shown in Table 2, various models were evaluated using images of diabetic retinopathy, undergoing multiple tests. EfficientNetV2 stood out, achieving averages

Table 3. Results obtained with EfficientNetV2 during the second diabetic retinopathy imaging test.

Evaluation Phase	Accuracy	Loss
Training	86.06%	0.4547
Validation	81.32%	0.4434
Test	**82.14%**	**0.5283**

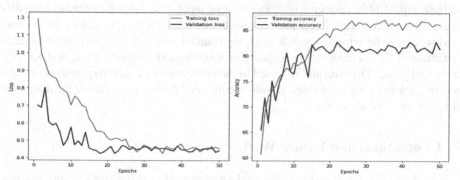

Fig. 1. Results of EfficientNetV2 in the second test. Left: loss reduction in training and validation. Right: Evolution of accuracy in training and validation.

above 82% across all four assessed metrics. Due to this high performance, EfficientNetV2 was selected as the model to continue training with images of leukemic retinopathy".

In the third test, a transfer learning approach focused on feature-extraction was applied using images of leukemic retinopathy. For this purpose, we used the weights resulting from the EfficientNetV2 model, which was previously trained on diabetic retinopathy images, orienting the model towards a binary classification of the images. In this scheme, 0 was assigned to individuals without the condition and 1 to those diagnosed with leukemic retinopathy. The results of this method are shown in Table 4.

Table 4. Results of the third test using leukemic retinopathy images.

Evaluation Phase	Accuracy	Precision	Recall	Loss
Training	89.06%	–	–	0.1574
Validation	100%	–	–	0.0871
Test	**93.33%**	**94%**	**93%**	**0.1487**

6 Discussion

In discussing the results of this research, it is essential to analyze the different tests performed. The first of these, focused solely on leukemia retinopathy images with limited data volume, revealed insufficient effectiveness of transfer learning under these circumstances. This finding led us to explore a dual-transfer learning approach. The second test, aimed at classifying diabetic retinopathy using a fine-tuning approach, revealed a remarkable diversity in the performance of different pre-trained CNN models. EfficientNetV2 outperformed the other models, achieving training and test accuracies of 86.06% and 82.14%, respectively, demonstrating its ability to discriminate between different disease categories. Regarding the results of the third test, a pre-trained model was used with diabetic retinopathy data, applying transfer learning with a focus on feature-extraction. This test achieved an accuracy of 89.06% in the training phase and 93.33% in the test phase. These results, obtained in the context of data scarcity, demonstrate the benefits of using prior knowledge of well-documented diseases to facilitate the diagnosis of lesser-known conditions.

7 Conclusions and Future Work

This study has demonstrated the value and efficiency of dual transfer learning in data-constrained settings. It also highlights the benefit of using prior knowledge of similar diseases, such as diabetic retinopathy, to improve the analysis of less documented diseases, such as leukemic retinopathy. It demonstrates the ability of this strategy to enhance the final results. Furthermore, the importance of proper CNN model selection and adaptation of the transfer learning approach to the specific needs of the dataset is highlighted. For future research, the use of zero-shot learning is considered as an alternative to transfer learning. This technique allows image classification without prior training and offers possibilities in data-limited situations.

References

1. Tang, Y.F., Chong, E.W.T.: Leukaemic retinopathy as the first manifestation in acute lymphoblastic leukaemia. BMJ **377**, e066969 (2022)
2. Benvenuto, F., Sgroi, M., Guillen, S., et al.: Ophthalmologic manifestations in Acute Leukemia. Integr. Cancer Sci. Ther. **7** (2020). https://doi.org/10.15761/icst.1000327
3. Khalil, M., Lobna, R., Amine, K.M., et al.: Leukemic retinopathy: a case report. Sch. J. Med. Case Rep. **11**, 711–715 (2023)
4. Yee, C., Scruggs, B.A., Flaxel, C.J.: Retinal infiltration in a case of chronic myeloid leukemia. Retin. Cases Brief Rep. (2022). https://doi.org/10.1097/ICB.0000000000001281
5. Vicini, G., Nicolosi, C., Malandrino, D., et al.: Leukostasis retinopathy with leukemic infiltrates as onset manifestation of chronic myeloid leukemia: a case report. Eur. J. Ophthalmol. **31**, NP116–NP121 (2021)
6. Bodhankar, P., Balakrishnan, D., Basheer, N., et al.: Leukemic retinopathy with rare presentation in B-cell acute lymphoblastic leukemia. J. Clin. Ophthalmol. Res. **9**, 138 (2021)
7. Gupta, A.K., Basnet, R., Yadav, R.D., Singh, S.: Leukemic retinopathy, a rare entity: a case report. Asian J. Med. Sci. **12**, 160–165 (2021)

8. Di Marino, M., Giannini, C., Mancino, R., et al.: Take a look in the eye: Long-term multimodal ophthalmological assessment of leukemic retinopathy, a case report. Ann. Case Rep. 7 (2022). https://doi.org/10.29011/2574-7754.100777
9. Cicinelli, M.V., Mastaglio, S., Menean, M., et al.: Retinal microvascular changes in patients with acute leukemia. Retina **42**, 1762–1771 (2022)
10. Beketova, T., Mordechaev, E., Murillo, B., Schlesinger, M.D.: Leukemic retinopathy: a diagnostic clue for initial detection and prognosis of leukemia. Cureus (2023). https://doi.org/10.7759/cureus.50587
11. Istrate, M., Ciubotaru, A., Hasbei-Popa, M., et al.: Leukemic retinopathy, the first expression in a case of chronic myelomonocytic leukemia - a case report. Rom J Ophthalmol **64**, 419 423 (2020)
12. Gim, Y., Kim, H.-J.: Ocular symptom can be the first presentation of differentiation syndrome in acute promyelocytic leukemia. Korean J. Ophthalmol. **35**, 94–96 (2021)
13. Lim, J., Kim, I., Sagong, M.: Leukostasis retinopathy as the first sign of chronic myeloid Leukemia with severe hyperleukocytosis: two case reports. Korean J. Ophthalmol. **37**, 266–269 (2023)
14. Sayadi, J., Gouider, D., Allouche, Y., et al.: Ophthalmic manifestations of newly diagnosed acute leukemia patients in a Tunisian cohort. Clin. Ophthalmol. **16**, 3425–3435 (2022)
15. Reddy, S.C., Jackson, N.: Retinopathy in acute leukaemia at initial diagnosis: correlation of fundus lesions and haematological parameters. Acta Ophthalmol. Scand. **82**, 81–85 (2004)
16. Pachade, S., Porwal, P., Thulkar, D., et al.: Retinal fundus multi-disease image dataset (RFMiD): a dataset for multi-disease detection research. In: International Conference on Data Technologies and Applications (2021). https://doi.org/10.3390/data6020014
17. Panchal, S., Naik, A., Kokare, M., et al.: Retinal fundus multi-disease image dataset (RFMiD) 2.0: a dataset of frequently and rarely identified diseases. Data (Basel) **8**, 29 (2023)
18. Nakayama, L.F., Restrepo, D., Matos, J., et al.: BRSET: a Brazilian multilabel ophthalmological dataset of retina fundus photos. bioRxiv (2024)
19. Larxel. Ocular Disease Recognition ODIR5K. In: Kaggle (2020). https://www.kaggle.com/andrewmvd/ocular-disease-recognition-odir5k. Accessed 30 Jan 2024
20. Rodriguez, M.A., AlMarzouqi, H., Liatsis, P.: Multi-label retinal disease classification using transformers. arXiv [cs.CV] (2022)
21. Hagis, D.R.: Diabetic retinopathy, hypertension, age-related macular degeneration and Glacuoma images. In: DR HAGIS (2016). https://paperswithcode.com/dataset/dr-hagis. Accessed 30 Jan 2024
22. Al-Smadi, M., Hammad, M., Baker, Q.B., Al-Zboon, S.A.: A transfer learning with deep neural network approach for diabetic retinopathy classification. Int J Elect. Comput. Syst. Eng. **11**, 3492–3501 (2021)
23. Jabbar, M.K., Yan, J., Xu, H., et al.: Transfer learning-based model for diabetic retinopathy diagnosis using retinal images. Brain Sci **12** (2022). https://doi.org/10.3390/brainsci1205 0535
24. Chilukoti, S.V., Maida, A.S., Hei, X.: Diabetic retinopathy detection using transfer learning from pre-trained convolutional neural network models. TechRxiv (2022). https://doi.org/10.36227/techrxiv.18515357.v1
25. Salvi, R.S., Labhsetwar, S.R., Kolte, P.A., et al.: Predictive analysis of diabetic retinopathy with transfer learning. In: 2021 4th Biennial International Conference on Nascent Technologies in Engineering (ICNTE), pp 1–6. IEEE (2021)
26. Gao, Y., Li, M., Peng, Y., et al.: Double stage transfer learning for brain-computer interfaces. IEEE Trans. Neural Syst. Rehabil. Eng. 1128–1136 (2023)
27. Mukhlif, A.A., Al-Khateeb, B., Mohammed, M.A.: Incorporating a novel dual transfer learning approach for medical images. Sens. (Basel) **23**, 570 (2023)

28. de Matos, J., Britto, A.D.S., Oliveira, L.E.S., Koerich, A.L.: Double transfer learning for breast cancer histopathologic image classification. In: 2019 International Joint Conference on Neural Networks (IJCNN), pp 1–8. IEEE (2019)

29. Dane, K.M.S.: APTOS 2019 blindness detection. In: Kaggle (2019). https://www.kaggle.com/competitions/aptos2019-blindness-detection/data. Accessed 2 May 2023

30. Llamas Ahumada, J.J.: Prevalencia de retinopatía leucémica y su asociación con el tipo de leucemia. In: Repositorio Institucional de la UNAM (2014). https://ru.dgb.unam.mx/handle/20.500.14330/TES01000717129. Accessed 24 June 2023

31. Kaggle. Diabetic Retinopathy (resized). In: Kaggle (2019). https://www.kaggle.com/tanlikesmath/diabetic-retinopathy-resized. Accessed 18 Jan 2024

32. The Retina Image Bank. Exudative Diabetic Maculopathy (2013). https://imagebank.asrs.org/file/11890/exudative-diabetic-maculopathy. Accessed 18 Jan 2024

33. Aliseda, D., Berástegui, L.: Retinopatía diabética. An. Sist. Sanit. Navar. **31**, 23–34 (2008)

34. Goyal, M.: Acute myeloid leukemia. In: Retina Image Bank (2012). https://imagebank.asrs.org/file/2175/acute-myeloid-leukemia. Accessed 18 Jan 2024

35. Heo, J., Ahn, J., Yoon, Y.H., et al.: Leukemia. In: Gupta, V., Nguyen, Q., LeHoang, P., Agarwal, A. (eds.) The Uveitis Atlas, pp. 637–644. Springer, New Delhi (2020). https://doi.org/10.1007/978-81-322-2410-5_101

36. Bekmez, S., Eris, D.: Retinal arterial macroaneurysm in leukemia. Eur. J. Ophthalmol. **32**, NP22–NP25 (2022)

37. Abadi, M., Agarwal, A., et al.: Transfer learning and fine-tuning. In: TensorFlow (2023). https://www.tensorflow.org/tutorials/images/transfer_learning. Accessed 21 Feb 2024

38. Tan, M., Le, Q.V.: EfficientNetV2: Smaller models and faster training. arXiv (2021). https://doi.org/10.48550/arXiv.2104.00298

39. Eckstein, W., Munkelt, O., Steger, C.A.: MVTec. In: HALCON - The Powerful Machine Vision Software: MVTec Software (1997). https://www.mvtec.com/products/halcon. Accessed 31 Jan 2024

40. Sheng, H., O'Keeffe, B.: Deep learning development platform. In: Medicmind (2021). https://www.medicmind.tech/. Accessed 31 Jan 2024

Classification of Breast Lesions Using Mammary Sinograms and Deep Learning

Estefania Ruiz Muñoz⑩, Leopoldo Altamirano Robles(✉)⑩,
and Raquel Díaz Hernández⑩

Instituto Nacional de Astrofísica, Óptica y Electrónica, Luis Enrique Erro #1, Sta. María
Tonanzintla, 72840 San Andrés Cholula, Mexico
robles@inaoep.mx

Abstract. Breast cancer is a disease that affects many women worldwide. Therefore, early detection of breast lesions is essential for effective diagnosis and treatment. In this context, digital breast tomosynthesis (DBT) is a promising technique
for improving lesion detection compared to conventional mammography. However, image reconstruction can lead to a loss of information. Sinograms provide
sufficient information for identifying and localizing lesions while reducing the
noise and artifacts associated with the image reconstruction process. In this paper,
we propose to employ image processing and deep learning techniques, especially
convolutional neural networks (CNN), to identify patterns and extract relevant
information from DBT sinograms. The objective is to facilitate diagnosis and
treatment through the analysis of sinograms, allowing the identification of patterns
and the extraction of useful information for continuous monitoring and evaluation of treatment over time. The results show that the ResNet50 and ResNet18
models have demonstrated a solid performance in classifying breast lesions from
sinograms, with outstanding results in accuracy, recall, and F1-score of 94.96%,
supporting their efficacy in this task. It is essential to highlight that although there
are studies on sinograms in other fields, their application in diagnosing breast
lesions has not yet been explored.

Keywords: sinograms · DBT · detection · classification · CNN · breast lesions

1 Introduction

Breast cancer is a disease that affects a large number of women worldwide. Early and
accurate detection of breast lesions is essential for effective diagnosis and treatment
[1]. In this regard, Digital Breast Tomosynthesis (DBT) has emerged as a promising
medical imaging technique that improves lesion detection compared to conventional
mammography [2].

DBT produces sinograms from thin-layer projections of the region of interest that
are combined to generate two-dimensional images with X-ray information from various
angles. These sinograms are then used to reconstruct three-dimensional images using
computational algorithms [3]. The reconstruction allows the use of image processing

E. Mezura-Montes et al. (Eds.): MCPR 2024, LNCS 14755, pp. 253–263, 2024.
https://doi.org/10.1007/978-3-031-62836-8_24

and data analysis tools, which are necessary for a correct interpretation of the images. However, the image reconstruction process from sinograms can cause a loss of information due to interpolation steps, suboptimal statistical weighting, shading, and other artifacts caused by the reconstruction process. These factors can lead to inaccuracies in lesion detection and localization [4].

The sinograms provide detailed and distributed information throughout the projection data. This information allows the detection and localization of lesions. In addition, they improve image quality by evaluating noise and spatial resolution, thus reducing possible errors in diagnosis [4]. This feature makes sinograms a valuable source of information for detecting and classifying breast lesions. Therefore, the need arises to develop a method to aid in diagnosis by detecting and classifying breast lesions using DBT sinograms.

This research aims to provide effective detection and characterization of these lesions. To address this problem, it is proposed to use image processing and deep learning techniques, specifically CNNs, to identify patterns and obtain relevant information about breast lesions in sinograms. In this way, the aim is to facilitate diagnosis, enable effective monitoring of treatments, and evaluate their success over time by classifying breast lesions in sinogram images.

This article contributes to the advancement of breast lesion detection and classification using DBT sinograms and CNNs, which may contribute to the accuracy of breast cancer diagnosis and treatment. Although previous research on sinograms has been conducted in other areas, their specific application in breast lesion detection has not yet been explored. During the study, several CNN model architectures, such as Res-Net, MobileNet, AlexNet, and Inceptionv3, were evaluated using transfer learning to adapt the pre-trained models to mammary sinograms. In addition, techniques such as learning rate adjustment and regularization were applied to improve model performance. Metrics used to evaluate the models included accuracy, recall, and F1-score. Among the models tested, ResNet50 and ResNet18 demonstrated high performance, with an accuracy, recall, and F1-score of 94.96%.

2 Related Work

Below are some relevant research studies in lesion detection and classification from sinograms, along with significant advances in other areas, such as computed tomography (CT) using CNNs. A 2018 study proposed the Machine Friendly Machine Learning approach, which uses CT sinogram data to train machine learning models. The results demonstrated an accuracy of 97.5% in pathology detection, comparable to traditional methods using reconstructed images [5]. In 2019, a method based on deep learning neural networks was presented to improve CT lung nodule detection using sinogram space, achieving an AUC of 91%. This method significantly outperformed existing approaches regarding sensitivity and accuracy [6]. In 2023, an automated process was proposed to detect and classify intracranial hemorrhages directly from sinograms using deep learning, with an accuracy of 94%. This approach eliminated the need for image reconstruction, reduced noise and artifacts, and improved accuracy and robustness [7].

On the other hand, sinogram analysis has been used to improve image quality before image reconstruction. In 2017, a study proposed a method to enhance low-dose computed tomography (CT) images. They used maximum posteriori estimation (MAP) in sinogram preprocessing, considering the statistical properties of the noise. The results showed that the proposed method improves the quality of the images compared to previous methods [8]. In 2018, super-resolution imaging was employed to enhance the quality of PET scanners from sinograms, demonstrating the potential for efficient and cost-effective PET systems [9]. In 2019, a deep learning framework was proposed to reconstruct PET images directly from sinograms, prioritizing quality and speed and demonstrating superior performance in image quality, reconstruction speed, and robustness [10]. In 2020, a neural network was used to reconstruct high-quality PET images from sinogram data, generating high-quality images faster and with fewer artifacts than traditional PET image reconstruction methods [11]. Another study from the same year investigated the generation of full-dose PET images from low-dose images and sinograms using deep learning techniques, finding that the PET images generated in projection space had better quality and lower variation in SUV values than those generated in image space [12]. In 2021, brain PET/CT data were used to create low-dose (LD) and full-dose (FD) sinograms and then generated FD images from LD using neural networks, finding that the sinogram-space method produced higher quality images and lower bias compared to the image-space method [13]. Another study from the same year compared a sinogram-based image reconstruction algorithm (DLIR) with ASIR-V in abdominal computed tomography. DLIR outperformed ASIR-V, and DLIR-H had the best scores in image quality, noise, contrast, and sharpness [14]. Finally, in 2022, The study presents a PET reconstruction method using deep learning from sinogram in long axial field-of-view PET. It improves image quality and reduces reconstruction time without additional CT imaging [15].

The literature review reveals a remarkable scarcity of specific studies on the detection and classification of breast lesions using DBT sinograms, despite advances in other medical imaging modalities. This study presents a breakthrough by proposing and evaluating methods to address this task, notable for its comprehensive comparison with the state of the art and meticulous analysis of metrics such as accuracy, recall, and F1-score. The results show outstanding performance in detecting and classifying breast lesions in DBT sinograms, supporting the effectiveness of this innovative approach. The ResNet50 and ResNet18 models obtained an accuracy, recall, and F1-score of 94.96%, suggesting their potential as a valid alternative in this field, thus filling an important gap in digital mammography.

3 Method

3.1 Model Selection

The ResNet, MobileNet, and AlexNet models benefited from the transfer of learning by using ImageNet's pre-trained weights, while InceptionV3 was initialized with random weights. Among the models used, ResNet18 and MobileNet stand out for their efficiency and low resource consumption. On the other hand, ResNet50 and InceptionV3 offer higher accuracy when adequate resources are available. It is important to mention that MobileNet stands out for its faster inference speed (Table 1).

Table 1. Description of the CNNs models used in the training. Information on each model's number of layers, description, size, and parameters is presented [8].

Model	Layers	Size	Parameters	Top1-Accuracy	Top5-Acuraccy
ResNet50	50	96 MB	26 M	0.749	0.921
ResNet18	18	44–47 MB	11.7 M	0.69–0.71	0.89–0.91
AlexNet	8	320 MB	60 M	0.57	.80
MobileNet	57	7–18 MB	1.6 a 3.4 M	0.70–0.74	0.89–0.95
InceptionV3	48	92 MB	23.9 M	77.9	93.7

3.2 Computer Equipment

The hardware and software used in conducting the experiments are as follows: an NVIDIA GeForce GTX 1060 Ti card, with CUDA version 11.8 and CUDNN version 11, an Intel(R) Core (TM) i7-10750H CPU @ 2.60 GHz 2.59 GHz, backed by 16.0 GB of RAM (15.8 GB usable), all running on the Windows 11 operating system. The models were evaluated in both Python and the Deep Learning tool platform.

3.3 Databases

The study is based on a DBT dataset from Duke Health [16], available at: https://jam anetwork.com/journals/jamanetworkopen/fullarticle/2783046. This dataset comprises 4,829 studies of 4,348 patients, generating 19,230 reconstruction volumes. Of these, 22,032 volumes correspond to 5,060 patients, but only 224 DBT images are labeled and will be used for training CNNs. The images, being real reconstructions, are used to calculate sinograms using the inverse radon transform, as seen in Fig. 2.

The data set is divided into 70% for training, 15% for validation, and 15% for testing. Given the limited size of the data set, data augmentation techniques are applied, generating a total of 2,460 augmented images. Of these, 1,722 are used for training, 369 for validation, and 369 for testing.

3.4 Preprocessing

A detailed evaluation of the various preprocessing techniques used to detect and classify breast lesions in DBT sinograms is performed. These techniques, ranging from data normalization to smoothing and contrast enhancement, were systematically applied and their effect on classification accuracy was analyzed. Each step of the image processing process was performed in MATLAB and has specific objectives that contribute to improving the quality of the images and preparing them for further analysis, as seen in Fig. 1:

Smoothing. The main objective is to remove noise and imperfections from images and smooth transitions between pixels, facilitating subsequent analysis and improving visual quality.

Equalization. Seeks to enhance image contrast by redistributing pixel intensities, which can highlight details and improve image display in areas of low-intensity difference.

Contrast Adjustment. This step focuses on highlighting features of interest by adjusting the range of pixel intensities, which can make essential details more noticeable and facilitate visual interpretation of the image.

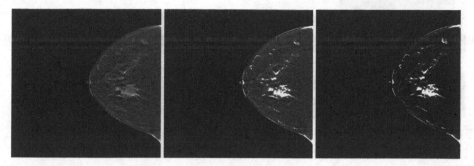

Fig. 1. Image preprocessing steps: smoothing, equalization, and contrast adjustment.

Sinogram Generation: A sinogram represents the information of the image projections from different angles, which is essential for DBT applications and three-dimensional image reconstruction.

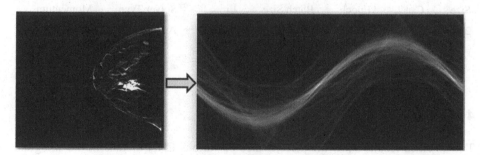

Fig. 2. Conversion of a Real Image to Sinogram Space through the Inverse Radon Transform.

Image enhancement. As an additional step, image augmentation was implemented in the sinogram images. This step involves applying transformations to existing images to generate new instances that enrich the data set. Some standard image augmentation techniques include Flipping, rotation, noise, shearing, shimmering, transforming, solarizing, and scaling and rotation.

Resizing. The objective is to resize the images to be compatible with the algorithm or processing requirements, simplifying their handling and analysis. In this case, they were resized to 224×224 pixels.

Label. The images were organized in two folders, one for benign and one for malignant lesions. Subsequently, manual editing was performed to subcategorize them in each corresponding folder. In addition, "benign" and "malignant" labels were assigned with values 1 and 2, respectively, as shown in Fig. 3.

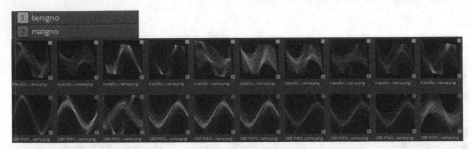

Fig. 3. Labels for each class (Benign 1, Malignant 2).

Hyperparameters. The following are the parameters used during the training process as shown in Table 2. These hyperparameters were selected through experimentation and fine-tuning to achieve a balance between accuracy and model performance.

Table 2. Hyperparameters are used to perform the training.

Size	Canal	Epoch	Batch Size	Lr	Solver Type	Momentum
224	1	70	8–32	0.0001	Adam	0.9

4   Results

The obtained results show the performance of various CNN models in the sinogram classification task. Metrics such as accuracy, recall, F1-score, top1-error, inference time, and preprocessing time are presented for each model.

According to the data in Table 3, it is highlighted that models such as ResNet50, ResNet18, and MobileNet show remarkably high accuracy and recall. Among them, ResNet18 and ResNet50 exhibit the most outstanding accuracy along with low top-1 error. Although AlexNet exhibits competitive performance on all metrics, it is slightly inferior to the ResNet models. On the other hand, InceptionV3 shows a more modest performance in terms of F1-score and recall, despite having a longer inference time.

The analysis of breast lesion classification using sinograms and deep learning shows significant differences in the performance of the models evaluated. This study is based on a dataset composed of a total of 2,460 breast sinograms, balanced between "Benign" and "Malignant" classes, with 1,230 samples for each.

Table 3. Analysis of Sinogram Classification Performance Metrics. The two most prominent results have been highlighted in bold.

Model	Accuracy	Recall	F1-score	Top1-error	Inference Time	Preprocess Time
ResNet50	**94.96%**	**94.96%**	**94.96%**	**5.04%**	**7.39 ms**	**0.63 ms**
ResNet18	**94.96%**	**94.96%**	**94.96%**	**5.04%**	**3.75 ms**	**0.66 ms**
AlexNet	91.6%	91.6%	91.58%	8.4%	2.52 ms	0.62 ms
MobileNet	94.73%	94.75%	94.75%	5.25%	8.55 ms	0.5 ms
InceptionV3	75%	38%	53%	25%	15 ms	0.30 ms

The ResNet50, ResNet18, AlexNet, and MobileNet architectures show accuracy, recall, and F1-score above 90%, accurately capturing the relevant features of breast sinograms and improving lesion classification capability. These results suggest that, for sinogram classification, ResNet50 and ResNet18 may be preferable due to their balance between accuracy, recall, F1-score, and top1-error, also considering inference time. These results are consistent because they share significant similarities in their underlying architecture and design approach, despite differences in network depth and complexity. Both models share numerous fundamental features, such as convolutional layers, ReLU activations, and regularization techniques.

In contrast, InceptionV3 exhibits significantly lower performance, with accuracy, recall, and F1-score values around 75%, 38%, and 53% respectively, suggesting that its architecture may not be suitable for capturing the relevant features of mammary sinograms. Inference and preprocessing time are also important considerations, as more complex models require more inference time, but offer higher accuracy and recall, while lighter models have shorter inference times but slightly lower performance. Regarding the classification of "Benign" and "Malignant" classes, both ResNet50 and ResNet18 show equal results, suggesting that both models have robust and nearly equivalent performance in classifying breast lesions (Tables 4 and 5).

Table 4. Analysis of sinogram classification performance metrics using the ResNet50 model by class.

Class	FP/Predicted	Precision	FN/Labeled	Recall	F1-Score
Benign	17/248	93.15%	7/238	97.06%	95.06%
Malignant	7/228	96.93%	17/238	92.86%	94.85%

Based on the confusion matrices presented in Table 6 and Table 7, both ResNet50 and ResNet18 perform robustly in classifying "Benign" and "Malignant" classes. Both models have a low number of false positives and false negatives compared to true positives, suggesting a practical ability to discriminate between classes and classify mammary lesions as benign or malignant.

Table 5. Analysis of sinogram classification performance metrics using the ResNet18 model by class.

Class	FP/Predicted	Precision	FN/Labeled	Recall	F1-Score
Benign	17/248	93.15%	7/238	97.06%	95.06%
Malignant	7/228	96.93%	17/238	92.86%	94.85%

Table 6. Confusion matrix of the ResNet50 model.

	Benign	Malignant	FP
Benign	231	17	17
Malignant	7	221	7
FN	7	17	24

Table 7. Confusion matrix of the ResNet18 model.

	Benigno	Malignant	FP
Benign	231	17	17
Malignant	7	221	7
FN	7	17	24

Evaluation of ResNet50 and ResNet18 indicates a reasonable ability to differentiate between benign and malignant breast lesions. The majority of benign observations (231) were correctly identified as true positives, although 17 were misclassified as malignant (false positives), highlighting the need for improved specificity. Likewise, 17 malignant observations were incorrectly identified as benign (false negatives), suggesting an opportunity to improve sensitivity. Although the number of false positives and false negatives is relatively low, there are areas where both models could be improved, especially in the accurate identification of malignant lesions. In summary, both ResNet50 and ResNet18 show reasonable performance in classifying breast lesions from sinograms.

Regarding the evolution of loss during training and validation, it was observed that ResNet18 presents a lower loss (0.00282968) compared to ResNet50 (0.0411653). This low loss suggests that ResNet18 might have a better generalization ability on this specific dataset, as shown in Figs. 4 and 5. Although ResNet50 is deeper and has a higher representation capability, the results indicate that ResNet18 achieves a lower minimum loss, suggesting a better generalization ability and possibly a lower propensity to overfit on this dataset.

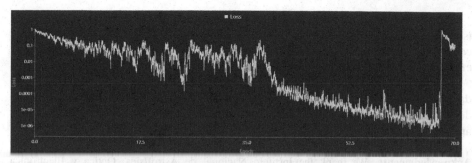

Fig. 4. Loss graph of the ResNet50 model.

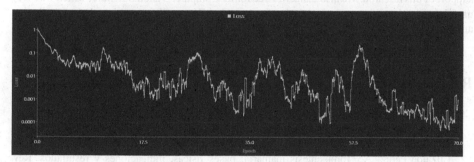

Fig. 5. Loss graph of the ResNet18 model.

5 Discussion

Breast lesion detection from sinograms offers significant advantages in providing information about breast structure and capturing features that might be missed in other medical imaging modalities, including reconstructed images. The results of this research highlight the performance of both ResNet50 and ResNet18 in classifying breast lesions from sinograms. Both models showed high accuracies, recalls, and F1-scores, demonstrating their effectiveness in this specific task. Recognition from sinograms presents significant potential in breast lesion detection and classification. Although the ResNet50 and ResNet18 models have proven to be effective, continued research and exploration of new strategies are required to advance this field.

6 Conclusion

In this study, the potential of breast lesion recognition and classification using sinograms and deep learning in the medical field has been demonstrated. Sinograms provide detailed information about the breast structure, which makes them a valuable tool for breast lesion detection and classification. The results show that the ResNet50 and ResNet18 models perform robustly in classifying breast lesions from sinograms. Both models achieved high levels of accuracy, recall, and F1-score, demonstrating their efficacy in this task. It is suggested to explore van-guard techniques, such as Transformer-based networks and capsular networks, for future research and comparison.

This research supports the idea that recognition and classification from sinograms is a valuable tool in the diagnosis of breast lesions. The combination of sinograms and convolutional neural network models shows great potential for improving accuracy and efficiency in the early diagnosis of breast disease.

For future work, we plan to optimize the neural network models, expand the available datasets, explore advanced data augmentation techniques, and clinically validate the developed models. These additional steps will allow further refinement of the algorithms and a better understanding of their performance in real clinical settings.

Acknowledgments. We thank the Instituto Nacional de Astrofísica, Óptica y Electrónica (INAOE), and the Consejo Nacional de Ciencia y Tecnología (CONAHCYT) for their financial support of this research. We also thank MVTec for its Computer Vision Software, which was very useful for the development and analysis of our results. We greatly appreciate their contribution and thank them for their continued support in future research.

References

1. Bhushan, A., Gonsalves, A., Menon, J.U.: Current state of breast cancer diagnosis, treatment, and theranostics. Pharmaceutics **13**(5), 723 (2021). https://doi.org/10.3390/PHARMACEU TICS13050723
2. Elizalde Pérez, A.: Tomosíntesis mamaria: bases físicas, indicaciones y resultados. Rev. Senología Patología Mamaria – J. Breast Sci. **28**(1), 39–45 (2015). https://doi.org/10.1016/J. SENOL.2014.10.004
3. Teuwen, J., et al.: Deep learning reconstruction of digital breast tomosynthesis images for accurate breast density and patient-specific radiation dose estimation. Med. Image Anal. **71** (2021). https://doi.org/10.1016/j.media.2021.102061
4. De Man, Q., et al.: A two-dimensional feasibility study of deep learning-based feature detection and characterization directly from CT sonograms. In: Medical Physics, pp. e790–e800. Wiley (2019). https://doi.org/10.1002/mp.13640
5. Lee, H., Huang, C., Yune, S., Tajmir, S.H., Kim, M., Do, S.: Machine friendly machine learning: interpretation of computed tomography without image reconstruction (2018). http://arxiv.org/abs/1812.01068
6. Gao, Y., Tan, J., Liang, Z., Li, L., Huo, Y.: Improved computer-aided detection of pulmonary nodules via deep learning in the sinogram domain. Vis. Comput. Ind. Biomed. Art **2**(1) (2019). https://doi.org/10.1186/s42492-019-0029-2
7. Sindhura, C., Al Fahim, M., Yalavarthy, P.K., Gorthi, S.: Fully automated sinogram-based deep learning model for detection and classification of intracranial hemorrhage. Med. Phys. (2023). https://doi.org/10.1002/mp.16714
8. Xie, Q., et al.: Robust low-dose CT sinogram preprocessing via exploiting noise-generating mechanism. IEEE Trans. Med. Imaging **36**(12), 2487–2498 (2017). https://doi.org/10.1109/TMI.2017.2767290
9. Hong, X., Zan, Y., Weng, F., Tao, W., Peng, Q., Huang, Q.: Enhancing the image quality via transferred deep residual learning of coarse PET sinograms. IEEE Trans. Med. Imaging **37**(10), 2322–2332 (2018). https://doi.org/10.1109/TMI.2018.2830381
10. Liu, Z., Ye, H., Liu, H.: Deep-learning-based framework for PET image reconstruction from sinogram domain. Appl. Sci. **12**(16), 8118 (2022). https://doi.org/10.3390/APP12168118

11. Whiteley, W., Luk, W.K., Gregor, J.: DirectPET: full-size neural network PET reconstruction from sinogram data. J. Med. Imaging **7**(03), 1 (2020). https://doi.org/10.1117/1.jmi.7.3.032503

12. Sanaat, A., Arabi, H., Mainta, I., Garibotto, V., Zaidi, H.: Projection space implementation of deep learning-guided low-dose brain PET imaging improves performance over implementation in image space. J. Nucl. Med. **61**(9), 1386–1396 (2020). https://doi.org/10.2967/JNUMED.119.239327

13. Sanaat, A., Shooli, H., Ferdowsi, S., Shiri, I., Arabi, H., Zaidi, H.: DeepTOFSino: a deep learning model for synthesizing full-dose time-of-flight bin sinograms from their corresponding low-dose sinograms. Neuroimage **245**, 118697 (2021). https://doi.org/10.1016/J.NEUROIMAGE.2021.118697

14. Parakh, A., Cao, J., Pierce, T.T., Blake, M.A., Savage, C.A., Kambadakone, A.R.: Sinogram-based deep learning image reconstruction technique in abdominal CT: image quality considerations. Eur. Radiol. **31**(11), 8342–8353 (2021). https://doi.org/10.1007/S00330-021-07952-4

15. Ma, R., et al.: An encoder-decoder network for direct image reconstruction on sinograms of a long axial field of view PET. Eur. J. Nucl. Med. Mol. Imaging **49**(13), 4464–4477 (2022). https://doi.org/10.1007/S00259-022-05861-2/TABLES/3

16. Buda, M., et al.: A data set and deep learning algorithm for the detection of masses and architectural distortions in digital breast tomosynthesis images. JAMA Netw. Open **4**(8), e2119100–e2119100 (2021). https://doi.org/10.1001/JAMANETWORKOPEN.2021.19100

Ultrasound Bone Surface Segmentation for Hip Joint Arthroscopy: Evaluating a Local Phase-Based and a Rigid Object Filtering in a Simulated Environment

Eduardo de Avila-Armenta[1]([✉]), Jose M. Celaya-Padilla[1],
Robert B. A. Adamson[2], Gamaliel Moreno-Chavez[1],
Antonio Martinez-Torteya[3], Manuel A. Soto-Murillo[1],
Diana L. Jácome-Cadena[4], Jorge I. Galván-Tejada[1],
M. Hazael Guerrero-Flores[1], and Miguel A. Cid-Baez[5]

[1] Unidad Académica de Ingeniería Eléctrica, Universidad Autónoma de Zacatecas,
Jardín Juarez 147, Centro, 98000 Zacatecas, Mexico
edavilaa@uaz.edu.mx
[2] Electrical and Computer Engineering Department, Dalhousie University, Halifax,
NS B3H 4R2, Canada
[3] Escuela de Ingeniería y Tecnologías, Universidad de Monterrey, Avenida Ignacio
Morones Prieto 4500 Pte., Jesús M. Garza, 66238 San Pedro Garza García, Nuevo
León, Mexico
[4] Unidad Académica de Medicina Humana y Ciencias de la Salud, Universidad
Autónoma de Zacatecas, Jardín Juarez 147, Centro, 98000 Zacatecas, Mexico
[5] Módulo de Salud Integral, Área de Ciencias de la Salud, Universidad Autónoma de
Zacatecas, Jardín Juarez 147, Centro, 98000 Zacatecas, Mexico

Abstract. Arthroscopy is a well-known procedure, classified as a minimally invasive procedure, the objective is to image inside the joints, as the hip joint. Although its use is being prioritized over others, this procedure is not exempt from certain complications, such as disorientation, reduced area of vision and loss of depth perception. To address this problem, clinicians relays on imaging systems for guidance, as Ultrasound (US). However, US presents some challenges, including a low signal-to-noise ratio, the need to address speckle noise, and a considerable learning curve. Efforts have been made to improve US-based bone detection so that it can be integrated into computer-assisted orthopedic surgery (CAOS) systems. In this paper, a bone surface segmentation algorithm based on local phases and combined with a rigid object filtering is presented. This algorithm is implemented in a simulated environment, where a 3D print of the hip joint is used as a target and a low-cost mannequin is made for soft tissue simulation. The evaluation metrics are presented, being a F-Score (0.979), Accuracy (0.9796), Recall (0.9883), and Hamming Loss (0.024).

Keywords: Ultrasound (US) imaging · hip joint segmentation · local phase · rigid object filtering · simulated environment

E. Mezura-Montes et al. (Eds.): MCPR 2024, LNCS 14755, pp. 264–273, 2024.
https://doi.org/10.1007/978-3-031-62836-8_25

1   Introduction

Arthroscopy is a well-known procedure, classified as a minimally invasive procedure (MIP), where the objective is to image inside of the joints, such as the hip, knees and shoulders [1]. The adoption of arthroscopic procedures, has significantly grown in recent decades, since they are preferred by the patients and clinical institutions due to the rapid recovery, and the minimal soft tissue damage [2]. In the case of hip arthroscopy alone, its use has significantly increased more than 25 times since the early 2000's [3].

Although its use is being prioritized over others, this procedure is not exempt from certain complications, such as disorientation, reduced area of vision and loss of depth perception [3]. To address this problem, clinicians relays on imaging systems for guidance, such as fluoroscopy and ultrasound (US). Due to its use of non-ionizing radiation and its affordability and portability, US is being selected over fluoroscopy for bone detection tasks in orthopedic procedures [4].

Despite the advantages of the US, it presents some challenges, such as a low signal-to-noise ratio, the need to address speckle noise, and a considerable learning curve [5]. However, efforts have been made to improve US-based bone detection so that it can be integrated into computer-assisted orthopedic surgery (CAOS) systems [6,7].

In the state of the art, various methods have been proposed for the segmentation of the bone surface with ultrasound images. These range from applications of machine learning, deep learning and image processing techniques. Alsinan et al. [6], proposed a methodology based on convolutional neural networks (CNN) and local phase filtered images, fusioning feature maps and employing the original B-mode US images and the local phase responses as multi-modal input images. They validated their results with various metrics, comparing the resulting segmentation with the segmentation performed manually by an expert. The best achieved metrics were an Intersection over Union (IoU) of 0.9728 and a F-Score of 0.9783.

Authors Wang et al. [7], presents a method for segmenting bone surfaces from ultrasound images using CNNs guided by a local phase tensor. Here, authors combine the local phase tensor and the global context tensor, in order to produce the final segmentation map. They achieved a F-score of 0.882 and a precision of 0.920, compared with manually segmentation masks created by experts. The research group lead by Bak [8], presented a method for detecting bone and skin regions in ultrasound images of joints, they used a pure image processing filtering stage, as well as machine learning classification algorithms. The best results were achieved by the Random Forest classifier with a recall score of 0.96, and an accuracy of 0.92.

In this paper, a bone surface segmentation algorithm based on local phases is presented, where in the first stage features such as phase symmetry and asymmetry are obtained, and unlike other methodologies in the state of the art, it is intended to obtain the bone surface through a process of rigid filtering of objects in the image, obtaining features such as area and depth. This algorithm is implemented in a simulated environment, where a 3D print of the hip joint is used as a target and a low-cost mannequin is made for soft tissue simulation.

2   Material and Methods

The proposed method is intended to be applied first in a simulated environment. Various researches have shown that low-cost mannequins can be made aiming to simulate the soft tissue in ultrasound imaging, a technique that is preferred for teaching and practice methods [9]. The mannequin made consists of a 3D print of the hip joint area, immersed in a solidified gelatin mixture. A total of 10 ultrasound series of 100 images each, were taken with the wireless linear doppler ultrasound probe model SONOWIRELESS-SONOMED. All the images had the acquisition parameters of 10MHz frequency, 59 dB of Gain and a depth of 60mm. Once the images were taken, 100 random images were selected to create the segmentation masks manually by an expert and by the algorithm, this in order to create a validation stage. The proposed method is shown in Fig. 1, in the following subsections the entire process will be described in detail.

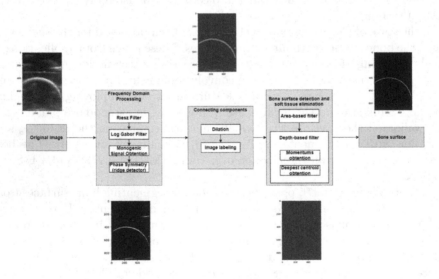

Fig. 1. Proposed experimental design.

2.1   Frequency Domain Processing

In the Medical Image Processing field, spatial domain processing is mostly used. However, some algorithms could present trouble in pattern recognition tasks, such as the differentiation between anatomical structures and anatomical border delimitation. Specifically, US has a poor signal to noise ratio (SNR) [7].

Due to the nature of the acoustic waves interacting with tissue structures, US images leads with the speckle noise. This noise is characterized for the presence of granular texture, being a random patterns of bright and dark spots. Due of the variability on intensity all over the image, traditional spatial domain algorithms are not suitable to process US images, thus, frequency domain processing becomes a viable option [5,7]. A well established methodological framework corresponds to the monogenic signal processing. This paper uses the mathematical framework proposed by Rajpoot et al. [10], and Mulet et al. [11], for frequency domain processing.

Analytic Signal. In order to understand monogenic signal firstly is necessary to study the analytic signal, which is a signal processing methodology introduced by Felsberg and Sommer [12]. The analytic signal, is represented mathematically as:

$$f_A(x) = f(x) + iH[f(x)] \tag{1}$$

In terms of frequency domain, the representation of analytic signal is:

$$F_A(\omega) = F(\omega) + F_h(\omega) \tag{2}$$

where, F_h is the original signal after the Hilbert transform has been applied, being:

$$F_h(\omega) = \begin{cases} F(\omega) & \omega > 0 \\ -F(\omega) & \omega < 0 \\ 0 & \omega = 0 \end{cases} \tag{3}$$

Thus, the analytic signal can be understand as a signal without negative frequency components, which is important for a local phase analysis. In the other hand, the monogenic signal is based on the analytic signal being its 2D extension, where instead of using the Hilbert Transform the Riesz filter and quadrature filters are used. The monogenic signal are designed to highlight certain details, such as specific edges, textures, or patterns present in the images. Specifically in medical imaging, the monogenic signal is used to facilitate the detection of anatomical structures, such as specific tissues, borders or lesions.

Riesz Transform. Riesz transform is a generalization of Hilbert transform in 2D, and is used to decompose an image into multiple scales. In monogenic signal framework, the Riesz Filter is a valued odd filter, and in terms of Fourier domain, can be expressed as:

$$(H_1(u,v), H_2(u,v)) = \left(i\frac{u}{\sqrt{u^2 + v^2}}, i\frac{v}{\sqrt{u^2 + v^2}} \right) \tag{4}$$

Quadrature Filters. As mentioned before, in the monogenic signal framework, quadrature filters are also important. They consists of a pair of linear filters whose outputs are 90° out of phase with each other. Also, quadrature filters are commonly given as filter banks, therefore this makes them suitable to analyse the image in different frequencies and directions.

One of the most used quadrature filters, corresponds to Log-Gabor filter, since this filters captures features in different frequency bands and different orientations. Additionally, this type of filters are radially symmetric about the origin in both, the frequency and the spatial domain. Log-Gabor filter in the frequency domain is expressed as:

$$G(\omega) = exp\left(-\frac{(log(\frac{\omega}{\omega_0}))^2}{2(log(\frac{k}{\omega_0})^2}\right), \tag{5}$$

where, ω_0 is the central frequency of the band pass filter and k is related to the bandwidth filter.

Monogenic Signal. Once the concepts of Riez Transform and Log-Gabor filters are introduced, is possible to formulate the math expression of monogenic signal. Since the interpretation in spatial domain of Log-Gabor filter and Riesz Transform could be difficult to implement correctly, is feasible to express the formulation in frequency domain by transforming the image in the Fourier space. Thus, having the expression:

$$F_M = \begin{bmatrix} \mathcal{F}[f(x,y)] \cdot [G_\omega] \\ \mathcal{F}[f(x,y)] \cdot [G_\omega] \cdot H_1(u,v) \\ \mathcal{F}[f(x,y)] \cdot [G_\omega] \cdot H_2(u,v) \end{bmatrix} = \begin{bmatrix} F_{M1} \\ F_{M2} \\ F_{M3} \end{bmatrix} = \begin{bmatrix} even \\ odd_1 \\ odd_2 \end{bmatrix}, \tag{6}$$

where $\mathcal{F}[f(x,y)]$ is the Fourier Transform of the original image $f(x,y)$. It is easy to see that the resulting tensor will be composed of an even part F_{M1} and two odd parts (F_{M2} and F_{M3}). In order to obtain just one even and one odd part, it would be expressed as:

$$even_{MG} = F_{M1} \tag{7}$$

$$odd_{MG} = \sqrt{F_{M2}^2 + F_{M3}^2} \tag{8}$$

Rajpoot et al. [10], argues that by obtaining the real part of the odd signals, then one can construct an analytical signal like:

$$F_{MG} = even_{MG}(x,y) + i * odd_{MG}(x,y) \tag{9}$$

It is worth mentioning that, the proposed method of this authors losses the local orientation information, but the local phase information is unaffected, and it simplifies calculations and power computation.

Phase Symmetry and Phase Asymmetry. The advantage of using the monogenic signal framework, is that various features can be obtained that can highlight or suppress certain information in the image. In the state of the art, many researchers uses the Phase Symmetry (PS) and Phase Asymmetry (PA) features. PS, works basically as a ridge detector, capturing the information near to the central frequency. In the other hand, PA captures the phase response near 0 or π, which can be interpreted as a edge detector. This features are expressed by the equations:

$$PS(x,y) = \frac{\lfloor |even_{MG}(x,y)| - |odd_{MG}(x,y)| - T \rfloor}{\sqrt{even_{MG}^2(x,y) + odd_{MG}^2(x,y)}} \qquad (10)$$

$$PA(x,y) = \frac{\lfloor |odd_{MG}(x,y)| - |even_{MG}(x,y)| - T \rfloor}{\sqrt{even_{MG}^2(x,y) + odd_{MG}^2(x,y)}} \qquad (11)$$

where T is a threshold proposed by Rajpoot et al. [10], that is obtained by applying:

$$T = exp^{log\left(mean\left(\sqrt{even_{MG}^2 + odd_{MG}^2}\right)\right)} \qquad (12)$$

The T threshold and the $\lfloor ... \rfloor$ operator, removes negative values by putting a zero value, which helps to have a better response from either the PS or PA.

2.2 Bone Surface Detection

After applying frequency domain processing and obtaining the phase symmetry (PS) feature, the resulting image may exhibit highlighted areas, including the bone, which is expected to have one of the strongest signals. However, it may also contain noise generated by soft tissue or acoustic echoes. Consequently, a connected components analysis and rigid filtering stage are performed. This stage is termed rigid filtering because it operates based on two primary assumptions: that the bone surface will be one of the largest areas and that it will also be one of the deepest objects in the image.

Connecting Components. Due to the bone morphology and the sound properties, when imaging the bone, some parts are not connected. That happens, especially when capturing a highly curved part, such as the femoral head. To face this problem, first the morphological operation of dilation needs to be applied. The dilation is obtained by windowing the image ($f(x,y)$) with a structuring element, also called kernel ($K(s,t)$), whose domain can be expressed as $K^{S \times T}$. The math expression of the dilation operator is given by:

$$(f \oplus K)(x,y) = \max_{S \times T} f(x-s, y-t) \qquad (13)$$

After the dilation with a rectangular 3×3 kernel. All the objects in the image are labeled. This by using the connected components properties, looking for a full connectivity in the neighbourhood, this process is implemented with *skimage.morphology.label* function.

Rigid Filtering Stage. As mentioned before, is pretended to implement a rigid filter of objects in the image based on the assumptions of the bone surface being the deepest and larger (based on area) object in the image. Firstly, the central moments of each labeled object needs to be obtained. In an image, the central moments can be calculated with the math expression:

$$M_{pq} = \sum_x \sum_y (x - \bar{x})^p (y - \bar{y})^q f(x,y) \tag{14}$$

where M_{pq}, represents the moments of the specific p and q orders. And $\bar{x}$ and $\bar{y}$ are the mean of x and y. It is possible to see that the moment M_{00}, is going to result on the area of an object, since is a binary image, being:

$$M_{00} = \sum_x \sum_y (x - \bar{x})^0 (y - \bar{y})^0 f(x,y) = \sum_x \sum_y f(x,y) \tag{15}$$

Thus, the larger the number of M_{00} corresponds to the larger object areas. In order to obtain the depth, it is necessary to follow the math formulation of the centroid in y, that is given by:

$$C_y = \frac{M_{01}}{M_{00}} = \frac{\sum_x \sum_y (y - \bar{y}) f(x,y)}{\sum_x \sum_y f(x,y)} \tag{16}$$

3   Results

Prior to the full implementation, fine-tuning the parameters of the Log-Gabor filter bank was required. Empirically, it was noticed that the best ω_0 frequencies for the images, were 30, 33, and 36, as well as a κ/ω_0 equals to 0.55. Additionally, due to the segmentation masks created by the expert being lines with a thickness of 3 pixels, a skeletonization step was essential for the final outcome of the object filtering process.

In order to validate the results, some metrics as F-Score, Accuracy, Recall and Hamming Loss were obtained. The overall results of the proposed algorithm

Table 1. Validation metrics results

Metric	Formulation	Interpretation	Validation Result
F-Score	$\frac{2*TP}{2*TP+FP+FN}$	Describes the harmonic mean of precision and sensitivity	**0.9798** (SD 0.0021)
Accuracy	$\frac{TP+TN}{TP+TN+FP+FN}$	Ratio of number of correct predictions to the total number of samples	**0.9796** (SD 0.0021)
Recall	$\frac{TP}{TP+FN}$	Portion of actual positives correctly identified	**0.9883** (SD 0.0018)
Hamming Loss	$\frac{1}{m}\sum_1^m 1_{P_l \neq A_l}$	Fraction of wrongly identified labels on the image	**0.0204** (SD 0.0021)

are shown in Table 1, where the bold number denotes the mean of the scores obtained per image, and SD refers to standard deviation.

Figure 2 shows some qualitative results. The images include the original mannequin image, the frequency domain processing result, the skeleton obtained, and a comparison between the manually segmented image by the expert and the segmentation results produced by the algorithm.

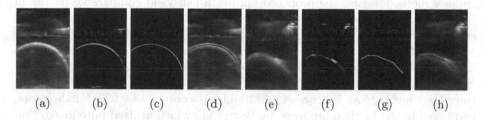

   (a)   (b)   (c)   (d)   (e)   (f)   (g)   (h)

Fig. 2. Image results. a) and e) show the original images; b) and f) correspond to the phase symmetry results; c) and g) present the skeletonization; d) and h) compares the segmentation made by the expert (highlighted in red) and the segmentation obtained by the algorithm (highlighted in green). (Color figure online)

4   Discussion

The proposed algorithm demonstrates a high level of accuracy in detecting the bone surface within a simulated environment. The proposed methodological framework, successfully handles the speckle noise present in the image, which arises from simulating soft tissue, even when utilizing ultrasound probes with less optimal features.

The obtained validation metrics, reflect the effectiveness of the approach when segmenting the bone surface. The values of F-Score and Accuracy, indicate the model capability to achieve a balance between precision and recall resulting in accurate and reliable segmentation task. Also, it needs to be mentioned that the preference for utilizing the F-Score metric stems from its inherent harmonic properties, particularly advantageous in scenarios with substantial abundance of black pixels (0) in contrast to white pixels (1). The Recall score of 0.9883 further underscores the proficiency of the algorithm in correctly identifying positive instances. The low Hamming Loss of 0.0204 signifies the model's ability to precisely segment the bone surface compared with the segmentation made by the expert.

Compared to methods that utilize CNNs, the proposed approach offers distinct advantages. Firstly, it operates effectively without the necessity for a large volume of images for training, making it more accessible and feasible for scenarios where collecting extensive datasets may be challenging or impractical. Additionally, the proposed method minimizes the demand for computational resources, both in terms of processing power and time. This efficiency is particularly advantageous in real-time applications or environments where computational resources are limited.

Specifically, compared to the work of Alsinan et al., who employed more complex local phase calculations and CNNs, the proposed algorithm achieves a slightly higher F-score and a lower Hamming Loss. They achieved a F-Score of 0.9783 and a Hamming Loss of 0.0271. This suggests that despite utilizing simpler methodologies, the proposed approach can yield comparable results in terms of segmentation when the proposed method is applied in a simulated environment.

Similarly, when comparing the obtained results to those of Wang et al., who utilized CNNs and a more intricate mathematical framework, the validation metrics indicate that the proposed method has a significantly higher performance, since they reported an F-Score of 0.882 and an accuracy of 0.920. Furthermore, compared to the method proposed by Bak et al., which utilized pure image processing and machine learning classificators, the proposed framework showcases superior performance in terms of recall and accuracy, as they obtained a recall of 0.96 and an accuracy of 0.92.

5   Conclusions

A local phase-based with a rigid object filtering framework has been proposed to segment bone surfaces in a simulated environment, using US images as an input source. The simulated environment comprises a 3D printed hip joint submerged in gelatin to replicate soft tissue conditions realistically. The proposed method has demonstrated promising results, as evidenced by the obtained metrics, showing its effectiveness in bone surface segmentation compared to existing state of the art techniques.

As a direction for future research, it is important to implement the proposed method using real in-vivo patient data. Furthermore, to further validate the robustness and effectiveness of the approach, additional images from different probes, and also, more segmentation masks obtained by experts should be incorporated for comparison. This comparative analysis will help to confirm the reliability of the method across different cases.

Acknowledgements. We gratefully acknowledge the support and founding provided by the Consejo Zacatecano de Ciencia y Tecnología (COZCyT), under the leadership of Dr. Hamurabi Gamboa Rosales. We also extend our sincere appreciation to Dalhousie University and Nova Scotia Health Authority (NSHA) for their invitation to collaborate on this research. And finally, we express our gratitude to the Consejo Nacional de Humanidades Ciencia y Tecnología (CONAHCYT) for their invaluable support through the postgraduate scholarship.

References

1. Marmol, A., Banach, A., Peynot, T.: Dense-ArthroSLAM: dense intra-articular 3-D reconstruction with robust localization prior for arthroscopy. IEEE Robot. Autom. Lett. **4**(2), 918–925 (2019). https://doi.org/10.1109/LRA.2019.2892199
2. Rees, J.L., Craig, R., Nagra, N., et al.: Serious adverse event rates and reoperation after arthroscopic shoulder surgery: population based cohort study. BMJ **378**, e069901 (2022). https://doi.org/10.1136/bmj-2021-069901
3. Williams, B.T., Vadhera, A., Maheshwer, B., et al.: Is there a role for ultrasound in hip arthroscopy? A systematic review, arthroscopy. Sports Med. Rehabil. **2**(5), e655–e660 (2020). https://doi.org/10.1016/j.asmr.2020.06.001
4. Pandey, P.U., Quader, N., et al.: Ultrasound bone segmentation: a scoping review of techniques and validation practices. Ultrasound Med. Biol. **46**(4), 921–935 (2020). https://doi.org/10.1016/j.ultrasmedbio.2019.12.014
5. Duarte-Salazar, C.A., Castro-Ospina, A.E., Becerra, M.A., et al.: Speckle noise reduction in ultrasound images for improving the metrological evaluation of biomedical applications: an overview. IEEE Access **8**, 15983–15999 (2020). https://doi.org/10.1109/ACCESS.2020.2967178
6. Alsinan, A.Z., Patel, V.M., Hacihaliloglu, I.: Automatic segmentation of bone surfaces from ultrasound using a filter-layer-guided CNN. Int. J. CARS **14**, 775–783 (2019). https://doi.org/10.1007/s11548-019-01934-0
7. Wang, P., Vives, M., Patel, V.M., et al.: Robust real-time bone surfaces segmentation from ultrasound using a local phase tensor-guided CNN. Int. J. CARS **15**, 1127–1135 (2020). https://doi.org/10.1007/s11548-020-02184-1
8. Bak, A., Segen, J., Wereszczyński, K., et al.: Detection of linear features including bone and skin areas in ultrasound images of joints. PeerJ **6**, e4411 (2018). https://doi.org/10.7717/peerj.4411
9. Shin, K.C., Ha, Y.R., Lee, S.J., et al.: Review of simulation model for education of point-of-care ultrasound using easy-to-make tools. World J. Clin. Cases **8**(19), 4286–4302 (2020). https://doi.org/10.12998/wjcc.v8.i19.4286
10. Rajpoot, K., Grau, V., Noble, V.: Local-phase based 3D boundary detection using monogenic signal and its application to real-time 3-D echocardiography images. In: 2009 IEEE International Symposium on Biomedical Imaging: From Nano to Macro, pp. 783–786 (2009). https://doi.org/10.1109/ISBI.2009.5193166.
11. Mulet-Parada, M., Noble, J.A.: 2D+T acoustic boundary detection in echocardiography. Med. Image Anal. **4**(1), 21–30 (2000). https://doi.org/10.1016/s1361-8415(00)00006-2
12. Felsberg, M., Sommer, G.: The monogenic signal. IEEE Trans. Signal Process. **49**(12), 3136–3144 (2001). https://doi.org/10.1109/78.969520

Comparison of CNNs and ViTs for the Detection of Human Skin Lesions

Nohemí Sánchez-Medel⬤, Víctor Romero-Bautista⬤, Raquel Díaz Hernández⬤, and Leopoldo Altamirano Robles⁽✉⁾⬤

Instituto Nacional de Astrofísica, Óptica y Electrónica, Luis Enrique Erro #1, Sta. María Tonantzintla, 72840 San Andrés Cholula, Puebla, Mexico
robles@inaoep.mx

Abstract. This study aims to evaluate the effectiveness of eight deep-learning models in skin lesion detection using dermatoscopic images. For this purpose, two architectures have been rained and compared: Convolutional Neural Networks (CNN) with models such as EfficientNet B0, B1, B2, and B3 and Vision Transformer (ViT) with the models base 16, base 32, large 16, and large 32. These models were trained using the HAM10000 dataset, a widely recognized database containing diverse dermatoscopic images with labeled clinical diagnoses. The main objective of this research is to evaluate the performance of these models in the classification and differentiation of malignant and benign skin lesions to determine which one might offer superior performance. After training the eight network models, it was determined that the EfficientNet B1 model, after 2000 epochs, achieved the best accuracy with 80%. In second place is the ViT base_patch_32 model with 76.67%. The performance of the ViT model improved significantly by adjusting the learning rate parameters and the number of epochs, achieving 85%. However, Vit required more computational resources to achieve these results than the CNNs.

Keywords: Convolutional Neural Networks (CNN) · Transformer Networks (ViT) · Skin lesions · Skin cancer

1 Introduction

Modern dermatology faces the constant challenge of detecting skin lesions early and accurately, which is essential to ensure timely diagnosis and effective treatment of various dermatological conditions. The importance of this early detection lies in its ability to identify disease, which can not only significantly improve clinical outcomes but also save lives. In this context, the advent of artificial intelligence, especially in neural networks, has revolutionized the diagnostic approach in dermatology. These advances have enabled the development of sophisticated computational models capable of analyzing large volumes of dermoscopic image data with unprecedented accuracy and speed. The ability of these network models to detect subtle patterns and features indicative of skin disease has opened up new possibilities in dermatological diagnosis.

E. Mezura-Montes et al. (Eds.): MCPR 2024, LNCS 14755, pp. 274–283, 2024.
https://doi.org/10.1007/978-3-031-62836-8_26

This paper compares convolutional neural networks and the latest transformer network architectures in skin lesion detection. It examines the performance and efficiency of both approaches in accurately identifying dermatological abnormalities from dermatoscopic images. The analysis focuses on assessing the ability of each model to detect and distinguish between benign and malignant lesions, thus providing a comparative view that can guide future research and applications in this medical field.

1.1 Deep Learning

This work employs deep learning models inspired by the workings of the human brain. These networks comprise processing units known as artificial neurons or nodes organized in interconnected layers. Each neuron receives inputs, performs computations based on these inputs, and produces outputs that can be passed on to other neurons. The connections between neurons are adjusted through a learning process so the network can learn to perform specific tasks based on input data, such as classification, pattern recognition, or prediction [1]. Neural networks are used in various applications, including computer vision, natural language processing, and speech recognition.

Convolutional neural networks (CNNs) are particularly effective artificial neural networks for processing images and other graph-like data. They are commonly used in image classification due to their ability to capture relevant patterns and features of images in an automated manner. CNNs are composed of multiple layers of artificial neurons organized at different levels. The main feature of CNNs is the convolutional layer, which applies convolution operations to the network's input. These convolution operations use filters or kernels applied to the input image, allowing relevant features, such as edges, textures, or shapes, to be extracted at different levels of abstraction. Convolutional neural networks are very effective in image classification due to their ability to automatically extract relevant features from the input data, their translational invariance, their ability to learn from relatively small data sets, and their ability to generalize pattern recognition from limited training examples [2].

On the other hand, Transformers is a type of neural network initially proposed to solve problems in the field of natural language processing (NLP); due to the good results, this architecture has been adapted for computer vision tasks, therefore called Vision Transformer (ViT) [3]. A ViT typically consists of a multi-head attention layer and a Multi-Layer Perceptron (MLP), with a normalization and residual connection layer. The fundamental core of the ViT is the attention mechanism, which consists of two crucial parts; in the first part, the input vector is transformed into three different vectors named q, k, and v. These vectors are then grouped into three matrices: Q, K, and V. In the second part, the attention function between the different input vectors is calculated; this process can be expressed as follows:

$$Attention(Q, K, V) = softmax\left(Q \cdot K^T / \sqrt{d_k}\right) \cdot V$$

where d_k represents the dimensionality of the key vectors.

The multi-head attention mechanism projects the input into multiple feature subspaces and processes them using several layers of attention. Since ViT only accepts sequential inputs, the input image is divided into sub-images.

Compared to CNN, which focuses on local features (using convolution operation), ViT can capture long-distance features, which makes it easier to derive global information from the image.

2 Related Works

In the work presented by Alexey Dosovitskiy et al. [3], they use a Transformer architecture designed specifically for large-scale image recognition. Their innovative approach treats images as sequences of pixel patches and transforms them into word representations. This methodology allows for efficient scalability in large-scale image recognition and has shown promising results compared to CNNs. On the other hand, Gan Cai et al. [4] propose a multimodal transformer to fuse images and metadata to classify skin diseases. It seeks to integrate visual and contextual information to improve classification accuracy. It uses a Transformer architecture to process multiple data modalities simultaneously. And a skin disease classification library. Subsequently, Jasil, S.P.G & V. Ulagamuthalvi [5] address the presentation of a new Convolutional Neural Network (CNN) architecture called DenseNet and a residual network that uses contextual data. To test how well the model worked, they analyzed examples from the HAM10000 dataset. To increase the classifier's effectiveness, they sampled and supplemented the data with additional information. Experimental results showed that the proposed approaches improved the automatic classification of skin lesions with an accuracy of 95%. On the other hand, Mingxing Tan, Quoc V. Le [6] present EfficienNetV2, a new convolutional network family with faster training speed and better parameter efficiency than previous models. They jointly combined search and training-aware neural architecture scaling to optimize training speed and parameter efficiency. The models were enriched with new operations such as Fused-MBConv. Their experiments show that EfficientNetV2 models train much faster than state-of-the-art models and are up to 6–8 times smaller. They mention they can further accelerate the training by increasing the image size. Although this would cause a drop in accuracy, it would be compensated by adjusting some parameters. Their results significantly outperform previous models, achieving an accuracy of over 87.3%. Some time later, Verónica Angélica-Villalobos Romo, et al. [8]. Based on deep learning, they developed an algorithm for skin cancer detection using the HAM10000 database, which contains 10015 images of different categories of pigmented lesions, which have been confirmed by pathology. They attacked the problem by evaluating different convolutional neural networks and programming the algorithms in Python 3.7 language. They performed the model's design, construction, and adaptation to achieve high accuracy. They provided the datasets used for training, validation, and testing. Their algorithm achieved an accuracy of 89% in melanoma detection. Finally, Md. Sazzadul Islam Prottasha, et al. This study aimed to diagnose two types of skin diseases, eczema, and psoriasis, using state-of-the-art CNN architectures; they analyzed their performance by cross-validation. With the Inception architecture, ResNetv2, and the Adam optimizer, they achieved an accuracy of 97.1%. This implies that the model performs significantly well in diagnosing skin diseases. Furthermore, the study demonstrates two approaches for practically applying the implemented model. After performing the literature review, we can observe that the authors are using deep learning with different architectures to perform classifiers, so in this paper we compare CNN and ViT architectures for detecting malignant and benign skin lesions. With CNN networks, up to 80% accuracy is achieved using the EfficientNet B1 model for 2000 epochs. On the other hand, with ViT networks, an accuracy of up to 76.67% is achieved with the ViT_base_Patch_32 model over 1000 epochs.

3 Methodology

3.1 Data Set

The HAM10000 database [6] is an essential reference in dermatology and computer vision, used extensively to research and develop detection algorithms for skin diseases.

This resource hosts high-resolution dermatoscopic images covering both benign and malignant skin lesions. For this particular study, 200 images were carefully selected equally distributed between benign and malignant lesions of the most common lesion classes, such as Actinic Keratosis (AK), Benign Keratosis (BKL), Basal Cell Carcinoma (BCC), Seborrheic Keratosis (SK), Carcinoma (C), Dermatofibroma (DF) and Melanoma (MEL), among others. These images were mainly collected by the ViDIR Group of the Department of Dermatology at the Medical University of Vienna and from a skin cancer office in Australia, specifically from the Faculty of Medicine at the University of Queensland. The Fig. 1 shows images of this dataset's most common skin lesions.

3.2 Characteristics of Images with Skin Lesions

In this section, a detailed analysis of the features present in the images of skin lesions under investigation was performed. Various aspects, such as asymmetry, border, color, dimension, and evolution of the lesions, are examined in detail using the ABCDE test [7]. Dermatologists commonly use this assessment to analyze moles and skin lesions suspected of developing into skin cancer. The main objective is to identify distinctive patterns that differentiate benign and malignant lesions. This analysis provides essential information for creating an artificial intelligence-based classification system with high accuracy and reliability.

3.3 General Outline of the Proposal

The methodology proposed in this research involves performing different tests using images of skin lesions to evaluate the effectiveness of deep-learning models. Two architectures and eight neural network models previously trained on the ImageNet dataset were selected. These tests analyze how both architectures can contribute to skin lesion detection and determine which allows for more accurate classification. After the test, the models were retrained by fine-tuning.

Skin lesions labeled in the HAM10000 dataset

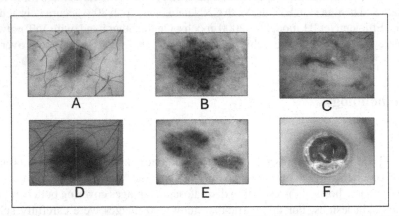

Fig. 1. Most common skin lesions: (A) Dermatofibroma (DF), (B) Melanoma (mel), (C) Benign Keratosis (BKL), (D) Melanocytic Nevus (NV), (E) Basal Cell Carcinoma (BCC), (F) Vascular Lesion (VASC).

3.4 Integration of the Pre-training Model into the Eight Final Models

In this research, eight pre-trained models were employed. The ImageNet data set was used for the training of the models. These models include four Convolutional Neural Network models (EfficientNet B0, B1, B2, and B3) and four Transformer Network models (ViT base 16, base 32, large 16, and large 32), implemented using the Pytorch framework. This approach leveraged graphics processing power and high-level functions, significantly accelerating the model training process and producing a more computationally efficient artificial neural network development option. These models were applied and evaluated in the classification of skin lesion tasks. Each of them was adapted by adjusting different parameters, such as the number of epochs, which varied between 30, 100, 500, 1000, 1500, and 2000, thus taking advantage of the unique characteristics of each architecture. We used an NVIDIA Geforce GTX 1660 Ti GPU and an Intel Core i7 10th GEN processor for the experiments.

4   Experiments and Results

This section details the experiments and results obtained using the methodology described in the previous section. The training results of the CNN and ViT architectures are presented with the eight respective models. Finally, an analysis of the evaluation is carried out.

4.1 Retrained Architectures

Two hundred images from the HAM10000 dataset were used, equally distributed between malignant and benign categories, with 100 images in each category (the number of images is reduced to facilitate training without excessive use of computational resources). The images were divided into training and validation sets, with a 90% and 10% ratio. At this stage of the work, the eight models were retrained and adjusted using the transfer learning technique.

4.2 Results

Firstly, the following Tables 1, 2, 3 and 4 show the training results of the CNN models. These tables detail the epoch, accuracy, and loss for each model.

Table 1. Model CNN EfficientNet B0

EfficientNet B0 (200 images)				
Architecture	Dataset	Epoch	Accuracy	Loss
CNN	HAM10000	30	55.00%	0.73
		100	40.00%	1.52
		500	69.00%	0.86
		1000	55.00%	0.73
		1500	65.00%	0.65
		2000	70.00%	0.859

Table 2. Model CNN EfficientNet B1

EfficientNet B1 (200 images)				
Architecture	Dataset	Epoch	Accuracy	Loss
CNN	HAM10000	30	50.00%	1.12
		100	56.00%	1.01
		500	55.00%	0.73
		1000	35.00%	0.7
		1500	60.00%	0.69
		2000	80.00%	0.63

Table 3. Model CNN EfficientNet B2

EfficientNet B2 (200 images)				
Architecture	Dataset	Epoch	Accuracy	Loss
CNN	HAM10000	30	75.00%	0.815
		100	55.00%	1.04
		500	70.00%	0.859
		1000	50.00%	0.866
		1500	50.00%	0.78
		2000	50.00%	0.86

Secondly, in the following Tables 5, 6, 7 and 8, the training results of the ViT models are shown. These tables detail the epoch, accuracy, and loss for each model.

Table 4. Model CNN EfficientNet B3

EfficientNet B3 (200 images)				
Architecture	Dataset	Epoch	Accuracy	Loss
CNN	HAM10000	30	45.00%	1.224
		100	55.00%	0.949
		500	65.00%	0.608
		1000	65.00%	0.65
		1500	65.00%	0.66
		2000	**70.00%**	**0.63**

Table 5. Model ViT base patch_16_244

ViT base patch_16_244 (200 images)				
Architecture	Dataset	Epoch	Accuracy	Loss
ViT	HAM10000	30	56.11%	0.68
		100	59.44%	0.67
		500	67.59%	0.59
		1000	**75.41%**	**0.48**
		1500	66.23%	0.62
		2000	66.11%	0.62

Table 6. Modelo ViT base patch_32_244

ViT base patch_32_244 (200 images)				
Architecture	Dataset	Epoch	Accuracy	Loss
ViT	HAM10000	30	56.11%	0.68
		100	59.44%	0.65
		500	68.89%	0.58
		1000	**76.67%**	**0.41**
		1500	65.77%	0.61
		2000	65.43%	0.62

Table 7. Modelo ViT large patch_16_244

ViT large patch_16_244 (200 images)				
Architecture	Dataset	Epoch	Accuracy	Loss
		30	75.00%	0.65
		100	70.00%	0.64
ViT	HAM10000	500	60.00%	0.63
		1000	65.00%	0.63
		1500	65.00%	0.63
		2000	55.00%	0.63

Table 8. Modelo ViT large patch_32_244

ViT large patch 32_244 (200 images)				
Architecture	Dataset	Epoch	Accuracy	Loss
		30	65.00%	0.66
		100	60.00%	0.65
ViT	HAM10000	500	55.00%	0.69
		1000	55.00%	0.71
		1500	50.00%	0.72
		2000	60.00%	0.74

4.3 Results Comparison

As can be seen in the results, for the CNN architecture, the best performance is achieved with the EfficientNet B1 model, reaching an accuracy of 80% after 2000 training epochs. On the other hand, for the ViT architecture, the best performance model is ViT base_patch_32, with an accuracy of 76.67% after 1000 epochs.

The following tables compare the two architectures and the eight models (Tables 9 and 10).

Table 9. Results of the four models of the CNN architecture.

Model CNN	Epochs					
	30	100	500	1000	1500	2000
EfficientNet B0	55.00%	40.00%	69.00%	55.00%	65.00%	70.00%
EfficientNet B1	50.00%	56.00%	55.00%	35.00%	60.00%	80.00%
EfficientNet B2	75.00%	55.00%	70.00%	50.00%	50.00%	50.00%
EfficientNet B3	45.00%	55.00%	65.00%	65.00%	65.00%	70.00%

Finally, it is essential to note that an additional test was carried out in which the learning rate was adjusted and the number of epochs was increased.

Table 10. Results of the four models of the ViT architecture.

Model ViT	Epochs					
	30	100	500	1000	1500	2000
ViT_base_Patch_16	56.11%	59.44%	67.59%	**75.41%**	66.23%	66.11%
ViT_base_Patch_32	56.11%	59.44%	68.89%	**76.67%**	65.77%	65.43%
ViT_large_Patch_16	**75.00%**	70.00%	60.00%	65.00%	65.00%	55.00%
ViT_large_Patch_32	**65.00%**	60.00%	55.00%	55.00%	50.00%	60.00%

With these adjustments, an accuracy of 85% was achieved with 5000 training epochs. This result suggests promising prospects for future research.

The table below presents the test results by adjusting the learning rate to 0.00001 and increasing the epochs from 30 to 5000 epochs (Tables 11).

Table 11. A test was performed on the ViT base 16 model, adjusting the learning rate and the number of epochs.

Test conducted with more epochs on ViT base_Patch_16 and with LR = 0.00001		
Epochs	Accuracy	Loss
30	50.00%	0.686
100	50.00%	0.684
500	55.00%	0.681
1000	55.00%	0.675
1500	55.00%	0.67
2000	60.00%	0.664
3000	80.00%	0.655
4000	85.00%	0.647
5000	**85.00%**	**0.64**

Based on the results obtained, and considering that the study aims to classify skin lesions (malignant or benign), it is noteworthy that an accuracy of 85% was achieved with ViT. With this accuracy and the inclusion of transforming blocks and self-attention, the ViT model is considered more potent in addressing classification tasks in this context.

5   Conclusion

Classification of skin lesions represents a significant challenge due to the vast diversity of appearances between the different classes. In this study, CNN and ViT architectures were compared, and the effectiveness of their respective models for this classification task was evaluated. Significant results were achieved through parameter selection and tuning. Specifically, 85% accuracy was performed using the ViT architecture, while Sufi A. [4] achieved 83% accuracy, and Budhiman [7] achieved 75% accuracy using CNN models.

These results indicate the superiority of the ViT architecture in this particular context. Overall, this work highlights the potential of ViT to achieve reliable classification of skin lesions, which has significant implications in dermatological computer-aided diagnosis. Using a larger dataset, including at least the 10,000 images available from the HAM dataset, is recommended, as well as adjusting the learning rate and increasing the number of epochs during training to further improve the accuracy of these models.

6 Future Work

In future research, it is suggested that other network architectures be explored, in addition to the ones analyzed in this study, to evaluate their performance in skin lesion detection. It is worthwhile to include experimenting with new or emerging architectures, refining data pre-processing techniques, or adapting existing models to address the challenge of class recognition. In addition, it is recommended that the evaluation be conducted on more extensive and diverse datasets than the HAM10000 database used in this work.

References

1. Qamar, R., Zardari, B.A.: Artificial neural networks. Mesopotamian J. Comput. Sci. **2023**, 130–139 (2023)
2. Nash, R.: An introduction to convolutional neural networks. arXiv. /abs/1511.08458 (2015)
3. Dosovitskiy, A., et al.: An image is worth 16 × 16 words: transformers for image recognition at scale. arXiv. /abs/2010.11929 (2020)
4. Sufi, A.: Skin Cancer Classification Using Deep Learning (2022). http://dspace.uiu.ac.bd/handle/52243/2483. Accessed 15 Sept 2022
5. Hosny, K.M., Kassem, M.A., Foaud, M.M.: Skin cancer classification using deep learning and transfer learning. In: Proceedings of the 2018 9th Cairo International Biomedical Engineering Conference (CIBEC), Cairo, Egypt, 20–22 December 2018, pp. 90–93 (2018)
6. Dorj, U.O., Lee, K.K., Choi, J.Y., Lee, M.: The skin cancer classification using deep convolutional neural network. Multimed. Tools Appl. **77**, 9909–9924 (2018)
7. Budhiman, A., Suyanto, S., Arifianto, A.: Melanoma cancer classification using resnet with data augmentation. In: Proceedings of the 2019 International Seminar on Research of Information Technology and Intelligent Systems (ISRITI), Yogyakarta, Indonesia, 5–6 December 2019, pp. 17–20 (2019)
8. Arshed, M.A., Mumtaz, S., Ibrahim, M., Ahmed, S., Tahir, M., Shafi, M.: Multi-class skin cancer classification using vision transformer networks and convolutional neural network-based pre-trained models. Information **14**(7), 415 (2023). https://doi.org/10.3390/info14070415
9. Skin Cancer MNIST: HAM10000|Kaggle. https://www.kaggle.com/datasets/kmader/skin-cancer-mnist-ham10000. Accessed 01 Jan 2024
10. Tan, M., Le, Q.V.: EfficientNetV2: smaller models and faster training. arXiv. /abs/2104.00298 (2021)
11. Duarte, A.F., et al.: Clinical ABCDE rule for early melanoma detection. Eur. J. Dermatol. **31**(6), 771–778 (2021). https://doi.org/10.1684/ejd.2021.4171. PMID: 35107069

Language Processing and Recognition

Text-Independent Speaker Identification with Glottal Flow and 1D Convolutional Neural Networks

Antonio Camarena-Ibarrola$^{(\boxtimes)}$, Erick Ruiz-Gaona , and Karina Figueroa

Facultad de Ingeniera Elctrica, Universidad Michoacana de San Nicolás de Hidalgo,
Morella, Mexico
{antonio.camarena,2026226a,karina.figueroa}@umich.mx

Abstract. We propose a method for Text-Independent Speaker Identification that consists in searching for the voiced frames of the speech signal, which are the ones emitted while the vocal cords vibrate, then estimate the glottal flow of each voiced frame using our own iterative inverse filtering technique, we use these glottal flows along with their corresponding speaker labels to train a 1D Convolutional Neural Network (1DCNN). Our specific 1DCNN lacks of dense layers, different from the conventional 1DCNN architecture, it is made of all convolutional layers. In the last layer the number of filters equals the number of speakers, and use global maximum pooling to predict the identity of the speaker that uttered each specific voiced frame. For identifying a speaker we also detect all voiced frames in his/her speech; then estimate the glottal flow of each of these voiced frames; use the trained 1DCNN for identifying the speaker each voiced frame belongs to; and finally, use a voting scheme for deciding the identity of the speaker. We first used our method in the English Language Speech Database for Speaker Recognition (ELS-DSR) corpus achieving perfect results (100% accuracy), then we used our technique in the TIMIT database which include audio-files from 630 speakers, using all of them in our tests, achieving an accuracy of 99.52%.

Keywords: Text-Independent Speaker Identification · 1D Convolutional Neural Networks · Glottal Flow Extraction

1 Introduction

When an individual is willing to be recognized, he would cooperate in uttering some specific word or phrase because he is claiming an identity that needs to be verified. Such recognition task is known as Text-Dependent Speaker Verification (TD-SV) and is typically addressed by modeling the speakers as sequences of feature vectors and comparing these sequences with Dynamic Time Warping, Hidden Markov Models, or other matching tools. In TD-SV the features extracted from the individual whose identity is being verified are compared only with the features belonging to the claimed identity. In another problem, known

E. Mezura-Montes et al. (Eds.): MCPR 2024, LNCS 14755, pp. 287–296, 2024.
https://doi.org/10.1007/978-3-031-62836-8_27

as Text-Dependent Speaker Identification (TD-SI) an individual is not claiming any identity but we still need to identify him/her among a collection of known individuals using his/her voice for that purpose, after we have asked previously to each speaker being enrolled in the database to utter some specific phrase. TD-SI is harder than TD-SV as the database grows; TD-SI systems frequently use a proximity index avoiding sequential search. Another problem, known as Text-Independent Speaker Verification (TI-SV), consists in: given two speech signals, we need to decide if both signals belong to the same speaker even when they contain different phrases. The speakers cannot longer be modeled as sequences of features and are commonly modeled as point clouds where time is disregarded since phonemes may appear in different order and some of them may not even appear at all. A more general and more complex problem than TI-SV is the Text-Independent Speaker Identification (TI-SI), where a speaker needs to be identified regardless of what he/she says as one of the members of a possibly big collection of known speakers.

Our approach for the TI-SI problem uses a 1D Convolutional Neural Network (1DCNN). Not directly with the speech signal since it has too much information within, it is too complex and chaotic, so in helping the 1DCNN we eliminate information from the speech signal that is not related to the identity of the speaker but to the content of the speech (i.e. specific sentences, phrases, or words uttered). We aim to preserve only speaker identity information, in a much simpler signal. To achieve that, from the speech signal, we extract the train of glottal pulses (i.e. the glottal flow) and only from those frames of speech identified as voiced speech, which are the ones uttered while the vocal cords vibrate. So we use a low level classifier that separates voiced from unvoiced speech. The glottal flow extracted from every voiced frame, along with the corresponding label of the speaker is used as training data for the 1DCNN. Once the 1DCNN has been trained it is used for identifying the speaker as follows: Each frame of the speech signal from the unknown speaker is first classified as voiced or unvoiced speech; From the voiced frames, the glottal flow is estimated and fed to the trained 1DCNN, obtaining a single vote for one of the registered speakers (speakers whose speech was used for training); The decision rule is: decide for the speaker that obtains the majority of the votes, one vote for each voiced frame in the speech.

2   Related Work

In 2019, for the TI-SI problem, Luque *et al.* characterized speakers as point-clouds where the points within a cloud are 16-dimensional vectors containing the distribution of entropy in the frequency domain for each frame of the speech signal, they used a proximity index to speed up a K-nearest neighbor classifier achieving about 95% accuracy in a dataset of almost 1000 speakers [1]. Also in 2019, Bunrit *et al.* characterized speakers by their spectrogram which is an image that shows the amount of energy both in frequency and time, the spectrogram is fed to a 2D Convolutional Neural Network (CNN) for TI-SI showing results that outperformed MFCC based recognizers [2]. In 2020, instead of spectrograms, "entropygrams" (i.e. spectrograms of entropy) were used as images for using 2D-CNN for TD-SI, entropygrams are images that show how the level of information (i.e. entropy) distributes both in time and frequency, it was found that entropygrams outperformed spectrograms for low resolution images which allowed for CNN with much fewer parameters to be determined during training and worked much better for noisy speech signals [3], In 2021, the voiced segments of the speech were first detected, from them the firsts three formants were estimated, both their central frequencies and their bandwidths, then used this information to build an image and identify the speakers using a 2D convolutional neural network [16]. In 2023, the glottal flow was estimated from the voiced segments of the speech, and it was used for classifying the speech signal as spoof or genuine, preventing attacks on speaker verification systems [17].

3   Our Proposal

We believe it is a good idea to benefit from the excellent recognition performance of convolutional neural networks. However, to use 2D CNN, speakers would have to be modeled as images such as spectrograms, wavelet scalagrams, or even entropygrams which show simultaneously how energy, or entropy respectively distribute in frequency and evolve in time. That may be a good approach when dealing with the TD-SI and TD-SV problems assuming the dynamics of the features vary from one speaker to another, but for the TI-SI problem, speakers have to be modeled disregarding time, it should not matter the order in which particular voiced sounds appear in the speech signal, some of them may not even appear at all. Our approach consists in extracting the glottal flow waveform from each voiced segment of the speech; The glottal flow has been used for speaker recognition before and it is a far less complex signal than the speech signal. Then we use a 1D convolutional neural network for identifying the speaker each voiced frame belongs to, and use a voting scheme among the frames for the final decision of the identity of the speaker.

3.1   Glottal Flow Estimation

Our method for extracting the glottal flow is iterative and yet simpler than Murphy's [4] or Alku's Iterative Adaptive Inverse Filtering [5] techniques, that is because our method does not require any model of the glottal pulse. We depict our method in Fig. 1, the solid lines represent control flow and the dotted lines represent data flow (i.e. signal flow). It is known that the lips shape the sound wave at the end of the vocal tract before it is radiated to the environment, this phenomenon is modeled by a radiation filter, which is really a first-order high-pass filter, then our first step consists in applying the inverse of this radiation filter which is a low-pass filter to obtain an estimate of the sound wave just before it was radiated outside the mouth through the lips, in Fig. 1 it is referred as the "radiation compensated voice" ($s^{(i)}(n)$), since at this point $i = 0$, you should

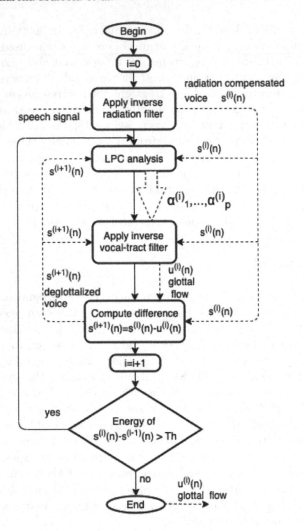

Fig. 1. Our Glottal Flow Estimation Technique. Solid lines represent control flow and dotted lines depict data (i.e. signals) flow

considered it as $s^{(0)}(n)$. A good model for the vocal tract is an all-pole filter, which is really a multi-band pass filter, one band for each resonant frequency of the vocal tract, the parameters of such filter are normally found through Linear Prediction Coding (LPC) analysis based on the autocorrelation of the speech signal, these parameters are $\alpha_1, \alpha_2, ..., \alpha_p$ where p is the order of the predictor. By applying a filter that is the inverse of this filter that models the vocal tract, we obtain a first estimate of the sound wave at the beginning of the vocal tract which is the glottal flow waveform denoted as $u^{(i)}(n)$. We have to take into account that the first LPC analysis delivered parameters $\alpha_1, \alpha_2, ..., \alpha_p$ that do not depend exclusively on the shape of the vocal tract but also on the glottal flow waveform itself. So in order to determine parameters that depend exclusively on the vocal tract we need to deglottalize the voice and repeat the LPC analysis. We deglottalize the voice simply by substracting the estimate of the glottal flow $u^{(i)}(n)$ from the voice $s^{(i)}(n)$ from which the parameters of the filter that models the vocal-tract were obtained. Once this "deglottalized voice" was estimated, we replace $s^{(i)}(n)$ by $s^{(i+1)}(n)$ and repeat all LPC analysis; inverse filtering; and deglottalization until the voice signal does not change enough for another iteration to be worth. To measure the change in the voice signal between iterations we compute the energy of the difference of two consecutive voice waveforms as:

$$E = \sum_{n=1}^{N}(s^{(i)}(n) - s^{(i-1)}(n))^2 \tag{1}$$

where N is the length of the frame in samples

In Fig. 2 we show the speech signal of a segment of voiced speech, this particular segment correspond to vowel /a/ and is the kind of signal that would be the input of the procedure shown in Fig. 1, the output of this procedure for the same signal is shown in Fig. 3.

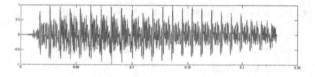

Fig. 2. Speech signal of vowel /a/

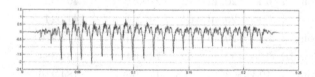

Fig. 3. Glottal Flow obtained from the speech signal of vowel /a/

3.2   Our 1D Convolutional Neural Network

In the classic convolutional neural network architecture, the first layers (the convolutional layers) act as feature extractors, while the last layers (the dense layers) conform the actual classifier, also the number of neurons of the last dense layer normally equals the number of classes and the softmax activation function is used in this last layer. However, dense layers are prone to overfitting, so we decided to avoid them and use the Global Max Pooling strategy, which replaces the dense layers with additional convolutional layers which act as nonlinear function approximators that generate a feature map for each class in the last layer where

Global Max Pooling is used for class selection. Global average pooling enforces correspondences between feature maps and categories being more natural to the convolution structure than dense layers and is more robust to time shifts in the input signal [6]. Detailed information about our model is provided in Table 1, the last layer of this table has a number of filters that equals the number of speakers of the data set, for example in the case of the English Language Speech Database for Speaker Recognition (ELSDSR) [7] there are 22 speakers, so the number of filters of the last layer is 22. Another particularity of our architecture is that we do not use local maxpooling, except after the fifth convolutional layer, but instead we gradually increase the kernel size from 3 in the first convolutional layer to 30 in the last convolutional layer, that way we do not loose information, as it is the case when local max pooling is used, at the expense of gradually making the convolutional layers more expensive in terms of computations.

Table 1. Specifics for the 1DCNN used for the ELSDSR database with 22 speakers. ks = kernel size; fs = number of filters; ws = window size

Layer	Tensor Shape	Parameters
Input layer	480,1	0
Conv1d_1 ks = 3, nf = 32	478,32	128
Conv1d_2 ks = 3, nf = 64	476,64	6,208
Conv1d_3 ks = 7, nf = 32	470,32	14,368
Conv1d_4 ks = 7, nf = 64	464,64	14,400
Conv1d_5 ks = 7, nf = 64	458,64	28,736
MaxPooling ws = 2	229,64	0
Conv1d_6 ks = 20, nf = 32	210,32	40,992
Conv1d_7 ks = 20, nf = 64	191,64	41,024
Conv1d_8 ks = 20, nf = 96	172,96	122,976
Conv1d_9 ks = 30, nf = 64	143,64	184,384
Conv1d_10 ks = 30, nf = 96	114,96	184,416
Conv1d_11 ks = 30, nf = 128	85,128	368,768
Conv1d_12 ks = 30, nf = 22	56,22	84,502
GlobalMaxPooling	22	0
		Sum 1,090,902

4   Experiments and Results

We used two known datasets for text-independent speaker recognition, one of them is the English Language Speech Database for Speaker Recognition (ELS-DSR) [7] created in the Technical University of Denmark, this corpus is divided in training and test sets. For the training set, each of the 22 speakers uttered 7 sentences, so there are 154 recordings. For the test set, each speaker uttered 2 sentences, so there are 44 recordings. The sentences for the test set are different from those of the training set, so this dataset is ideal for text-independent speaker recognition tests. From the 22 speakers 12 are male and 10 are female, with ages in the range of 24 to 63 and different nationalities. For most of them english is not their native language. The other dataset used in our experiments is the well-known TIMIT database which was built from 630 American-English speakers from several regions of the United States of America. The corpus was the result of the joint effort of the Massachusetts Institute of Technology (MIT), SRI International (SRI) and Texas Instruments, Inc. (TI). In fact, TIMIT is the acronym of Texas Instrument/Massachusetts Institute of Technology [8]. TIMIT has 6300 sentences, 10 different sentences spoken by each of the 630 speakers from 8 major regions of the United States. This corpus is also divided into test set and training set, 168 speakers out of the 630 conform the test set. However, we believe that, in order to better assess our speaker identification technique, all 630 speakers should be involved in our tests, then we took 8 sentences from each of the 630 speakers to conform our training dataset and the remaining 2 sentences from each of the 630 speakers to conform the test dataset.

The length of our frames is 30 ms and they are overlapped by 20 ms. At a sampling frequency of 16,000 Hz 30 ms means frames of 480 samples, which is why the input size of our 1D Convolutional Neural Network is precisely 480. For each sentence uttered by a speaker many voiced frames may be detected, all of them are used for training.

For the speaker identification phase we also detect every frame with voiced speech in the sentence that was uttered by the speaker and estimate the glottal flow from each of these frames, then using the trained 1D Convolutional network we identify the speaker each frame belongs to. Finally we use a voting scheme for the final decision regarding the identity of the speaker.

4.1 Results with the ELSDSR Corpus

With the ELSDSR dataset we achieved 100% accuracy. In Table 2 we include our result along with results reported by several researchers that have used that corpus to assess their methods.

4.2 Results with the TIMIT Corpus

The TIMIT dataset was built from 630 speakers and since the original purpose was for testing speaker independent speech recognizers it comes as two separate subsets of 168 speakers for testing and 432 for training. But we did not want to assess our method with just the 168 speakers that belong to the test subset but with all 630 speakers. For every speaker there are 10 different spoken sentences, so we took 5040 audio-files for training out of the 6300 that conform the TIMIT dataset and the remaining 1260 for testing. We achieved an accuracy of 99.52% with the TIMIT dataset, this result is shown in Table 3 along with the accuracy

Table 2. Comparison results with other methods also tested on ELSDSR corpus

Features	Classifier	Acc
Resonant freq of vocal tract	Nearest neighbor/ Polygon Matching [9]	90%
Wavelet Packet	Neural Network [10]	95.7%
Discrete Zak Transform	Nearest Neighbors/ Euclidean distance [11]	100%
Glottal Flow	1DCNN (our proposal)	100.0%

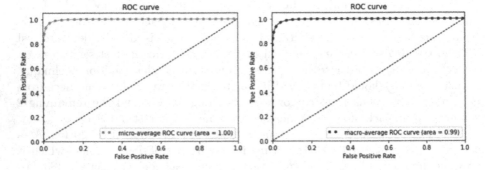

Fig. 4. ROC Curves for the TIMIT dataset

reported by several researchers that also used the TIMIT corpus to assess their respective methods on the TI-SI problem.

Table 3. Comparison results with other methods also tested on TIMIT corpus

Features	Model	Accuracy
MFCC Eigenspace with PCA and MLE	NN classifier using eigendistance [12]	92.5%
Multitaper MFCC	GMM [13]	95.0%
Histogram of the DCT Cepstrum	GMM [14]	99.0%
MFCC	GMM [15]	99.5%
Glottal Flow	1DCNN (our proposal)	99.52%

In Fig. 4 we show the micro-average (left), and macro-average (right) ROC curves that we obtained for the TIMIT corpus, these results show how well a single voiced frame would do at identifying the speaker. However, our proposed method uses not just one but all voiced frames found in the speech signal and decide upon the identity of the speaker after each frame has voted for a speaker, that is why our TI-SI system achieves 99.52% accuracy with the TIMIT corpus. The fact that both ROC curves shown in Fig. 4 are practically identical is an evidence that any imbalance of the classes due to the fact that the number of voiced frames is not the same for all speakers does not affect the performance of the recognizer. Remember we are testing a text-independent speaker identifier and in the TIMIT corpus the speakers do not utter the same sentences, only two sentences were uttered by every speaker, the remaining 8 sentences were assigned to each speaker from a collection of 2340 sentences.

5 Conclusions

We combined three key concepts to implement our TI-SI system. First, the known fact that the glottal flow signal varies from one speaker to another; Second, the glottal flow changes depending on the specific voiced sound uttered by the speaker, still we use the same label for the different glottal flows since they belong to the same speaker, but neural networks benefit from the richness of the training set, turning an inconvenient into an advantage; Third, at identifying the speaker, each frame containing voiced speech in the uttered phrase is fed to the trained neural network, obtaining one decision for each of these frames, we use a voting scheme for achieving a final decision regarding the identity of the speaker.

Unlike the traditional classifiers that use a front-end (i.e. feature extraction module) based on designed features, the first layers of 1D Convolutional Neural Networks extract features that are not designed but learned during training. However the speech signal is way too complex even for these powerful tools, then we used 1D-CNN for identifying speakers with signals such as the glottal flow that compared to the speech signal is much simpler.

Also, we should remark that the architecture of the 1D-CNN that we use is not the classic one (convolutional layers followed by dense layers) but one made out of all convolutional layers combined with the Global Max Pooling strategy which is less prone to overfitting, with a number of filters in the last layer that equals the number of speakers in the training dataset.

Our glottal flow estimator is iterative but simpler than the one proposed by Murphy since we do not use a model for the glottal pulse and then we do not have to estimate its parameters. Still our glottal flow extractor manages to produce a good estimation of the glottal flow that allows for good results in identifying speakers with both ELSDSR and TIMIT.

Disclosure of Interests. The authors have no competing interests to declare that are relevant to the content of this article.

References

1. Luque-Suárez, F., Camarena-Ibarrola, A., Chávez, E.: Efficient speaker identification using spectral entropy. Multimed. Tools Appl. **78**(12), 16 803–16 815 (2019). https://doi.org/10.1007/s11042-018-7035-9
2. Bunrit, S., Inkian, T., Kerdprasop, N., Kerdprasop, K.: Text-independent speaker identification using deep learning model of convolution neural network. Int. J. Mach. Learn. Comput. **9**, 143–148 (2019)

3. Camarena-Ibarrola, A., Figueroa, K., García, J.: Speaker identification using entropygrams and convolutional neural networks. In: Martínez-Villaseñor, L., Herrera-Alcántara, O., Ponce, H., Castro-Espinoza, F.A. (eds.) MICAI 2020. LNCS (LNAI), vol. 12468, pp. 23–34. Springer, Cham (2020). https://doi.org/10.1007/978-3-030-60884-2_2
4. Murphy, K.: Digital signal processing techniques for application in the analysis of pathological voice and normophonic singing voice. Ph.D. dissertation, Universidad Politecnica de Madrid (2008). https://oa.upm.es/1079/
5. Alku, P.: Glottal wave analysis with pitch synchronous iterative adaptive inverse filtering. Speech Commun. **11**, 109–118 (1992)
6. Lin, M., Chen, Q., Yan, S.: Network in network. In: International Conference on Learning Representations, Banff, Canada (2014)
7. Feng, L., Hansen, L.K.: A new database for speaker recognition. Informatics and Mathematical Modeling, Technical University of Denmark, Technical report (2005)
8. Garofolo, J., et al.: Timit acoustic-phonetic continuous speech corpus. Linguist. Data Consortium (1992)
9. Camarena-Ibarrola, A., Castro-Coria, M., Figueroa, K.: Cloud point matching for text-independent speaker identification. In: IEEE International Autumn Meeting on Power, Electronics and Computing (ROPEC), pp. 1–6 (2018)
10. Saady, M.R., El-Borey, H., El-Dahshan, E.-S.A., Yahia, A.S.: Stand-alone intelligent voice recognition system. J. Signal Inf. Process. **5**, 179–190 (2014)
11. Hossen, A., Al-Rawahi, S.: A text-independent speaker identification system based on the Zak transform. Signal Process. Int. J. **4**, 68–74 (2010)
12. Thyes, O., Kuhn, R., Nguyen, P., Junqua, J.C.: Speaker identification and verification using eigenvoices. In: Proceedings of the ICSLP, pp. 242–245 (2000)
13. Veena, K.V., Mathew, D.: Speaker identification and verification of noisy speech using multitaper MFCC and Gaussian mixture models. In: 2015 International Conference on Power, Instrumentation, Control and Computing (PICC), pp. 1–4 (2015)
14. Al-Rawahy, S., Hossen, A., Heute, U.: Text-independent speaker identification system based on the histogram of DCT-cepstrum coefficients. Int. J. Knowle.-Based Intell. Eng. Syst. **16**, 141–161 (2012)
15. Reynolds, D.: Large population speaker identification using clean and telephone speech. IEEE Signal Process. Lett. **2**(3), 46–48 (1995)
16. Camarena-Ibarrola, A., Reynoso, M., Figueroa, K.: Text-independent speaker identification using formants and convolutional neural networks. In: Batyrshin, I., Gelbukh, A., Sidorov, G. (eds.) MICAI 2021. LNCS (LNAI), vol. 13068, pp. 108–119. Springer, Cham (2021). https://doi.org/10.1007/978-3-030-89820-5_9
17. Camarena-Ibarrola, A., Figueroa, K., Plancarte Curiel, A.: Spoofing detection for speaker verification with glottal flow and 1D pure convolutional networks. In: Rodríguez-González, A.Y., Pérez-Espinosa, H., Martínez-Trinidad, J.F., Carrasco-Ochoa, J.A., Olvera-López, J.A. (eds.) MCPR 2023. LNCS, vol. 13902, pp. 149–158. Springer, Cham (2023). https://doi.org/10.1007/978-3-031-33783-3_14

Towards the Automatic Construction of Multimodal Graphical and Voice Interfaces

Juan C. Olivares-Rojas[1]($\boxtimes$) (iD), Gabriel González-Serna[2] (iD),
J. Guadalupe Ramos-Díaz[1] (iD), Noe A. Castro-Sánchez[2] (iD),
and Johan W. González-Murueta[1]

[1] Tecnológico Nacional de México/I. T. de Morelia, 50120 Morelia, Michoacán, Mexico
juan.or@morelia.tecnm.mx
[2] Tecnológico Nacional de México/CENIDET, 62490 Cuernavaca, Morelos, Mexico

Abstract. The development of natural language processing is popularizing the use of voice interfaces in current applications. However, many of the interfaces currently developed are graphical interfaces that have been surpassed for the new needs of users. Hence, the use of multimodal interfaces, both visual and voice, is necessary to be more friendly and easy to use by final users. To do this, it would be necessary to redesign current graphic systems to integrate voice interfaces. This work shows that it is possible to develop multimodal interfaces starting from existing graphical interfaces by adding voice interfaces through previously designed dialogue and interactions. Tests were carried out through Web forms using feature extraction techniques, where satisfactory results were obtained.

Keywords: Multimodal · GUI · VUI · Machine Learning

1 Introduction

To end users, computer systems are what they see. Hence, user interfaces are important since they are the entry and exit point of information [1].

When the first computers started, they had very difficult to manage interfaces, in many cases related very directly to the computer hardware. With the appearance of input mechanisms such as the keyboard and output mechanisms such as the monitor, interfaces became simpler, facilitating the use of computers through what was called command line interface (CLI). However, to handle even a CLI the end user must learn commands and syntax that are, in many cases, difficult to learn since it requires knowing many parameters and ways of use, as well as having a manual at their side, so initially, computers were only used by computer experts [2].

Since the beginning of the computer era, efforts have been made to make interfaces more natural, intuitive, and friendly to the end user, which is why it is necessary to try to use the various human senses, not only the visual aspect but also the touch, sound, taste, and smell if possible [3].

A multimodal system allows the use of more than one way, form, or sense so that the user can interact with the computer and its environment [4].

© The Author(s), under exclusive license to Springer Nature Switzerland AG 2024
E. Mezura-Montes et al. (Eds.): MCPR 2024, LNCS 14755, pp. 297–307, 2024.
https://doi.org/10.1007/978-3-031-62836-8_28

The use of multimodal interfaces to improve human-computer interaction has been studied for many years. Since the first graphic systems appeared, as well as the use of multimedia (mainly audio) in computers, the first multimodal interfaces emerged. With the appearance of mobile devices, firstly handheld computers, and then smart mobile phones, it became necessary to improve the interaction between users and the devices since their limited capabilities, especially screen and processing, make it very difficult to work with interfaces [5]. Traditional user graphs. For this reason, schemes such as gestures using hands-on touch screens were designed [6].

With the proliferation of artificial intelligence and machine learning techniques, voice-based natural language interfaces (NLI) have begun to be used massively, such as digital assistants such as Alexa, Siri, Cortana, etc., presented in various devices such as smart speakers and cell phones, among others [7].

Various authors have focused on improving human-machine interaction using various human senses through multimodal interfaces. For example, multimodal interfaces have been designed in robots, allowing better interaction with humans [8]. This has contributed to the development of social service robots [9].

The interaction of humans with machines has also been studied for many years in various ways to ensure better user experiences (UX) using various metrics to do so. For example, in [10], a comparison of voice assistants and graphical interfaces for virtual reality environments using performance metrics is shown. Various authors have worked on multimodal systems that combine voice and graphical interfaces, such as [11].

For some time now, particularly with the appearance of mobile devices, work has been done on architectures for the adaptation of multimodal interfaces using the Web using dialog modelling [12].

Other authors have focused on the use of artificial intelligence techniques to improve voice interfaces (VUI) and NLI and make them more intuitive for the end user [13].

However, we have talked about multimodal interfaces and their evolution up to this point. As has been seen, these interfaces are designed from scratch, but what happens when you already have existing systems and interfaces that need to add more natural modes of interaction? In most cases, the interfaces and systems would have to be redone.

Few works focus on adapting already existing interfaces to add multi-mode aspects automatically. For example, in [14], a framework for working with multimodal systems in mobile applications with Android is presented.

This work aims to help convert existing graphical user interfaces, particularly designed through Web forms with HTML, towards multimodal interfaces that automatically integrate recognition and speech synthesis. To this end, a study of the characterization of the various types and controls of Web forms was developed in the first instance and then validated using automatic classification techniques that allow the construction of a natural language dialogue that helps improve human-computer interaction when obtaining a multimodal GUI/NLI (VUI) system.

2   Materials and Methods

Figure 1 describes a traditional Web system that implements a traditional GUI through a form. If you wanted to integrate a voice interface, you would have to design and add a new one to the existing system. This work intends to analyze existing GUIs to automatically obtain the VUIs and integrate them directly into a multimodal system.

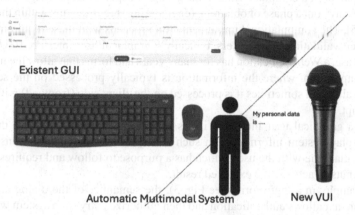

Fig. 1. Multimodal system problem construction.

To solve this problem, the following steps were followed. First a Dialogue modeling of the previous interfaces. Second a manual collection and classification of web pages interface. Third, an automatic classification and understanding of dialogue of Web pages. Finally, and automatic conversion and integration of natural voice interfaces.

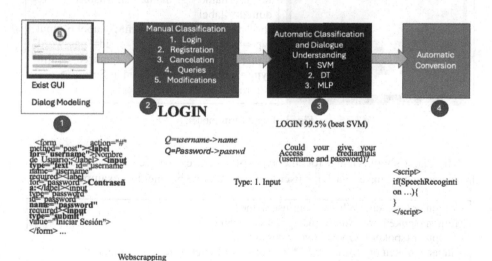

Fig. 2. Methodology solution

Figure 2 shows the general process of the steps followed in the methodology. Each step is described below, and Sect. 3 shows the results.

2.1 Dialogue Modeling

Returning to some concepts of user interface management. It is assumed that, during the development of a computer system, the group of experts that participate in its initial phase must carry out a phase of obtaining (engineering) requirements within the analysis process [15]. The computational implementation proceeds with these requirements and, through their validation by end users, typically a graphical user interface (GUI).

In our case, a Web application has for many years had forms that allow the interaction of input/output data, where the information is typically processed on the server side (backend), although sometimes it is processed on the client side (frontend) with the help of JavaScript.

Given a graphical user interface, it has a dialog and interaction with the user to capture/display system information in such a way that each screen is considered an interaction dialogue with the user, which has a purpose to follow and requires inputs as well as outputs to achieve the expected result.

For example, in a login form (see Fig. 3), the semantics of the dialog are to enter information that allows authentication and then authorize entry for a system with predetermined privileges. In this case, the input is typically the username (which may or may not be public) and a password.

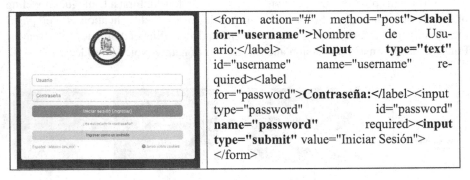

Fig. 3. Login form model.

This dialog should change for other types of interfaces. In the case of a voice interface, the system would have to ask the user to input data one by one. For example:

Computer (spoken): What is your username?
Human (spoken or written): juan.perez@correo.com
Computer (spoken): Give me your password?
Human (spoken or written*): ****** (password in clear text with a mask)
Computer (spoken, successful scenario): Welcome, Juan Perez; what can I do for you today?
Computer (spoken, failure scenario): Invalid username or password. Please try again

Some elements, such as passwords, are inappropriate to be displayed in a voice interface for privacy and security reasons.

Output interfaces have another semantics of displaying process results to end users. When it is text, the output is easy to process for a voice system, but when it is a graphic element or a table, the output is more complicated to say by voice, even though you have the element on the screen (if it is a multimodal VUI interface-GUI).

In this other example, the results of a process are shown. For example, when inserting an item into the catalog. An output interface would be generated as follows:

> Computer (spoken and written): The item was successfully registered.
> Computer (spoken and written*): Displays a table of items and reads it row by row

Note that the interface could vary to, for example, only show the first part of the process. In general, there are also both input and output interfaces simultaneously. For example, a student withdrawal form. You have the following interface (Table 1).

Table 1. Example of an input/output dialog.

Seq	Interaction	Mode	Information
1*	Computer	Spoken/Screen	Which student do you want to remove?
2	User	Spoken/Screen*	*******
3	Computer	Spoken/Screen*	Do you want to eliminate so-and-so?
4	User	Spoken/Screen*	Yes (press button)
5	Computer		Student successfully removed

Note that the interface could be different, for example, when placing a table resulting from a student query for a given criterion and having the word delete highlighted or, more intuitively, an X icon to delete.

Interfaces can mix both inputs and outputs. So, the interface must handle both modes. You must have the context of what should be entered as input and what is displayed as output.

Although there are various processing languages on the server side, such as PHP, ASP, Python, JSP, etc., at the end of the day, it falls on HTML-based technology. HTML marks the document's structure, while CSS defines the behavior of the elements. So, more weight is given to HTML.

Most web applications are generally oriented towards business, which can be various types. However, they are generally transactional systems based on data-centric architectures, so their basic operations fall into registrations, cancellations, queries, and modifications (CRUD). So, their input/output interfaces, in most cases, fall into these forms.

Web systems are also informative, showing detailed information to the end user, but in this context, they are not very interactive so that a voice interface would reproduce the text shown with a screen reader.

Therefore, our variables of interest are the type of form: entry, exit, hybrid, the category of the form: login, registration, cancellations, queries, modifications; as well as the text content of the page (for example, questions and answers).

2.2 Manual Collection and Classification

Through the web programming projects of the computer systems engineering and information and communications technology engineering careers from 2015 to 2023, a total of 600 web development projects that have the characteristics of the data were requested since, as a final project, a project is left that covers the management of databases (relational and lately non-relational) to register, cancel, queries, and modifications, and a security system based on login and sessions.

Of the 600 sites, a sample of 500 was chosen for the training/validation process and 100 for the system in production. Where each page has a form of each type.

As we know which category they belong to, each website was cataloged with its type and respective category using a CSV. As shown in Table 2.

Table 2. Example of the dataset.

Site	Type	Mode	Information
Flower Shop	1	1	Login/User/Password/Forgot/...
Book store	2	2	Register successfully/...
Private School	3	3	Do you want to eliminate this student?

The webform type is given by the values 1) Login, 2) Registrations, 3) Cancellations, 4) Queries, and 5) Modifications, while the mode is given by 1) Input, 2) Output and 3) Input/output. The process described in Sect. 2.3 was used to obtain the information field.

2.3 Automatic Classification and Understanding of Dialogue

It was necessary to analyze each form on the website to carry out the automatic classification process. To do this, it is necessary to decompose the website into its HTML elements represented by its different types of tags marked by tags such as form, input, select, and option, among others that mark the HTML5 standard and earlier.

The website structure analysis was done using the Python language using the BeatifullSoap library, following these heuristic rules:

1. If the webform only have input tags is for input
2. If the webform does not have input tags is for output
3. If the webform have input with
4. Check if the text in tags mentions input/output in explicit forms, these is the final mode.
5. The webform component order is so important to get the dialog
6. All the text is getting and putting in a single text to conform a natural language dialog

2.4 Automatic Conversion

Once the websites' structure and type have been recognized, the extracted dialogue is automatically converted to a voice interface.

To do this, we implement the simplest dialogue, the question/answer dialogue. To do this, the first question is detected in an input interface, placing the focus on the first cursor. The system will wait for the user to speak or manually select the result. Passing the focus to another control or the user entering the jump word "over" at the end will continue the interaction or word "over and end" to finish the dialogue.

For an output interface, it is simpler since you only put a screen reader so that the computer can speak the result. The input and output interfaces are combinations, so only knowing the current context is required to place the appropriate dialog type.

The JavaScript Web Speech API library was used for synthesis (speech synthesis) and speech recognition (Speech recognition). Following is an example of the convertion and integration:

```
...    <p id="voice-response"></p>
<script>
    const form = document.getElementById('multimodal-form');
    const voiceResponse = document.getElementById('voice-response');
    form.addEventListener('submit', function(event) {
        event.preventDefault();
        const username = form.elements.username.value;
        const password = form.elements.password.value;
        // Here, you can add logic to process the form data.
        // For now, we will only show a voice response
        voiceResponse.textContent = ` Logging in as ${username}`;
        // Here is the logic to send the data to a server
    });
    // Speech Recognition Section
    if ('SpeechRecognition' in window || 'webkitSpeechRecognition' in window) {
        const SpeechRecognition = window.SpeechRecognition || window.web-
kitSpeechRecognition;
        const recognition = new SpeechRecognition();
        recognition.lang = 'es-ES'; // Set the language for Speech Recognition
        recognition.onresult = function(event) {
            const transcript = event.results[0][0].transcript;
            const confidence = event.results[0][0].confidence;
            // Here is the logic to interpret the voice command and complete the form
            // As mentioned, we use a simple question-answer interaction.
            document.getElementById('username').value = transcript;
        };
        recognition.onerror = function(event) {
            console.error('Error in speech Recognition:', event.error);
        };
        document.getElementById('username').addEventListener('focus', function() {
            recognition.start();
        });
    } else {
        console.error(' Voice recognition is not supported in this browser.);
    }
</script> ...
```

3 Results and Discussion

3.1 Dialog Modelling (Semi-automatic)

The retrieved tags are used to try to identify the type of dialog using heuristics, typically using the headers (h1-h6) to detect the type of form, for example, High (with synonyms such as register, add, etc.) and extending to the others, as well as see if metadata is marked as the meta tag. This applies to all 5 types of forms.

To determine whether the mode of the form is input, output, or input/output, it is checked if it contains an action attribute of a form tag, which indicates that it is input;

if it does not, it is assumed that it is output. The input/output type must have an action, and we consider that there are too many texts or other elements on the page. It is also considered an input and output form if form fields are disabled or read-only.

The text of each question is obtained by reviewing the plain text or label tags before or after the form. The order followed is how the form controls and other components on the Web page are marked, following the default flow from top to bottom, from left to right, unless there is a default order with the tab index attribute.

These rules were obtained from direct observation and analysis of the 600 sites reviewed.

Depending on the type of form and its mode, the dialogue is constructed in the text that will be passed to the voice synthesizer, and the pauses between questions and answers will be captured by the voice recognizer.

3.2 Automatic Classification and Understanding of Data (Dialogue)

The feature extraction in Sect. 3.1 is somewhat time-consuming, performed manually, and error prone. The idea is that, with the data collected and classified, the developed converter can automatically infer the type and mode of the form by analyzing its content. Therefore, an automatic classifier was implemented to support and complement the modeling and understanding of conversational dialogue.

The SVM, Decision Trees, and Multilayer Perceptron Neural Network classifiers were used for the automatic classification of Web sites, obtaining the results shown in Table 3.

Table 3. Classification results.

Model	Accuracy	Precision	Recall	F1 Score
SVM	91.1%	92.51%	98.17%	95.23
Decision Tree	99.49%	99.66%	99.87%	99.72%
MLP	99.83%	99.91%	99.9%	99.89%

The results obtained are very homogeneous, with the neural network having greater performance. Already in the production system, the 100 results were used, obtaining an accuracy like that reported in the training and validation process.

3.3 Automatic Conversion (Multimodal)

To validate the automatic converter and its integration with the existing graphical interface to obtain a multimodal system, a set of tests was developed to verify whether the generated natural language interface can coexist well with the existing graphical interface.

To do this, students from the Selected Web Topics subject were used to evaluate user interaction, simply measuring the effectiveness of whether the natural language interface could be used alone and in combination. In most cases it could be used without problems (95%), only with some complications in very elaborate dialogues and in forms classified as incorrectly classified input/output (around 5%).

It was observed that, in general terms, the natural language interface works adequately, but the dialogue in some cases, such as in the contact data form, is extremely slow, given that various elements can be grouped, such as address (which is a composite piece of information) in several simple elements such as street, exterior number, neighborhood, etc.

4 Conclusions and Future Works

The present work shows that it is possible to implement the automatic conversion of graphical interfaces in Web systems towards multimodal systems that add natural interfaces such as voice. However, it can still be seen that it deals with a more in-depth analysis of the written context for a better understanding of the dialogue, but above all, to better manage the interaction of the dialogue, since a question-answer dialogue, although functional, it is not the most friendly and fast for the end user.

To improve the best automatic construction of multimodal interfaces from GUI, it is recommended to consider the following. The analysis of dialogue modeling can be improved using natural language processing techniques to perform a better classification through topic modeling. In addition, it is necessary to structure the forms with metadata in a better way so that they are more useful, considering that today, support for HTML5 in browsers has been present for many years (this is because the design of most of the considered websites does not consider these best practices). Finally, care must be taken when managing legacy systems since some technologies could be obsolete today, and when updated to use voice interfaces, they could no longer be functional.

Acknowledgments. This project is supported by Tecnológico Nacional de México under grant 19382-24.P. Juan C. Olivares-Rojas thanks Tecnológico Nacional de Mexico for the support provided to carry out a postdoctoral stay within his sabbatical year.

References

1. Ilyas, Q., et al.: Localized text-free user interfaces. IEEE Access **10**, 2357–2371 (2022)
2. Moore, A.: Python GUI Programming with Tkinter: Design and Build Functional and User-Friendly GUI Applications. Packt Publishing (2021)
3. Sharma, R., et al.: Toward multimodal human-computer interface. In: Proceedings of the IEEE, vol. 86, no. 5, pp. 853–869 (1998)
4. Furht, B.: Multimodal interfaces. In: Furht, B. (ed.) Encyclopedia of Multimedia, pp. 651–652. Springer, Boston (2008). https://doi.org/10.1007/978-0-387-78414-4_159
5. Dumas, B., Lalanne, D., Oviatt, S.: Multimodal interfaces: a survey of principles, models and frameworks. In: Lalanne, D., Kohlas, J. (eds.) Human Machine Interaction. LNCS, vol. 5440, pp. 3–26. Springer, Heidelberg (2009). https://doi.org/10.1007/978-3-642-00437-7_1
6. Hsu, W., et al.: Adaptive virtual gestures for GUI testing on smartphones. IEEE Softw. **34**(5), 22–29 (2017)

7. Singh, N., et al.: Operating system command execution using voice command. In: Proceedings of 3rd Asian Conference on Innovation in Technology (ASIANCON), Ravet IN, India, pp. 1–5 (2023)
8. Goyzueta, D., et al.: Analysis of a user interface based on multimodal interaction to control a robotic arm for EOD applications. Electronics **11**(11) (2022)
9. Hoang, V., et al.: Socially aware robot navigation framework: where and how to approach people in dynamic social environments. IEEE Trans. Autom. Sci. Eng. **20**(2), 1322–1336 (2023)
10. Buchta, K., et al.: NUX IVE - a research tool for comparing voice user interface and graphical user interface in VR. In: Proceedings of 2022 IEEE Conference on Virtual Reality and 3D User Interfaces Abstracts and Workshops (VRW), Christchurch, New Zealand, pp. 982–983 (2022)
11. Zhou, Bo., Li, L.: GVUI: graphic-assisted voice user interface based on multi-modal human-machine conversation. In: Ahram, T.Z., Falcão, C.S. (eds.) AHFE 2021. LNNS, vol. 275, pp. 833–842. Springer, Cham (2021). https://doi.org/10.1007/978-3-030-80091-8_99
12. Steele, R., Khankan, K.: Towards the Mobile Web - An Architecture for Multimodal Interface Auto-Generation for Web Pages and Services, University of Technology, Sydney, Australia (2005)
13. Polyakov, E., et al.: Investigation and development of the intelligent voice assistant for the Internet of Things using machine learning. In: 2018 Moscow Workshop on Electronic and Networking Technologies (MWENT), Moscow, Russia, pp. 1–5 (2018)
14. Griol, D., Molina, J.M.: A framework to develop adaptive multimodal dialog systems for android-based mobile devices. In: Polycarpou, M., de Carvalho, A.C.P.L.F., Pan, J.-S., Woźniak, M., Quintian, H., Corchado, E. (eds.) HAIS 2014. LNCS (LNAI), vol. 8480, pp. 25–36. Springer, Cham (2014). https://doi.org/10.1007/978-3-319-07617-1_3
15. ISO/IEC/IEEE Draft International Standard - Systems and Software Engineering – Life Cycle Processes –Requirements Engineering. In ISO/IEC/IEEE P29148_FDIS, pp. 1–104 (2018)

An Analysis of the Impact of Gender and Age on Perceiving and Identifying Sexist Posts

Martha Paola Jimenez-Martinez[1]([⊠]) [iD], Irvin Hussein Lopez-Nava[1] [iD], and Manuel Montes-y-Gómez[2] [iD]

[1] Centro de Investigación Científica y de Educación Superior de Ensenada, Ensenada, Mexico
{jimenezmp,hussein}@cicese.edu.mx
[2] Instituto Nacional de Astrofísica, Óptica y Electrónica, Puebla, Mexico
mmontesg@inaoep.mx

Abstract. This research addresses the challenge of detecting sexism in Spanish-language tweets on social media. Our analysis explores labeling differences among annotators with diverse sociodemographic attributes, emphasizing their relevance in automated model development. Using a dataset enriched with labels from six diverse profiles, our study revealed nuanced perceptions of sexism across different genders and age ranges. Although there is considerable agreement between genders, instances of disagreement persist. Similarly, while there is a better consensus in terms of age, disagreements still arise. We use a RoBERTuito model fine-tuned on sexism identification, reaching an F1-score of 0.856 when training the model considering only the labels of the oldest age profile. These instances underscore the necessity for continuous model refinement to effectively capture subtle language variations.

Keywords: Sexism detection · Text Classification · Natural language processing · Transformers · Social Media

1 Introduction

Sexism in language refers to the use of expressions that favor one gender over the other, perpetuating stereotypes and prejudices that can be deemed harmful, especially towards women [13]. This form of discrimination is rooted in biological differences and manifests through attitudes, prejudices, and stereotypes suggesting the inferiority of one gender to another [15].

Those born or residing in Mexico understand that our culture, like many Latin cultures, is strongly imbued with "machismo"[1]. It is common to encounter numerous sexist expressions prevalent in the Spanish language. Statements

---

[1] It encompasses a collection of attitudes and actions that unfairly undermine the dignity of women when compared to men.

include phrases like "You run like a girl" or "You throw like a girl". Men can also be subjected to victimization, as there are expressions designed to "test" their masculinity. Moreover, women often face phrases like "You look prettier when you're quiet", which serves to minimize and silence them [2].

A study has highlighted that areas with higher rates of misogynistic tweets also show higher rates of domestic and family violence [1]. Another study has pointed out that the increase in the use of misogynistic language on Twitter is correlated with an increase in real-life rates of sexual violence [4]. This underscores the significance of conducting thorough research from diverse perspectives, including computational methods focused on automatically identifying messages with such demeaning content. The integration of these methods becomes pivotal in addressing and mitigating the impact of online misogynistic language over offline incidents of gender-based violence.

Hate speech is widely recognized as highly intricate, even among those familiar with the subject and the variety of definitions proposed [9]. Accordingly, several notable workshops have played a crucial role in advancing the field of hate speech detection, these include, but are not limited to, The Workshop on Computational Approaches to Subjectivity, Sentiment & Social Media Analysis (WASSA); The Workshop on Online Abuse and Harms (WOAH); and The International Workshop on Semantic Evaluation (SemEval). In the context of the latter, a task on Explainable Detection of Online Sexism (EDOS) was introduced in which approximately 90% of participants, across various subtasks, opted for applying a transformer-based architecture. They used well-known models such as RoBERTa, DeBERTa, BERT, BERTweet, and DistilBERT. Some submissions leveraged prompted language models like GPT-2, GPT-3, PaLM, and OPT [3].

Unfortunately, the majority of research focuses on detecting misogyny in English tweets, therefore the automatic detection of misogynistic tweets in Spanish is notably scarce [10]. A significant effort in this regard is the recent organization of the EXIST (sEXism Identification in Social neTworks) shared task [8,11,12]. In 2021, with a focus on two primary tasks (Identification and Categorization), approaches for detecting sexism in Spanish utilized a pre-trained multilingual BERT model as well as monolingual BERT models [7]. In 2022, also centering on the two tasks, a novel bi-ensemble approach based on RoBERTa and BERT was introduced. This method combined transformers pretrained in both Spanish and English [16]. By 2023, the scope expanded to include three tasks (Identification, Intention, and Categorization). A cascaded system was developed using GPT-NeoX and BERTIN-GPT-J-6B [14].

Despite the encouraging results reported by the EXIST task, there is a lack of analysis regarding the differences in the perception of sexism by different groups of people. At this point it is worth noting that the EXIST corpus stands out from previous ones by making the labels of all annotators available, making this type of analysis possible. Nonetheless, all the studies using this corpus have predominantly concentrated on proposing novel methods for the automatic detection of sexism, and none have carried out an in-depth analysis of the differences on the annotators' labels. Accordingly, our primary contribution involves a detailed analysis of labels from six annotator profiles in the EXIST corpus, examining agreement levels and identifying themes causing discordant perceptions. Our second contribution focuses on automatically identifying sexist comments. We explore the consequences of training models on data labeled by a homogeneous group and assess their effectiveness in detecting comments marked as sexist by the majority opinion. Using state-of-the-art methods, we analyze top-performing models, particularly transformers, to evaluate their ability to identify sexism in real tweets labeled by gender and age profiles. This multifaceted approach enhances our understanding of sexism detection, considering diverse annotator perspectives and model effectiveness on homogeneous data.

2 The EXIST Corpus

To conduct our analysis and experiments, we utilized the corpus from the sEXism Identification in Social neTworks task at CLEF 2023 [8]. It comprises 10,000 entries in both English and Spanish [6]. From the 4,209 labeled instances in Spanish, 3,660 were utilized for training, with 20% reserved for validation purposes. The models underwent testing with 549 instances.

The EXIST' tasks encompass three distinct objectives, with the initial task involving binary classification (Sexist or Not Sexist) of the tweet. The subsequent two tasks further delve into the content identified as sexist. Task two aims to classify the message based on three types of author intentions (Direct; Reported; and Judgemental). Meanwhile, the third task requires categorizing the tweet into one or more of five different categories: Ideological and Inequality; Role Stereotyping and Dominance; Objectification; Sexual Violence; and Misogyny and Non-Sexual Violence. However, our primary focus lies on the first task [8].

Unlike typical datasets, this corpus lacks a single, definitive label. Instead, it includes labels from six different profiles of individuals. Having 725 annotators, these profiles consist of three women and three men from distinct age groups: 18–22, 23–45, and 46+. Consequently, each text is associated with six labels.

The "hard label", or the consensus label, is determined through the agreement of the six different profiles, regardless of whether the consensus is unanimous or based on a majority, the label remains unchanged. For instance, consider the example where annotators unanimously agreed (Table 1).

Table 1. Tweet where annotators unanimously agreed.

Tweet	@BestKabest Esta gringa sigue llorando por el gamergate, que "coincidencia" que tenga pronombres en su perfil
Gender Annotators	"F", "F", "F", "M", "M", "M"
Age Annotators	"18-22", "23-45", "46+", "46+", "23-45", "18-22"
Labels Task1	"YES", "YES", "YES", "YES", "YES", "YES"
Consensus Label	"YES"

On the contrary, consider the example where annotators had varying opinions (Table 2). From this example, only the 18–22 female and 23–45 male profiles identified the tweet as not sexist. By employing rigid labels, valuable information pertaining to annotator profiles is foregone. Based on all this, prior to model construction, we focused on conducting a thorough examination of discrepancies in individual annotations, particularly with respect to gender and age perspectives.

Table 2. Tweet where annotators had varying opinions.

Tweet	Alejandro Saavedra, violador parte de #laManada en SCZ finalmente sentenciado a 20 años #SeVaACaer
Gender Annotators	"F", "F", "F", "M", "M", "M"
Age Annotators	"18-22", "23-45", "46+", "46+", "23-45", "18-22"
Labels Task1	"NO", "YES", "YES", "YES", "NO", "YES"
Consensus Label	"YES"

3   Sexism Perception by Different Annotators

We conducted a qualitative assessment of agreement and disagreement between men and women (Fig. 1) based on labeled tweets. Out of 3660 texts, 36% showed agreement between men and women stating they are sexist, while 39% agreed that they are not sexist. In 12% of texts, men claimed they were sexist while women denied it, and in 13%, women affirmed they were sexist while men denied it. This discrepancy implies potential variations in perception and sensitivity towards sexist content between genders (in total 25%).

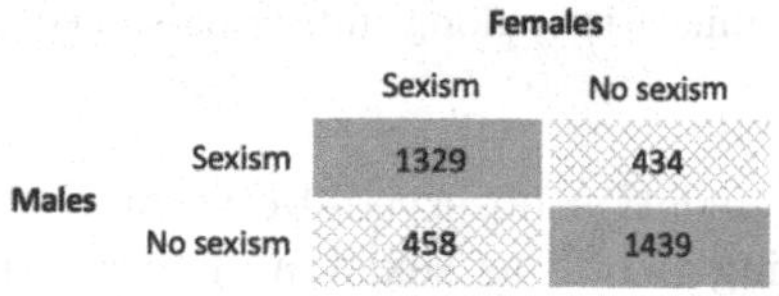

		Females	
		Sexism	No sexism
	Sexism	1329	434
Males			
	No sexism	458	1439

Fig. 1. Coincidence and disagreement in sexism labels between Men and Women.

Noteworthy examples of disagreement occur in scenarios in which women label the posts as "sexist" while men label them as "non-sexist". Many of these cases revolve primarily around women, presenting as "facts" the opinions of men towards them, as exemplified by Table 3.

Similarly, instances where men categorize a text as "Sexist" while women categorize it as "Not Sexist" are more directed towards men (Table 3), often conveyed with subtlety or in a "joking" manner, which tends to be more widely

Table 3. Tweets where women and men differ in labeling.

Label Task1	Tweet
female: YES **male: NO**	- *Nadie te va a tratar tan bien como un hombre que te quiere cog*r por primera vez. #BuenosDías* - *@gishel_paola @PaveloRockstar @giov_ Las mujeres no deben opinar, no porque varias lo hagan, tu también andes haciéndolo*
female: NO **male: YES**	- *No todos los hombres son iguales, siempre llega uno más cul*ro que el anterior.* - *buena foto teodoro pareces una p*ta en decadencia* https://t.co/1LecSxbGKi

accepted by people. This is because there is a common perception that sexism is predominantly directed at women when in reality, it affects both genders.

In cases where men identify content as sexist and women disagree, it typically pertains to mockery directed towards men, as demonstrated in the examples. These patterns underscore the nuanced and diverse perceptions of sexism in discourse, emphasizing the need for sensitivity and understanding when addressing these issues.

Our second analysis focuses on the annotators' age groups, where differences, although more subtle, can also be observed between people aged 18 to 22 years, 23 to 45 years and 46+ (Fig. 2).

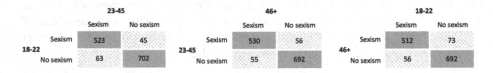

Fig. 2. Differences and similarities among individuals aged 18–22, 23–45 and 46+.

A considerable agreement is observed between the 18–22 and 23–45 age groups, with 39% labeling tweets as sexist and 53% agreed that they are not sexist; conversely, the total disagreement rate was 8%. These levels of agreement were presented when comparing the other groups, 23–45 with 46+, and 46+ with 18–22, registering a total level of agreement of 92% and 90%, respectively.

Despite disagreement rates being below 10% it is important to thoroughly examine instances where these varied age groups hold differing views on the concept of sexism. Table 4 illustrates tweets on which the age groups diverged in their labels of sexism.

As expected, these results indicate coherence in opinions within certain age groups but highlight discrepancies in the perception of sexism, especially when comparing younger participants (18–22) with older participants (46+).

Table 4. Tweets where individuals ages 18–22, 23–45 and 46+ differ in labeling.

Label Task1	Tweet
18–22: YES **23–45:** NO	- *@ParentiSol cheto florida 40 te voy a re acosar ahora.*
18–22: NO **23–45:** YES	- *@KtaNaldo_Bucara El hacerlo con una mujer embarazada levanta un morbo increíble...Que buen vídeo muchachos.*
18–22: YES **46+:** NO	- *@PamelaAlemapq @AustinPalao obvio que sii , es guapisimo, chicas un grito saooooooo!!!*
18–22: NO **46+:** YES	- *@23_Shephard GORDA P*TA Y TIRA CAUCHO. VOMITIVA.*
23–45: YES **46+:** NO	- *@LeiiVaquella Que nai jajaja! Hasta se me aflojaron las caderas de nuevo, que se prepare el 31 y primero jajajaja.*
23–45: NO **46+:** YES	- *@PerroChusko @MineduPeru @congresoperu Que el de todas el feminismo es cáncer.*

It's important to note that this analysis was conducted with a dataset of only 1333 instances due to information loss in each age group, requiring the identification and selection of common tweets. These disagreements represent a minority within the dataset. Therefore the perception of sexism is more uniform and similar across different age groups than across different genders.

4 On the Automatic Identification of Sexism

We focus on revealing nuanced perceptions of sexism across different genders and age ranges through our model, comparing both groups with the consensus of all. Due to our focus on Spanish data, we chose to work with a pre-trained language model designed for social media text in Spanish, specifically "pysentimiento/robertuito-base-uncased" from Hugging Face[2].

In the gender sorting, we utilized 3,021 examples for training, 638 for development, and 549 for testing. Regarding age, the training set varied: 2,064 examples for ages 18 to 23; 2,039 for ages 23 to 45; and 1,981 for ages 46 and above. The dataset decreases based on gender and age as annotators come to a consensus. In specific, when training a model on gender opinions, we consider only three labels. If 2 out of 3 annotators agree on the label of a tweet (sexist or not-sexist), it's labeled as such. Similarly, when training models on individuals' ages, we only have two labels. In this case, the label is required to be mutually agreed upon by the two annotators; otherwise, the tweet is removed.

Given that the dataset comprises Twitter texts, which are mainly informal and often contain tags or links irrelevant to the model's learning, we conducted pre-processing on mentions and links. Mentions were replaced with "@USER," and links were replaced with "HTTPURL". This step aimed to enhance the model's performance by removing non-informative elements from the text.

---

[2] https://huggingface.co/pysentimiento/robertuito-base-uncased.

We will present the outcomes yielded by our model, taking into account the profiles associated with the six distinct labels present in each text. The experiments are structured in two phases: the initial phase focuses on visualizing accurate predictions and inaccurate predictions based on gender. The subsequent phase involves comparing outcomes based on age.

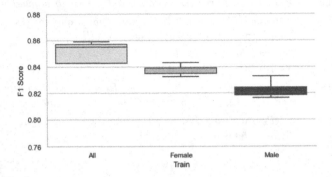

Fig. 3. Classification results by gender. Comparison based on the consensus of men, women and consensus of all annotators.

Our model, was trained using three different approaches, considering the opinions of all six profiles per tweet, only the opinions of the three female profiles, or only the opinions of the three male profiles, and using a hard label evaluation scheme (see Fig. 3). The boxplot with the opinions of all six profiles will be taken as a reference. However, focusing on training with men and women groups, we obtained F1 scores of 0.822 ($\sigma = 0.005$) and 0.837 ($\sigma = 0.003$), respectively, compared to the overall consensus of the six profiles that achieved 0.851 ($\sigma = 0.007$). To assess whether there is a distinction between models trained with gender-specific labels, we conducted a t-test on F1 scores for women and men, revealing a significant difference ($p < 0.05$). Consequently, there is also a notable distinction between the consensus and the female and male groups ($p < 0.05$).

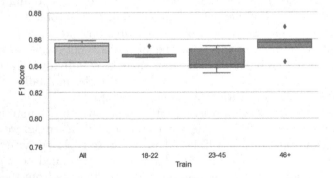

Fig. 4. Classification results by age. Comparison with different age groups and the consensus rankings from all annotators.

The study delves deeper into age groups and, initially assuming gender as the primary factor for identifying sexism, strategically opts to evaluate models customized for each age group (see Fig. 4). The model achieved an F1 score of 0.848 ($\sigma = 0.003$) for group 18 to 22; 0.844 ($\sigma = 0.008$) for the group of 23 to 45; and for individuals aged 46 and above, the F1 score reached 0.856 ($\sigma = 0.008$). The ANOVA analysis reveals that there are no statistically significant differences between the consensus across various age groups ($p > 0.05$). It is essential to underscore that no statistically significant differences ($p > 0.05$) were ascertained in the context of any other inter-group comparisons.

It is imperative to draw attention to the notable loss of data within the consensus, comprising 1,128 texts for the age bracket of 18 to 22; 1,124 instances for the range of 23 to 45; and 1,216 instances for the age group of 46 and above. This data loss occurs because we exclusively engage with two annotators; therefore, to retain an instance, both annotators must reach an agreement. Instances are forfeited in cases where concordance is not achieved. We propose that the improved performance, despite the reduced dataset, can be attributed to the incorporation of both female and male perspectives in all models.

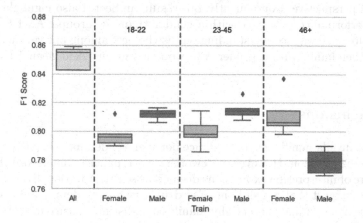

Fig. 5. Classification results for each profile. Comparison with different gender-age profiles and the consensus rankings from all annotators.

Finally, a set of models was trained individually by age and gender profile, as shown in Fig. 5. For the age group 18 to 22, the F1 scores were 0.797 for women and 0.811 for men. For ages 23 to 45, women achieved an F1 score of 0.799, while men scored 0.815. For individuals aged 46 and above, women achieved an F1 score of 0.811, while men obtained 0.779. The ANOVA analysis ($p < 0.05$) indicates a statistically significant difference in the F1 scores between women and men in the age range of 46+, but not for the other age groups.

Remarkably, our analysis reveals statistically significant differences within the group of all annotators when compared to several other subgroups: males aged 18 to 22, males aged 23 to 45, males aged 46 and above, females aged 18 to 22, females aged 23 to 45, and females aged 46 and above. These results underscore the diversity inherent in our dataset and highlight the statistical significance of the observed distinctions among these specific groups. It is crucial to emphasize that comprehensive training, considering annotations from all groups, is essential for identifying general instances of perceived differences. Each perspective needs to prove sufficient in capturing a consensus, underscoring the importance of a holistic approach in model development and evaluation.

Navigating the intricacies of the classification task becomes particularly challenging when addressing cases where gender and age groups exhibit divergent labeling preferences within the dataset. Despite a notable consensus between men and women in text classification, significant disparities highlight the subtleties in perceiving sexism. The model generally demonstrates strong predictive agreement, yet instances of disagreement underscore the imperative for ongoing refinement to capture the intricate nuances of language.

As analyzed in Sect. 3, there is a more noticeable consensus within age groups compared to gender. The prevalence of agreement on sexism across age categories was 39.12%, with 52.16% indicating a non-sexist perspective. In contrast, within gender categories, the agreement rate on sexism is 36.31%, and 39.31% express a non-sexist perspective. Consequently, our results in Sect. 4 also highlight a more distinct performance difference within gender than age groups. An F1 score of 0.856 for 46+ age was scored, standing out as the best among our various groups. On the other hand, within gender, the women's group yielded an F1 score of 0.837.

5   Conclusions

The study unveils significant concordance between gender and age participants in content categorization. However, noteworthy discrepancies underscore the intricate nature of interpreting expressions deemed as sexist. Additionally, age-related disparities suggest that perceptions of sexism vary among demographic cohorts, with younger individuals potentially manifesting distinct sensitivities. While the model's overall performance remains robust, it accentuates the imperative for continual refinement to effectively capture subtle language nuances. Furthermore, this refinement ensures the model's adaptability to the dynamic landscape of evolving digital discourse. The incorporation of soft labels, addressing categorization or intention tasks, data augmentation, and exploration of alternative language models represent avenues for further enhancement and comprehensive exploration within this study's scope.

This study highlights the challenges of detecting sexism in social media content and emphasizes the ongoing need to refine models to effectively address the complex changes in language use. To delve into the potential roots of these variations, it is crucial to factor in cultural or sociological influences that could impact content perception. Variables such as cultural disparities in gender norms, shifting social dynamics, and specific linguistic expressions within certain communities may contribute to the observed discrepancies in classification. For subjective tasks it is crucial to consider the opinions of various annotators [5], for instance, age ranges and genders; and if possible non-binary perspectives. One potential approach is to train separate models and then merge their outputs at the end, e.g., through ensemble modeling. This aims to improve the effectiveness of sexist content by ensuring inclusivity and accuracy across diverse perspectives.

References

1. Blake, K.R., O'Dean, S.M., Lian, J., Denson, T.F.: Misogynistic tweets correlate with violence against women. Psychol. Sci. **32**(3), 315–325 (2021)
2. Comisión Nacional para Prevenir y Erradicar la Violencia Contra las Mujeres, Gobierno de México: Frases sexistas que hombres y mujeres debemos dejar de decir para promover la igualdad de género (2018). https://www.gob.mx/conavim/articulos/frases-sexistas-que-hombres-y-mujeres-debemos-dejar-de-decir-para-promover-la-igualdad-de-genero
3. Kirk, H.R., Yin, W., Vidgen, B., Röttger, P.: Semeval-2023 task 10: explainable detection of online sEXism. arXiv preprint: arXiv:2303.04222 (2023)
4. Menczer, F., et al.: Misogynistic language on twitter and sexual violence. In: Proceedings of the ACM Web Science Workshop on Computational Approaches to Social Modeling (ChASM) (2015)
5. Mokhberian, N., Marmarelis, M.G., Hopp, F.R., Basile, V., Morstatter, F., Lerman, K.: Capturing perspectives of crowdsourced annotators in subjective learning tasks. arXiv preprint: arXiv:2311.09743 (2023)
6. Muti, A., et al.: Enriching hate-tuned transformer-based embeddings with emotions for the categorization of sEXism. In: CEUR Workshop Proceedings, vol. 3497, pp. 1012–1023. CEUR-WS (2023)
7. de Paula, A.F.M., da Silva, R.F., Schlicht, I.B.: SEXism prediction in Spanish and English tweets using monolingual and multilingual BERT and ensemble models. arXiv preprint: arXiv:2111.04551 (2021)
8. Plaza, L., et al.: Overview of exist 2023: sEXism identification in social networks. In: Kamps, J., et al. (eds.) Advances in Information Retrieval. Lecture Notes in Computer Science, vol. 13982, pp. 593–599. Springer, Cham (2023). https://doi.org/10.1007/978-3-031-28241-6_68
9. Poletto, F., Basile, V., Sanguinetti, M., Bosco, C., Patti, V.: Resources and benchmark corpora for hate speech detection: a systematic review. Lang. Resour. Eval. **55**, 477–523 (2021)
10. Rodríguez, D.A., Díaz-Ramírez, A., Miranda-Vega, J.E., Trujillo, L., Mejia-Alvarez, P.: A systematic review of computer science solutions for addressing violence against women and children. IEEE Access **9**, 114622–114639 (2021)
11. Rodríguez-Sánchez, F., et al.: Overview of exist 2021: sEXism identification in social networks. Procesamiento del Lenguaje Natural **67**, 195–207 (2021)
12. Rodríguez-Sánchez, F., et al.: Overview of exist 2022: sEXism identification in social networks. Procesamiento del Lenguaje Natural **69**, 229–240 (2022)
13. Secretaría de Salud, Gobierno de México: Manual para el uso no sexista del lenguaje (2011). https://www.gob.mx/salud/documentos/manual-para-el-uso-no-sexista-del-lenguaje-cnegsr
14. Tian, L., Huang, N., Zhang, X.: Efficient multilingual sEXism detection via large language models cascades. Working Notes CLEF (2023)

15. Vallecillo-Rodríguez, M.E., del Arco, F., Ureña-López, L.A., Martín-Valdivia, M.T., Montejo-Ráez, A.: Integrating annotator information in transformer fine-tuning for sEXism detection. Working Notes CLEF (2023)
16. Villa-Cueva, E., Sanchez-Vega, F., López-Monroy, A.P.: Bi-ensembles of transformer for online bilingual sEXism detection. In: CEUR Workshop Proceedings, vol. 3202 (2022)

Relevance of Sentence Features for Multi-document Text Summarization Using Human-Written Reference Summaries

Verónica Neri Mendoza[✉][iD], Yulia Ledeneva[✉][iD],
René Arnulfo García-Hernández[iD], and Ángel Hernández Castañeda[iD]

Autonomous University of the State of Mexico, Instituto Literario No. 100, 50000
Toluca, State of Mexico, Mexico
vnerim001@alumno.uaemex.mx,
{ynledeneva,reagarciah,anhernandezc}@uaemex.mx

Abstract. For multi-document text summarization, text features are fundamental because they determine the importance of each sentence from source documents. Therefore, selected sentences create a summary that represents the most essential information. In the state-of-the-art, several techniques and methods have been proposed that use different text features and select sentences. However, some features may be more important than others. Thus, differentiating between important and unimportant features is a difficult task. This work proposes a method to generate extractive multi-document text summaries based on statistical and linguistic text features. We calculated the relevance coefficient of each feature to determine its degree of importance through the human-written reference summaries. To perform such calculus, we use 19 text features. After this calculus, we employ a Genetic Algorithm (GA) that selects sentences to generate summaries. In a general way, the proposed method consists of three steps: feature weighting, concatenation and pre-processing of source documents, and feature extraction with sentence selection. In our experiments, we used the DUC01 dataset in two different lengths to evaluate the performance of the proposed method. The results show improvement over state-of-the-art methods.

Keywords: Sentence features · Multi-document text summarization · Statistical and linguistic text features · Human-written reference summaries · Genetic algorithm

1 Introduction

The Internet is a useful tool for spreading information of public interest, but its extensive use has caused an enormous growth of digital information. This situation causes information overload among Internet users, which is usually addressed by generating text summaries [23]. The general summarization process involves rewriting the full text into a brief version. Based on this process, Automatic Text Summarization (ATS) consists of selecting the most important content from a document or a collection of documents using state-of-the-art methods.

ATS is classified according to how it is generated. This categorization involves abstractive, extractive, and hybrid summarization [7, 20]. In **abstractive summarization**, the content of source documents should be interpreted. Usually, generated summaries contain new words obtained from external resources to depict the main idea from source documents. For **extractive text summarization**, summaries are generated by selecting sentences from the source documents. Each sentence is assigned a score, and the sentences with higher scores are selected to be included in the final summary. In **hybrid summarization**, summaries are produced through a combination of abstraction and extraction approaches. Commonly, this approach is generated in two steps: extraction-abstraction and abstraction-abstraction [7].

Depending on the number of input documents, the ATS can be divided into the following tasks: ATS of Individual Documents (ATSID) and ATS of Multiple Documents (ATSMD) [20]. The research of the ATS began approximately 60 years ago [13], focusing on the ATSID. Nevertheless, the to generate of this task occurred in the 90 s, when ATSMD research also began, to provide the user with a brief and informative summary of a set from documents related to a particular topic.

Generally, ATS involves creating a summary by a machine to present the most important content in a brief version of the original text [20, 22]. This process significantly differs from human writing text summarization since humans can capture and relate deep meanings and topics of written documents. Automation of such a skill is challenging to implement [7, 18]. Therefore, it is necessary to design cognitive processes of language comprehension. In ATS, this design consists of preprocessing the text to create an intermediate representation of the original text. After this, two stages are identified: Feature modeling and sentence selection [1].

The quality of a summary depends on the relevance of presented information and a set of text features. One of the essential questions in ATS is what features should be considered in the summarization process and what importance each should have [1, 7, 18, 20]. In the state-of-the-art, several text features have been proposed, which are classified into statistics and linguistics. The statistical features deal with the distribution of words or topics without understanding the document. On the other hand, linguistic features refer to using linguistic knowledge to analyze sentences [7].

In this work, we proposed a method to generate extractive multi-document text summarization. Then, we analyzed a set of 19 statistical and linguistic features. We calculated a relevance coefficient of each feature to determine the importance according to the information presented in the human-written summaries. Finally, we used a Genetic Algorithm (GA) to select sentences from source documents.

The rest of the paper is organized as follows: Sect. 2 presents the related work. Then, Sect. 3 describes the proposed summarization method. In Sect. 4, we show experimental results. Finally, the conclusions are drawn in Sect. 5.

2 Related Works

The use of statistical and linguistic features in the ATS depends on how they are exploited and combined to differentiate the relevance of each sentence from the source documents. The statistical features are sentence position, coverage, similarity to the title, sentence length, redundancy reduction, term frequency, and positive/negative words. In linguistic features, we usually incorporate named entities and part-of-speech tagging (POS).

Determining text features' importance helps generate a better summary, considering sentence relevance, coverage, and redundancy reduction. Moreover, When writing a summary, humans consider both the meaning, semantic relationships of sentences, and structural properties of the text (i.e., at word, sentence, paragraph, and document levels). For this reason, in the methods proposed in the state-of-the-art, we have sought to include features in different language structure levels. Thus, the lexical and syntactic levels analyze the distribution of features at the word and sentence levels, respectively [7]. At the semantic level, however, the meaning of the words and sentences has been taken into account, as well as their semantic relationships [7,15].

In the state-of-the-art, there are different ways to calculate the relevance of text features. Some of them are focused on scoring the sentences of input documents and assigning a relevance coefficient for each feature.

Relevance Based on Sentence Punctuation From Input Documents: The relevance of the features is constructed from the input documents. That is, weights will be generated for each feature based on the provided text. For instance, in [12], a simple but effective method for generating summaries based on the term frequency was introduced. Generally, it was shown that term frequency could serve as a criterion to detect more relevant sentences. In addition, the roots of the words were identified, and finally, the sentences were ordered by their scoring. While in [3], the position of the sentences and the frequency of words to summarize were considered, later in [6], text features such as emblematic words and similarity to the title were introduced.

Relevance Based on Coefficients Calculated Through Optimization: In [9], a Genetic Algorithm (GA) is used to weigh the importance of eight text features, among them are the position of the sentence in the paragraph, term frequency, sentence length, sentence inverse document frequency, sentences including numbers, and sentence similarity. Chromosome size represents the total number of features. Each chromosome combines eight relevance coefficient values calculated from 0 to 1. Subsequently, each relevance coefficient participates in the generation of summaries. On the other hand, in [25], combinations of relevance coefficients were generated to extract sentences. The initial relevance coefficients of the features were generated randomly, in the range of 0 to 1. Subsequently, these coefficients were updated through the GA.

In [8], a GA was used to obtain an adequate combination of relevance coefficients for ten features, among which are the following: position of the sentences, similarity with the title, inclusion of named entities, and length of sentences. The effect of each feature was first investigated to generate summaries. Subsequently, they considered all the above features to train a GA and a mathematical regression algorithm to obtain a suitable combination of features and relevance coefficients. In these works, the sentences are evaluated using the relevance coefficients multiplying the score of the sentence a through the following fitness function:

$$F(s) = \sum_{j=1}^{C} f_j(s) \tag{1}$$

where, f_j is the relevance coefficient for each jth feature, s is the sentence score, and C is the total number of features.

Relevance Based on Manual Coefficients: As in relevance based on coefficients calculated through optimization, the coefficient of text features have been calculated manually. In [17], a method was proposed based on the combination of semantic and statistical features, including key sentences, length of the key sentence, the inclusion of proper nouns, the position of the sentence, similarity with the title, the centrality of the sentence, and the inclusion of numbers. Sentences were evaluated using a linear sum in the sentence selection stage, whose coefficients were manually determined.

On the other hand, in [14], a set of features independent of the domain and language was used to determine the quality of a summary. Among them are sentence position, similarity to the title, sentence length, cohesion between sentences, and coverage. These features were maximized through a memetic algorithm. While [24] proposed a GA to select sentences using four features: coverage, sentence position, sentence length, and similarity with the title. The obtained results show improvements in sentence selection. However, they obtained these coefficients manually, assuming these values are appropriate for improving sentence selection. Therefore, these alternatives require using subjective criteria to determine coefficients.

Sentence Selection: It is the crucial stage to generate the summary. This is where selected features (with their assigned relevance coefficients) establish what sentences represent the document. In the state-of-the-art, this stage has been addressed by techniques such as decision trees, lexical chains, clustering, latent semantic analysis, neural networks, and optimization. However, these techniques have some limitations. For example, although clustering is a simple and intuitive method, the elements are limited to being assigned to a single group [4,7].

On the other hand, graph-based methods produce understandable models to represent documents. However, their construction and storage are complex. In addition, they do not reflect the meaning of the words or sentences [7]). While deep learning-based methods perform well, they require large amounts of training data [7,25,27]. Concerning methods based on latent semantic analysis, the generated summary depends on the quality of the semantic representation of the input text [4]. In decision trees, it is only possible to identify the relationships between sentences by discovering the shared phrases between these sentences [4,7].

Due to the above, it is necessary to model the features by obtaining weighting coefficients through a method that estimates the balance between the quality of the summary and the cost of generating it. Throughout the ATS research, various datasets have been created that include reference summaries written by humans to evaluate the performance of the proposed methods. The goal is for the summaries generated by software to be similar to those written by humans. As mentioned, relevance coefficients have been generated by optimization or manual assignment. However, in the state of the art, summaries written by humans have not been studied as an objective reference to calculate these coefficients.

3   Proposed Method

From the lack of knowledge of how useful the calculation of relevance coefficients from a set of statistical and linguistic features obtained from summaries written by humans can be, we propose a methodology that consists of three steps: feature weighting, concatenation and preprocessing of source documents, and feature extraction with sentence selection.

3.1   Feature Weighting

This stage aims to obtain the relevance coefficients for each feature from the human-written reference summaries. These relevance coefficients affect how sentences from the source text were evaluated for selection and inclusion in the final summary.

The input to this stage is human-written reference summaries. These documents were preprocessed by normalizing and deriving text and filtering stop words. Subsequently, each word was tagged by assigning grammatical categories (POS Tagging) and Named Entity Recognition (NER) tags. Additionally, the text was vectorized using the Word2vec word embedding model to encode the meaning of the words and construct linguistic concepts of the sentences. After this, we consider a set of statistical and linguistic features representing the language structure levels and requirements: relevance, coverage, and redundancy reduction. These features are described as follows:

Thematic Words (TW): This feature is related to domain-specific words frequently appearing in the document. For the proposed method, we considered percentage values from 5% to 15%. However, we empirically noticed that 7% of the most frequent words are the most representative words of each document.

Positive Keywords (PW): Since words are the building blocks of a sentence, the more content keywords a sentence has, the more important it is. Therefore, we defined the positive keywords as 7% of the most frequent words in the summary since this value performs well in determining thematic words.

Inclusion of Title Words (ITW): The sentence receives a high score if it contains more words that appear in the document's title.

Inclusion of Tagged Words (POS, NER): The frequency of POS or NER tags may indicate the relevance of words that compose a sentence. We may capture the frequency of all available POS or NER tags (54). Still, we considered the most common ones (14), which are coordinating conjunction (CC), cardinal number (CD), determiner (DT), preposition or subordinating conjunction (IN), adjective (JJ), singular noun (NN), plural noun (NNS), the verb in base form (VB), the verb in the past (VBD), past participle verb (VBN), personal (PERSON) and organizational names (ORG), names of countries, cities, states (GPE). Finally, dates or periods (DATE).

TF-IDF: Term frequency (TF) measures the number of times a word appears in the document, while inverse document frequency (IDF) processes the number of sentences in which the word appears. When the word is more frequent in the sentence but less frequent in the entire document, the TF-IDF value is higher.

Similarity With the Main Sentence (SMS): It is defined as the similarity between a sentence and other sentences in the document. The use of centrality increases diversity. In the proposed method, the topic sentence obtained the highest score in the TF-IDF calculation. Once the main sentence was identified, we calculated its similarity to other sentences using cosine similarity and Word2vec vectorization.

Based on the calculation of the previously explained features, the following steps were carried out:

1. For each human-written reference document, a feature matrix was generated. The columns represent the calculation of each feature (C_i), and the rows represent the sentences from the source document.
2. After calculating the features of all the sentences of the source document, a sum of each characteristic was obtained $\sum(C_i)$.
3. Then, the average of the features of the source documents $\frac{\sum(C_i)}{d}$, (where d is the number of source documents) was obtained, to have a representative value of each feature.
4. Considering the averages calculated from the previous step, the relevance coefficients of each feature were calculated using the Bayesian probability of each value. This conception of probability has an essential advantage because it allows the assignment of probabilities to single events and calculates the probability of an event from known values of other probabilities related to the event, as shown in the following equation:

$$relevance\ coefficients = \frac{\frac{(\sum C_i)}{d} * 1}{\sum \frac{\sum C_i}{d}} = 1 \qquad (2)$$

where: $\frac{\sum C_i}{d}$ is the average of each feature. The vector of relevance coefficients was generated based on the previous calculation. Each coefficient obtained a value between 0 and 1.

As output, a vector of coefficients is obtained, called w_i. This vector is subsequently used as input for feature extraction and sentence selection.

3.2 Concatenation and Preprocessing of Source Documents

This step takes as input a set of documents to be summarized (source documents). Next, the following processes are considered for each set of source documents:

1. Concatenation: The order of the input documents should be considered according to the occurrence of events. Therefore, the documents in the collection were concatenated hierarchically to create a meta-document, considering their chronology, from the oldest news to the most recent.
2. Preprocessing: This process is applied once the documents have been concatenated. The text was normalized, considering lemmatization and stopword removal. In addition, POS and NER labeling was carried out. Finally, the sentences were vectorized with Word2vec to encode the meaning of the words and build linguistic concepts. The output of this stage was a set of preprocessed, labeled, and vectorized meta-documents.

3.3 Feature Extraction and Sentence Selection

In this step, we applied the GA to address sentence selection as a combinatorial optimization problem, considering selection, crossover, and mutation operators. Moreover, a fitness function is necessary to explore and present a better selection of sentences. Therefore, the input for this stage is the output described in Sect. 3.2, a set of preprocessed, labeled, and vectorized documents. Next, the following steps were carried out:

1. From the input documents, the initial population is randomly generated with binary encoding, where a gene represents a sentence and an individual represents a summary. Consecutively, candidate summaries are generated from the population to calculate their features (see Sect. 3.1) subsequently.
2. A feature matrix is generated based on the features calculated for each candidate summary. The columns represent each feature's S_i score values, and the rows represent the candidate summary's sentences.
3. From the S_i scores, the features score vector is generated through the calculation of the summary of each feature $(\sum S_i)$.
4. Then, the candidate summary is evaluated as follows:

$$FA(D = Max \sum (\sum s_i * w_i) \tag{3}$$

where the weighting of the candidate document D_i is the maximization of the linear sum of the scores obtained $\sum s_i$ multiplied by their corresponding relevance coefficients $W = \{w_i\}$ (vector of relevance coefficients).

Subsequently, the candidate summaries were generated through the selection, crossover, and mutation operators. The stop criterion was established as the number of generations. The output of this stage is a summary obtained from a set of documents.

4   Experiments and Results

With the experimentation carried out, we seek to test the following hypothesis. If relevance coefficients are obtained from statistical and linguistic features of human-written reference summaries, then sentence selection for extractive ATSMD will be improved.

The relevance coefficients obtained from the proposed method were the following: CC 0.019, CD 0.030, DT 0.040, IN 0.050, JJ 0.050, NN 0.120, NNS 0.060, VB 0.005, VBD 0.030, VBN 0.010, PERSON 0.010, ORG 0.005, DATE 0.015, TF-IDF 0.080, TW 0.350, PW 0.005, SMS 0.090, ITW 0.02

To evaluate the proposed method's performance, the DUC01 corpus was considered. This corpus is considered an open benchmark for evaluating summaries written in English and consists of 309 documents divided into 30 collections. This task aims to generate an informative summary of a certain period of time at compression rates of 200 and 400 words. Additionally, this corpus includes two reference summaries written by humans for evaluation.

The summaries generated by the proposed method were evaluated using the ROUGE (Recall-Oriented Understudy for Gisting Evaluation) system. This system measures the quality of a summary created by the proposed method by contrasting it with ideal summaries created by humans using n-grams. In particular, we focused on using Rouge-1 since it is considered a well-known evaluation measure for these summaries.

Next, the heuristics used to compare the performance of the proposed method are briefly described.

- **Topline:** It is a heuristic that aims to generate the best extractive summaries. The results of these summaries are used as a reference to establish the upper limit, which can be achieved using state-of-the-art methods [19].
- **Baseline-first:** This heuristic takes the first sentences from the collection of documents in chronological order to generate extractive summaries until the target summary size is reached. Any state-of-the-art method that generates better summaries than Baseline-first may be considered intelligent.
- **Baseline-random:** Unlike Baseline-first, this heuristic randomly selects sentences from the source document to incorporate them as an extractive summary until the required length is achieved.
- **Baseline-first-document:** Unlike Baseline-first, this heuristic extracts the first sentences from the first document until the target summary size is met. In other words, it takes the sentences from the first document.
- **Lead Baseline:** Take the first 200 and 400 words of the last (most recent) document to include as a summary. For this heuristic, documents must be ordered chronologically.

In addition to the heuristics, the following list describes the state-of-the-art methods in which the proposed method is compared. These methods were considered since they have been a general benchmark for evaluating generic summaries. Each method considers both supervised and unsupervised machine learning approaches.

- **CBA:** This method generates extractive summaries based on sentence clustering. This clustering assumes that each sentence is considered a topic. In particular, CBA uses two types of clustering, hierarchical and partitioning (K-means), to select sentences for the final summary [5].
- **NeATS:** This method considers the following text features to weight each sentence of the source documents: frequency of terms, position of the sentence, stigma words, and a simplified version of Maximum Marginal Relevance. Moreover, NeATS uses term clustering, a "buddy system" of paired sentences, and explicit temporal annotation for sentence selection [10].
- **GA:** In [10], it was proposed to optimize the selection of sentences using a GA. However, in this work, only two characteristics were used for sentence selection: coverage and position of sentences.
- **RBM:** It is an approach with deep learning through the Restricted Boltzmann Machine (RBM). Unlike traditional neural networks such as Multilayer Perceptron (MLP), the RBM has a low computational cost and is useful for discovering new relationships between text features [26].
- **Baldwin:** This method is based on the concept of using "interesting phrases and words", which are considered candidates for sentence extraction [2]. According to the authors of this method, a sentence is relevant if it contains words whose relative entropy is low concerning the collection of documents.

Table 1 compares the proposed method with heuristics and state-of-the-art methods. The results show that the proposed method outperforms all state-of-the-art methods and heuristics in both word lengths. The proposed method improves sentence selection by including more text features than the GA. Moreover, it shows proximity to the Topline, representing an improvement gap.

Table 1. Comparison of the proposed method with heuristics and state-of-the-art methods. The best results are highlighted in bold.

200 WORDS		400 WORDS	
Method	ROUGE-1	Method	ROUGE-1
Topline	53.630	Topline	60.691
Proposed Method	**41.432**	Proposed Method	**49.533**
GA	40.372	GA	47.619
RBM	39.584	RBM	47.275
Baseline-first	39.280	Baseline-first	47.198
NeATS	37.883	NeATS	45.551
Baldwin	35.890	Baldwin	43.812
Baseline-first-document	35.472	Baseline-first-document	41.161
CBA	34.108	CBA	41.259
Baseline-random	34.057	Baseline-random	42.131
Lead Baseline	34.009	Lead Baseline	39.961

On the other hand, it is essential to mention that we experimented with GA parameters to improve the selection of sentences. The best parameters are the following: Number of individuals: 2 * Number of sentences. Selection operator: Tournament operator (k=2). Number of Elite: 3 individuals. Cross operator: Cross Uniform (98%). Mutation operator: Mutation Inversion (0.012%). Number of Generations (200 words):135, number of Generations (400 words):180

5 Conclusions and Future Works

In this research, statistical and linguistic feature modeling was performed from human-written reference summaries for the extractive ATSMD, aiming to generate summaries similar to how humans would perform them. The proposed method considers 19 text features that process diverse information, relevance, and coverage of the main idea of the sets of documents. In the state-of-the-art, the reference summaries were only used to assess the ATSMD methods, not to determine the relevance of features. Once the relevance coefficients of the reference summaries written by humans were obtained, the selection of sentences was optimized through the GA.

The results show that the proposed method improves sentence selection for the ATSMD task, according to the ROUGE evaluation system (Rouge-1); however, ROUGE depends on creating human-written summaries. For this reason, it is important to analyze this method's performance using evaluation methods that do not depend on human references [11, 21].

References

1. AL-Khassawneh, Y.A., Hanandeh, E.S.: Extractive Arabic text summarization-graph-based approach. Electronics **12**(2), 437 (2023)
2. Baldwin, B., Ross, A.: Baldwin language technology's DUC summarization system. In: Proceedings of the 1st Document Understanding Conference, New Orleans, LA (2001)
3. Baxendale, P.B.: Machine-made index for technical literature-an experiment. IBM J. Res. Dev. **2**(4), 354–361 (1958)
4. Belwal, R.C., Rai, S., Gupta, A.: Extractive text summarization using clustering-based topic modeling. Soft. Comput. **27**(7), 3965–3982 (2023)
5. Boros, E., Kantor, P.B., Neu, D.J.: A clustering based approach to creating multi-document summaries (2001)
6. Edmundson, H.P.: New methods in automatic extracting. J. ACM **16**(2), 264–285 (1969)
7. El-Kassas, W.S., Salama, C.R., Rafea, A.A., Mohamed, H.K.: Automatic text summarization: a comprehensive survey. Expert Syst. Appl. **165**, 113679 (2021)
8. Fattah, M.A., Fattah, M.A.: A hybrid machine learning model for multi-document summarization. Appl. Intell. **40**, 592–600 (2014)

9. Jain, A., Arora, A., Morato, J., Yadav, D., Kumar, K.V.: Automatic text summarization for Hindi using real coded genetic algorithm. Appl. Sci. (Switzerland) **12**(13), 6584 (2022)
10. Lin, C.-Y., Hovy, E.: NEATS: a multidocument summarizer (2001)
11. Louis, A., Nenkova, A.: Automatically assessing machine summary content without a gold standard. Comput. Linguist. **39**(2), 267–300 (2013)
12. Luhn, H.P.: The automatic creation of literature abstracts. IBM J. Res. Dev. **2**(92), 159–165 (1958)
13. Mendoza, G.A.M., Ledeneva, Y., Hernández, R.A.G., Alexandrov, M., Castañeda, Á.H.: Ground truth Spanish automatic extractive text summarization bounds. Computación y Sistemas **24**(3), 1241–1250 (2020)
14. Mendoza, M., Cobos, C., León, E., Lozano, M., Rodríguez, F., Herrera-Viedma, E.: A new memetic algorithm for multi-document summarization based on CHC algorithm and greedy search. In: Gelbukh, A., Espinoza, F.C., Galicia-Haro, S.N. (eds.) Human-Inspired Computing and Its Applications. Lecture Notes in Computer Science(), vol. 8856, pp. 125–138. Springer, Cham (2014). https://doi.org/10.1007/978-3-319-13647-9_14
15. Mohamed, M., Oussalah, M.: SRL-ESA-TextSum: a text summarization approach based on semantic role labeling and explicit semantic analysis. Inf. Process. Manage. **56**(4), 1356–1372 (2019)
16. Neri-Mendoza, V., Ledeneva, Y., García-Hernández, R.A.: Unsupervised extractive multi-document text summarization using a genetic algorithm. J. Intell. Fuzzy Syst. **39**(2), 2397–2408 (2020)
17. Qaroush, A., Abu Farha, I., Ghanem, W., Washaha, M., Maali, E.: An efficient single document Arabic text summarization using a combination of statistical and semantic features. J. King Saud Univ. - Comput. Inf. Sci. **33**(6), 677–692 (2021)
18. Rajalakshmi, R., Vidhya, S., Harina, D., Karna, R., Sowmya, A.: Text summarization for news articles using latent semantic analysis technique. In: 2023 4th International Conference on Electronics and Sustainable Communication Systems, ICESC 2023 - Proceedings, pp. 1421-1425 (2023)
19. Rojas Simón, J., Ledeneva, Y., García Hernández, R.A.: Calculating the upper bounds for multi-document summarization using genetic algorithms. Computación y Sistemas **22**(1) (2018)
20. Rojas-Simon, J., Ledeneva, Y., Garcia-Hernandez, R.A.: Fundamentals of the ETS. In: Evaluation of Text Summaries Based on Linear Optimization of Content Metrics. Studies in Computational Intelligence, vol. 1048. Springer, Cham (2022). https://doi.org/10.1007/978-3-031-07214-7_3
21. Rojas-Simón, J., Ledeneva, Y., García Hernández, R.A.: Evaluation of text summaries without human references based on the linear optimization of content metrics using a genetic algorithm. Expert Syst. Appl. **167**, 113827 (2021)
22. Sanchez-Gomez, J.M., Vega-Rodríguez, M.A., Pérez, C.J.: A multi-objective memetic algorithm for query-oriented text summarization: medicine texts as a case study. Expert Syst. Appl. **198**, 116769 (2022)
23. Torres-Moreno, J.-M.: Automatic Text Summarization. ISTE Ltd and John Wiley & Sons Inc., London (2014)
24. Vázquez, E., García-Hernández, R.A., Ledeneva, Y.: Sentence features relevance for extractive text summarization using genetic algorithms. J. Intell. Fuzzy Syst. **35**(1), 353–365 (2018)
25. Verma, P., Om, H.: MCRMR: maximum coverage and relevancy with minimal redundancy-based multi-document summarization. Expert Syst. Appl. **120**, 43–56 (2019)

26. Verma, S., Nidhi, V.: Extractive summarization using deep learning. Res. Comput. Sci. **147**(10), 107–117 (2018)
27. Xiong, Y., Yan, M., Hu, X., Ren, C., Tian, H.: An unsupervised opinion summarization model fused joint attention and dictionary learning. J. Supercomput. **79**(16), 17759–17783 (2023)

Classification of Human and Machine-Generated Texts Using Lexical Features and Supervised/Unsupervised Machine Learning Algorithms

Jonathan Rojas-Simón[(⊠)] [iD], Yulia Ledeneva[(⊠)] [iD],
and René Arnulfo García-Hernández[(⊠)] [iD]

Autonomous University of the State of Mexico, Instituto Literario No. 100,
50000 Toluca, State of Mexico, Mexico
{jrojass,ynledeneva,reagarciah}@uaemex.mx

Abstract. In today's digital information era, distinguishing between human- and machine-generated texts has become a focus of study in academia and industry. This is because Large-Language Models (LLMs) can produce high-quality texts, posing a challenge to the legitimacy and authenticity of texts. In this regard, it is essential to create methods and models that can differentiate whether a human or an LLM wrote a text. Therefore, this paper explores the effectiveness of supervised and unsupervised machine learning algorithms using lexical features. Mainly, we focused on traditional algorithms, such as Multilayer Perceptron (MLP), Naive Bayes (NB), Logistic Regression (LR), Agglomerative Hierarchical Clustering (AHC), and K-means Clustering (KC). Obtained results have been compared to state-of-the-art approaches presented in the Automated Text Identification (AuTexTification) shared task, serving as reference methods. Moreover, we have found that both NB and KC may achieve competitive results in the before-mentioned task.

Keywords: Large-Language Models (LLMs) · AuTexTification · Lexical Features · Supervised/Unsupervised Learning Algorithms · Text representation models

1 Introduction

In recent times, Natural Language Processing (NLP) has experienced significant advances since the implementation of Large-Language Models (LLM). Current LLMs, such as Generative Pre-trained Transformer (GPT) [11, 15], Pathways Language Model (PaLM) [4], BLOOM [18], and ChatGPT, have boosted the research of cutting-edge applications, producing texts of high quality in terms of grammaticality, fluency, coherence, and usage of real-world knowledge [7, 15]. However, these models can also be used maliciously (*e.g.*, spreading untruthful news, reviews, or opinions), manipulating people's interests.

E. Mezura-Montes et al. (Eds.): MCPR 2024, LNCS 14755, pp. 331–341, 2024.
https://doi.org/10.1007/978-3-031-62836-8_31

According to the latest studies [21], the content generated by LLM usually provides more accurate information than human-written texts, but it shows more compelling disinformation. This situation leads humans to not distinguish information generated by LLM from information written by other humans [25]. Therefore, the government, academy and industry have discussed the need to implement ethical regulations regarding the use of these models [23]. Moreover, it motivates researchers to develop new methods and approaches to detect human- and machine-generated texts [17].

In the state-of-the-art, several works have been done to detect machine- and human-generated texts. Some of them include employing classifiers trained from a Bag-Of-Words (BOW) representation [20], zero-shot approaches [10, 25], supervised systems [6], large-scale shared tasks [8, 19], such as AuTexTification (**Au**tomatic **Text** Iden**Tification**) [17]. Regarding AuTexTification, several efforts have been made to develop methods and techniques to detect human- and machine-generated texts or documents across multiple domains, focusing on using LLMs [1, 2]. However, they still struggle to explain how the proposed model works and their underlying textual features (*e.g.*, what text features are relevant to achieve desirable results and how they contribute to the task).

Although traditional machine learning algorithms usually achieve lower results than LLM, they provide a more comprehensive explanation of their parameters and the textual features used to represent the content of documents. In this sense, we have explored the effectiveness of traditional supervised and unsupervised machine learning algorithms using lexical features in this paper. We assume that by using lexical features, such as the probability of characters, and the use of traditional machine learning algorithms, we can obtain more explainable models for the AuTexTification shared task.

In addition of using lexical features, we seek a more comprehensive comparison of proposed methods and approaches in the task, including supervised learning algorithms, such as the Multilayer Perceptron (MLP), Naive Bayes (NB), and Logistic Regression (LR). In the case of unsupervised learning algorithms, we have included clustering algorithms, such as the Agglomerative Hierarchical Clustering (AHC), and K-means Clustering (KC).

The rest of the paper is organized as follows: Sect. 2 presents a brief description of the background and related works. In Sect. 3, a description of the supervised and unsupervised learning methods is shown. Additionally, we describe the lexical features used to represent each document. In Sect. 4, the experiments and obtained results are explained. Besides, we compare them to other state-of-the-art and baseline methods. Finally, the conclusions and future works are drawn in Sect. 5.

2 Background and Related Works

Initially, the necessity of detecting human- and machine-generated texts started in the context of the automatic detection of fake news. According to [21, 25], disinformation generated by LLMs is rated by humans as trustworthy, even more so than human-written disinformation. Considering this situation, the authors in [25] proposed GROVER as a generative model to generate and detect fake news.

Regarding the generation of fake news, GROVER can automatically generate the text of the news article (body) from the context given by the *domain, date, authors,* or *headline.* On the other hand, GROVER was also proposed to detect machine-written fake news, placing a special [CLS] token at the end of each article and then extracting the final hidden state at that point. The hidden state is fed to a linear neural layer to predict the label assigned to each article (*Human* or *Machine*).

Afterward, other studies have been focused on determining whether a human or a machine wrote a set of given texts. Firstly, Solaiman et al. [20] implemented a baseline model representing each text document using TF-IDF vectors obtained from BOW and bigrams. Resultant representations were later introduced into an LR algorithm to distinguish WebText articles (online web pages) from text generated using GPT-2 models.

Besides Solaiman's studies, other reference works include the study done by Ippolito et al. [6], which focused on the differences in the ability of humans and automated detectors (like GROVER [25], GLTR [5], and EBMs [3]) to identify text generated by LLMs. They observed that (i) human detectors can notice contradictions or semantic errors (*e.g.*, incoherence) in text generated by LLMs; in contrast, automatic detectors are weak on this due to the lack of semantic understanding. Moreover, they found that (ii) automatic detectors can distinguish LLM texts when they over-represent high-likelihood words.

Despite such efforts, no assumptions existed about how different the documents' domains may affect the task's performance. For this reason, large-scale tasks were carried out in the state-of-the-art, such as DagPap22 [8], RuATD [19], and AutoTexTification [17]. The AutoTexTification task, also known as *Automatic Text Identification*, has been of recent interest due to text generation models (*e.g.*, GPT [11, 15], PaLM [4], BLOOM [18], and ChatGPT) can automatically generate synthetic texts in different domains. Based on this, AutoTexTification addressed the following two subtasks [17]:

- **Subtask 1 – Human or Generated:** Participant teams must build systems that distinguish between machine- or human-generated text of different domains. Moreover, organizers provided a balanced dataset.
- **Subtask 2 – Model Attribution:** Unlike subtask 1, participant teams must build systems able to attribute authorship to six LLMs, which are labeled with six classes (A, B, C, D, E, and F), but participants do not know what LLMs are behind the classes. To achieve this, the organizers provided a balanced dataset.

As a result, several teams around the world participated in the task of developing methods able to perform Subtask 1. Some of them include using individual LLMs [2] and ensemble classifiers of LLMs [1], achieving competitive results. On the other hand, other teams proposed methods that employ stylometric and linguistic features [9]. Finally, several baselines were included in the task that usually consider lexical features (see Sect. 4.3).

3   Supervised and Unsupervised Machine Learning Algorithms

In this section, we provide an overall description of supervised and unsupervised machine learning algorithms used in this work. Moreover, we provide a description of lexical features considered for each algorithm.

3.1 Supervised Learning Algorithms

Multilayer Perceptron (MLP). Also known as a *multilayer neural network*, it is a deep learning model consisting of three fully connected types of neuron layers: an input layer, one or more hidden layers, and an output layer. The MLP is flexible and can learn complex data representations, making it suitable for Pattern Recognition (PR) tasks. Moreover, it is the basis of modern deep-learning models (*e.g.*, transformers [22]).

Logistic Regression (LR). LR is an algorithm based on the *logistic function* that models the relationship between the features and a binary outcome. Formally, LR is defined as $\frac{1}{1+e^{-z}}$, where z is the linear combination between the input features (x_i) and model parameters (w_i). Resultant values of LR vary from 0 to 1, representing the degree of probability the input belongs to the positive class (1).

Naive Bayes (NB). The NB algorithm is based on *Bayes' theorem*, which addresses the probability theory. It allows the use of subjective information and combines it with empirical information to estimate the probability of events. For any classification task, NB calculates the probability of each class, given the input features, and selects the class with the highest probability, which is the predicted class.

3.2 Unsupervised Learning Algorithms

K-means Clustering (KC). In unsupervised learning, KC is the most popular machine learning algorithm for grouping data into K clusters based on distance calculations. This algorithm aims to create pattern clusters depending on the proximity among patterns and the centroids' proximity.

Agglomerative Hierarchical Clustering (AHC). AHC is an algorithm that starts by considering each pattern as a single cluster and then iteratively merges the clusters closest to each other until all data points are grouped into one cluster. As groups merge, a *dendrogram* that represents the relationship among patterns or clusters is created.

3.3 Lexical Features Used in This Work

Lexical features have played an essential role in many NLP tasks since they can represent important information from documents to perform PR tasks, such as clustering or classification. In the case of text classification, one of the most used representations is the n-grams at character or word levels [13]. However, it usually has high dimensionality, causing higher computation costs. Considering this situation, we seek a lower dimensionality representation that can capture stylistic and lexical features from a document. Therefore, we calculated the probability that each character in ASCII format may appear in the document. Equation (1) displays this representation:

$$ASCII(d) = \left[p(c_1), p(c_2), \ldots, p(c_{255})\right], p(c_i) = \frac{f(c_i)}{len(d)} \tag{1}$$

where $ASCII(d)$ is a function that receives the input document d without any preprocessing. Afterward, this function produces a vector of 255 values[1], where each represents the probability that character c_i may appear in d. . This probability $(p(c_i))$ is calculated by dividing the frequency of character c_i $(f(c_i))$ and the length of d measured in characters $(len(d))$. Additionally, we added a probability value $(p(c_{256}))$ to this vector in case unknown characters may appear. This is because input documents would contain emojis or other characters outside the ASCII code.

4 Experiments and Obtained Results

This section is organized as follows: First, we describe the AuTexTification dataset and evaluation metrics used to measure the performance of each algorithm. Second, we show the most relevant experiments from each machine learning algorithm and their obtained results. Finally, we compared the performance of these methods against state-of-the-art approaches and baseline methods.

4.1 Dataset Description

Regarding subtasks of AuTexTification (see Sect. 2), we have focused on Subtask 1. Thus, the dataset comprises 55677 documents written by humans and LLMs in five domains: tweets, reviews, how-to articles, news, and legal documents. Table 1 shows the number of documents per class and set. As observed, 33845 documents compose the training set, which is balanced per class. For the test set, 21832 documents were used, and it is also balanced per class. To evaluate the performance of proposed methods, the Macro F-measure was used.

Table 1. Number of documents per class of the AuTexTification dataset (Subtask 1).

Class	Training set	Test set
Human	17046	10642
Generated	16799	11190
Total	33845	21832

4.2 Experiments of Machine Learning Algorithms

To test the performance of supervised and unsupervised machine learning algorithms, we performed several experiments to fine-tune generated models. The input of each algorithm was the vector representation of lexical features explained in Sect. 3.3. Below, it is described the best parameters of each algorithm.

---

[1] We have based on the ASCII code table, which is available at https://elcodigoascii.com.ar.

- MLP: The best model generated by MLP consists of implementing five hidden layers, each containing 350, 300, 500, 150, and 10 neurons. Each of these neurons operated under the ReLu activation function, and the sigmoid function was used in the output layer. The Stochastic Gradient Descendent (SGD) algorithm was used for the learning process, iterating it in 15 epochs to avoid overfitting.
- LR: In the case of LR, we employed the default parameters, which were provided by the scikit-learn Python library [12].
- NB: For the NB algorithm, we experimented with the following variants: Gaussian NB, Multinomial NB, Bernoulli NB, and Complement NB. However, we selected Multinomial NB because it obtained the best results.
- KC: As the subtask requires the classification of documents into two classes (*Human* and *Generated*), the KC algorithm operated with $K = 2$. Resultant clusters were associated with the corresponding class according to the features of each cluster.
- AHC: We used the Euclidean distance to measure the separability between patterns and clusters. The resultant dendrogram is shown in Fig. 1, where we clearly observe the separability of documents when the distance is set to 8000. Therefore, we used this value to create two clusters.

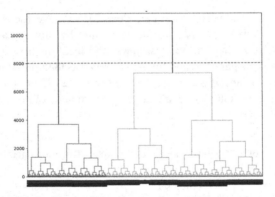

Fig. 1. Obtained dendrogram from AHC algorithm.

Once we have described the best parameters from each algorithm, explaining their efficacy using confusion matrices is essential. Figure 2 shows the confusion matrices obtained by the MLP (A) and LR (B) algorithms. According to the results, the MLP distinguishes human-written texts better than LR, classifying 8409 texts correctly. This is because the LR is focused on better distinguishing machine-generated texts, classifying 2216 texts. However, LR obtained a similar F-measure score to MLP (see results in Table 2).

On the other hand, Fig. 3 shows the confusion matrices obtained by the NB (A) and KC (B) algorithms. Notice that the NB shows the best classification, particularly in detecting human-generated texts (9280), but it struggles in detecting machine-generated texts. This is because the NB only classified 3099 texts as Generated, but the remaining 8091 texts were classified as Human. On the other hand, the KC is better at detecting

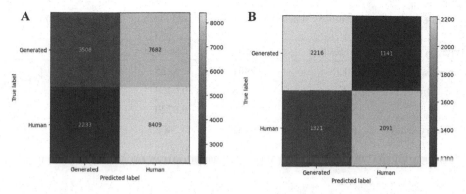

Fig. 2. Confusion matrices obtained by the MLP (A) and LR (B) algorithms.

machine-generated texts because it correctly classifies 5192 texts as Generated and 7068 texts as Human-written documents.

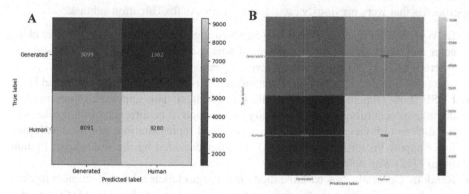

Fig. 3. Confusion matrices obtained by the Multinomial NB (A) and KC (B) algorithms.

Table 2 shows the obtained results by supervised and unsupervised machine learning algorithms. According to the results, the NB has achieved the best performance, obtaining the highest F-measure (0.6626) and Precision (0.8720) scores, which far surpasses the other models. Besides, the LR and MLP present similar performance in terms of F-measure score. In particular, the MLP has achieved the best Recall performance because it correctly classifies more machine-generated texts. On the other hand, as expected, unsupervised machine learning algorithms have obtained the lowest F-measure scores. Still, it is important to highlight that these algorithms do not require training data. Even the KC has achieved a closer performance than MLP and LR.

Table 2. Obtained results by supervised and unsupervised machine learning algorithms.

Type	Algorithm	Recall	Precision	F-measure
Supervised	MLP	**0.7901**	0.5225	0.6291
	LR	0.6128	0.6469	0.6294
	NB	0.5670	**0.8720**	**0.6626**
Unsupervised	KC	0.6652	0.5408	0.5966
	AHC	0.4126	0.6004	0.4891

4.3 Comparison Between the Obtained Results and State-Of-The-Art/baseline Methods

Once we have experimented with different parameters across the before-mentioned algorithms, it is necessary to compare the performance of the best parameters of each algorithm against the baseline and state-of-the-art methods. Below, we describe the baseline approaches that were previously considered for the AuTexTification subtask.

- BOW+LR: This baseline is based on representing each document in a BOW at character and word levels. For word level, it was used the most frequent 5K n-grams, where $n \in \{1,2\}$. At the character level, n-grams were used, where $n \in \{2, \ldots, 6\}$ (see [13]). Finally, resultant representations are used as inputs to an LR model [12].
- LDSE (Low-Dimensionality Semantic Embeddings): This approach represents text documents according to the probability distribution of occurrence of their tokens in the different classes LDSE [16]. Then, obtained representations are used as inputs to a Support Vector Machine (SVM) classifier provided by the scikit-learn Python library [12] with default parameters.
- Random: Generally, this baseline randomly assigns labels to each document to classify. However, in this task, the value of the baseline random is set to 0.5000 because it considers the class balance, which is calculated as $1/C$, where C is the number of classes (in this task $C = 2$).
- SB-FS and SB-ZS: The AuTexTification organizers have employed the Few-shot (SB-FS) and Zero-shot (SB-ZS) Symanto Brain API to classify each document into Hum and Gen labels [17].
- Transformer: It is a baseline approach based on the HuggingFace ecosystem to fine-tune the pre-trained transformers [24]. Moreover, it considers a random classification head for five epochs and default parameters [17].

In addition to the baseline methods, we briefly describe the state-of-the-art classification methods that have achieved the best results in the subtask.

- TALN-UPF: This team implemented a method centered on measuring "predictability". That is, how likely a given text is according to several LLMs [14]. In addition, linguistic and semantic information was used to train a neural network.
- CIC-IPN-CsCog and Drocks: The team CIC-IPN-CsCog implemented a method based on BERT and GPT-2 Small [2] models. On the other hand, the teams

Drocks used an ensemble of neural models that generates probabilities from different pretrained LLMs, which are used as features of a traditional machine learning classifier.

According to the results shown in Table 3, the NB model performed better than all baseline approaches. The main difference between our experimentation and all baselines lies in using lexical features described in Sect. 3.3. Therefore, only 256 features are considered for each document, whose calculus is based on character probability distributions. In addition, this representation has lower dimensionality than BOW + LR (10,000 features) as the baseline.

Compared to the LDSE baseline (0.6035), which is a model based on dimensionality reduction, the performance of the proposed representation with NB as a classifier is better. Despite this, its performance is still far from TALN-UPF, CIC-IPN-CsCog, and Drocks because their underlying methods employ more modern language models, such as GPT-2 and pre-trained deep representations (*e.g.*, BERT). However, we seek this representation to be the basis of more modern machine learning algorithms, such as transformers or Long Short-Term Memory (LSTM) neural networks.

Table 3. Comparison between the best results and state-of-the-art/other baseline approaches.

Name	F-measure	Name	F-measure
TALN-UPF [14]	0.8091	LDSE (Baseline [17])	0.6035
TALN-UPF [14]	0.7416	**KC (this work)**	**0.5966**
CIC-IPN-CsCog [2]	0.7413	SB-FS (Baseline [17])	0.5944
Drocks [1]	0.7330	Transformer (Baseline [17])	0.5710
NB (this work)	**0.6626**	Random [17]	0.5000
BOW + LR (Baseline [17])	0.6578	**AHC (this work)**	**0.4891**
LR (this work)	**0.6294**	SB-ZS (Baseline [17])	0.4347
MLP (this work)	**0.6291**		

On the other hand, we included unsupervised algorithms in the comparison since they do not require training data to determine the separability between human- and automatic-generated texts. According to the results obtained from clustering algorithms, KC shows a competitive performance (0.5966) concerning other baselines (*e.g.*, SB-FS: 0.5944, Transformer 0.5710, Random: 0.5000, and SB-ZS: 0.4347).

5 Conclusions and Future Works

In this paper, we explored and analyzed the performance of supervised and unsupervised machine learning algorithms using lexical features, which are based on character probability distributions. These features have been used as inputs to supervised/unsupervised machine learning algorithms, such as MLP, LR, NB, KC, and AHC. In particular, the

NB models based on Multinomial distribution of text features performed best in the task. Compared to baseline approaches, it provides a better classification between manual- and machine- generated texts. As future work, we focus on more advanced classifiers, including convolutional neural networks, LSTM, or transformers. Moreover, we seek the implementation of more advanced and explainable text features.

Acknowledgements. The authors of this paper thank the support of the following postgraduate students: Marco Antonio Hernández Galicia, María Azucena Torres Flores, and Efraín Macedo González.

References

1. Abburi, H., et al.: Generative AI text classification using ensemble LLM approaches (2023)
2. Aguilar-Canto, F., et al.: GPT-2 versus GPT-3 and bloom: LLMs for LLMs generative text detection (2023)
3. Bakhtin, A., et al.: Real or fake? Learning to discriminate machine from human generated text (2019)
4. Chowdhery, A., et al.: PaLM: scaling language modeling with pathways. J. Mach. Learn. Res. **24**, 1–113 (2023)
5. Gehrmann, S., et al.: GLTR: statistical detection and visualization of generated text. In: Proceedings of the 57th Annual Meeting of the ACL: System Demonstrations, pp. 111–116. Association for Computational Linguistics, Stroudsburg, PA, USA (2019)
6. Ippolito, D., et al.: Automatic detection of generated text is easiest when humans are fooled. In: Proceedings of the 58th Annual Meeting of the ACL, pp. 1808–1822. Association for Computational Linguistics, Stroudsburg, PA, USA (2020)
7. Jawahar, G., et al.: Automatic detection of machine generated text: a critical survey. In: Proceedings of the 28th International Conference on Computational Linguistics, pp. 2296–2309. International Committee on Computational Linguistics, Stroudsburg, PA, USA (2020)
8. Kashnitsky, Y., et al.: Overview of the DagPap22 shared task on detecting automatically generated scientific papers. In: Cohan, A., et al. (eds.) Proceedings of the Third Workshop on Scholarly Document Processing, pp. 210–213. ACL, Gyeongju, Korea (2022)
9. Mikros, G., et al.: AI-writing detection using an ensemble of transformers and stylometric features (2023)
10. Mitchell, E., et al.: DetectGPT: zero-shot machine-generated text detection using probability curvature (2023)
11. Ouyang, L., et al.: Training language models to follow instructions with human feedback. In: 36th Conference on Neural Information Processing System (NeurIPS 2022), pp. 1–15 (2022)
12. Pedregosa, F., et al.: Scikit-learn: machine learning in Python. J. Mach. Learn. Res. **12**, 2825–2830 (2011)
13. Pizarro, J.: Using N-grams to detect bots on Twitter, Lugano, Switzerland (2019)
14. Przybyła, P., et al.: I've seen things you machines wouldn't believe: measuring content predictability to identify automatically-generated text (2023)
15. Radford, A., et al.: Language models are unsupervised multitask learners. OpenAI Blog **1**(8), 1–24 (2019)
16. Rangel, F., Franco-Salvador, M., Rosso, P.: A low dimensionality representation for language variety identification. In: Gelbukh, A. (ed.) Computational Linguistics and Intelligent Text Processing. LNCS, vol. 9624, pp. 156–169. Springer, Cham (2018). https://doi.org/10.1007/978-3-319-75487-1_13

17. Sarvazyan, A.M., et al.: Overview of AuTexTification at IberLEF 2023: detection and attribution of machine-generated text in multiple domains. Proces. del Leng. Nat. **71**, 275–288 (2023)
18. Le Scao, T., et al: BLOOM: A 176B-parameter open-access multilingual language model (2022)
19. Shamardina, T., et al.: Findings of the the RuATD shared task 2022 on artificial text detection in Russian. In: Computational Linguistics and Intellectual Technologies, pp. 497–511. RSUH (2022)
20. Solaiman, I., et al.: Release strategies and the social impacts of language models (2019)
21. Spitale, G., et al.: AI model GPT-3 (dis)informs us better than humans. Sci. Adv. **9**(26), 1–28 (2023)
22. Vaswani, A., et al.: Attention is all you need. In: Proceedings of the 31st International Conference on Neural Information Processing Systems, New York, USA, pp. 6000–6010 (2017)
23. Widder, D.G., et al.: Limits and possibilities for "Ethical AI" in open source: a study of deepfakes. In: 2022 ACM Conference on Fairness, Accountability, and Transparency, pp. 2035–2046. ACM, New York, NY, USA (2022)
24. Wolf, T., et al.: Transformers: state-of-the-art natural language processing. In: Proceedings of the 2020 Conference on Empirical Methods in NLP: System Demonstrations, pp. 38–45. Association for Computational Linguistics, Stroudsburg, PA, USA (2020)
25. Zellers, R., et al.: Defending against neural fake news. In: NIPS'19: Proceedings of the 33rd International Conference on Neural Information Processing Systems, pp. 9054–9065 (2019)

Identification of Deceptive Texts Using Cascade Classification

María del Carmen García-Galindo[1]([⊠])[iD], Ángel Hernández-Castañeda[1,2][iD],
René Arnulfo García-Hernández[1][iD], and Yulia Ledeneva[1][iD]

[1] Autonomous University of the State of Mexico, Instituto Literario 100, Col. Centro.
C.P., 50000 Toluca, Mexico State, Mexico
marycarmeng142@gmail.com, angelhc2305@gmail.com, renearnulfo@hotmail.com,
yledeneva@yahoo.com
[2] Cátedras CONACyT, Av. Insurgentes Sur 1582, Col. Crédito Constructor. C.P.,
03940 Mexico City, Mexico

Abstract. Online reviews of products, hotels, restaurants, and other
services play an important role for both sellers and buyers. Through
these reviews, potential buyers can get an idea of what to expect before
making a purchase. However, not all reviews are authentic, as there are
companies that pay their employees to generate reviews that discredit
their competitors. To address this task, this study presents a computational method based on cascade classification that first automatically
detects the distribution of latent emotions in the text. Subsequently, the
emotion distribution vectors, in combination with lexical features, are
used to identify signs of deception. Our experimental results demonstrate
that the proposed method of this study show good performance on different datasets analyzed. In addition, our method automatically provides
information about the emotions that influence the act of deception.

Keywords: Deception text · Emotion detection · BERT embeddings ·
Natural Language Processing

1 Introduction

Online reviews of products, hotels, restaurants, and other services play an important role for both sellers and buyers [7,13]. For example, in online purchases they
provide potential buyers with valuable information about the product or service
they are going to receive [8,13]. Additionally, these opinions can significantly
impact the reputation and sales of a product or service, because users tend to
buy products with good reviews [12].

Textual reviews allow the consumer to openly describe their opinion about
the product or service received. These types of reviews can reveal consumers'
deep thoughts or feelings and their detailed experiences. In this sense, Li et al.
[10] claim that reviews can express emotions that significantly influence sales.

However, since anyone is free to write a review, this can lead to negative
consequences such as insults, spam, or deception [12]. According to Caspi &

E. Mezura-Montes et al. (Eds.): MCPR 2024, LNCS 14755, pp. 342–352, 2024.
https://doi.org/10.1007/978-3-031-62836-8_32

Gorsky [3], deception is defined as the conscious transmission of messages to a receiver with the intention of fostering a false belief or conclusion.

For example, some companies incentivize people to post deceptive opinions [13]. These types of reviews are often classified as false positives and false negatives [13]. The former aim to improve the image of a product or service to increase its own sales [8]; while the goal of false negative reviews is to damage the reputation and reduce the sales of the competition [6]. Therefore, not all opinions shared online are authentic [3].

Currently, in the computational area, several approaches have been developed to automate and improve the detection of deceptive text. These approaches have employed a variety of feature extraction methods, machine learning algorithms, and more recently, the use of large language models (LLMs).

This study proposes the use different feature generation methods, including LLMs, in a cascade classification framework. Our proposed approach shows good performance in evaluating multi-domain datasets.

2 Related Works

Generally, the task of identifying deceptive text is to determine whether the opinion is deceptive or genuine based on the words used [13]. However, some studies have considered the analysis of additional features, for instance, sentiment polarity and emotional aspects that influence deception.

In this regard, Saini & Sharan [16] analyzed the emotions and sentiments expressed in genuine and sanctioned deceptive hotel reviews, in relation to various specific aspects, such as food, location, service quality, price, and others. The authors analyzed different types of features, including unigrams, parts of speech (POS), language formality, sentence subjectivity, sentiment polarity, and specific emotions associated with product aspects. The authors manually assign the corresponding emotion to the text based on the words used. Subsequently, they combine the features and perform the classification process. The authors' findings conclude that combining unigrams with emotions aspects creates a more complete set of features that improves the ability of the support vector machine (SVM) classifier to identify deceptive reviews.

In the research of Hernández-Castañeda et al. [7], the impact of polarity on deceptive text detection was addressed. In this study, a polarity classifier was implemented to generate subsets of positive and negative opinions. Then, feature vectors with lexical-semantic information were constructed. Finally, these vectors were input into an naïve Bayes (NB). The authors conclude that using only lexical information achieves acceptable results for deception detection. Interestingly, incorporating polarity information worsens performance. For future work, the authors propose exploring emotional states instead of only analyzing polarities (positive or negative).

García-Galindo et al. [5] propose a cascade classification method to detect signs of suicidal ideation in texts by identifying latent emotional distributions. The authors' proposed method uses two classifiers, where the first determines the latent emotional distribution and the second uses this output to determine suicidal thoughts. This approach does not directly analyze words to determine class membership, but instead uses the distribution of emotions obtained from the text.

Currently, pretrained LLMs are the subject of great interest in various researches, due to their ability to perform bidirectional contextual analysis. In the work of Aggarwal et al. [1], the performance of long-short-term-memory (LSTM), a Gradient Boosted Tree, and the Bidirectional Encoder Representations from Transformers (BERT) language model was compared for fake news classification. The results show that the fine-tuned BERT model achieved an accuracy of 97.021%.

Different studies emphasize the importance of analyzing a variety of emotions in deceptive texts instead of simply addressing their polarity. Therefore, our proposed approach performs a cascade classification that process a distribution of latent emotions combined with lexical features to finally identify deception.

3   Proposed Architecture

In this study, an ensemble of cascade classifiers are implemented to detect deceptive text. In addition, lexical, semantic, contextual and emotional features are concatenated. Figure 1 presents an overview of the proposed method, which is described below. The first stage consists of term weighting in which each text is converted into a numerical vector. Then, the first classifier analyzes these representations to determine the emotional distribution of each text. Next, the distributions are concatenated with lexical features. Finally, the second classifier receives the concatenated vectors to identify deceptive texts.

The datasets used are described in Subsect. 3.1. Feature extraction methods are briefly explained in Subsect. 3.2.

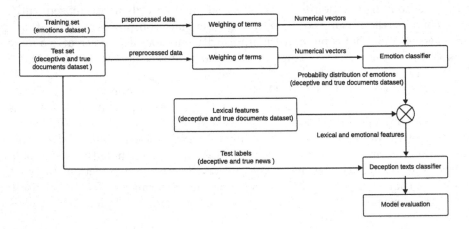

Fig. 1. General scheme of the proposed method.

3.1 Datasets

The proposed approach requires determining the distribution of latent emotions presented in text. To achieve this, we used the emotional intensity training dataset from the WASSA-2017 shared task. The WASSA-2017 collection [11] consists of 3,613 sentences, labeled with four emotions, distributed as follows: anger (857), fear (1147), joy (823) and sadness (786).

The evaluation of our proposed framework was conducted using three different datasets, on deceptive text, which are briefly described below.

DeRev Dataset. (DEception in REViews) [4] is a collection that includes both deceptive and truthful book reviews, sourced from the Amazon website. This gold-standard corpus contains 236 texts, evenly split between truthful and deceptive categories (118 each).

Since the opinions were obtained after the participants lied, this corpus is considered of sanctioned deception [6,7].

OpSpam Dataset. (Opinion Spam) [14] is a corpus composed of 400 deceptive and 400 truthful reviews about different hotels. The deceptive reviews were sourced from Amazon Mechanical Turk (AMT), while truthful reviews were collected from TripAdvisor.

The deceptive texts were created as a form of unsanctioned deception, as the participants were asked to lie in order to create them [6,7].

Opinions on Controversial Topics. [15] is a dataset that includes 600 opinions on the following three controversial topics: abortion, the death penalty, and best friend. Each topic consists of 100 truthful and 100 deceptive opinions. These opinions were extracted using AMT.

The method of collecting deceptive notes is based on unsanctioned deception, as participants were asked to lie about their true opinions [6,7].

This dataset includes texts in American English, Indian English, and Mexican Spanish; however, only those documents written by American users were used in this study.

The Table 1 summarizes the related statistical information about each dataset.

Table 1. Description of the corpus used

Dataset	No. of docs
DeRev	236
OpSpam	800
Abortion	200
Best friend	200
Death penalty	200

As a preprocessing stage, we expand contractions, convert words to lowercase, remove special characters, symbols, punctuation marks, stop words, whitespace, and numbers.

3.2 Feature Generation

Previous research has shown that deceptive text detection can be improved by combining semantic and lexical features [6,7].

In this study, five feature generation methods were used. Below is a brief description of each method.

One-Hot Representation (OHR). Performs *lexical* encoding at the individual word level. This encoding transforms the texts into a numerical vector of binary representation. For this reason, a list of all the unique words in the document set is created. It subsequently analyzes each document and assigns a value of one if the word Wn is present in the document; otherwise, it assigns a zero, indicating its absence [6,7]. This representation only considers the presence of each word, without considering its frequency and relevance.

Term frequency - Inverse document frequency (TF-IDF), similar to the previous method, analyzes words at the *lexical* level. However, TF-IDF considers the frequency with which each term appears in a document and in the collection of documents.

Latent Dirichlet Allocation (LDA). [2] is a probabilistic model that represents documents as a mixture of different latent topics. Each topic consists of a set of words that are related to each other. The method produces numerical vectors that capture the probability with which each word is associated with a particular topic [6,7]. This approach performs an analysis at the *semantic* level.

Doc2Vec (D2V) [9]: Captures the *semantic* meaning of an complete document. This is possible because it uses a neural network architecture that allows it to learn vectors of words and documents, considering the context.

Bidirectional Encoder Representations from Transformers (BERT) [17]: Is a language representation model that processes information in a bidirectional manner [1]. BERT allows the analysis of documents at a *semantic* and *contextual* level. In this study, the *distilbert-base-uncased* model was employed.

4   Experimentation and Results

The proposed approach of this study uses a cascade classification approach. Furthermore, it examines different feature generation methods to determine the latent emotional distribution in each text. Finally, it concatenates lexical and emotional features to identify deceptive text.

The classifiers analyzed in this study were the Support Vector Machine (SVM), Naive Bayes (NB), and Multilayer Perceptron (MLP). All classifiers were used with their default hyperparameter values according to the *Scikit-learn* library. These classifiers were selected based on their previous use in various tasks.

In this section, we compare the results of two cascade classification approaches for identifying deceptive text. Both methods determine the latent emotional distribution in the texts, but they differ in how they use this information. On the one hand, the baseline approach uses only emotional distributions to identify deceptive texts. On the other hand, the proposed approach concatenates the emotional distribution with lexical features and uses this combination to determine which texts are deceptive.

To evaluate the classification performance, we employ five-fold cross-validation and choose Precision (P), Recall (R), and the F-measure (F) as evaluation measures. The percentage of selected texts that are correct is shown by precision. Recall shows the percentage of correct texts that are selected. Finally, F-measure is the metric that evaluate the balance between P and R [6].

Below a table of classification results for each dataset is presented. These tables compare the performance of the two cascade classification methods (baseline and proposed) with different feature generation methods and the classifiers used. Each results table highlights the best F-measure in bold.

Table 2 shows the classification results for the DeRev dataset. As can be seen, the proposed method that considers the concatenation of lexical-emotional features achieves the best performance with an F-measure of **91.25%**. On the other hand, the baseline cascade classification obtained an F-measure of 70.77%.

Table 2. Classification of the DeRev corpus

Method	Classifier	Baseline			Proposed method		
		P	R	F	P	R	F
TF-IDF	SVM	56.23%	51.01%	52.00%	78.05%	85.62%	80.93%
	NB	58.28%	52.07%	51.24%	97.03%	78.77%	86.72%
	MLP	56.15%	75.43%	64.97%	89.80%	91.49%	90.11%
LDA	SVM	30.86%	58.33%	40.25%	78.05%	85.62%	80.93%
	NB	31.93%	57.50%	40.77%	96.97%	77.93%	86.16%
	MLP	42.73%	60.07%	56.90%	89.54%	91.45%	**91.25%**
D2V	SVM	69.53%	65.98%	66.71%	79.93%	86.45%	82.51%
	NB	81.80%	44.96%	57.68%	97.24%	65.40%	78.04%
	MLP	70.15%	71.92%	**70.77%**	90.33%	90.62%	91.02%
BERT	SVM	60.09%	49.24%	52.77%	78.78%	86.45%	81.84%
	NB	63.94%	72.93%	68.03%	97.98%	79.64%	87.65%
	MLP	55.11%	51.88%	53.51%	89.84%	91.49%	90.46%

When comparing the feature generation methods that achieve better results (LDA and D2V), it is observed that D2V outperforms LDA in most cases. This advantage is attributed to the ability of D2V to capture contextual information, which LDA does not consider. Other observations are that the incorporation of lexical features improves the classification process in all cases, and that both approaches highlight the use of the MLP classifier to classify deceptive book reviews.

Table 3. Classification of OpSpam

Method	Classifier	Baseline			Proposed method		
		P	R	F	P	R	F
TF-IDF	SVM	57.46%	78.50%	66.28%	85.57%	83.75%	84.62%
	NB	64.21%	71.75%	67.52%	90.28%	85.25%	87.67%
	MLP	62.18%	78.50%	68.37%	88.80%	84.50%	86.06%
LDA	SVM	50.86%	99.00%	67.18%	85.59%	83.75%	84.63%
	NB	51.18%	98.00%	67.24%	90.04%	85.25%	87.56%
	MLP	56.44%	69.25%	58.99%	87.86%	83.50%	86.53%
D2V	SVM	66.06%	68.00%	67.00%	85.28%	84.25%	84.69%
	NB	50.46%	99.25%	66.90%	73.26%	74.50%	73.83%
	MLP	66.73%	69.25%	**67.89%**	87.60%	84.00%	86.13%
BERT	SVM	55.08%	71.50%	61.93%	85.04%	83.00%	83.96%
	NB	59.94%	55.75%	57.70%	90.74%	85.25%	**87.88%**
	MLP	56.39%	29.50%	40.66%	87.66%	83.75%	85.98%

The results from the OpSpam dataset reveal the effectiveness of the proposed method in classifying intentionally deceptive hotel reviews. According to Table 3, the proposed approach outperforms the baseline method in terms of F-measure by 19.99% in the best case. The proposed method achieves an F-measure of 87.88%, in contrast to the baseline method that achieves an F-measure of 67.89%.

The classifier that achieves the best performance is NB, followed by MLP. The table show that extracting latent emotions from texts using semantic-contextual analysis improves the classification process when this information is concatenated with lexical features, compared to considering only semantic information.

The results of the classification of opinions on the controversial topic of abortion are compared in the Table 4. The table shows that for this dataset the baseline method achieves the best F-measure result 69.90% with semantic features of D2V and the NB classifier.

The best results obtained with the proposed method show a minimum difference of 0.54% compared to those achieved with the base method. This difference indicates that the classification of opinions on the topic of abortion from a small dataset does not require the implementation of more complex methods that consider additional features to discriminate between the analyzed texts.

The Table 5 shows that, in general, the proposed method improves the classification of deceptive texts related to the controversial topic of the best friend.

Table 4. Classification of abortion opinions

Method	Classifier	Baseline			Proposed method		
		P	R	F	P	R	F
TF-IDF	SVM	62.05%	75.00%	67.24%	67.31%	64.00%	64.51%
	NB	58.61%	66.00%	61.73%	80.44%	58.00%	66.81%
	MLP	56.86%	66.00%	65.03%	70.89%	65.00%	**69.36%**
LDA	SVM	57.11%	69.00%	62.45%	66.44%	60.00%	61.94%
	NB	50.00%	100.00%	66.67%	76.79%	58.00%	65.60%
	MLP	51.56%	68.00%	62.73%	69.93%	66.00%	67.77%
D2V	SVM	62.61%	67.00%	64.37%	68.94%	65.00%	66.25%
	NB	55.44%	95.00%	**69.90%**	63.86%	74.00%	68.53%
	MLP	61.35%	66.00%	63.16%	71.32%	71.00%	**69.36%**
BERT	SVM	54.74%	76.00%	63.25%	68.83%	65.00%	65.79%
	NB	48.93%	70.00%	57.06%	75.88%	58.00%	65.2%
	MLP	59.09%	63.00%	60.56%	67.96%	67.00%	66.43%

Table 5. Classification of best friend opinions

Method	Classifier	Baseline			Proposed method		
		P	R	F	P	R	F
TF-IDF	SVM	63.64%	65.00%	64.28%	74.87%	70.00%	71.44%
	NB	73.11%	68.00%	**70.02%**	78.92%	79.00%	78.11%
	MLP	65.64%	72.00%	68.09%	71.48%	73.00%	71.39%
LDA	SVM	52.45%	97.00%	68.06%	76.22%	71.00%	72.31%
	NB	50.00%	100.00%	66.67%	78.92%	79.00%	78.11%
	MLP	59.17%	71.00%	63.08%	72.22%	74.00%	71.54%
D2V	SVM	54.95%	70.00%	61.41%	75.59%	69.00%	71.27%
	NB	52.61%	95.00%	67.66%	65.48%	68.00%	66.49%
	MLP	57.41%	72.00%	64.14%	71.86%	72.00%	71.70%
BERT	SVM	50.91%	82.00%	62.73%	75.58%	70.00%	72.04%
	NB	46.92%	68.00%	54.98%	79.00%	80.00%	**78.78%**
	MLP	56.17%	81.00%	66.34%	71.89%	73.00%	71.70%

In the best case, the base method achieves an F-measure of 70.02%, compared to the proposed method that achieves an F-measure of 78.78%.

The baseline method achieves the above mentioned performance by using lexical features, while the proposed method employs semantic-contextual features extracted from BERT. In both cases, the use of NB classifier stands out.

Table 6 shows the results of the classification of opinions on the controversial topic Death penalty. The table reveals that the base method achieves superior performance with F-measure 66.89%, in contrast to the proposed method (58.82%). These results suggest that for this dataset, semantic features obtained from D2V together with an NB classifier are the best option to detect deceptive opinions.

The classification results of the death penalty topic indicate that including emotional information on the patterns (as extra feature) worsens the classification process.

Overall, it is shown that the proposed method achieves the best performance on the DeRev dataset with F-measure of **91.25%**, using LDA + OHR concatenation and MLP classifier.

Table 6. Classification of death penalty opinions

Method	Classifier	Baseline			Proposed method		
		P	R	F	P	R	F
TF-IDF	SVM	52.95%	71.00%	60.47%	62.29%	54.00%	57.65%
	NB	51.77%	72.00%	60.10%	58.05%	50.00%	53.51%
	MLP	51.75%	72.00%	60.27%	57.99%	52.00%	53.69%
LDA	SVM	50.26%	99.00%	66.67%	62.88%	55.00%	58.51%
	NB	50.51%	99.00%	**66.89%**	57.40%	49.00%	52.65%
	MLP	49.09%	38.00%	65.08%	56.03%	51.00%	53.30%
D2V	SVM	52.35%	59.00%	54.21%	64.19%	55.00%	**58.82%**
	NB	53.40%	90.00%	**66.89%**	50.23%	50.00%	50.03%
	MLP	51.78%	66.00%	57.00%	56.11%	50.00%	51.96%
BERT	SVM	49.11%	52.00%	49.82%	62.26%	55.00%	58.19%
	NB	45.62%	39.00%	33.95%	57.19%	48.00%	52.63%
	MLP	44.12%	43.00%	47.39%	55.90%	46.00%	52.79%

5   Conclusions

Deceptive text detection is a relevant topic that can be addressed through the analysis of various features, including emotional and contextual ones. Emotions play an important role in deception texts, even when not explicitly expressed. Their relevance is due to the fact that they can persuade in the act of deception to convince.

Experimental results demonstrate that cascade classification method, which combines lexical and emotional features, outperforms the approach that only uses emotional distributions in 3 out of 5 datasets analyzed.

This study shows that depending on the nature of the dataset, the feature vectorization method and the classifier that achieves the best performance differ. Among the proposed method's successful cases, BERT emerged as the feature vectorization method with the best performance. This behavior is attributed to BERT is capable of analyzing the context of texts bidirectionally, compared to the other methods used.

BERT was used only as a feature generation method in this study, due to its ability to semantically and contextually analyze texts. Therefore, its use cannot be directly compared to the performance of the pre-trained and fine-tuned model. Because fine-tuning a model to a specific task has the advantage of adapting the classification process to a particular topic.

As an advantage, the cascade method is structured in several stages, this allows a simpler understanding of the classification process, unlike neural networks or LLMs, where the process is a black box. Another advantage is that the proposed approach does not use a large amount of resources as advanced models do.

Acknowledgement. We thank Autonomous University of the State of Mexico and CONAHCyT.

References

1. Aggarwal, A., Chauhan, A., Kumar, D., Verma, S., Mittal, M.: Classification of fake news by fine-tuning deep bidirectional transformers based language model. EAI Endorsed Trans. Scalable Inf. Syst. **7**(27), e10–e10 (2020)
2. Blei, D.M., Ng, A.Y., Jordan, M.I.: Latent Dirichlet allocation. J. Mach. Learn. Res. **3**(Jan), 993–1022 (2003)
3. Caspi, A., Gorsky, P.: Online deception: prevalence, motivation, and emotion. Cyberpsychol. Behav. **9**(1), 54–59 (2006)
4. Fornaciari, T., Poesio, M.: Identifying fake amazon reviews as learning from crowds. In: Proceedings of the 14th Conference of the European Chapter of the Association for Computational Linguistics, pp. 279–287. Association for Computational Linguistics (2014)
5. García-Galindo, M.D.C., Hernández-Castañeda, Á., García-Hernández, R.A., Ledeneva, Y.: Automatic identification of suicidal ideation in texts using cascade classifiers. In: Pichardo Lagunas, O., Martínez-Miranda, J., Martínez Seis, B. (eds.) Advances in Computational Intelligence. Lecture Notes in Computer Science(), vol. 13613, pp. 114–126. Springer, Cham (2022). https://doi.org/10.1007/978-3-031-19496-2_9
6. Hernández-Castañeda, Á., Calvo, H.: Deceptive text detection using continuous semantic space models. Intell. Data Anal. **21**(3), 679–695 (2017)
7. Hernández-Castañeda, Á., Calvo, H., Gambino, O.J.: Impact of polarity in deception detection. J. Intell. Fuzzy Syst. **35**(1), 549–558 (2018)
8. Kim, J., Kang, J., Shin, S., Myaeng, S.H.: Can you distinguish truthful from fake reviews? user analysis and assistance tool for fake review detection. In: Proceedings of the First Workshop on Bridging Human–Computer Interaction and Natural Language Processing, pp. 53–59 (2021)
9. Le, Q., Mikolov, T.: Distributed representations of sentences and documents. In: International Conference on Machine Learning, pp. 1188–1196. PMLR (2014)
10. Li, X., Wu, C., Mai, F.: The effect of online reviews on product sales: a joint sentiment-topic analysis. Inf. Manag. **56**(2), 172–184 (2019)

11. Mohammad, S.M., Bravo-Marquez, F.: WASSA-2017 shared task on emotion intensity. arXiv preprint: arXiv:1708.03700 (2017)
12. Mohawesh, R., Xu, S., Springer, M., Al-Hawawreh, M., Maqsood, S.: Fake or genuine? Contextualised text representation for fake review detection. arXiv preprint: arXiv:2112.14343 (2021)
13. Mohawesh, R., et al.: Fake reviews detection: a survey. IEEE Access **9**, 65771–65802 (2021)
14. Ott, M., Choi, Y., Cardie, C., Hancock, J.T.: Finding deceptive opinion spam by any stretch of the imagination. arXiv preprint: arXiv:1107.4557 (2011)
15. Pérez-Rosas, V., Mihalcea, R.: Cross-cultural deception detection. In: Proceedings of the 52nd Annual Meeting of the Association for Computational Linguistics (Volume 2: Short Papers), pp. 440–445 (2014)
16. Saini, M., Sharan, A.: Identifying deceptive opinion spam using aspect-based emotions and human behavior modeling. Int. J. Hybrid Inf. Technol. **10**(1), 447–456 (2017)
17. Vaswani, A., et al.: Attention is all you need. In: Advances in Neural Information Processing Systems, pp. 5998–6008. Search PubMed (2017)

Deep Learning and Neural Networks

LCAM-Net: Local Context Attention Network for Diabetic Retinopathy Severity Classification

Dora E. Alvarado-Carrillo[1]([⊠]) [iD], Emmanuel Ovalle-Magallanes[2] [iD],
and Oscar S. Dalmau-Cedeño[1] [iD]

[1] Department of Computer Science, Center for Research in Mathematics (CIMAT),
Jalisco S/N, Guanajuato, 36000 Guanajuato, Mexico
{dora.alvarado,dalmau}@cimat.mx
[2] Dirección de Investigación y Doctorado, Facultad de Ingeniería y Tecnología,
Universidad La Salle Bajío, Av. Universidad 602. Col. Lomas del Campestre, León,
37150 Guanajuato, Mexico
eovalle@lasallebajio.edu.mx

Abstract. Diabetic Retinopathy (DR) is a chronic condition caused by microvascular complications of diabetes mellitus. DR is the leading cause of blindness in working-age adults globally. Hence, early diagnosis and precise treatment are paramount to prevent visual impairment. However, the task's difficulty and the high demand for ophthalmological services often lead to delays and inaccuracies in DR severity assessment. Deep Learning (DL) techniques have emerged as a promising solution to address this challenge and provide timely and unbiased DR analysis. This paper proposes a novel local-context attention mechanism (LCAM) to enhance the identification of salient elements such as lesions in DR severity classification. LCAM leverages spatial context information to emphasize abnormal regions in intermediate feature maps of a convolutional neural network by learning context weights to integrate multi-level features effectively.

Experimental results on the benchmark dataset IDRiD show that incorporating the proposed module over five backbone classification architectures enhances performance, achieving state-of-the-art results: 64.08% for Quadratic Weighted Kappa score and 69.13% for Accuracy. Additionally, the LCAM-based architectures show explainability qualities to highlight lesion-related areas in the fundus image, as evidenced by using Grad-CAM.

Keywords: Context Attention · Convolutional Neural Network · Deep Learning · Diabetic Retinopathy · Image Classification

1 Introduction

Diabetic Retinopathy (DR) is a chronic progressive disease derived from diabetes, with worldwide prevalence among people between 20 and 79 years old at

E. Mezura-Montes et al. (Eds.): MCPR 2024, LNCS 14755, pp. 355–367, 2024.
https://doi.org/10.1007/978-3-031-62836-8_33

34.6%. Since it represents the main cause of visual disability in adults of working age (between 20 and 69 years old), DR is considered a severe public health problem that increases the cases of disability pension and generates a tremendous economic expense for countries, regardless of their incomes [5,21].

Given the asymptomatic behavior of DR at an early stage, it is essential to facilitate periodic retinal monitoring to rapidly treat complications and prevent blindness [25,26].

To contribute to timely and unbiased DR recognition, Deep Learning (DL) systems have recently achieved more significant results. These techniques have demonstrated proficiency in identifying the degree of DR with greater precision, following the international clinical scale [11,13,20,29]. Despite the high classification rates of DL-based methods, recent studies have criticized the lack of interpretability and the tendency to learn wrong associations, such as matching severe damage with the location of the optic disc in the image [1].

Herein, a local-context attention mechanism integrates general and salient features such as lesions, which enhances the DR severity classification. Experiment results demonstrate that incorporating the attention mechanism into different backbone architectures achieves outstanding performance with fewer parameters than the existing state-of-the-art methods. Particularly, the proposed approach achieves the best Quadratic Weighted Kappa score (64.08%) and the second-best Accuracy (69.13%) concerning state-of-the-art methods.

The following are the main contributions of this work:

- A novel attention module based on spatial context information is proposed to emphasize salient regions in intermediate feature maps of a convolutional neural network by resembling a local Z-normalization process where context weights are automatically learned.
- The robustness of the proposed module is validated through an ablation study in which multiple backbone architectures are evaluated with a benchmark dataset, verifying the ability of the mechanism to increase performance, regardless of the classifier architecture.

2   Related Works

Explaining decision criteria is desirable and necessary in computerized healthcare systems. Therefore, recent research has focused on developing models that can reasonably justify their classification rules.

For instance, Foo et al. [7] designed a multi-task DL network using a hybrid architecture consisting of a VGG16-based encoder and a UNet-based decoder. The model was trained simultaneously for lesion segmentation and severity grade classification. Alyoubi et al. [3] proposed to perform an explicit localization of heterogeneous lesions using a YOLOv3-type fine-tuned network and a dense three-layer block that was added at the end of the model to perform the classification, taking the patches of the previously localized lesions as input.

Attention-based models adopt an indirect strategy, aiming to enhance informative regions adaptively within the model training. Farag et al. [6] proposed to include a Convolutional Block Attention Module (CBAM) on top of a pre-trained DenseNet169, freezing the DenseNet backbone and only training the attention module and the classification head to boost the classification performance. Miao *et al.* [15] introduced a multiscale DL network model with hybrid attention for DR classification, consisting of a Residual-Inception double attention module (channel and spatial attention modules); in such a way, the module was able to extract the importance of different channels and focus on areas with high-frequency information simultaneously. Alahmadi *et al.* [2] designed a texture and spatial recalibration mechanism inside an Inception network; the module passed intermediate outputs from the model through a Laplacian pyramid to highlight high-frequency information related to the texture while complementary features were generated using the CBAM.

As described in the previous paragraphs, DR classification approaches solve the problem by employing a DL object detection framework (lesion-based) to improve the interpretability of their results, and others incorporate a generic attention mechanism to highlight more informative DR regions and patterns.

3 Proposed Method

The proposed local context-based attention module identifies spatially salient regions of intermediate feature maps by exploiting the variability between background and foreground features, thus distinguishing them as objects of interest for a correct DR classification.

Let $\mathbf{A} \in \mathbb{R}^{H \times W}$ be a two-dimensional field, where H and W refer to the height and width of the map, respectively. For a point $\mathbf{u} = (a, b)$ in the domain of $\mathbf{A}$, a local statistic can be computed as specified below.

$$\mu(\mathbf{u}) = \mathbf{A}(\mathbf{u}) * \mathbf{W} \tag{1}$$

subject to restrictions:

$$\mathbb{1}^\top \mathbf{W} \mathbb{1} = 1, \tag{2}$$
$$\mathbf{W}(\mathbf{v}) \geq 0 \tag{3}$$

where $*$ denotes the convolution operator, $\mathbf{W}$ is a matrix with dimensions $\ell \times \ell$ ($\ell << H, \ell << W$), ℓ is the size of the neighborhood to calculate the local statistic, $\mathbf{A}(\mathbf{u})$ denotes an element in the a-th row and b-th column of $\mathbf{A}$, $\mathbf{v} = (c, d)$ represents a point in the domain of $\mathbf{W}$, $\mathbf{W}(\mathbf{v})$ represents an element in the c-th row and d-th column of $\mathbf{W}$, and $\mathbb{1}$ is a column vector of all-ones.

The elements of $\mathbf{W}$ play the role of a density function, which could be adjusted automatically to capture context relevance. In this regard, $\mathbf{W}$ must be restricted by conditions of non-negativity in all its elements and normalization over its grand sum, with the intent that $\mu(\mathbf{u})$ can be seen as the first moment of a random variable with density function $\mathbf{W}$.

Ergo, the variance in the neighborhood of $\mathbf{u}$ can also be obtained by:

$$\sigma^2(\mathbf{u}) = (\mathbf{A}(\mathbf{u}^2) * \mathbf{W}) - \mu(\mathbf{u})^2, \tag{4}$$

Consequently, normalizing $\mathbf{A}(\mathbf{u})$ is equivalent to performing the following operation:

$$\bar{\mathbf{A}}(\mathbf{u}) = (\mathbf{A}(\mathbf{u}) - \mu(\mathbf{u}))/\sigma(\mathbf{u}). \tag{5}$$

Extending this idea to a convolutional neural network context, an analogous operation to Eq. (1) is to apply a convolutional layer on an input feature map $\mathbf{I} \in \mathbb{R}^{C \times H \times W}$, such that:

$$\mathcal{M}(\mathbf{I}; \mathcal{W}) = \text{C\_Conv2D}_{\ell \times \ell}^{(C/r)}(\mathbf{I}; \mathcal{W}), \tag{6}$$

where $\text{C\_Conv2D}_{\ell \times \ell}^{C/r}(\mathbf{I}; \mathcal{W})$ represents a two-dimensional constrained convolutional layer (values in each filter are restricted by non-negativity and normalization conditions on their grand sum) with C/r filters, r is a reduction scalar factor, typically used in attention models [16,17], $\mathcal{W} = \{\mathbf{W}_1, \mathbf{W}_2, ..., \mathbf{W}_{C/r}\}$ denotes the set of weights (parameters) of the layer, and $\mathcal{M}(\mathbf{I}; \mathcal{W}) \in \mathbb{R}^{C/r \times H \times W}$ is the local mean feature map. Parameters in $\mathcal{W}$ are learnable, and each element acts as a weight determining the importance of the corresponding spatial location within the neighborhood.

Moreover, to compute local statistics in spatial and per-channel terms while keeping the number of parameters low, the filter grouping configuration of this layer has been set to C/r groups (see [28] for more information on grouped convolutions), reducing the number of parameters of this layer from $C \times (C/r) \times \ell^2$ to $C \times \ell^2$.

Afterwards, a map of local variances $\mathcal{V}(\mathbf{I}; \mathcal{W}) \in \mathbb{R}^{C/r \times H \times W}$ can be obtained as follows:

$$\mathcal{V}(\mathbf{I}; \mathcal{W}) = \mathcal{M}(\mathbf{I}^{\circ 2}; \mathcal{W}) - \mathcal{M}(\mathbf{I}; \mathcal{W})^{\circ 2}, \tag{7}$$

where $(\cdot)^{\circ 2}$ denotes the 2-th Hadamard power. In this case, the Hadamard power is applied to calculate the element-wise square of $\mathbf{I}$. This operation is utilized to capture higher-order statistics within the feature map.

Finally, the normalization of the feature map is given by:

$$\bar{\mathbf{I}}(\mathcal{W}) = \left(\text{Conv2D}_{k \times k}^{(C/r)}(\mathbf{I}) - \mathcal{M}(\mathbf{I}; \mathcal{W})) \right) \oslash (\mathcal{V}(\mathbf{I}; \mathcal{W})^{\circ \frac{1}{2}} + \epsilon), \tag{8}$$

where $\oslash$ denotes Hadamard division and $\text{Conv2D}_{k \times k}^{(C/r)}(\cdot)$ is a conventional convolutional layer with C/r filters of arbitrary kernel size $k \times k$. The purpose of Hadamard division is to normalize the feature map $\mathbf{I}$ based on the local context information encoded by $\mathcal{M}(\mathbf{I}; \mathcal{W})$ and the local variances represented by $\mathcal{V}(\mathbf{I}; \mathcal{W})$. It is important to note that Hadamard division is performed element-wise, allowing for independent scaling of each element in the normalization process, instead of mitigating internal covariate shift and stabilizing network training, such as batch, instance, and group normalization [24]. $\mathrm{Conv2D}_{k \times k}^{(C/r)}(\cdot)$ is employed to match the dimensions between $\mathbf{I}$ and $\bar{\mathbf{I}}$, given the reduction in channels that affects the dimensions of $\mathcal{M}(\mathbf{I}; \mathcal{W})$ and $\mathcal{V}(\mathbf{I}; \mathcal{W})$.

Notice that $\bar{\mathbf{I}}$ is intended to be a map where background elements are dimmed and foreground elements are boosted. Therefore, to keep as much information from the input map as possible while providing the network with an indication of the spatial features to highlight, the local context attention module is defined as:

$$\mathbf{I}_{LCAM}(\mathcal{W}) = \mathbf{I} \otimes \mathrm{Conv2D}_{k \times k}^{(C)} \left(\bar{\mathbf{I}}(\mathcal{W}) \right) + \mathbf{I}, \tag{9}$$

where $\otimes$ denotes the Hadamard product.

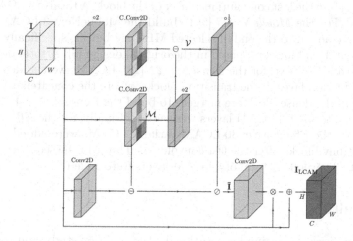

Fig. 1. Local Context Attention Module (LCAM). The attention weights are obtained by local normalization at the spatial level of an input feature map $\mathbf{I}$ by estimating their local expected values and variances.

Figure 1 shows an overall diagram of LCAM module: at the channel level, the input feature map is passed through a process of reduction (or squeezing) and excitation, which allows the extraction of contextual information efficiently since it maintains the number of parameters dependent of a reduction factor r; at spatial level, attention weights are obtained from two local statistical maps, $\mathcal{M}(\mathbf{I}; \mathcal{W})$ and $\mathcal{V}(\mathbf{I}; \mathcal{W})$, which are extracted through operations including Hadamard power layers, conventional convolutional layers, and two constrained convolutional layers (all weights must be greater than or equal to zero and the grand sum of each filter must equal one). It is worth mentioning that, although in terms of the number of operations these two constrained convolutional layers count as independent layers, in terms of parameters, they must be seen as a single layer since their weights are shared.

3.1 Backbone Architectures with LCAM

In order to evaluate the effectiveness of the proposed attention module LCAM, a group of convolutional neural models known for their strong performance in image classification tasks were selected as the baseline. These models were pre-trained on the ImageNet dataset.

First, for the *InceptionV3* [22], to build the InceptionV3-LCAM variant, LCAMs were attached to the end of each group of factorization blocks (block type A and C), considering that these parts of the network are richer in terms of spatial features than features in the transition blocks or grid size reduction (block type B, D, E), which remain unchanged. A total of 2 LCAM layers were added. Secondly, for the *ResNet50* [8], to assemble the ResNet50-LCAM variant, an LCAM was included in the last block of each sequence of residual blocks with the same spatial resolution before the last convolutional layer of the block. A total of 4 LCAM layers were added. For the *MobileNetV3* [9] to build the MobileNetV3-LCAM variant, LCAMs were added to the end of selected MBConv blocks, specifically after the squeeze-excitation blocks proposed in the original design [9]. A total of 5 LCAM layers were added. Next, for the *DenseNet121* [10], LCAMs were added after the channel reduction layer in the transition blocks, where the concatenated maps of each layer in the dense block are merged, to build the DenseNet121-LCAM variant. Hence, a total of 3 LCAM layers were added. Finally, for the *EfficientNetB0* [23], to build the EfficientNetB0-LCAM variant, LCAMs were added at the end of the MBConv blocks after the last convolutional layer in the sequence, as in the MobileNetV3 variant. A total of 3 LCAM layers were added.

4 Results

This section presents the implementation details, ablation study, and comparison with state-of-the-art methods. Accuracy (ACC), ROC Curve (AUC), F1-score (F1), and Quadratic Weighted Kappa (Kappa) scores were considered to evaluate the classification performance of the proposed LCAM-based architectures. For AUC and F1-score, Weighted and Macro variants are evaluated.

4.1 Implementation Details

The proposed architectures were evaluated on the IDRiD [18] dataset. The original training-test partition was used, *i.e.*, 413 and 103 images, respectively, and the validation set was created randomly, by taking 10% of the training set. The International Clinical Diabetic Retinopathy Scale was used to label the dataset into five severity groups manually: 1) no apparent DR, 2) mild nonproliferative DR, 3) moderate nonproliferative DR, 4) severe nonproliferative DR, and 5) proliferative DR.

For the training part, partial transfer learning was used; regardless, the original models were modified to create new variants. No layers in the original baseline models were removed or modified. Instead, the only change made was the addition of LCAM mechanisms in specific parts of the models, as discussed in Sect. 3.1. Consequently, the layer weights in the original models were initialized using the weights from the pre-trained ImageNet models. In contrast, the LCAM layers were initialized with random weights.

The optimization setup consisted of an Adam optimizer, which started with a value of $1e-5$ and increased linearly at each epoch until reaching a value of $1e-4$, allowing the ImageNet pretrained weights to transition from natural images to fundus data gradually. The training was carried out for 200 epochs, with a minibatch of size 32. In each epoch, the validation set was evaluated, and the model with the best performance in the Kappa metric was kept. All models used in the experiments were developed using Pytorch and a 24 GB NVIDIA Titan RTX GPU. The source code will be available upon paper publication[1].

4.2 Ablation Study for LCAM

An ablation study was performed to evaluate the impact of the proposed LCAM module and the different architectures built with it. The experiments were conducted using the IDRiD dataset, selected for having well-established training-test partitions and a size that facilitates the analysis of multiple configurations in a reasonable time. The original architectures of InceptionV2, ResNet50, MobileNetV3, DenseNet121, and EfficientNetB0 were compared with their LCAM-based counterparts. For LCAM-based Networks (LCAM-Nets), configurations with receptive field size $\ell \times \ell$, with ℓ equal to 3, 5, and 7 in the constrained convolutional layers were evaluated to study the effect of the neighborhood size for the attention layer. Henceforth, the notation Backbone-LCAM-L refers to an LCAM-Net architecture, where the base model is specified at the beginning (Backbone) and with hyperparameter $\ell = L$.

Comparative results, presented in Table 1, show that the incorporation of LCAM has a positive impact on the performance of the baseline networks: there was a notable increase in the Kappa index for all cases, being the most significant InceptionV3-LCAM-7 and MobileNetV3-LCAM-5, with a gain around 20% and 12%, respectively; in ACC, scores increased for LCAM-3 and LCAM-5 variants in all cases except the DenseNet121 architecture; for M-AUC and W-AUC, improvements of 2% to 6% were observed in most of the models, except for the three variants of EfficientNetB0-LCAM and DenseNet121-LCAM-7; in M-F1 and W-F1 metrics, the best results were obtained with the DenseNet121-LCAM-5 and EfficientNetB0-LCAM-5 variants, which used a using a receptive field of 5×5 in the LCAM module.

Regarding the variation of the receptive field size in the LCAM module, a fair benefit was observed in increasing up to 5×5 the size of the field in backbone architectures such as MobileNetV2-LCAM, DenseNet121-LCAM, and EfficientNetB0-LCAM. In general, most metrics declined as the size of the receptive field increased to 7×7 for all models. The best configuration was the DenseNet121-LCAM-5, which obtained the best values in 4 of 6 metrics

---

[1] https://github.com/dora-alvarado/lcam-diabetic-retinopathy-classification.

Table 1. Ablation study of LCAM on IDRiD dataset. M- and W- stands for Macro and Weighted metrics. The symbol ✗ denotes that the baseline model does not include the LCAM.

Baseline	LCAM	Results (%)					
	($\ell \times \ell$)	Kappa	ACC	M-AUC	W-AUC	M-F1	W-F1
InceptionV3	✗	47.12	47.57	79.61	77.16	35.01	46.65
	3 × 3	64.85	56.31	85.51	84.12	48.71	55.81
	5 × 5	64.30	59.22	85.37	82.55	**54.61**	59.24
	7 × 7	**71.00**	50.49	82.37	81.11	41.79	51.72
ResNet50	✗	64.22	55.34	83.89	81.63	40.25	53.43
	3 × 3	68.95	*62.14*	86.62	83.50	48.84	60.57
	5 × 5	65.48	61.17	86.96	83.86	44.97	58.09
	7 × 7	64.28	**64.08**	87.29	85.20	45.96	59.96
MobileNetV3	✗	56.30	55.34	82.55	80.93	44.56	53.17
	3 × 3	60.78	56.31	85.15	82.81	37.53	50.30
	5 × 5	69.09	59.22	83.85	80.66	44.77	57.00
	7 × 7	59.12	52.43	83.63	80.97	42.62	51.80
DenseNet121	✗	64.85	**64.08**	87.12	85.24	47.05	*61.12*
	3 × 3	67.11	58.25	*87.47*	*85.47*	45.83	56.71
	5 × 5	68.24	**64.08**	**87.66**	**86.48**	48.22	**61.48**
	7 × 7	60.50	52.43	84.22	81.03	38.33	49.82
EfficientNetB0	✗	65.65	59.22	86.64	83.77	42.07	55.51
	3 × 3	67.15	*62.14*	84.52	81.48	*51.25*	60.73
	5 × 5	*69.13*	61.17	85.73	83.04	45.82	58.25
	7 × 7	67.37	57.28	85.44	82.72	42.70	55.08

evaluated (ACC, M-ROC, W-ROC, and W-F1). However, InceptionV3-LCAM-5, ResNet50-LCAM-3, and EfficientNetB0-LCAM-5 models also had notable improvements over the baseline, obtaining the best evaluation in M-F1 and the second-best evaluations in ACC and Kappa, respectively. These configurations have been selected for further experiments.

4.3 Classification Results

The five-class classification performance of LCAM-Nets was evaluated and compared with state-of-the-art methods in terms of Accuracy (ACC), Weighted Quadratic Kappa (Kappa), number of epochs (Epochs), input size, number of parameters (Params), and number of multiply-accumulate operations (Ops.). The backbones used were InceptionV3, ResNet50, DenseNet121, and Efficient-NetB0, selected from the ablation study (see Sect. 4.2).

The performance analysis of the IDRiD dataset is presented in Table 2, where a comparison is made against state-of-the-art methods, and outstanding results are obtained. In terms of accuracy score, all four LCAM variants either match or surpass the performance of their respective vanilla models and outperform the results reported by [12,27]. Notably, the DenseNet121-LCAM-5 model achieves the second-best accuracy score among all models considered. All four LCAM-based models demonstrate significant improvements over the corresponding baseline models regarding the Kappa index. The EfficientNetB0-LCAM-5 model outperforms the others, achieving a four-percentage-point increase compared to the lowest-scoring LCAM variant, InceptionV3-LCAM-5. Additionally, it outperforms the best-performing baseline architecture, EfficientNetB0, by three percentage points.

Additionally, Grad-CAM (Gradient-weighted Class Activation Mapping) [19] heatmap visualizations were created to explore the regions with the greatest relevance in the learning process of the baseline and LCAM-based models. Figure 2 show Grad-CAM results for images of the five classes, showing the original image and Grad-CAM heatmaps (warmer colors indicate higher values, and cooler colors indicate lower values). The results show better intuition than LCAM-based models to highlight areas with the presence of both blood and lipid lesions given by a medical counterpart. In particular, in examples (c) and (d) of Fig. 2, the Grad-CAM of the baseline model fails to recognize the largest lesions as an important part of the classification decision, whereas the LCAM variant identifies these as strong regions.

Table 2. Five-class classification performance comparison on IDRiD dataset

Method	Year	Results (%)	
		ACC	Kappa
InceptionV3 [22]	2016	47.57	47.12
ResNet50 [8]	2016	55.34	64.22
DenseNet121 [10]	2017	64.08	64.85
EfficientNetB0 [23]	2019	59.22	65.65
SKD [14]	2020	**67.96**	-
CF-DRNet [27]	2020	56.19	-
ExplainDR [12]	2021	60.19	-
SA-NSVM [4]	2022	63.24	-
InceptionV3-LCAM-5 (Proposed)	-	59.22	64.30
ResNet50-LCAM-3 (Proposed)	-	62.14	*68.95*
DenseNet121-LCAM-5 (Proposed)	-	*64.08*	68.24
EfficientNetB0-LCAM-5 (Proposed)	-	61.17	**69.13**

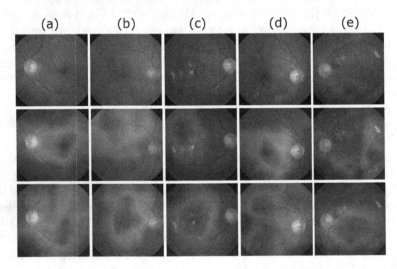

Fig. 2. Grad-CAM visualization for IDRiD images. Rows from top to bottom: Original image, overlapping Grad-CAM heatmap using baseline model, and overlapping Grad-CAM heatmap using LCAM-based model. Examples from all five classes were used for this visualization and are listed in left-to-right order.

5   Conclusion

This paper presented a new deep-learning module based on local spatial context information. The LCAM attention module was designed to prioritize identifying salient elements within feature maps. By guiding indirect classification toward lesions and abnormalities in fundus images, it significantly enhanced the performance of lightweight models. In terms of performance, LCAM-based models have achieved state-of-the-art results in the Kappa score and the second-best result in Accuracy.

The proposed LCAM-Nets focused on achieving a performance gain by using local spatial information without exploring or combining other deep learning techniques, such as other attention mechanisms proposed in the literature. However, in future work, it is intended to exploit the ordinal nature of the problem, as well as to address the marked class imbalance that exists in different public databases. A cost function, for example, that leverages a *priori* knowledge about these conditions could significantly enhance the performance of the models proposed here.

Acknowledgments. This research was partially supported by the Mexican Council of Humanities, Science and Technology CONAHCyT (Grant no. 626155/719327), and by the Bajio Supercomputer Laboratory (Grant no. 300832).

References

1. Abràmoff, M.D., et al.: Improved automated detection of diabetic retinopathy on a publicly available dataset through integration of deep learning. Invest. Ophthalmol. Visual Sci. **57**(13), 5200–5206 (2016). https://doi.org/10.1167/iovs.16-19964
2. Alahmadi, M.D.: Texture attention network for diabetic retinopathy classification. IEEE Access **10**, 55522–55532 (2022). https://doi.org/10.1109/ACCESS.2022.3177651
3. Alyoubi, W.L., Abulkhair, M.F., Shalash, W.M.: Diabetic retinopathy fundus image classification and lesions localization system using deep learning. Sensors **21**(11), 3704 (2021). https://doi.org/10.3390/s21113704
4. Bodapati, J.D.: Stacked convolutional auto-encoder representations with spatial attention for efficient diabetic retinopathy diagnosis. Multimed. Tools Appli. 1–24 (2022). https://doi.org/10.1007/s11042-022-12811-5
5. Cheloni, R., Gandolfi, S.A., Signorelli, C., Odone, A.: Global prevalence of diabetic retinopathy: protocol for a systematic review and meta-analysis. BMJ Open 9(3), e022188 (2019). https://doi.org/10.1136/bmjopen-2018-022188
6. Farag, M.M., Fouad, M., Abdel-Hamid, A.T.: Automatic Severity classification of diabetic retinopathy based on DenseNet and convolutional block attention module. IEEE Access **10**, 38299–38308 (2022). https://doi.org/10.1109/ACCESS.2022.3165193
7. Foo, A., Hsu, W., Lee, M.L., Lim, G., Wong, T.Y.: Multi-task learning for diabetic retinopathy grading and lesion segmentation. In: Proceedings of the AAAI Conference on Artificial Intelligence. vol. 34, pp. 13267–13272 (2020). https://doi.org/10.1609/aaai.v34i08.7035
8. He, K., Zhang, X., Ren, S., Sun, J.: Deep residual learning for image recognition. In: Proceedings of the IEEE Conference on Computer Vision and Pattern Recognition, pp. 770–778 (2016). https://doi.org/10.1109/CVPR.2016.90
9. Howard, A., et al.: Searching for MobileNetV3. In: Proceedings of the IEEE/CVF International Conference on Computer Vision, pp. 1314–1324 (2019). https://doi.org/10.1109/ICCV.2019.00140

10. Huang, G., Liu, Z., Van Der Maaten, L., Weinberger, K.Q.: Densely connected convolutional networks. In: Proceedings of the IEEE Conference on Computer Vision and Pattern Recognition, pp. 4700–4708 (2017). https://doi.org/10.1109/CVPR.2017.243

11. Ioannou, G., Papagiannis, T., Tagaris, T., Alexandridis, G., Stafylopatis, A.: Visual interpretability analysis of deep CNNs using an adaptive threshold method on diabetic retinopathy images. In: Proceedings of the IEEE/CVF International Conference on Computer Vision, pp. 480–486 (2021). https://doi.org/10.1109/ICCVW54120.2021.00058

12. Jang, S.I., Girard, M.J., Thiéry, A.H.: Explainable diabetic retinopathy classification based on neural-symbolic learning. In: NeSy, pp. 104–114 (2021)

13. Kwasigroch, A., Jarzembinski, B., Grochowski, M.: Deep CNN based decision support system for detection and assessing the stage of diabetic retinopathy. In: 2018 International Interdisciplinary PhD Workshop (IIPhDW), pp. 111–116. IEEE (2018). https://doi.org/10.1109/IIPHDW.2018.8388337

14. Luo, L., Xue, D., Feng, X.: Automatic diabetic retinopathy grading via self-knowledge distillation. Electronics 9(9), 1337 (2020). https://doi.org/10.3390/electronics9091337

15. Miao, Y., Tang, S.: Classification of diabetic retinopathy based on multiscale hybrid attention mechanism and residual algorithm. Wirel. Commun. Mobile Comput. **2022** (2022). https://doi.org/10.1155/2022/5441366

16. Mustaqeem, Kwon, S.: Att-Net: enhanced emotion recognition system using lightweight self-attention module. Appl. Soft Comput. **102**, 107101 (2021). https://doi.org/10.1016/j.asoc.2021.107101

17. Park, J., Woo, S., Lee, J.Y., Kweon, I.S.: A simple and light-weight attention module for convolutional neural networks. Int. J. Comput. Vision **128**(4), 783–798 (2020). https://doi.org/10.1007/s11263-019-01283-0

18. Porwal, P., et al.: Indian diabetic retinopathy image dataset (IDRiD): a database for diabetic retinopathy screening research. Data **3**(3), 25 (2018). https://doi.org/10.3390/data3030025

19. Selvaraju, R.R., Cogswell, M., Das, A., Vedantam, R., Parikh, D., Batra, D.: Grad-CAM: visual explanations from deep networks via gradient-based localization. In: Proceedings of the IEEE International Conference on Computer Vision, pp. 618–626 (2017). https://doi.org/10.1109/ICCV.2017.74

20. Shaik, N.S., Cherukuri, T.K.: Hinge attention network: a joint model for diabetic retinopathy severity grading. Appl. Intell. 1–17 (2022). https://doi.org/10.1007/s10489-021-03043-5

21. Stewart, M.W.: Diabetes and Diabetic Retinopathy: Overview of a Worldwide Epidemic. chap. 1, pp. 1–27. Springer, Singapore (2017). https://doi.org/10.1007/978-981-10-3509-8_1

22. Szegedy, C., Vanhoucke, V., Ioffe, S., Shlens, J., Wojna, Z.: Rethinking the inception architecture for computer vision. In: Proceedings of the IEEE Conference on Computer Vision and Pattern Recognition, pp. 2818–2826 (2016)

23. Tan, M., Le, Q.: EfficientNet: rethinking model scaling for convolutional neural networks. In: International Conference on Machine Learning, pp. 6105–6114. PMLR (2019)

24. Tian, Y., Zhang, Y.: A comprehensive survey on regularization strategies in machine learning. Inf. Fusion **80**, 146–166 (2022)

25. Ting, D.S.W., Lamoureux, E., Wong, T.Y.: Innovative approaches in delivery of eye care: diabetic retinopathy. In: Khanna, R.C., Rao, G.N., Marmamula, S. (eds.)

Innovative Approaches in the Delivery of Primary and Secondary Eye Care. EO, pp. 127–145. Springer, Cham (2019). https://doi.org/10.1007/978-3-319-98014-0_9

26. Tsiknakis, N., et al.: Deep learning for diabetic retinopathy detection and classification based on fundus images: a review. Comput. Biol. Med. 104599 (2021). https://doi.org/10.1016/j.compbiomed.2021.104599

27. Wu, Z., et al.: Coarse-to-fine classification for diabetic retinopathy grading using convolutional neural network. Artif. Intell. Med. **108**, 101936 (2020). https://doi.org/10.1016/j.artmed.2020.101936

28. Xie, S., Girshick, R., Dollár, P., Tu, Z., He, K.: Aggregated residual transformations for deep neural networks. In: Proceedings of the IEEE Conference on Computer Vision and Pattern Recognition, pp. 1492–1500 (2017). https://doi.org/10.1109/CVPR.2017.634

29. Yaqoob, M.K., Ali, S.F., Bilal, M., Hanif, M.S., Al-Saggaf, U.M.: Resnet based deep features and random forest classifier for diabetic retinopathy detection. Sensors **21**(11), 3883 (2021). https://doi.org/10.3390/s21113883

Image Classification with Recurrent Spiking Neural Networks

Andres Cureño Ramirez$^{(\boxtimes)}$ ⓘ, Balam García Morgado,
and Luis Gerardo de la Fraga ⓘ

Computer Science Department, Cinvestav, Av. IPN 2508, 07360 Mexico City, Mexico
andres.cureno@cinvestav.mx, fraga@cs.cinvestav.mx

Abstract. In this work we test some state of the art works in Spiking Neural Networks (SNN) to train them using surrogate gradients and using different loss functions to perform classification tasks using recurrent SNN and with our own datasets. We show that this kind of networks can accomplish in a good way the classifications tasks, but can not generalize the features of the incoming images.

Keywords: Spiking Neural Networks · Classification · Machine Learning

1 Introduction

Neuromorphic computing will be important in the future, and we can define it as non-von Neumann computers whose structure and functions are inspired by brains and that are composed of neurons and synapses [10]. IBM has recently presented a processor called NorthPole with a neuromorphic architecture, inside it has two dense networks-on-chip that are inspired by long-distance white-matter and short-distance gray-matter pathways and this chip outperforms some of the newest GPU in some benchmarks [6]. Programming a neuromorphic computer often entails creating a Spiking Neural Network (SNN), and have been in the focus of the development of novel computing hardware for AI, partially because the giant SNN of the brain with about 100 billion neurons consumes just 20 W [11].

Image classification in machine learning aims to predict the label of unknown data on an image, using previous knowledge that was obtained using some training data with known labels. Nowadays there exists a lot of techniques to perform this tasks and one of the best approaches is the Deep Learning techniques, in the work [9], the authors mentioned that is is still a challenge to perform classification tasks using neuromorphic approaches.

1.1 Spiking Neural Networks

This kind of neural networks do not use the non-linear functions as sigmoid, atan or Relu, instead they produce a spike and the these spikes are time dependent.

E. Mezura-Montes et al. (Eds.): MCPR 2024, LNCS 14755, pp. 368–376, 2024.
https://doi.org/10.1007/978-3-031-62836-8_34

This type of neuron model can handle the generation of spikes, and these models are generally expressed in the form of ordinary differential equations. A variety of spiking neural models have been proposed, and those models display the trade off between the biological accuracy and computational feasibility [12]. In this work we are going to use the model Leaky Integrate and Fire (LIF), because of its simplicity and low computational cost. The LIF model is described as follows:

$$C_m \frac{dv_m}{dt} = -G_L(v_m - E_L) + I_{syn}(t),$$

$$\text{if } v_m \geq v_\theta, \; v_m \leftarrow v_{peak} \text{ then } v_m \leftarrow v_{reset}; \tag{1}$$

where C_m is the membrane capacitance, v_m is the membrane potential, I_{syn} is the synaptic input current, G_L represents the leak conductance, E_L represents the leak reversal potential, where v_θ is the threshold voltage, v_{peak} is the action potential, and v_{reset} is the resetting membrane potential. Then it is necessary to solve (1) for v_m. We implemented this model in snnTorch, that is a Python package for performing gradient-based learning with spiking neural networks and extends the capabilities of PyTorch [2], as follows:

$$v_m(t+1) = \beta v_m(t) + I_{syn}(t) - s(t)v_\theta,$$

$$\text{if } v_m > v_\theta \Rightarrow s(t) = 1 \text{ else } s(t) = 0, \tag{2}$$

where $s(t)$ is the presence or absence of a spike and β is the membrane potential decay rate. The Eq. (2) is named snn.Leaky in snnTorch and there is a recurrent model, that is described in the Eq. (3), where the main difference is the V term, that is a matrix with the recurrent weights, and this model is named snn.RLeaky in snnTorch.

$$v_m(t+1) = \beta v_m(t) + Vs(t) + I_{syn}(t+1) - s(t)v_\theta,$$

$$\text{if } v_m(t) > v_\theta \Rightarrow s(t) = 1 \text{ else } s(t) = 0 \tag{3}$$

1.2   Training of Spiking Neural Networks

One of the main problems of the SNNs is because the spike is a hard function to differentiate, and it is also possible that some neurons in the network did not activate during the simulation, so we can not update all the weights in every step in the network because the spikes are time depend. There exist some methods like converting an artificial neural network to an SNN, also gradient descent methods [1,3,7]. The surrogate gradient that we utilize, was proposed in the work [4], and is described as follows :

$$s = \begin{cases} 1 & \text{if } v_m \geq v_\theta \\ 0 & \text{else} \end{cases}, \tag{4}$$

$$s \approx \frac{1}{\pi} \arctan(\pi v_m \frac{\alpha}{2}), \tag{5}$$

$$\frac{\partial s}{\partial v_m} = \frac{1}{\pi} \frac{1}{(1 + (\pi v_m \frac{\alpha}{2})^2)}, \tag{6}$$

where $\alpha = 2$. Equation (4) is the one that produces a spike in the Eq. (2) and (3) and in order to use the derivative, it can be approximate using the Eq. (5) then its derivative is in the Eq. (6) and this surrogate gradient is also available in snnTorch.

2   Results

First, we create our own dataset of images with eight classes, and with 200 different samples for each class. The size of each picture is 64×64 pixels, so in total we have 1600 images. A sample image of each class can be seen in Fig. 1. All samples shown in images Fig. 1a–1d and 1f are only rotated of the same shown object. The other samples are taken with different ellipses, rectangles, or triangles. All the figures lie inside a circle of radius of 30 pixels centered on each image. To start the preprocessing of the data, each image was first crop to a new image of size 53×53 pixels because on the margins there is no information. Then, each image was binarized using a threshold equal to 127, and then pixel values were normalized in range [0,1], this simulates a spike, then the images are flatten to a vector of size 2809, that is going to be the input of our network. We divided this dataset in a training set with 80% of the data and a testing set with 20% of the remaining data. We also use an augmented dataset as another testing set with 480 images, with the same classes than previous one dataset, but the forms are scaled and translated, an image of each class of this new dataset is shown in Fig. 2.

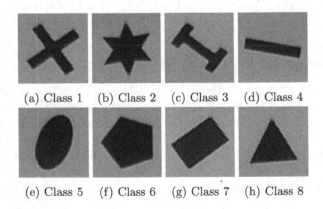

(a) Class 1   (b) Class 2   (c) Class 3   (d) Class 4

(e) Class 5   (f) Class 6   (g) Class 7   (h) Class 8

Fig. 1. Eight sample images of our dataset.

We took the proposed architecture for a Recurrent Spiking Neural Network (RSNN) from the work [1] that is described as follows:

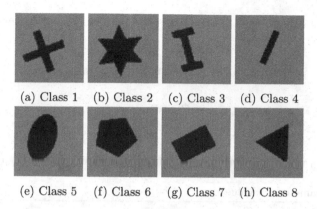

(a) Class 1   (b) Class 2   (c) Class 3   (d) Class 4

(e) Class 5   (f) Class 6   (g) Class 7   (h) Class 8

Fig. 2. Example of images in the augmented dataset.

$$v_j^{t+1} = \alpha v_j^t + \sum_{i \neq j} W_{ji}^{\text{rec}} z_i^t + \sum_i W_{ji}^{\text{in}} x_i^t - z_j^t v_{\text{th}}$$

$$z_j^{t+1} = H(v_j^{t+1} - v_{\text{th}})$$ (7)

$$y_k^{t+1} = \kappa y_k^t + \sum_j W_{kj}^{\text{rec}} z_j^{t+1} + b_k^{\text{out}}$$

At $t = 0$, $v_j^t = 0$, $z_j^t = 0$ and $y_k^t = 0$, where the observable state $z_j^t \in \{0,1\}$ is binary, indicating a spike when $z_j = 1$ or no spike when $z_j = 0$, and the hidden state or membrane potential is v_j^t, H denotes the Headviside step function, α is the decay factor, κ the leak factor, v_{th} the threshold potential, y_k^t is the output potential, and x_i^t are the features of the samples.

For the experiments the size of the matrices are: $W^{\text{in}} \in \mathbb{R}^{\text{in} \times \text{rec}}$, $W^{\text{rec}} \in \mathbb{R}^{\text{rec} \times \text{rec}}$, $W^{\text{out}} \in \mathbb{R}^{\text{rec} \times \text{out}}$, $v \in \mathbb{R}^{\text{rec}}$, $y \in \mathbb{R}^{\text{out}}$, $z_{\text{out}} \in \{0,1\}^{\text{out}}$, and $z \in \{0,1\}^{\text{rec}}$. All the network was implemented using PyTorch and snnTorch, in the computer with the specifications that are shown in Table 2. To obtain the hidden state v and the visible state z from Eq. (7) we use the model described in Eq. (3). And to obtain the output potential we use Eq. (2) without the term $-s(t)v_\theta$. The set of parameters for the training is presented in Table 1. In the work [3], the authors mentioned that it is possible to use the spikes count or the membrane potential of the output layer for the loss function, as it is shown in Eq. (8) and (9), in Fig. 3 we present a comparison of the loss function using both outputs. The loss function using the membrane potential decrease more than the one using the spikes, but their accuracy with the testing set it is almost the same, as we can see in second column of Table 3, and their confusion matrices in Tables 4 and 5. Once the network was trained, we use the augmented dataset to perform another test with all the same preprocessing, to analyze if the network after the training can generalize the features of the figures, their accuracy is presented in the third column of Table 3 and their confusion matrices are shown in Tables 6 and 7, and we can see that in both cases the performance of the network is not the best.

$$\text{loss}_{\text{spikes}} = \text{CrossEntropy}(z_{out}, y_{\text{target}}) \qquad (8)$$

$$\text{loss}_{\text{potential}} = \text{CrossEntropy}(y, y_{\text{target}}) \qquad (9)$$

Table 1. Training parameters.

Parameter	Value
seed	42
in	2809
rec	50
out	8
α	0.90
κ	0.90
v_{th}	1
b^{out}	0
epochs	30
batch size	80
number steps	10
loss function	Cross Entropy Loss
optimizer	Adam (learning rate = 5e−4, betas= (0.9,0.999))

Table 2. Computer settings.

Processor	Intel i7-10700 (16) 4.800GHz
GPU	NVIDIA RTX 4060
RAM	8 GB
Operating System	Ubuntu 22.04

Table 3. Accuracy comparison.

Loss function	Accuracy testing dataset	Accuracy augmented dataset
Output spikes	99.06%	23.12%
Output potential	100%	26.04%

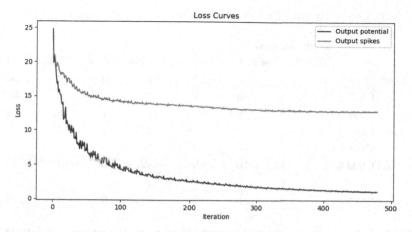

Fig. 3. Comparison between the output potential and the output spikes as loss function.

Table 4. Confusion matrix with output potential using the testing dataset.

		Predicted label							
		Class 1	Class 2	Class 3	Class 4	Class 5	Class 6	Class 7	Class 8
True label	Class 1	50	0	0	0	0	0	0	0
	Class 2	0	36	0	0	0	0	0	0
	Class 3	0	0	35	0	0	0	0	0
	Class 4	0	0	0	37	0	0	0	0
	Class 5	0	0	0	0	46	0	0	0
	Class 6	0	0	0	0	0	42	0	0
	Class 7	0	0	0	0	0	0	40	0
	Class 8	0	0	0	0	0	0	0	34

Table 5. Confusion matrix with output spikes using the testing dataset.

		Predicted label							
		Class 1	Class 2	Class 3	Class 4	Class 5	Class 6	Class 7	Class 8
True label	Class 1	50	0	0	0	0	0	0	0
	Class 2	0	36	0	0	0	0	0	0
	Class 3	0	0	35	0	0	0	0	0
	Class 4	0	0	0	37	0	0	0	0
	Class 5	0	0	0	0	43	2	0	1
	Class 6	0	0	0	0	0	42	0	0
	Class 7	0	0	0	0	0	0	40	0
	Class 8	0	0	0	0	0	0	0	34

Table 6. Confusion matrix with output potential using the augmented dataset.

		Predicted label							
		Class 1	Class 2	Class 3	Class 4	Class 5	Class 6	Class 7	Class 8
True label	Class 1	3	4	0	2	1	0	0	50
	Class 2	0	0	0	0	1	0	0	59
	Class 3	2	5	9	13	7	2	8	14
	Class 4	0	2	0	29	2	0	7	20
	Class 5	4	6	0	4	5	0	0	41
	Class 6	2	14	0	0	12	6	4	22
	Class 7	0	6	0	1	7	2	9	35
	Class 8	1	3	0	5	0	0	1	50

Table 7. Confusion matrix with output spikes using the augmented dataset.

		Predicted label							
		Class 1	Class 2	Class 3	Class 4	Class 5	Class 6	Class 7	Class 8
True label	Class 1	6	7	0	5	2	0	0	40
	Class 2	1	1	0	0	1	0	0	57
	Class 3	10	9	10	11	7	3	4	6
	Class 4	2	1	0	34	5	0	4	14
	Class 5	3	4	0	3	11	1	0	38
	Class 6	3	11	0	0	14	8	2	22
	Class 7	4	8	0	1	6	3	5	33
	Class 8	0	1	0	7	1	0	1	50

3   Discussion

Firstly, we do not know yet how a change in the hyperparameters of the network described in Table 1: α, κ, v_{th}, b_{out} and the number of steps, will impact in the performance of the network. The v_{th} can change during the training instead of being constant as it is described in the work [1]. And also it is not possible to observe a big difference in the accuracy obtained between using the output potential or the spikes in the loss functions, we can see that the accuracy in Table 3 are really similar, in the work [3] the authors mentioned that with a sufficient number of steps passing the spikes counts it is more adopted as loss function, the main advantage that we observe in using the spikes instead of the output potential, is that we only need 0 and 1 to predict the output, instead of using a real number from the output potential, but we do not know what it is a sufficient number of steps as mentioned by the authors.

We also tried to use the first four convolutional layers of the SimpleNet [5], before the architecture described in Eq. (7), to extract the characteristics, and we obtained a 100% accuracy using the testing dataset but only 40% of accuracy using the augmented dataset. Despite of we saw a little improvement in accuracy, it is not an acceptable result. As a consequence of this, we decided to merge both datasets, and train the network. And we obtained 85% of accuracy only using the architecture in Eq. (7), and 93% of accuracy using the convolutional network before Eq. (7).

It is important to mention that this problem can be solved satisfactorily using a support vector machine (SVM) with the first four Hu moments as the set of characteristics for each form. The SVM used has a radial basic functions kernel, with $\gamma = 0.8$ and $C = 1000$ for the implementation in the python module sklearn.svm.SVC.

Another important thing, is that we would like to look for the best way to initialize the weights of the network, currently all the test were performed using the same seed for the pseudo random number generator. But we would like to know how dense the matrices of the network need to be to achieve a good result in these tasks. If the matrices of the network can be sparse matrices this can help to reduce the storage, and some computations can be done quicker than using a dense matrix.

To sum up, it is not clear if this kind of networks outperforms classical methods, the main advantage it seems to be the implementation of these kind of networks in hardware, because they do not use any activation functions, they only produce spikes as an activation function.

Lastly, it is no clear how an static image needs to be pass through the network, because this networks are supposed to work with spikes, but in some works the image is normalized in the range [0,1] and then make the propagation, and in other works the image is encoded to spikes [3] and then passed through the network. In the work [8] they described a method to pass an static dataset of images to a neuromorphic dataset, but there is not a consensus yet how process the images before the propagation through the network.

4   Conclusions

We created our own datasets to test and compare different methods to do classification tasks with RSNN. For future work we would like to explore the search of the best architecture to solve classification and regression tasks and how to tuning the hyperparameters of the network. And we leave as open question in which kind of tasks this kind of networks can achieve better results than the current state of the art machine learning methods.

References

1. Bellec, G., et al.: A solution to the learning dilemma for recurrent networks of spiking neurons. Nat. Commun. **11**(1), 3625 (2020)
2. Eshraghian, J.K.: snnTorch documentation (2021). https://snntorch.readthedocs. io/en/latest/. Accessed 08 Feb 2024
3. Eshraghian, J.K., et al.: Training spiking neural networks using lessons from deep learning. In: Proceedings of the IEEE (2023)

4. Fang, W., Yu, Z., Chen, Y., Masquelier, T., Huang, T., Tian, Y.: Incorporating learnable membrane time constant to enhance learning of spiking neural networks. In: Proceedings of the IEEE/CVF International Conference on Computer Vision, pp. 2661–2671 (2021)
5. Hasanpour, S.H., Rouhani, M., Fayyaz, M., Sabokrou, M.: Lets keep it simple, using simple architectures to outperform deeper and more complex architectures. arXiv preprint arXiv:1608.06037 (2016)
6. Modha, D.S., et al.: Neural inference at the frontier of energy, space, and time. Science 382(6668), 329–335 (2023)
7. Neftci, E.O., Mostafa, H., Zenke, F.: Surrogate gradient learning in spiking neural networks: bringing the power of gradient-based optimization to spiking neural networks. IEEE Signal Process. Mag. 36(6), 51–63 (2019)
8. Orchard, G., Jayawant, A., Cohen, G.K., Thakor, N.: Converting static image datasets to spiking neuromorphic datasets using saccades. Front. Neurosci. 9, 437 (2015)
9. Reynolds, J.J., et al.: A comparison of neuromorphic classification tasks. In: Proceedings of the International Conference on Neuromorphic Systems, pp. 1–8 (2018)
10. Schuman, C.D., et al.: Opportunities for neuromorphic computing algorithms and applications. Nature Comput. Sci. 2(1), 10–19 (2022)
11. Stöckl, C., Maass, W.: Optimized spiking neurons can classify images with high accuracy through temporal coding with two spikes. Nat. Mach. Intell. 3(3), 230–238 (2021)
12. Yamazaki, K., Vo-Ho, V.K., Bulsara, D., Le, N.: Spiking neural networks and their applications: a review. Brain Sci. 12(7), 863 (2022)

Reducing Parameters by Neuroevolution in CNN for Steering Angle Estimation

José-David Velazco-Muñoz[✉], Héctor-Gabriel Acosta-Mesa,
and Efrén Mezura-Montes

Artificial Intelligence Research Institute, University of Veracruz,
Veracruz 91097, Mexico
zs22000515@estudiantes.uv.mx, {heacosta,emezura}@uv.mx

Abstract. Convolutional Neural Networks (CNNs) are becoming increasingly popular in autonomous driving. Researchers are focused on optimizing these models to work on smaller control devices, which can allow for more performance of vehicle steering. A lot of attention is being paid to reducing the number of parameters in a CNN so that it can predict steering angles more efficiently for autonomous vehicles. To tackle this challenge, we have adopted a neuroevolution approach, which is a fusion of neural networks and evolutionary algorithms. This approach can help us find models that are less complex but still have adequate predictive capacity and a lower number of parameters compared to existing networks. The results show that the neuroevolution approach was successful in producing an architecture with only 35,972 evaluated parameters. This is a significant reduction in the number of parameters compared to established models like PilotNet with 233,701 parameters, RestNet50 with 25,636,699 parameters, PSO-CNN with 1,335,758 parameters, VGG16 with 138,357,456 parameters, and VGG16-LSTM with 156,223,443 parameters. Despite having fewer parameters, our model's performance is similar to some of the other CNNs.

Keywords: Steering angle · neuroevolution · CNN · autonomous driving car

1 Introduction

The development of Convolutional Neural Networks (CNNs) has had a significant impact on autonomous driving systems in recent years. These networks have the ability to process complex visual information and have become a critical technology for vehicular autonomy [6]. The incorporation of CNNs in self-driving car control systems has the potential to revolutionize the automotive sector and urban transportation. These systems rely on the steering angle to control the trajectory of the vehicle. By enabling precise control, the vehicle can safely and efficiently follow its intended path, steer clear of accidents, and stay in the correct lane. Designing a CNN can be a challenging task. Determining its parameters

© The Author(s), under exclusive license to Springer Nature Switzerland AG 2024
E. Mezura-Montes et al. (Eds.): MCPR 2024, LNCS 14755, pp. 377–386, 2024.
https://doi.org/10.1007/978-3-031-62836-8_35

is equally important as it significantly influences the performance of the results and convergence. The main parameters and hyperparameters of a CNN include the learning rate, the number of epochs, the batch size, the activation function, the number and sequence of layers (convolutional, pooling, and fully connected), the number of neurons in the fully connected layers, and the number and size of filters in each convolutional layer. All these parameters play an essential role in ensuring the correct performance of the network. Addressing these challenges and optimizing fundamental aspects within a network could open up new possibilities in architecture design. Integrating neural networks with evolutionary algorithms through neuroevolution presents a novel approach to enhancing neural networks [5,14].

This paper is divided into four main sections. Section 2, related works, explores previous research related to the study topic. Section 3, methods and materials, explains the process used for conducting this study, including the dataset and algorithm used. Section 4 presents the experiments conducted and a discussion of each of them. Finally, Sect. 5 provides conclusions and a discussion of the overall findings.

2   Related Works

In the field of steering angle prediction, there are two different research paths [12]. The first involves using established vision methods to process images and identify road boundaries or lane markings, and then calculating the steering angle based on this information. The second path involves using CNNs for imitation learning to predict steering angles in both real-world scenarios and simulated applications. Various CNNs have been explored for this purpose. Several CNNs have been developed and tested to improve the accuracy and performance of steering angle predictions for autonomous vehicles. One well-known network is PilotNet [1], which is a deep architecture that directly maps camera images in a vehicle to steering angles. This eliminates the need for manual feature design, making it more efficient. In a study presented in [4], an autonomous car prototype and CNNs on Raspberry Pi were used. Another proposal, [17], is based on CNN-LSTM to predict steering angles. This proposal uses future sequential information during training, which results in good performance with the Udacity dataset [15] and in real autonomous vehicle tests. Similarly, in [7,8], proposals and experiments with CNN using simulated data are presented. Researchers have also explored optimizing algorithms and employing transfer learning techniques with CNNs to enhance their capability in predicting steering angles. The study [9] evaluated the performance of pre-trained networks, including AlexNet, ResNet18, and DenseNet121, by applying transfer learning and adjusting the last layer. ResNet18 and DenseNet121 turned out to have a better error percentage than the others. Among the various optimization methods used in CNNs, there are compression and acceleration techniques [3]. These techniques include pruning, factorization, and knowledge distillation which reduce the model's depth without compromising its performance. When it comes to optimizing CNNs using evolutionary computation, there are various approaches available. One such approach is to use memetic algorithms, which refine the mutation step through a series of educated local-search moves. A study presented in [10] discusses this paradigm. Another approach is to use Particle Swarm Optimization (PSO), which was used in [13] to optimize the weights of a CNN for angle estimation in autonomous driving. The study compared PSO and bat algorithms, and demonstrated the quality of the predictions through Mean Squared Error (MSE). The Udacity dataset [15] was used to validate different sets of hyperparameters. Existing techniques for compressing CNNs have shown evidence of increased computational efficiency and improved generalization, particularly in pruning techniques. However, not all techniques work well for certain problems and may require fine-tuning. On the other hand, methods like particle swarm optimization (PSO), memetic algorithms, and transfer learning have shown to generate higher precision CNNs, but with greater depth in the architectures. A literature review summary indicates that hyperparameter optimization, transfer learning, and compression techniques are the main focus of research in this area. These methods have demonstrated positive results in improving model performance. However, there is a lack of detailed exploration of the internal parameters and network structure depending on the problem. This lack of attention highlights the need for further research, leading to the adoption of neuroevolution techniques, which are more adaptable compared to other techniques. It is essential to understand the impact of the quantity of parameters on the latency of control devices, emphasizing the importance of further research.

3 Materials and Methods

This methodology, illustrated in Fig. 1, compares various CNNs for estimating steering angles in autonomous driving. It distinguishes itself by considering the number of parameters used by these networks. The main objective is to examine how varying parameter counts in CNN architectures impact the accuracy

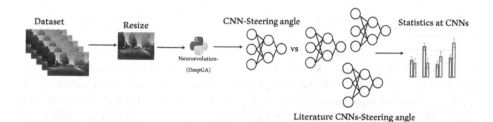

Fig. 1. This proposed methodology employs a dataset resized to 256 × 256, which is then fed into a neuroevolution algorithm to obtain a CNN architecture. This architecture is subsequently compared with the most relevant CNNs in the steering angle field. Finally, statistical comparisons are made between the CNNs and the proposed CNN to identify any significant differences.

of direction estimation while performing autonomous vehicle operations. This study emphasizes the significance of restricting the number of parameters used in architectures designed for predicting steering angles.

3.1   Dataset

This research proposes using the PilotNet dataset [2], as shown in Fig. 2, which is a representative dataset in autonomous vehicle research for predicting angles using only 1000 RGB images. The images were resized from 255×455 pixels to 255×255 pixels to accommodate the necessary features input of DeepGA. Out of all the images, 70% were used for model training, while the remaining 30% were used for testing during the neuroevolution process. Additionally, 10000 more images were used under the same conditions for model comparison.

Fig. 2. Images labeled with the required steering angle of the vehicle's steering wheel, related to the specific characteristics of the road observable in the image. In these images, the steering angle is associated with particular elements of the road environment, such as curves, lane changes, U-turns, among other factors that affect the vehicle's direction.

3.2   Neuroevolution

We utilized a neuroevolution algorithm to generate our network, specifically the Deep Genetic Algorithm (DeepGA) [16]. DeepGA is an evolutionary algorithm designed to optimize CNNs for visual recognition tasks, such as classifying. It employs a hybrid encoding to represent complex neural network structures and automatically improves the architecture through genetic algorithms instead of manual design. Unlike other neuroevolution methods [11], optimization and compression techniques, DeepGA has great adaptability and few tuning parameters. For the design of our network, primarily focused on regression CNNs, modifications were made to the DeepGA algorithm. The algorithm was adapted to generate designs for regression networks by altering the maximization criteria to minimization. The objective was to discover networks with the lowest values in

Mean Absolute Percentage Error (MAPE) (Eq. 1) which is a measure that evaluates the accuracy of a model by calculating the average percentage difference between predicted values and actual values, relative to the actual values.

$$MAPE = \frac{1}{N} \sum_{i=1}^{N} \left| \frac{\hat{y}_i - y_i}{y_i} \right| \tag{1}$$

We modified the algorithm to find networks that are both accurate in their predictions and efficient in their use of resources. This means we aim to obtain models that are compact and effective. To introduce more diversity, we use a variant of elitism, which considers the greater among the lesser as a means of generating diversity. Our objective is to discover efficient networks that use fewer parameters but still deliver high predictive performance.

4   Experiments and Results

Using the first 1000 images from the dataset [2], neuroevolution was performed. The initial ranges used by DeepGA to evolve CNNs (minimum and maximum counts for convolutional and fully connected layers, number of filters, filter dimensions, pooling methods, pool sizes, and neuron quantities) are summarized in Table 1. CNN models were trained using the parameters and hyperparameters specified in Table 1, they were taken concerning [16], given the promising results observed in the internal constructions of CNNs in classification. Those DeepGA parameters in Fig. 2 were fine-tuned by a grid search process. After conducting

Table 1. Initialization parameters and hyperparameters in CNNs

Parameter	Values
Minimum Convolutional Layers	2
Maximum Convolutional Layers	6
Minimum Fully Connected Layers	2
Maximum Fully Connected Layers	4
Number of Filters	2, 4, 8, 16, 32
Filter Size	2, 3, 4, 5, 6, 7, 8
Pooling Type	Max, Avg
Pooling Size	2, 3, 4, 5
Number of Neurons	4, 8, 16, 32, 64, 128
Training Epochs	30
Learning Rate (Adam Optimizer)	1×10^{-4}
Batch Size	10

Table 2. DeepGA Parameters

Parameter	Values
Population Size	20
Number of Generations	30
Tournament Size	5
Crossover Percentage	0.9
Mutation Percentage	0.7

ten DeepGA independent runs on a Tesla V100 in Google Colab with 16 GB with 13 h to complete one run, we obtained the following statistical results: the best value was 0.090, the worst value was 0.123, the mean value was 0.108, and the standard deviation was 0.007. Such values indicate a competitive and robust performance on DeepGA based on the fitness values reached. Moreover, the run located in the median value of the ten runs is plotted in Fig. 3. The MAPE convergence plot on the top left side of Fig. 3 shows that DeepGA improves result quality by avoiding local optimum solutions. Similarly, on the top right side of Fig. 3, the behavior of MSE exhibits a similar trend to MAPE. This leads us to consider that the fitness function is more representative in terms of information regarding prediction quality in CNN construction within DeepGA. After exploring different configurations in CNN parameters, DeepGA finds more compact designs without compromising regression quality across generations, as shown in the bottom part.

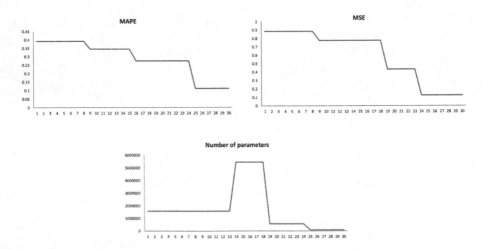

Fig. 3. Convergence plot of the run located at the median value of 10 executions across 30 generations of the fitness function (MAPE), MSE, and the number of parameters.

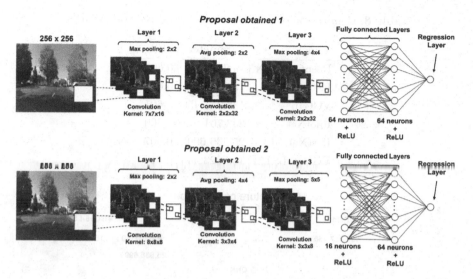

Fig. 4. Best architectures obtained by DeepGA. In the first proposal, the architecture consists of three convolutional layers using convolution kernels of sizes 7×7, 2×2, with pooling kernel sizes of 2×2 and 4×4. Additionally, there are two fully connected layers, each with 64 neurons. In the second proposal, the architecture includes three convolutional layers using convolution kernels of sizes 8×8, 3×3, with pooling kernel sizes of 2×2, 4×4, and 5×5. Similarly, there are two fully connected layers, one with 16 neurons and the other with 64 neurons.

The details of the best two architectures are depicted in Fig. 4. For comparison purposes with those state-of-the-art approaches, the first one was chosen. The models used for comparison include PilotNet [1], RestNet50 [8], VGG16, and VGG16-LSTM [17], and the optimized by PSO in [13]. All compared architectures will undergo an identical training process, using a batch size of 10 for 50 epochs and a fixed learning rate of 0.0001. This experimental design will ensure a fair and comprehensive comparison of the learning performance of different architectures.

In Fig. 5, a detailed comparison of those considered CNN architectures is conducted through the logarithmic distribution of their parameters. The aim is to visualize and analyze the differences in complexity among those architectures. Each parameter value is transformed using the log_{10} function to distribute the scale and highlight variations. Those evaluated architectures include PilotNet [1] with 233,701 parameters, RestNet50 [8] with 25,636,699, PSO-CNN [13] with 1,335,758, VGG16 with 138,357,456, VGG16-LSTM [17] with 156,223,443, and the proposed DeepGA-CNN (from Fig. 4) with 35,972 parameters (see Table 3). Considering the significant differences in the number of parameters required by the compared networks, the parameter axis is represented by its logarithm value for better visualization, emphasizing the performance of DeepGA-CNN with a low number of parameters. Despite the diversity in the absolute number of parameters, each architecture was trained, achieving a MSE in a range

Table 3. Comparison of Convolutional Neural Network Models

Model	Parameters	MSE
DeepGA-CNN	35,972	0.601
PSO-CNN	1,335,758	0.604
VGG16	138,357,456	0.601
PilotNet	233,701	0.600
RestNet-50	25,636,699	0.607
VGG16-LSTM	156,223,443	0.610

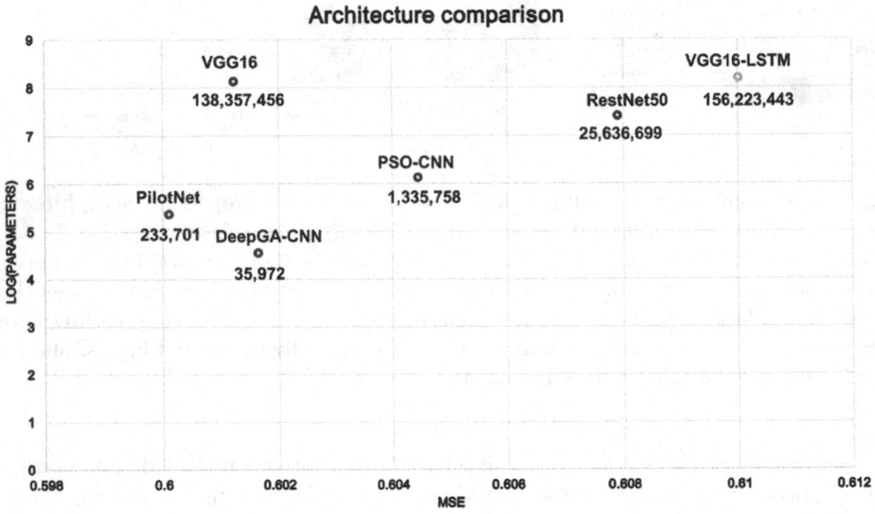

Fig. 5. Architecture distribution through its MSE and number of parameters

between 0.602 and 0.612, attributed to the number of images used. Ten experiments were conducted for each CNN. We conducted 10 runs to ensure a more solid and comprehensive sampling, encompassing different partitions and thus ensuring a more thorough and reliable evaluation of the results, divided into 70% for training and 30% for testing Training the CNNs involved specific conditions for each run, including 50 training epochs, a batch size of 10 samples per iteration, and a learning rate of 0.0001, 10,000 images. After the ten independent runs, ten sets of MSE values were obtained. A $Kolmogorov - Smirnov$ test indicated non-normality in the MSE data samples, and a $Kruskal - Wallis$ test revealed statistically significant differences in medians among the evaluated groups. To analyze differences between the DeepGA-RNC model and others, the $Mann - Whitney$ U-test was employed. Those results suggest that DeepGA-RNC performed similarly to PSO-RNC, VGG16, and VGG16-LSTM, despite having a significantly lower number of parameters (i.e., a competitive smaller model was obtained).

5   Discussion and Conclusion

The neuroevolution approach based on DeepGA has proven to be a good alternative, highlighting its potential for predicting steering angles. The study emphasizes the importance of exploring internal parameters and network structure to achieve smaller architectures with a competitive performance compared to state-of-the-art CNNs. The study has found that DeepGA-CNN, proposed as shown in Fig. 4, is an architecture with 35,972 parameters that can perform similarly to other complex models predicting steering angles. Getting smaller models favor the addition of possible explainable mechanisms and lead to include them in restricted hardware architectures. The integration of neuroevolution and the DeepGA algorithm [16] has shown promising results in predicting steering angles. Part of the future work considers using a multi-objective version of DeepGA to verify if better solutions can be obtained. Finally, experiments in a small car in controlled conditions is also expected. In future work, the intention is to work with established vision methods for angle prediction, as well as different compression methods to compare them with neuroevolution.

Acknowledgments. The first author acknowledges support of the National Council of Humanities, Science, and Technology (CONAHCYT) through a scholarship with no. CVU 1220680 to pursue graduate studies at Universidad Veracruzana.

References

1. Bojarski, M., et al.: End to end learning for self-driving cars (2016). https://doi.org/10.48550/arXiv.1604.07316
2. Bojarski, M., et al.: PilotNet: end-to-end learning for self-driving cars (2016). https://github.com/lhzlhz/PilotNet
3. Cheng, Y., Wang, D., Zhou, P., Zhang, T.: A survey of model compression and acceleration for deep neural networks. CoRR (2017). http://arxiv.org/abs/1710.09282
4. Do, T.D., Duong, M.T., Dang, Q.V., Le, M.H.: Real-time self-driving car navigation using deep neural network, pp. 7–12 (2018). https://doi.org/10.1109/GTSD.2018.8595590
5. Galván, E., Mooney, P.: Neuroevolution in deep neural networks: current trends and future challenges. IEEE Trans. Artif. Intell. **2**(6), 476–493 (2021). https://doi.org/10.1109/TAI.2021.3067574
6. Gidado, U.M., Chiroma, H., Aljojo, N., Abubakar, S., Popoola, S.I., Al-Garadi, M.A.: A survey on deep learning for steering angle prediction in autonomous vehicles. IEEE Access **8**, 163797–163817 (2020). https://doi.org/10.1109/ACCESS.2020.3017883
7. Hwang, K., Park, J.H.: Steering control of an autonomous vehicle using CNN. J. Korean Inst. Inf. Commun. Eng. **24**, 834–841 (2020). https://api.semanticscholar.org/CorpusID:226447140
8. Khanum, A., Lee, C.Y., Yang, C.S.: End-to-end deep learning model for steering angle control of autonomous vehicles. In: 2020 International Symposium on Computer, Consumer and Control (IS3C), pp. 189–192 (2020). https://doi.org/10.1109/IS3C50286.2020.00056

9. Khidhir, Y.G., Morad, A.H.: Comparative transfer learning models for end-to-end self-driving car. Al-Khwarizmi Eng. J. **18**(4), 45–59 (2022). https://doi.org/10.22153/kej.2022.09.003, https://alkej.uobaghdad.edu.iq/index.php/alkej/article/view/814

10. Lorenzo, P.R., Nalepa, J.: Memetic evolution of deep neural networks. In: Proceedings of the Genetic and Evolutionary Computation Conference, pp. 505–512. GECCO 2018, Association for Computing Machinery, New York, NY, USA (2018). https://doi.org/10.1145/3205455.3205631

11. Papavasileiou, E., Cornelis, J., Jansen, B.: A systematic literature review of the successors of "neuroevolution of augmenting topologies". Evol. Comput. **29**(1), 1–73 (2021). https://doi.org/10.1162/evco_a_00282

12. Saleem, H., Riaz, F., Mostarda, L., Niazi, M.A., Rafiq, A., Saeed, S.: Steering angle prediction techniques for autonomous ground vehicles: a review. IEEE Access **9**, 78567–78585 (2021). https://doi.org/10.1109/ACCESS.2021.3083890

13. Saleem, H., et al.: Optimizing steering angle predictive convolutional neural network for autonomous car. Computers. Mater. Continua **71**(2), 2285–2302 (2022). https://doi.org/10.32604/cmc.2022.022726, http://www.techscience.com/cmc/v71n2/45840

14. Stanley, K.O., Clune, J., Lehman, J., Miikkulainen, R.: Designing neural networks through neuroevolution. Nat. Mach. Intell. **1**(1), 24–35 (2019). https://doi.org/10.1038/s42256-018-0006-z

15. Udacity: Udacity self-driving car datasets (Año). https://github.com/udacity/self-driving-car/tree/master/datasets

16. Vargas-Hákim, G.A., Mezura-Montes, E., Acosta-Mesa, H.G.: Hybrid encodings for neuroevolution of convolutional neural networks: a case study. In: Proceedings of the Genetic and Evolutionary Computation Conference Companion, pp. 1762–1770. GECCO 2021, Association for Computing Machinery, New York, NY, USA (2021). https://doi.org/10.1145/3449726.3463133

17. Wu, T., Luo, A., Huang, R., Cheng, H., Zhao, Y.: End-to-end driving model for steering control of autonomous vehicles with future spatiotemporal features. In: 2019 IEEE/RSJ International Conference on Intelligent Robots and Systems (IROS), pp. 950–955 (2019). https://doi.org/10.1109/IROS40897.2019.8968453

Learnable Gabor Filters in CNNs: Avoiding Filter Degeneration via Early Stopping Based on Similarity Metrics

Carlos Orozco-Solis[1], Alfonso Rojas-Domínguez[1]([⊠]) [ID], Héctor Puga[1] [ID],
Manuel Ornelas Rodríguez[1] [ID], Martín Carpio[1] [ID],
and Valentín Calzada-Ledesma[2] [ID]

[1] Tecnológico Nacional de México, campus León, 37290 Gto., Mexico
alfonso.rojas@gmail.com
[2] Tecnológico Nacional de México, campus Purísima del Rincón, 36425 Gto., Mexico

Abstract. The advent of Deep Learning introduced a paradigm shift in the design and implementation of machine learning models, from the *feature engineering* paradigm towards the *feature learning* one; nowadays much less effort is dedicated to the manufacture of feature extraction methods, albeit at the expense of requiring larger volumes of training data and extended training times for deep models to learn the meaningful features. Nonetheless, it has been observed that the initial layers of many image models tend to converge to some of the earlier engineered feature extractors, mainly in the form of Gabor filters and other spatial filters, thus generating a growing interest in replacing the first layers in CNNs with learnable spatial filters, and in particular, Gabor filters. In this work we investigate the problem of parameter convergence in learnable Gabor filters, discover that the filters can exhibit degradation after a few epochs of training, and propose a method based on similarity metrics between the Gabor filters to address this issue. This research can contribute to the design of more efficient training strategies of networks employing learnable spatial filters, to leverage their intrinsic advantages over the more popular non-engineered convolutional filters.

Keywords: Learnable spatial filters · Gabor filters · Convolutional Neural Networks · Early Training-Stopping

1 Introduction

Convolutional Neural Networks (CNNs) [8] possess a powerful learning capability, based on multiple stages of feature extraction, allowing them to automatically learn complex data representations [6]. Before the popularization of CNNs, feature extraction relied on manually designed filters (spatial filters); these offer great flexibility, but these require laboriously manually tuning parameters.

It has been observed that after training CNNs there is a tendency of the convolutional filters in the first layer to converge towards spatial filters such as

© The Author(s), under exclusive license to Springer Nature Switzerland AG 2024
E. Mezura-Montes et al. (Eds.): MCPR 2024, LNCS 14755, pp. 387–396, 2024.
https://doi.org/10.1007/978-3-031-62836-8_36

Gabor filters [10]. In fact, a recent study states that "the early layer weights of diverse image models tend to converge to Gabor filters and color-contrast detectors" and "Spatially localized versions of canonical 2D Fourier basis functions, such as Gabor filters or wavelets, are perhaps the most frequently observed universal features in image models." [12].

In other words, the same attributes that are learned by the first convolutional layers can be captured using spatial filters designed specifically for that purpose. From this observation, the perspective arises of replacing some convolutional filters with Gabor filters, due to their flexibility in analyzing and representing features in an image. This idea has led to various strategies, reviewed in Sect. 2.

This work examines a CNN architecture where the filters of the first convolutional layer are replaced with trainable or *learnable* Gabor filters, referred to as a GaborNet. In particular, the convergence of the filter parameters is analyzed and it is found that a) the filter design is decided early in the training process; b) these filters exhibit degeneration after a certain training epoch; c) a point for early stopping can be identified via metrics of filter similarity, thus avoiding their degeneration and enabling ending the training after a few epochs.

2   Related Work

To take advantage of the benefits of spatial filters, some authors have proposed applying these on training images before given to a CNN. In [7], the authors apply spatial filters to detect features in faces, improving the accuracy of a CNN by 8.5%. In [4], the authors use spatial filters for handwritten digit classification, achieving competitive results against a LeNet network [8], which obtains 99.05% accuracy, while the authors' proposal achieves 99.16%.

The integration of spatial filters into CNNs is a recent trend that has shown to improve network performance in some cases. For example, the GCN network from [10] uses a bank of Gabor filters and achieves 99.37% accuracy on MNIST, comparable to 99.43% of the Oriented Response Network [17]. On CIFAR10/100, GCN achieves 96.12% and 79.87%, respectively, halving the required parameters compared to the Wide Residual Network [16], which achieves 96.00% and 80.95%.

To further integrate spatial filters into CNNs, it has been proposed that the first layer be composed exclusively of spatial filters, adjusted by the network in the same way as conventional convolutional layers. GaborNet [2] and PCFNet [11] employ this approach. However, the performance advantage of using spatial filters in the first layer diminishes as the size of the training dataset increases.

The same is demonstrated in tests conducted on a Predefined Filter CNN (PCF) [11], which implements spatial filters like Gabor (Ga), Sobel (So), and Schmid (Sc) in its initial layer. Using only 5% of the CIFAR10 dataset, PCF-GaSc-ResNet18 achieved an accuracy of 66.32%, surpassing ResNet18 (with 62.05%). Similarly, using only 20% of the CIFAR100 dataset, PCF-GaSc-WRN168 reached 55.15%, surpassing WRN168 (with 53.27%). However, when evaluating the complete CIFAR10/100 datasets, no significant differences were observed.

In [2], a simple CNN and AlexNet are compared with their respective Gabor variants. The results show that the Gabor-CNN outperforms the CNN by 6% accuracy on the "Dogs vs Cats" dataset. In the "AffectNet" dataset, the difference is 3%. In the "ImageNet" dataset, no significant difference is observed.

3   Methodology

3.1   Convolutional Neural Networks

A Convolutional Neural Network (CNN) is a type of deep neural network designed to process data organized in a grid, typically images. CNNs can learn hierarchical representations of data through convolutional layers [9]. The learned representations are then employed in image analysis tasks such as classification, segmentation, identity recognition, etc.

The architecture of a CNN is organized through several layers, each of which contains multiple filters or convolutional kernels. These kernels are applied to input images through convolution, an operation involving the shifting of a window over the image (1). This process facilitates feature extraction by utilizing a specific set of weights and multiplying them with the corresponding elements of the receptive field [3]. The convolution operation can be expressed as follows:

$$g(x,y) = w * f(x,y) = \sum_{i=-a}^{a} \sum_{j=-b}^{b} w(i,j)f(x-i, y-j) \tag{1}$$

where $g(x,y)$ is the filtered image, $f(x,y)$ is the original image, w is the convolution kernel, $\sum_{i=-a}^{a} \sum_{j=-b}^{b}$ denotes a double sum over all positions of the kernel, the indices i and j represent coordinates in the convolution kernel, and a and b are used to define the size of the kernel.

3.2   GaborNet Architecture

The base architecture employed in this work consists of a simple CNN composed of 3 convolutional layers, each followed by subsampling. In the first layer, 12 kernels of size 7 are used, while in the second layer, 16 kernels of size 5 are employed and finally the third layer contains 120 kernels, also of size 5. This simple architecture enables us to perform a detailed analysis that otherwise would be obfuscated by a larger and more complex CNN.

The first layer consists of 12 convolutional kernels w, each one a 7×7 matrix, implying a total of 49 parameters that the network must train for each kernel. Given the tendency of these filters to converge towards spatial patterns known as Gabor filters, replacing these w with Gabor functions is explored. Gabor functions are complex sinusoids modulated by a Gaussian envelope [2]:

$$g(x, y, w, \theta, \psi, \sigma) = \exp\left(-\frac{x'^2 + y'^2}{2\sigma^2}\right) \exp(i(wx' + \sigma)) \tag{2}$$

$$x' = x \cos(\theta) + y \sin(\theta) \qquad (3)$$

$$y' = -x \cos(\theta) + y \sin(\theta) \qquad (4)$$

Equation (2) can be expressed in its real and imaginary parts; in this work, we use the real part of the Gabor function:

$$g(x, y, w, \theta, \psi, \sigma) = exp\left(-\frac{x'^2 + y'^2}{2\sigma^2}\right) \cos(wx' + \psi) \qquad (5)$$

where (x, y) denotes the pixel position in the spatial domain, w represents the central angular frequency of a sinusoidal plane wave, θ indicates the counter-clockwise rotation of the Gaussian function (i.e., the orientation of the Gabor filter), and σ represents the sharpness of the Gaussian function along the x and y directions. We set $\sigma \approx \pi/w$ to define the relationship between σ and w as described in [13]. By combining multiple Gabor filters with different orientations and frequencies, what is known as a filter bank is formed.

To leverage these filters within the context of a CNN, we introduce a specialized convolutional layer designed to apply a bank of Gabor filters, through which the 49 parameters for a kernel are now reduced to just 4 parameters $(w, \theta, \psi, \sigma)$. Integrating this Gabor layer into the CNN yields the GaborNet architecture [2]. Notice that because we have modified the original GaborNet, and to avoid confusion, we refer to our own implementation as **GaborNet2**.

3.3   Implementation

To develop **GaborNet2** in Python, it is convenient to use the PyTorch library, which provides a dynamic interface for building and training deep learning models. With this tool, we can effectively implement a convolutional neural network (CNN) architecture in which a layer with Gabor filters is integrated.

The base architecture of the CNN in PyTorch is defined by creating a class that inherits from nn.Module. In the constructor of this class, the convolutional (nn.Conv2d), pooling (nn.MaxPool2d), normalization (nn.BatchNorm2d), and activation layers (nn.ReLU, nn.Sigmoid, etc.) are defined.

A notable feature of PyTorch is the integration of various optimizers, such as stochastic gradient descent (SGD), Adam, RMSprop, or Adagrad. These optimizers adjust the network weights to minimize a loss function through the iterative update of descending gradients automatically. For this reason, the Gabor layer was designed based on the traditional nn.Conv2d layer.

The convolutional layer nn.Conv2d is a subclass of _ConvNd, so the custom layer GaborConv2d also inherits from this. In the constructor of this custom layer, 4 main parameters of the Gabor filters are defined: spatial frequency, orientation, standard deviation, and phase. These parameters are trainable and are updated through SGD (Adam) just as the weights of a traditional layer.

Once the GaborConv2d layer is defined, it is easy to replace the first convolutional layer of the CNN base architecture with this custom layer. By doing so, the CNN will use Gabor filters instead of conventional filters in its initial layer.

4   Experimental Setup

The parameters and configuration used to evaluate **GaborNet2** and identify potential points for early stopping are detailed in Table 1. All experiments are repeated 50 times (i.e. crossvalidation folds) to make our conclusions as robust as possible. Also, to give greater relevance to the Gabor layer compared to the other convolutional layers, the latter remain frozen during training, preserving the initial values of all convolutional kernels.

Two types of initialization: *Independent* and *Same*, were evaluated. *Independent* means that filter $j \in 1,\ldots,12$ was randomly initialized with a different seed for each of the executions. Meanwhile, *Same* initialization means that the j-th filter was initialized using the same random seed every time, for the sake of increased repeatability and hoping to achieve a better (more clearly distinguishable) convergence of the trainable parameters. Due to space limitations only the results of the *Same* initialization are reported; however, those of the *Independent* initialization were qualitatively equivalent and lead to the same conclusions.

Datasets. - In our experiments we employ two datasets that are easily represented by spatial filters. The MNIST dataset is a large database of handwritten digits commonly used in the field of machine learning. It comprises 60,000 training images and 10,000 test images of size 28×28 pixels [1]. To make our results less dependent on the dataset, we repeated the experiments on a dataset of similar difficulty: Fashion-MNIST (FMNIST) [15], which shares the characteristics of MNIST (number of images, classes, size of images and training-test split).

Gabor Filter Parameters. - The initialization of the 4 parameters $(w, \theta, \psi, \sigma)$ of the Gabor layer is based on [13], as follows: $w_n = \frac{\pi}{2} \cdot 2^{\frac{-(n-1)}{2}}$, $n \in [1,5]$; $\theta_m = \frac{\pi}{8} \cdot m - 1$, $m \in [1,8]$; $\psi \sim \mathcal{U}(0,\pi)$; $\sigma \approx \frac{\pi}{w}$.

This configuration results in a Gabor filter bank with 5 different scales and 8 different orientations. This diversity in scales and orientations allows for optimal adaptability to a wide range of features in processed images.

Filter Similarity Metrics. - The procedure to identify an early stopping for the training consists in computing the pairwise distance between each of the filters in the Gabor layer, treated as data vectors, one iteration at a time. Several metrics can be employed. For two vectors $u, v \in \mathbb{R}^n$ with mean values $\bar{u}$ and $\bar{v}$, the following metrics were evaluated:

Entropy (η). - the entropy of a grayscale image (in this case, each Gabor filter) is a measure of randomness that can be used to characterize the image:

$$\eta = - \sum (p \cdot \log_2(p)) \tag{6}$$

where p contains the histogram counts for the input images, which were treated as grayscale images with an 8-bit depth, thus producing histograms of 256 bins.

Correlation-Based Distance.- One minus the sample correlation between points (i.e. the sequences of values in x and y):

$$d_{corr} = 1 - \frac{(u - \bar{u})(v - \bar{v})^{\mathrm{T}}}{\sqrt{(u - \bar{u})(u - \bar{u})^{T}}\sqrt{(v - \bar{v})(v - \bar{v})^{\mathrm{T}}}} \qquad (7)$$

Hamming Distance.- The percentage (fraction) of elements (coordinates or dimensions) that differ between u and v:

$$d_{Hamm} = \#(u_j \neq v_k)/n, \quad j, k \in \{1, \ldots, n\} \qquad (8)$$

where the $\#(\cdot)$ function represents the number of occurrences for which the condition in the argument is satisfied.

Table 1. Experimental configuration

Parameter	Description	MNIST	FMNIST
Epochs	Number of training iterations	25	50
Optimizer	Optimization algorithm used	Adam	Adam
Executions	Number of repetitions of the experiment	50	50
Batch size	Training batch size	256	256
Learning rate	Learning rate	0.001	0.001

5   Results

Convergence of the parameters in the Gabor layer was tested by performing 50 executions or folds, training the **GaborNet2** and recording the value of each of the filter parameters per iteration for the purposes of observing the average behavior of the parameters over the whole set of 12 filters, during training.

Figure 1 shows the results of the filters' parameters convergence using *Same* filter initialization. For a better interpretation, the mean value was centered at zero and we plot the difference in the mean value between iterations, per filter. This processing has the effect of displaying the displacement of each parameter, irrespective of their actual value; this is shown as dashed lines in Fig. 1. Furthermore, the standard deviation is presented as shaded regions around the mean. Observe that both the displacement and the change in the dispersion are negligible. However, Loss and Accuracy plots (shown in Fig. 2) are as expected and do not allow the identification of a problem in the **GaborNet2**.

The lack of convergence of the Gabor filters led us to examine each filter as it is trained, discovering that, after a few training epochs, the filters exhibit gradual degeneration, as shown in Fig. 3. The final step in our methodology is to compute similarity metrics between the filters, following the assumption that some of these could be used to detect the point at which filter degradation began, and thus identify a good time for early stopping of the training process.

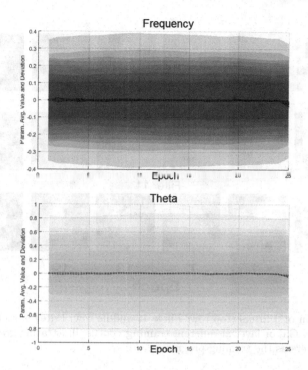

Fig. 1. Parameter convergence with *Same* filter initialization. These results are illustrative of the general behavior for all the filter parameters.

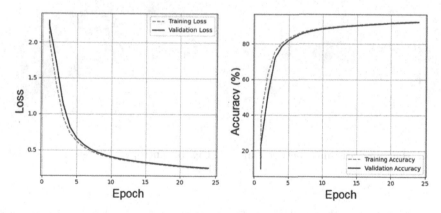

Fig. 2. Loss and Accuracy plots of training with *Same* filter initialization. These plots correspond to the MNIST dataset. Plots corresponding to FMNIST are very similar but are not shown due to space liminations.

The results of our procedure are shown in Figs. 4 5 and 6. All of the metrics tested in this experiment could allow for the identification of an "inflection" point (around epoch 16), but this is more clearly observed in the Correlation between

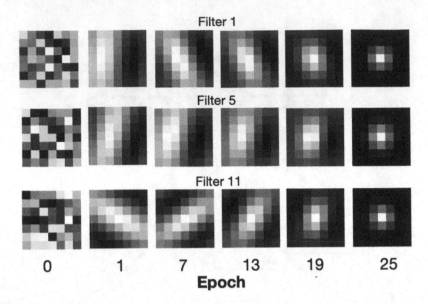

Fig. 3. Selection of 3 filters (top row: Filter 1, middle row: Filter 5, and bottom row: Filter 11) in the Gabor layer at different training epochs, illustrating gradual degeneration of the filters as the training progresses.

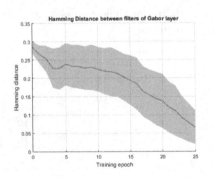

Fig. 4. Hamming distance between filters of the Gabor layer.

Fig. 5. Entropy of filters of the Gabor layer.

filters of the Gabor layer, shown in Fig. 6 where said point has been marked in black. This point in fact avoids significant filter degradation and, as said before, the network does not incur in any meaningful loss of performance.

In the experiments conducted on the MNIST dataset, an accuracy of 93.12% was achieved; meanwhile, evaluating the model on the FashionMNIST dataset produced an accuracy of 79.97%. A similar difference (about 10%-13%) between the results of MNIST and FMNIST has been observed before (see for instance [5]), even when the accuracy during training is well above 95%. This indicates that good generalization is harder to achieve on FMNIST.

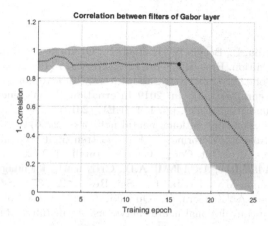

Fig. 6. Correlation-based distance between filters of the Gabor layer and inflection point (early stopping point) identified by a black dot.

6   Conclusion

Although several works have explored the use of spatial filters, and in particular that of Gabor filters [2,4,7,10,11,16,17], through our review of such works we found that a detailed analysis of the convergence of the filters had not been carried out. During our own analysis it was observed, not only a lack of convergence of the filter parameters, but a gradual degradation of the filters after a certain point in the training process. We have described our methodology and the proposed solution, based on the computation of a correlation-based distance metric between the Gabor filters, in order to identify the point at which training on the Gabor layer can be stopped to avoid filter degradation.

As to the reasons why the observed degradation takes place, we speculate that the Fully Connected (FC) layers have learned useful features that enable the adequate performance of the network, so that, as training continues, the network degrades the Gabor filters, as it does not need them any further. In other words, in lieu of the convolutional filters, a network can rely on many other neurons (e.g. 11,000 in the FC layers) to maintain or improve its performance. Compare this with [14], where CNN filters are compressed without significantly compromising accuracy (thus showing that not every filter is required to maintain performance).

In future work we will continue investigating the behavior of spatial filters as the initial layers of CNNs and design training strategies to leverage their intrinsic characteristics that make these desirable over the more popular kernels. Two aspects worthy of future study are the filters convergence and the decreased efficiency of GaborNet architectures when dealing with large datasets.

Acknowledgements. This work was supported by the National Council of Humanities, Science and Technology (CONAHCYT) of Mexico, via Postgraduate Scholarship 824517 (C. Orozco) and Grant CÁTEDRAS-2598 (A. Rojas).

References

1. LeCun, Y., Bottou, L., Bengio, Y., Haffner, P.: Gradient-based learning applied to document recognition. Proc. IEEE **86**(11), 2278–2324 (1998)
2. Alekseev, A., Bobe, A.: GaborNet: Gabor filters with learnable parameters in deep convolutional neural network. In: 2019 International Conference on Engineering and Telecommunication (EnT), pp. 1–4. IEEE (2019)
3. Bouvrie, J.: Notes on convolutional neural networks (2006)
4. Calderon, A., Roa, S., Victorino, J.: Handwritten digit recognition using CNNs and Gabor filters. Proc. Int. Congr. Comput. Intell., 1–9 (2003)
5. Kadam, S.S., Adamuthe, A.C., Patil, A.B.: CNN model for image classification on MNIST and fashion-MNIST dataset. J. Sci. Res. **64**(2), 374–384 (2020)
6. Khan, A., Sohail, A., Zahoora, U., Qureshi, A.S.: A survey of the recent architectures of deep convolutional neural networks. Artif. Intell. Rev. **53**, 5455–5516 (2020)
7. Kwolek, B.: Face detection using convolutional neural networks and Gabor filters. In: Duch, W., Kacprzyk, J., Oja, E., Zadrożny, S. (eds.) ICANN 2005. LNCS, vol. 3696, pp. 551–556. Springer, Heidelberg (2005). https://doi.org/10.1007/11550822_86
8. LeCun, Y., et al.: Backpropagation applied to handwritten zip code recognition. Neural Comput. **1**(4), 541–551 (1989)
9. Li, Z., Liu, F., Yang, W., Peng, S., Zhou, J.: A survey of convolutional neural networks: analysis, applications, and prospects. IEEE Trans. Neural Netw. Learn. Syst. **33**, 6999–7019 (2021)
10. Luan, S., Chen, C., Zhang, B., Han, J., Liu, J.: Gabor convolutional networks. IEEE Trans. Image Process. **27**(9), 4357–4366 (2018)
11. Ma, Y., Luo, Y., Yang, Z.: PCFNet: deep neural network with predefined convolutional filters. Neurocomputing **382**, 32–39 (2020)
12. Marchetti, G.L., Hillar, C., Kragic, D., Sanborn, S.: Harmonics of learning: universal Fourier features emerge in invariant networks (2023). arXiv:2312.08550
13. Meshgini, S., Aghagolzadeh, A., Seyedarabi, H.: Face recognition using Gabor filter bank, kernel principle component analysis and support vector machine. Int. J. Comput. Theory Eng. **4**(5), 767 (2012)
14. Wang, Y., Xu, C., You, S., Tao, D., Xu, C.: CNNpack: packing convolutional neural networks in the frequency domain. In: Advances in Neural Information Processing Systems, vol. 29 (2016)
15. Xiao, H., Rasul, K., Vollgraf, R.: Fashion-MNIST: a novel image dataset for benchmarking machine learning algorithms. arXiv preprint: arXiv:1708.07747 (2017)
16. Zagoruyko, S., Komodakis, N.: Wide residual networks. arXiv preprint: arXiv:1605.07146 (2016)
17. Zhou, Y., Ye, Q., Qiu, Q., Jiao, J.: Oriented response networks. In: Proceedings IEEE Conference on Computer Vision and Pattern Recognition, pp. 519–528 (2017)

Author Index

E. Mezura-Montes et al. (Eds.): MCPR 2024, LNCS 14755, pp. 397–398, 2024.
https://doi.org/10.1007/978-3-031-62836-8

Printed in the United States
by Baker & Taylor Publisher Services

Printed in the United States
by Baker & Taylor Publisher Services